Capturing The Aura

Integrating Science, Technology, and Metaphysics

I have discovered an unknown source of energy–
unlimited energy–that can be harnessed.
Throughout space there is an energy filling all space.

–Nikola Tesla

CAPTURING THE AURA

Integrating Science, Technology, and Metaphysics

C.E. Lindgren, DEd

MOTILAL BANARSIDASS PUBLISHERS
PRIVATE LIMITED • DELHI

First Indian Edition: Delhi, ***2008***

ISBN: 978-81-208-3361-6

MOTILAL BANARSIDASS
41 U.A. Bungalow Road, Jawahar Nagar, Delhi 110 007
8 Mahalaxmi Chamber, 22 Bhulabhai Desai Road, Mumbai 400 026
203 Royapettah High Road, Mylapore, Chennai 600 004
236, 9th Main III Block, Jayanagar, Bangalore 560 011
Sanas Plaza, 1302 Baji Rao Road, Pune 411 002
8 Camac Street, Kolkata 700 017
Ashok Rajpath, Patna 800 004
Chowk, Varanasi 221 001

Chapter 4 is from THE TAO OF PHYSICS by Fritjof Capra, © 1975, 1983, 1991. Reprinted by arrangement with Shambhala Publications, Inc., 300 Massachusetts Avenue, Boston, MA 02115

Fate Magazine, published by Llewellyn Worldwide, Ltd., has given permission to quote extensively from the article *Capturing Your Aura on Film* by Dr. C.E. Lindgren, Copyright 1995.

Special acknowledgement to TIMELESS BOOKS (Spokane, Washington) for the use of illustrations relating to Swami Radha. This is greatly appreciated. See Reference Section.

Illustrations by Chip Weston, William Mclellen, and Robert Bruce

PRINTED IN INDIA
By Jainendra Prakash Jain at Shri Jainendra Press,
A-45, Naraina, Phase-I, New Delhi 110 028
and Published by Narendra Prakash Jain for
Motilal Banarsidass Publishers Private Limited,
Bungalow Road, Delhi 110 007

ACKNOWLEDGMENTS

THANKS TO GUY COGGINS AND BURYL PAYNE for their technical support, and in particular to the other contributors to this work: Blythe Arakawa, Jacques Beauchamp, Robert Bruce, Fritjof Capra, Ruby Corder, Janice Dye, Gerald Owen Grow, Julia Jablonski, Arnold Keyserling, Ralph Losey, William McClellen, Rosalee Elizabeth McCurdy, Susana Madden, Andrine Morse, Margo von Phul, Chip Weston, and Richard Bernard Wigley. Thanks as well to Aura Imaging—Progen Co. for contributing photos and information to this book.

A special note of appreciation to Tammy Darby for her assistance in transcribing and typing certain chapters of this work. Lynn Jones McCullar is to be acknowledged for her near proofing of the individual chapters. Kristin Hansen, Esq., Attorney at Law, is to be recognized for her legal assistance regarding contractual agreements and legal consultations. Finally, our special thanks goes to all the authors and publishers for granting permission to reprint from their works.

In reading this work, readers will note certain variations in writing style, spelling, and grammar. Since the work is international in scope, with writers from France, Austria, Canada, Australia, and the States, grammar may vary. Originally we thought of changing this, but finally decided to bring our readers in contact with a variety of thoughts, writing styles, and grammatically "flavored" terms.

TABLE OF CONTENTS

FOREWORD
Jacques Beauchamp xiii

SECTION I: SCIENCE, HISTORY, AND TECHNOLOGY

1. **HUMAN ENERGY**
Historical Origins, Directions of Research, Investigating the Aura, Wave Particles, Time, and Light, Indeterminacy and Perception, Spirituality and Reality, Esoteric Occult Traditions, Technology Creating Spiritual Transformation, Mind and Body Connection, Sight, Photography, and Medicine
Richard Bernard Wigley, BA 3

2. **IN SEARCH OF AURAS**
Science Meets the Unknown, The Kirlian Experiment, Thelma Moss and Other Investigators, Conclusion
C. E. Lindgren, DLitt 13

3. **ELECTROPHOTOGRAPHY — AURA IMAGING PHOTOGRAPHY**
Body and Machine, The Future, *Full-body Imaging, Interactive Aura Imaging*, Conclusion
C. E. Lindgren, DLitt & Susana Madden 23

4. **THE NEW PHYSICS**
Modern Physics
Fritjof Capra, PhD 30

5. DISCOVERY OF THE BIOFIELD: A DIFFERENT TYPE OF MAGNETISM?
The SQUID, Animal Magnetism, Detecting the Biofield, Research Possibilities for the Biofield, Generalization of the Spin Force
Buryl Payne, PhD 55

6. NATURALLY INDUCED MAGNETIC ENERGY
Natural Magnetism, History, *Magnetic Therapy and Research Through the Ages*, Magnetism in Esoteric Literature, Magnets in Alternative Medicine, Finding Magnetic North, Magnetic Therapy, Using Magnets, Conclusion
C. E. Lindgren, DLitt & Ruby K. Corder 68

7. THE CHAKRAS: A KEY TO SUBTLE PHYSIOLOGY
The Sources, *Sources: Myth and Legend, Source: Classic Texts, Source: Experiences of Traditionally Trained Contemporary Experts, Source: Experiences of Sensitives, Healers, and Psychics, Source: Observation and Measurement by Conventional Science*, Cosmology: The Magical World-View, An Overview of the *Chakra-Kundalini-Nadi* System, *The Nadis, The Muladhara Chakra, Sahasrara* and Other Chakras, Inconclusive Postlude
William T. McClellan, PhD (cand.) 76

8. THE SEVEN ENERGY CENTERS
Summary of Knowledge of the Seven Energy Centers
Prof. Arnold Keyserling and Ralph Losey, JD 125

SECTION II: EFFECT OF SOUNDS AND MUSIC ON CHAKRAS AND AURIC FORMATIONS

9. THE IMPACT ON THE AURA OF MUSIC, SOUND, AND PRIMASOUNDS
PrimaSound, Indirect Impact of Music and Sound on the Aura,

How PrimaSounds Directly Impact the Aura, The Effects of Chakra Tones on the Aura, The Ultimate Meaning of Prima-Sounds and the Development of the Aura
Ralph Losey, JD 135

SECTION III: AURIC COLORS

10. THE INTERPRETATION OF AURIC COLORS USING AURA IMAGING PHOTOGRAPHY
Center, Right, Left colors, Throat, Heart, Solar plexus, Sex, Root
Guy Coggins and Susana Madden 153

11. COLOR AND THE AURIC ENERGY FIELD: EXPERIMENTS IN AURIC COLORS
Seeing Auras, *Remembering . . . , Daydreams, Stopping the World, Difficulty Seeing Auras, Trees and Stars, Other Methods*
Chip Weston, BA 187

12. AURIC AND EMOTIONAL STABILITY BASED ON COLOR TECHNIQUES
Color Organization of Auric Bands, Color Vibrations and Proper Living, *Depleting Mental and Emotional Energies*, Conclusion
Margo von Phul, BFA 197

SECTION IV: MENTAL, PHYSICAL, AND SPIRITUAL HEALING

13. PSYCHOPHYSICS: A HOLISTIC APPROACH TO ENERGY OR AURIC HEALING
Psychophysics: The Wave of the Future, Scientific Research Supporting Life Energy Fields, Interaction of Electromagnetic Fields, The Underlying Mechanism in Energy Healing—Thoughts are Energy, Thought Energy: Brain vs. Mind, Extra-sensory Perception: The Product of Extra-Sensitive Nervous Systems, Altered States of Consciousness and Extrasensory Perception, Healers: Receivers, Transmitters, and Directors of

Energy, Disease and Healing: Harmonizing Energy for Health, "As Above, So Below," Beyond Theory and Energy Healing, Tachyon Energy, The Creative Force of the Universe, Conclusion
Julia Melges Jablonski, BA 205

14. TOUCHING THE QI
Introduction, The Universal Energy, The Energy of Love and Light, *Exercises*, *The Candle Flame*, Auras in Nature, The Human Aura, Sensing Auras, Using Crystals, Healing Through the Aura
Janice Dye with Intro. by ***Richard Bernard Wigley, BA*** 218

15. ACUPUNCTURE THERAPY AND ITS POTENTIAL RELATIONSHIP TO AURIC ENERGY
A Western Approach to the Seven Layers of the Human Aura, Basic Principles of Chinese Medicine, Opening Points, *Case, Confluent Points, Window to the Sky Points*, Conclusion
Rosalee Elizabeth McCurdy, RN, DOM 230

16. AURAS IN THERAPY
The Crown of Air, The Auric Bodies and Dis-ease, The Aura and Energy Centers, Ways of Balancing the Aura, Chakras and Organ Imbalance, Emotional Trauma and the Aura, Releasing Energy Blocking Through Reflexology and Acupuncture, The Beamer®, Moving Energy Through Reiki and Sound
Andrine Morse 246

17. STRENGTHENING THE CHAKRAS THROUGH HERBAL THERAPY
The Seven Chakras
C. E. Lindgren, DLitt 257

18. BREATH — HEALING THE AURIC FORCE
Brucian Techniques, *Storage Centres, Moving the Seat of Awareness, Posture and Relaxation, Energy Movement Sensations*, The Mystery Schools, *Two-Four-Two, One-Four-Two, Six-Twelve-Six Technique*, Conclusion
Robert Bruce and C. E. Lindgren, DLitt 261

19. ALTERNATIVE ENERGY: AN INTRODUCTION FOR TEACHERS

Energy Healing, Energy in Education, *For the Teacher, Movement, Interpreting Energy Through Touch: An Experiment, Energy Through Art, Humor, Singing, Chanting, Breathing, Ritual, Silent Teaching Practices*, Mental Healing, *World View of Mental Healing, Self-Talk and Affirmations, Visualization, Mental Healing in Education, Teacher's Own Practices, Studying Cultural Images, Self-Talk, Art That Makes Us Whole, Mental Healing in Medicine*, Spiritual Healing, *Metaphysical Healing, Spirit Guide Healing, Shamanism, Reconnecting to the Higher Self, Spiritual Healing in Education, For the Teacher, Summon the Spirit of a Great Teacher, Goal Setting, Healing by Presence, The Study of World Views*, Conclusion

Prof. Gerald Owen Grow, PhD 270

SECTION V: MECHANICS AND EXERCISES

20. AURIC MECHANICS AND THEORY

What Is an Aura?, The Mechanics of Auric Sight, *Normal Sight, Auric Sight, The Complexity of Normal Vision, Line of Sight and Aura, Hidden Subject Test, Darkness and the Aura, Auric Sight and Aura Cameras, Three Basic Types of Non-physical Sight*, Energy Centres, *What They Are, The Brow and Crown, The Complexity of the Energy Body, The Energy Body's Effect on the Aura*, The Human Aura, *Etheric Aura, Main Aura, Spiritual Aura, Thoughts on the Aura*

Robert Bruce 291

21. AURIC SIGHT TECHNIQUE

All the Colors of Colors, *Uniqueness, Training Aid, Auras of Colors*, Afterimages and Aura, *Color Depletion, Slow Auric Drag, Living Aura and Afterimages*, Why Most People Fail: The Human Aura—Not a Good Training Ground, *The Auras of Color—Better for Learning*, Graduated Training Method, *Step 1—Preparations and Tips, Step 2—Brow Center Stimulation, Step 3—Viewing Technique, Step 4—Graduated Training Exercises, Step 5—The Human Subject, Step 6 — A Viewing for Two, Tips*, Close

Robert Bruce 304

SECTION VI: RESOURCES AND REFERENCES

22. RESOURCES FOR PERSONAL GROWTH
Intuitive Training, Schools and Foundations, Spiritual Healing Centers, Spiritual Travel, Books, Tapes, and Related Products, Recommended Reading List, *Aura Related Books,* Bioenergy and Magnetism, Aura Photography, Clairvoyant/Healing/ Psychic Readings, Psychic Investigator/Researcher
Blythe Arakawa 323

23. REFERENCES AND OTHER RELATED WORKS 336

CONTRIBUTORS 346

FOREWORD

You are not alone. . . . As you will see, perhaps feel, through this book, many people (i.e., scientists, inventors, scholars, and lay individuals) already spend considerable time exploring consciousness through different avenues. Using skills, talents, and innovative technology, these dedicated "searchers" explore the correlation between personal and collective consciousness and diverse phenomena such as quantum physics, wormholes, multi-dimensions, chakra sounds, electronics, and metaphysics. Often, initially motivated by curiosity, these individuals soon turn their avocations into lifelong passions.

At a time in history when the world is overshadowed by wars, natural disasters, and uncertainty, the sun continues shining for everyone who dares go beyond the visual linearity of mundane situations and accepts the potentiality that Creation is motivated by Love and a supreme universal intelligence. This intelligence is part of mankind, as mankind is a part of the God energy and auric fields of the Cosmos.

This work offers an opportunity for the reader to become a part of something bigger and more perfect than he/she could ever imagine—a world, a dimension, and a universe intermingled with energy fields, magnetic forces, and unimaginable electromagnetic vibrations of light and sound.

Capturing the Aura will introduce you to a new Era where humans are invited to use their creativity, love, passion, and mental ability constructively in making a better world for themselves and humanity as a whole. Let us, therefore, keep an open mind and heart in sharing a vision of a better potentiality. A potentiality which we each must activate through the reading of our Cosmic blueprint—life itself.

Jacques Beauchamp
St. Laurent, Quebec
September 1997

SECTION I:

SCIENCE, HISTORY, AND TECHNOLOGY

CHAPTER ONE

HUMAN ENERGY

Richard Bernard Wigley, BA

> I discovered a light appearing in my room, which continued to increase until the room was lighter than at noonday, when immediately a personage appeared at my bedside, standing in the air, for his feet did not touch the floor. He had on a loose robe of most exquisite whiteness. It was a whiteness beyond anything earthly I had ever seen; nor do I believe that any earthly thing could be made to appear so exceedingly white and brilliant. . . . The room was exceedingly light, but not so very bright as immediately around his person. (*The Book of Mormon*)

WAS THE LIGHT MENTIONED in this nocturnal visit that of an aura—an auric force produced by a divine being? Such manifestations have occurred throughout history and have been documented as far back as Egyptian times.

Once the sole property of esoteric study, the aura is no longer off limits to the scientific establishment. Its quest is now championed by academic researchers using the tools of modern technology to bring this former curiosity and enigma to the general public. With new and greater clarity, the human aura is being perceived as a viable and measurable energy field.

Humanity's evolution is requiring the introduction of a new scientific model, MetaScience. In this new model, the human aura stands out in brilliant radiance as the beacon to guide science and metaphysics into a new relationship and make possible a blending of science and metaphysics. It is gradually bringing the best of ancient philosophy in contact with modern technological advances. These advances will integrate the scientific study of auras, telepathy, precognition, and other forms of PSI into an accepted field of scientific investigation.

Historical Origins

In the past, shamans, and seers were the founders of medicine and science. Development of clairvoyance and clairaudience were prerequisites to the study of the ancient wisdom teachings. Wisemen and women relied upon their mind/body connection being in harmony with animistic life energies. Following ritual ceremonies of purification, they created inner sensitivities to perceive unseen emanations from the paranormal psychic reality.

As civilization developed, a new rational science with primitive technology came into power. This technology could not verify the psychic dimensions. Materialistic philosophy became more and more accepted, and religion and spirituality fell into controversy for lack of evidence. The ancient wisdom teachings became tainted with illusions and superstition. Its vision became blurred and myopic. With this new technology" came the loss of certain psychic powers, i.e., telepathy, clairvoyance, and the seeing of auric fields.

Directions of Research

The doctrines of religion and science and the long separation of the mind of science from the soul of knowing are coming closer together under the enormous technical advances and outpouring of new knowledge and information.

Former concepts solely the property of esoteric beliefs and ancient wisdom are being investigated by pragmatic scientists. From new research design and opening perspectives, the once large gap is a diminishing separation. Each of today's disciplines carries a load of history and experience, yet neither discipline can safely enter the 21st century until they agree to leave behind certain prejudices and disagreements.

According to A. A. Berezin, "One cannot exorcise unorthodox claims by repeating mantras that they are 'pseudoscience'" (Corliss 1996, 1). Echoing these sentiments in a letter to *Physics Today*, S. Malin states, "[Our] science . . . is based on objectivation, whereby it has cut itself off from an adequate understanding of the Subject of Cognizance, of the mind. But I do believe that this is precisely the point where our present way of thinking does need to be amended, perhaps by a bit of blood-transfusion from Eastern thought. . . ." (Corliss 1996, 1).

Investigating the Aura

Technology has created new tools to understand and test the human energy body. The MEG and EEG, magnetoencephalogram and electroencephalogram respectively, and other magnetic resonance imagining systems are very important in medical diagnosis using the electromagnetic pulsations of the body and brain. Biofeedback monitors, the SQUID (see Chapter 5), Kirlian energy transfer printing (see Chapter 2), and Aura Imaging Photography (see Chapter 3) are many of the new tools being used to understand the invisible electromagnetic fields of the body. Many of these ventures into human energy are using advanced technology to reveal bioplasmic energy (i.e., chakras and energy centers) and expose man's very aura.

To more completely understand the auric fields and the secrets of life, it is wise to understand the basic building blocks of matter and energy. The materialistic viewpoint of the past is giving way to the views of quantum physics, parallel universes, the superstring theory, wormholes, and multiple dimensions (Kaku 1994).

A methodical process of education and relearning has begun to reveal deeper fundamental physical principles in paranormal phenomena. The scientific and spiritual understanding of the human energy body will continue to be revised by the evolving discoveries of current researchers. Amid this crossover, newer paradigms are being discovered and are being synchronized with ancient wisdom. "An eternal flux of energy enfolds all processes in universal space-time at every scale from the sub-molecular to the galactic, so that there is a reflection of the whole in every fragment, at every time" (Mann 1991, 12).

Wave Particles, Time, and Light

Light is radiation. Understanding light as radiant energy that operates at various frequencies and wave lengths is a first step towards synthesis. Newton theorized that light is a shower of particles. James

Maxwell, following Newton's research, in 1873 concluded that "Light consists of electromagnetic waves."

Light is both visible and invisible. It is invisible as x-rays and radio waves. Visible light is discernible only because of magnetic interplay. In fact, we do not really see light itself. Light is the result of the processing of radiation wave lengths that penetrate our atmosphere and cause electromagnetic and electrochemical reactions to create an awareness in our neurochemical (physical) and analog or digital technological systems.

At the beginning of the 20th century, the science of quantum mechanics and Albert Einstein's theory of relativity crossed the bridge from real to unreal. Quantum physicists broke through the shell of the atom, discovered a vast array of indeterminate energies, and learned that electricity and magnetism were founding principles of all energy. The conclusions were that energy and matter were convertible through the theory of relativity.

Still, light remained the illusive particle/wave, and the *Æther*[1] was given over to imagination and disproof by the acceptance of Einstein's theory of relativity—with the speed of light being a constant in a complete vacuum. Without the *Æther*, all psychic phenomena continued to be unthinkable.

Æther is an ancient cross-cultural concept accepted by many civilizations as the only explanation for the stuff of the heavens. Newton could not explain gravity without the use of the invisible *Æther*. Later researchers explained that the *Æther* may also be responsible for electricity, magnetism, light, radiant heat, and motion.

Modern science denies the concept of *Æther*, as it does the concept of God or Universal Mind, but mathematically, science determines reality. Mathematics provides a mental grid, just as the *Æther* provides the essence and blueprint of the material strata and the emotional, mental, and spiritual connections.

Indeterminacy and Perception

Scientists are uncovering a constant relationship between the seen and unseen energies, the mundane and the spiritual, or as Hermes Trismegistus states, "As above, so below." This pure energy is recognizable and is becoming more and more visible as technical advances are used to investigate these sublime concepts. As we enter the 21st century, we are learning through a blending of science and philosophy that we are pure spirit (note Michio Kaku's *Hyperspace*).

Spirituality and Reality

In many cultures, there is strong evidence of an etheric or subtle layer of energy that pervades all existence. Modern researchers like Wilhelm Reich, who discovered orgone energy, and Nikola Tesla attempted to demonstrate the presence of this subtle energy (see Chapter Two). Of this immaterial phenomenon, the ancients speak of words such as *ch'i*, *ki*, and *prana,* which have no current scientific recognition but are connected with ancient teachings describing the movement of electromagnetic energies. In one example from the Hindu tradition, the tides are known as *Tattvas,* and the unseen medium in which they flow is known as *prana*. This is the state of matter that is the next stage above terrestrial essence, and it is referred to as "etheric matter." This etheric matter surrounds the sun, and in it, the earth and other planets move. This is referred to as free etheric substance. On the other hand, the prana surrounding our planet, as well as others in this solar system, is referred to as "bound ether" or the magnetic sphere of our plane (*Cosmic Awareness* 1969).

Auric fields, including the human aura, are part of this realm and have been mysteries to science because of their inability to be perceived by most individuals. According to Grof (1990, 145), "in non-ordinary states of consciousness it is possible to see and experience energy fields that have been described in the mystical traditions of the East but have not been objectively verified by western Science. I am speaking here of 'Auras,' 'subtle bodies,' 'acupuncture meridians,' 'nadis,' and 'Chakras.'"

Esoteric Occult Traditions

Esoteric healers, Shaman priests, Reiki Masters, and "lightworkers" understand this human energy field and see it as composed of an aura of many layers and chakras (Sanskrit word meaning "wheel" and, as such, is a wheel of energy within the body).

The common agreement is that ". . . the auric emanation consists of seven distinct units or waves of light encircling the subject in an oval shaped conformation. The extent and strength of the aura varies considerably from person to person, depending on his state of health, mental and emotional state, and evolutionary status" (Anderson 1975, 21).

There are other ancient teachings on the energy body. Taoism and its concepts of *ch'i,* or the life force that emanates the body, is a very notable and elaborate philosophy but uses energy centers that correlate with major organs. The commonality here is that the human aura is not a supernatural or metaphysical phenomena, but that it is the basis and foundation of physical life.

The etheric body is the state of energy that exists between pure energy and dense matter. From the spiritual viewpoint, it is divine energy that is the biomagnetic life force or bioplasma. All of this is under the spiritual and physical laws of energy, vibration, and relationship, so that the individual life force is connected and part of a greater whole. "The physical tissues exist only because of the vital field behind them. The field is prior to, not a result of, the physical body" (Brennan 1988, 49).

Technology Creating Spiritual Transformation

Knowing or feeling a person's energy must have a mechanism. This mechanism can be explained in various forms, but it has proven best to express this energy in terms of vibration. Each person is said to have his or her own frequency, which can be seen in colors (see Chapter Ten).

"Each energy wave consists of an electric and a magnetic field at right angles to each other, and both at right angles to the direction the wave is traveling. The number of waves formed in one second is the frequency; the distance the energy travels during one oscillation is its wavelength. The higher the frequency, the shorter the wavelength" (Becker 1985, 272).

Working with observable and repeatable factual data, the typical representative of modern science recognizes light and electromagnetic radiation as similar and equivalent. Currents of energy and magnetic fields are produced as electrons move around and within various fundamental physical elements and through space. This primal energy can be utilized and transformed into other sorts of electromagnetic radiation, both as high frequency invisible light (ultraviolet), visible light, color, and low frequency invisible infrared (heat) radiation.

Using standard methodology, some scientists have been able to create advanced technology (i.e., Aura Imaging Photography) to break through the formerly invisible barriers of the human aura. To these esoteric scientists (scientists who unravel the mysteries of the universe), light and consciousness are comparable and share basic similarities. Both are descriptive of the intelligence surrounding manifestation of physical existence. This image is shared by esoteric and psychic healers around the world. The aura is seen as a mixture of energies with distinctive layers relating to the different densities of electromagnetic frequency or bodies of consciousness. In these bodies there is the physical or etheric, the emotional or astral, and the mental, which connects into the spiritual bodies.

The emotional body contains the full spectrum of colors, extends outward beyond the etheric body, and produces vibrant and interesting patterns of colors. The emotional body changes constantly and is filled with mood swings, desires, fear, pain, joy, hate, love, anger, and all of the other emotions. It is a wild, chaotic jumble of colors when a person is agitated and a calm, relaxed, pastoral model of symmetry at other times.

The mental body contains the ideas and the forms of things that are logical and mathematical. It is the blueprint of the manifestation.

Mind and Body Connection

To understand that the aura is a vibrant reality in a scientific context, one begins with the mind and body connections. Kaplan (1987, ix) states that ". . . the relationship between the brain and the eyes led me to realize that the brain is really in control of the eyes."

The eyes have been called the "Window to the Soul," and light is the basic life force of nature. With proper training, the eyes can be taught by the mind to physically see beyond normal vision and witness the energy fields of thoughts, emotions, and life itself manifesting in every human being.

Vision must be transferred through an elaborate complex process to the occipital lobe in the back of the brain and then organized into images and forms. Each image is broken down into various packets of information and sent to different processors within the brain, similar to the way a computer processes information.

All sensory information, except smell, passes through the thalamus on the way to cerebral hemispheres. The hypothalamus, just under the thalamus, controls endocrine levels, water balance, sexual rhythms, the autonomic nervous system, and is the seat of emotion and hunger. The brain analyzes sensory input in the parietal, temporal, and occipital lobes and sends out messages to the body through the frontal lobes of the cerebrum. This is where vision takes place. The upper brain stem, the medulla or "magic inch," was not considered because of a lack of conceptual power, nor was the reticular formation, which is responsible for alertness but does not contain awareness in the dream state.

If there is such a place as a seat of consciousness, it is probably in the cerebral hemispheres, and many scientists theorize consciousness is bound up with language. This theory associates consciousness with the left cerebral cortex, the location of the language centers. It is known that dolphins possess cerebrums as big as human's and communicate in complex sound signals.

The ability to see is an incredible and complex system of changing images and lightning-fast reactions. In the mechanics of vision, the eyes receive light that is focused on the retina, the back of the eye. The retina contains light sensitive cells that send out signals when light shines on them. There are 120 million rod cells in each eye that distinguish shade and see in monochrome. There are seven million specialized cone cells, concentrated around the back of the retina where the main images fall, where details and colors are seen (note Kilner 1965; 1973).

Images received by the retina are processed in other regions besides the visual cortex. From the retina, an image is transferred into neuro-electrical signals and passed, via the optic nerve, along to the sight center of the brain, where it is interpreted as a sight picture. The process of transferring images to the occipital lobes requires the breakdown of the images into many levels of information to be reformed by the holistic action of the brain. Whenever a thought or perception emerges into conscious awareness inside the brain, it is like the mind observing itself.

The reaction of the aura to light is the only visible part of the aura. It is this reactionary field that is seen with auric sight. This fact explains why the aura can not be seen in the dark and needs light to make it visible (Bruce 1994). "It is possible, however, to see a small part of the energy body, etheric aura, in the dark and also light from any active chakras. These are seen as small points of intense light, the size and rightness of which depends on how active the chakra is at the time of observation." (Bruce 1994).

Physical sight is understood by science well enough, but clairvoyance, auric sight, interior imagination, dreaming, and memory are areas of understanding that are still beyond the acceptance of the traditional researcher and practitioners alike.

Understanding other forms of vision require a knowledge of the electron and the photon. This area of study is highly debatable and the world is no longer only made of black and white facts but of various shades of gray.

Newton speculated that the vibrations of an unseen *Æther* may be excited by the brain and that the human mind had psychic forces that transcend the material universe. This invisible field or *Æther* was important to his understanding of gravity and how movement is possible in space. "Newton had envisioned matter and light to be particulate in nature, though they appear continuous to the human eye. Gravity, however, seemed to be something else, acting invisibly—holistically—over the entire universe" (Stenger 1992).

The blue sky and the orange red glow of the setting sun are caused by selective scattering of sunlight by minute particles in the air. Without gases and dust in the atmosphere, the sky would appear black, as it always does from a point ten miles above the surface of the earth, where the stars are constantly visible regardless of the time of the day.

The eye's ability to see rests in the mind's ability to see. The mind rather than the eyes is in control of the process of vision. Most people do not have clairvoyant abilities and cannot see auras because they have not been trained to see them, and if they have seen colors, lights, shapes, and felt this energy, they have been told they were "merely seeing things."

Sight, Photography, and Medicine

In the orthodox medical field, the relative health and vibrancy of the etheric body presents the case for the beginnings of disease. Kirlian photography and Aura Imaging Photography can be main elements in the prevention and paradiagnosis process. The next step is understanding the source of diseases coming from the electric etheric interconnections between the physical, etheric, emotional, and mental bodies.

The common denominator between matter and energy is vibration. The human energy body is made of matter and vibrates at different frequencies. Dr. Harold S. Burr Yale, in 1940, found bioenergetic growth fields in salamanders and seeds. Similar experiments conducted by Dr. Robert O. Becker "measured electrical direct currents which seemed to indicate a connection to the nervous system. Each mass of nerve cells showed a positive, and all their nerve endings a negative, electrical potential" (Fisslinger 1994, 47). Kirlian or electrophotography professes to see these electromagnetic fields around living objects. The ability to see the etheric body and the forms, colors, and shapes of the layers of the aura will most likely become more commonplace with the aid of aura photographing techniques.

The effort of MetaScience is to bring about the synthesis of scientific formulas with spiritual concepts. Scientists have an inherent weakness in moving from the intellectual to spiritual while non-scientists have the same inability to move from the ethereal to the concrete. When this is accomplished and accepted by mainstream scientists, then this knowledge can be brought into full service by humanity. A new model is required that partakes of modern technological advances and ancient wisdom.

> It will be found that certain colours will definitely affect certain disease, cure certain nervous troubles, eradicate certain nervous tendencies, tend to the building of new tissues, or to the burning out of corruption. All this must be studied. Experiments can be made along the line of vitalization and magnetization, which involve direct action on the etheric, and this again will be found in the law of vibration and of colour. (Bailey 1922, 247)

The following chapters will provide greater insight into the history of auric research, the theory of magnetism and electricity, bioplasmic energy and biofields, chakras, light and color, sound and the aura, healing, and experiments for attuning oneself to sense auric fields.

Note

1. A Latin term referring to "a thin, subtile matter, much finer and rarer than air, which, some philosophers suppose, begins from the limits of the atmosphere, and occupies the heavenly space" (Newton). "There fields of light and liquid ether flow" (Dryden). Also referred to as Ether.

CHAPTER TWO

IN SEARCH OF AURAS

C.E. Lindgren, DLitt

KNOWN OVER THE CENTURIES BY MANY NAMES, *ch'i*, *prana*, *karnaeem*, and *Illiaster*, auric energy or bioplasmic fields have been documented for over 5,000 years. Astral lights alluded to by ancient Eastern Indians, Chinese, and Jewish mystics, are attributed to a universal energy that permeates all matter. In early esoteric writings and later in those of the Rosicrucians, American Indians, Zen Buddhists, and Christian mystics, these fields have been described as glowing clouds of light infused with diverse colors. Christian mystics feel that auric activity consists of two interconnecting energy patterns, i.e., the aureole, surrounding the entire being, and the nimbus or halo encircling the head. Many Eastern and Western esoteric writings strongly suggest that auric field intensity correlates to Chinese acupuncture locations of subtle energy. The Greek writer Plutarch expressed the notion that auras revealed the desires and vices of man through their color variation and movements. Gina Allan, author of a best seller, *Gifts of Spirit,* believes that:

> auras are like a signature, each as individual as the person they surround. There are two separate auras that are with all individuals. The physical aura's colours change with the moods/emotions of the moment. The spiritual aura has colours reflecting the evolution of the person. Both auras are changing constantly. In a survey (1987) at a private school in Singapore, 85% of the students, ages ranging from six years to twenty-two, could see the physical aura. Those people with the ability to truly see the physical aura can also

> diagnose medical problems. The spiritual aura is even more rarely seen as it requires a deep sense of integrity. This aura shows past lives and the potential for spiritual growth in this and future lives. (Allan 1996)

If the aura exists, as attested to by countless mystics and psychics, then it certainly manifests itself in the ultraviolet light spectrum.[1] Though imperceptible to most individuals, this radiation is visible only to a select few. According to some scientists, this ability is part of man's evolutionary development, and in time, all will be afforded this precious gift. This theory is advanced in Steve Richards' book, *Invisibility: Mastering the Art of Vanishing* (1992). According to Patrick Alessandra, author of *Seeing Auras:*

> these images are the testimony of those who see the world of energy around us and who seek to understand how we can all become more aware of these realities. Today, in the last decade of the twentieth century, there are far more people alive than ever before who can not only feel but also see the energies around them. This is a natural event in human evolution and as more years pass we will all find our abilities to sense auras and energies increasing.

Howard and Dorothy Sun (1993), in their acclaimed work, *Color Your Life*, propose that auric energy vibrates around all living things, absorbing sun and atmospheric light. This light is divided (similar to a prism) into "component color energies" (red, orange, yellow, green, turquoise, blue, purple, and pink). The color energies are then directed toward the body's energy transformers, the chakras.[2] These energy centers are "power points in the body through which energy flows and is transformed." Chakras, therefore, transform and balance the energy currents coming from the higher, finer energy fields so the material body can use this energy. Allan, a former Buddhist nun and currently a Naturopath and Natural Healer, provides personal insight into auric colors and their potentiality for change:

> Over the last fifteen years, I have been observing changes taking place in the spiritual colours of my own aura. I have had these colours confirmed by a friend who sees auras. Many times when I have been speaking publicly, people have commented on my colours. Fifty years ago my colours showed a very pale aqua green, indicating healing abilities. Today that colour is a deep sea green

> when I'm healing or speaking on the subject of healing. The field of colours changes in size and density the more the energy is balanced and in harmony within the seven Chakras. (Allan 1996; also see Chakra chapter)

The aura, Allan noted, besides providing an array of colors ranging from one end of the spectrum to the other, also has texture and shape variations. Some of these variations include: solid and brittle, thick and thin, light and heavy, and luminous and dark. Many times a brittle or broken aura is produced by fear, confusion, greed, envy, or doubt. These auric or electromagnetic bodies are also divided into seven bands or fields. These fields surrounding the body include: Etheric, Emotional, Mental, Astral, Etheric Template, Celestial, and Ketheric. Some psychics and healers state that there are other "finer" levels on the cosmic plane.

According to *Hands of Light*, by Barbara Ann Brennan (1987), when these energy fields become unbalanced, it is possible to reorganize and heal them by the clearing of the unhealthy or "blocked" energies (note healing chapters) by trained and gifted healers. Much of the healing process of auras, regardless of their condition, must also come from within. Auras are strengthened by pure thoughts, exercise, sunshine, fresh air, and proper nutrition and eating habits. More importantly, the Societas Rosicruciana in America stresses the importance of concentrating, visualizing, and meditating on an outpouring of Spiritual Fire which covers the physical and spiritual bodies in illumination, which is the healing power of God that heals and protects. An individual, according to Rosicrucian philosophy, must desire and will this light, which is always present but invisible, to immerse the body in its divine rays. To accomplish this goal, auric fields must first be seen. Although these human energy fields, described by mystic C.W. Leadbeater (1987) in *Man Visible & Invisible* as "very dense and solid-looking mist surrounded by an egg-shaped cloud of diaphanous mist," are visible to some psychics and mystics, the "spiritual skin" remains invisible to the average person. Therefore, some scientists and researchers have attempted to devise machines that will photograph and analyze the aura, then diagnose its condition.

For over a hundred years, researchers have tried to photograph these luminous fields. Since the 1890s, however, when the first aura photograph was taken by Nicola Tesla (whose body was attached to the output of his apparatus), this search has succeeded in producing mostly fraudulent, poor-quality prints and small, direct-contact Kirlian photos (high-voltage imaging process).

With recent "cutting-edge" technology, however, these auric fields, which bathe animals and other matter in electrical light energy, can be observed and photographed at a distance, revealing passionate reds, healing greens, sensitive blues, creative oranges, relaxing violets, and spiritual white.

Science Meets the Unknown

One of the first serious attempts at scientifically studying the aura was conducted by Dr. Walter Kilner of London's St. Thomas' Hospital. Through a series of objective and subjective experiments, Kilner was able to invent a crude detection device for observing auric activity.

By separating two pieces of glass, cementing them around the edges except for one small opening, pouring a bluish dye called dicyanin (coal-tar dye from Germany) into the hollow glass, and sealing it, Kilner invented an apparatus that was sensitive to the ultraviolet energy spectrum. Dr. Kilner could then observe, by peering through the lens, vaporous energy (auras) extending from living bodies. It seems, according to Kilner, that the longer one looks through the blue-colored lens, the more sensitive the eyes become to ultraviolet and higher light spectrums. It is in this range that Kilner believed auras occur. In his book, entitled *The Human Atmosphere* (1911), Dr. Kilner presents scientific evidence for the existence of the aura. According to Kilner's research, he and his associates were able, on many occasions, to perceive auric formations extending several inches from patients' naked bodies. Within the pages of Kilner's work, he also describes a series of experiments that the reader may try. The only drawbacks to Kilner's method are the extreme difficulty in obtaining the blue dye and the potential for serious injury to skin or eyes if the apparatus were to leak (i.e., blindness and burning).

In 1924, Ernest J. Stevens, PhD, opened a research laboratory for the investigation of odic and auric energy. During the next few years, Dr. Stevens (1924) attempted to harness these forces, but much of Dr. Stevens's work is no longer in existence.

Later, in 1937, Oscar Bagnall, BA (Cantab.), in his work *The Origin and Properties of the Human Aura*, expanded on Kilner's theory presenting a simple method of observing auric formations by substituting the dye pinacyanol (dissolved in triethanolamine) for dicyanin. This dye, like the aforementioned dicyanin, is also difficult to obtain, and cobalt blue and purple glass may be substituted for the dyes used by Kilner and Bagnall (see resource chapter).

In 1946, Harry Boddington, in his book *The University of Spiritualism*, announced that he had also discovered a method of viewing auras through glass made to the same spectroscopic tint as dicyanin. This process, using glass produced in Czechoslovakia, provided the user with a permanently colored and safer viewing apparatus.

Boddington (1946), within the pages of his work, also alluded to a process by a Harley Street specialist who invented an apparatus based on a step-down transformer connected to electrical current with high voltage, low amperage, and a handle connecting to the transformer, completing the subject-earth circuit. The researcher would approach the subject with an electrical bulb or tube of neon gas. The closer the tube came to the subject, the brighter it glowed. According to Boddington (1946, 107), the brightening of the tube was caused by ". . . some invisible emanation given off from the body of the subject . . . [an] aura."

Shortly after Bagnall's aforementioned experiments, a radically new technique for auric detection was created. Soviet scientists Semyon and Valentina Kirlian (c. 1939) developed a method for photographing and viewing the aura.

The Kirlian Experiment

This form of radiation field photography, introduced by the Kirlians, was later researched by V. M. Inyushin and Victor Adamenko. This technique, using electric current, exposes the presence of energy patterns which are then transferred to a photographic plate. More specifically, the subject places his fingertip on the condenser-like plate. As over-head lights are turned down, a bright, ghostly blue light rises from the plate area and a strong odor of ozone fills the room (produced by low-ampere high-electrical voltage). The pad produces a crackling sound as electrical current is transferred from the plate to the subject's finger. Small tentacles of white and bluish light jump in arcs, lighting the space between the skin tissue and cold metal (plate is insulated). Once the photograph is developed, the print reveals an array of brightly colored lights extending from the fingertip. In one print of a healer's finger, the center of the fingertip was dark, while from the upper portion, extending out about one-third inch, were a series of blue, hair-like strands of current-induced lights. Near the bottom was a bright, red and orange light extending from the finger, connecting with the blue upper corona[3] to form an outline of the darkened finger.

It was during these initial experiments that Kirlian accidently discover the therapeutic benefits of Kirlian photography. According to Susana Madden (1995), aura imaging photographer, Kirlian, while conducting a series of experiments, took a picture of his fingertip which revealed no corona discharge. Surprised, Kirlian once more attempted the experiment with the same results. Shortly thereafter, he came down with the flu. Soon after this experiment, his wife also exhibited similar effects while attempting to photograph her aura. She, too, only a few days later, contracted the flu.

According to Stan Krippner and Daniel Rubin's (1972) *Galaxies of Life*, researchers are divided in their evaluation of the Kirlian phenomena. Some call the manifestation "corona discharge," believing that the technique only reveals commonplace electrical occurrences, while others conceive of radiation field photography as revealing the "bioplasma body" or aura.

According to Viktor Adamenko, a Russian scientist (c 1970s), the discharge is "the cold emission of electrons." Relating to the bioplasmic theory, V. M. Inyushin of Kirov University felt that "the photographs reveal the 'bioplasmic body' of organisms, a patterning of electrons and photons that determines the structure of the physical body" (Moss 1974, 478). "Inside the 'bioplasmic' body," said Inyushin, "processes have their own labyrinthine motion, different from the energy pattern in the physical body, yet the bioplasmic body is not a chaotic, but a whole unified organism which acts as a unit, is polarized, gives off its own electromagnetic fields, and is the basis for 'biological' fields" (Tompkins and Bird 1989, 204).

Thelma Moss and Other Investigators

By the 1970s, the Psychical Research Foundation and Department of Electrical Engineering at Duke University began investigating not only Kirlian photography but a technique known as bioluminescence (Duncan and Roll, 1995). This procedure used highly sensitive light amplifiers to map very faint natural light that seems to be radiated by the body (Duncan and Roll 1995). Kirlian photography, however, possessed a near magical quality which continued to draw researchers. On the West

Coast at UCLA, Dr. Thelma Moss was just beginning her research with Kirlian photography.

Many of the early 1970s experiments by parapsychologists led them to believe that the Kirlian camera, which produces photographs of electrical corona, actually provided proof of the existence of an aura or soul (Robinson 1981). Scientists, such as Dr. Viktor Inyushin (State University of Kazakhstan, Russia), were inclined to believe, based on their experimentations, that bioluminescence represents auric manifestations.

Although being an indicator of moods, emotions (Singer 1981), and certain physiological changes, scientists soon discovered that the Kirlian process did not reveal the seat of the soul, but rather ultraviolet radiation arcing between the instrument, photographic plate, and subject. The Kirlian camera, earlier thought of as a means of psychic detection and perhaps an instrument for perceiving the soul, has recently been shown to merely measure sweat. As Duncan and Roll (1995) state, the effects produced by Kirlian technology "is due to an interaction between electromagnetic radiation from the camera, the air surrounding the hand, and perspiration from it." The variations in shape, size, and color of the photographed "aura" are due to variables such as moisture, salt content, and gases produced by the skin. More precisely, as electricity from the Kirlian apparatus enters the test subject, a gas ionization occurs around the moist (i.e., perspiration) object. Therefore, "during exposure, moisture is transferred from the subject to the emulsion surface of the photographic film and causes an alternation of the electric pattern on the film" (Pehek, Kyler, and Faust 1976). For this reason, a photograph taken in a vacuum does not produce an auric pattern (Hines 1988). In all, there are over twenty-five variables which may influence a final Kirlian photograph (Singer 1981).

Although many parapsychologists will agree to the non-psychical explanation of Kirlian's "auras," these explanations do not explain the so-called "phantom-leaf" effect, wherein a portion of a leaf is removed, and a Kirlian print is made revealing the intact configuration of the original leaf. These experiments were conducted by many researchers including I. Dumitrescu and Allen Detrick. According to L. E. Bartlett's *Psi Trek*, these effects were first noted by Soviet scientists and later confirmed by UCLA researcher, Dr. Thelma Moss.

Further, Lois Julien (1996), one of Dr. Moss' former lab assistants, says, "We wanted to make sure that we were on the right track. We did all sorts of tests to make sure that it wasn't something else like sweat. We studied the effects of moisture, temperature, the room, the atmosphere, the film. We eliminated all of these factors. What it came down to was energy."

In other words, Kirlian photos are not like the ever popular "mood sensors" that measure changes in your skin temperature. They actually measure the energy field around your body. Once she established this fact, Dr. Moss and her volunteers began various studies using the Kirlian photos.

One involved how the aura reacted in relationships. Julien relates the story of one young girl, sent to the lab by UCLA's psychology department. "The psych department sent us some teenagers in therapy with their parents. One girl came in and she and I put our fingertips down on the film (to take a Kirlian photo). We both had nice wide emanations of energy around our fingertips. Then I left the room and her parents came in. The resulting photo showed that the girl's aura got smaller around her fingertip, and the parents' had nice large energy fields." Being around her parents caused the girl to reduce the size of her aura—to shrink inward! "This was very consistent from family to family," notes Julien (1996). "They went back to therapy and discussed it—the photo became a jumping-off point to discuss the issue."

Dr. Moss also studied *energy transference* between people. Julien describes one experiment: "I tend to have quite an energetic outgoing personality. One day, Dr. Moss said, 'Lois, you are so bubbly today. I'd love to have some of that energy.' One of her assistants got an idea: 'Why don't you two go in and see if Lois can transfer her energy to Thelma?' So we tried it. At first, my fingertip photo had little tiny bubbles all round it, and hers didn't. We both concentrated on my transferring energy to her. In the second picture, bubbles from my fingertip went over to hers and surrounded her fingertip!"

Dr. Moss (1974) also did "green thumb" and "brown thumb" experiments. People with "green thumbs" held a damaged leaf in their hands and focused on "healing" the leaf. Before and after photos were taken of the leaf and of a "control" leaf that was not touched. She even tried "healing at a distance," where the healer simply focused his thoughts on the leaf in question without touching it. What she found was that the "healed" leaves had a brighter aura than the unhealed leaves. She also discovered that many of the people who volunteered as "brown thumbs," (aka plant killers) really were—the plants actually responded negatively to their touch!

Conclusion

As with all scientific endeavors, there are still disputes as to whether the Kirlian photograph reveals merely a physiological manifestation or an ever present bioplasmic electromagnetic energy field. Moss and Julien support one theory while other researchers and parapsychologists, such as Duncan and Roll, support another.

Duncan and Roll's theory, however, does not eliminate the potential which this technique, and the later-developed Aura Imaging Photography, may present toward personality and health diagnoses. As noted in the text, certain illnesses are inclined to produce perspiration or physiological changes which may be perceived by the Kirlian process.

Notes

1. Noted mystic, healer, writer, and metaphysical researcher, Robert Bruce, takes issue with this statement. According to Bruce: "For many years scientists have tried (and failed) to detect enough visible light to account for the human aura . . ."

2. According to Bruce: "My research shows that it is not the aura that gives and receives energy or light, but the energy body and its energy centres, energy exchange ports and bio-circuitry (networks of energy pathways and meridians). The physical aura is more of an energy reflection, or field, that can only be detected by the brow centre when it is tuned into a subject. The eyes are intimately linked to the brow centre and are used solely to tune the brow centre into the subject—but the eyes don't actually 'see' the aura. The energy of the subject is received by the brow centre (aided by the eyes) and passed to the sight centre of the brain—in a similar way as normal optical sight works. All energy received at the sight centre of the brain is interpreted in the same way: as a mental sight picture which can appear to be superimposed over the top of normal sight. Auric energy is received and interpreted by the sight centre of the brain as a mental sight picture—creating the illusion of coloured bands of light surrounding the subject [note the technique used by the Aura Camera 3000 and 6000].

"This energy field (commonly called an aura) definitely does exist—not as light of any type—but as a bio-electrical-spiritual-pranic type of living energy that has depth and feel and force. This field radiates from the complex energy activity within and around the physical organism (person), caused by the spirit manifesting through it and all the complex energy processes that define life as we know it. This is similar, in a way, as to how an electrical device radiates an electro-magnetic field around itself. Even when an electrical device is perfectly contained and insulated it still creates an electro-magnetic field around itself—which can be detected and measured" [For additional information, note Bruce's Chapter XX entitled "Auric Mechanics and Theory"].

3. The corona refers to the display of millions of electrons which are produced by an electronic discharge. As in Kirlian photography, these electrons travel to a photographic plate from the photographed object.

The writer wishes to thank *Fate* Magazine and Llewellyn Publications for permission to use certain portions of a January 1995 article written by the author.

CHAPTER THREE

ELECTROPHOTOGRAPHY
Aura Imaging Photography

C.E. Lindgren, DLitt & Susana Madden

TODAY THERE IS A NEW FORM of energy photography which many believe is far superior to Kirlian's energy transfer printing. Known as Aura Imaging Photography, this technique produces a full-spectrum color print of remote bioplasmic energy transfer. The resulting photographs show the upper segment of the subject's body including the head, neck, and shoulders. Experimentation is currently underway toward producing a full-body perimeter electro-field image. This system utilizes traditional biofeedback measuring combined with high-voltage field imaging. The camera displays the aura as colorful fields of light, providing the therapist or healer with quick recognition (of shape, color, and size) and processing (each color suggests a specific physical, emotional, or spiritual condition). With the introduction of aura cameras, these colorful luminous formations can easily and effortlessly be recorded.

According to Stephany Hurkos (1996), widow of famed psychic Peter Hurkos, these sensors measure the subject's "electromagnetic field, based on the Ayurvedic (acupressure points on the hand) system of meridians. The machine codes these energy readings into frequencies (which correspond to certain colors) and processes the photograph; a computer sorts the information and prints the Aura Photograph." These colors and their corresponding emotional states include passionate and joyful red, happy and creative orange, disciplined yellow, healing green, sensitive and solitary blue, relaxing violet, and spiritual white.

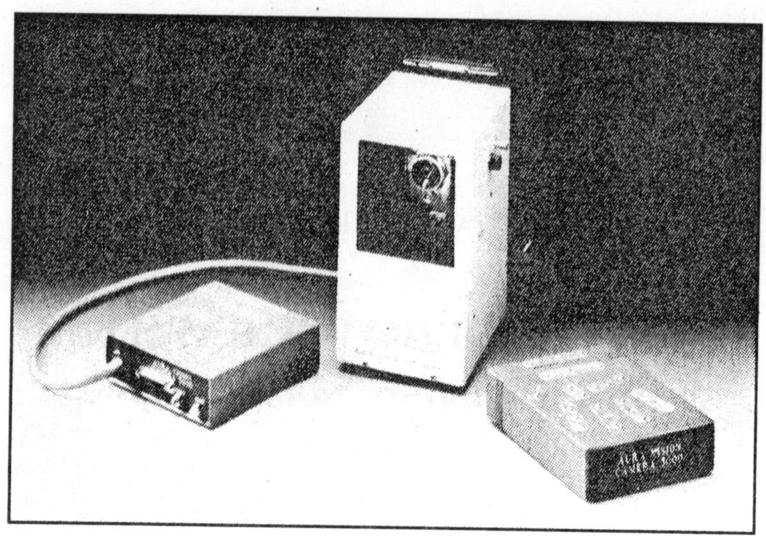

Aura Camera

The original researcher and designer in this new technology is Guy Coggins, inventor of the Aura Camera 3000, which he introduced in 1992. This camera represents a major step in biofeedback imaging. The Aura Camera 3000 (and the new 6000), according to its inventor, does not actually "see" auras, rather it perceives them electronically, converting energy impulses into an auric image with the help of a computer program. These images can then be viewed on a projection screen or photographically printed, creating a permanent record.

Coggins (1994) states this camera "transmits radio waves through the subject's electromagnetic field, then converts the waves into electrical energy which can be processed . . . as light and color." In utilizing his earlier, more complex camera, a subject, while sitting, is asked to place his/her hands on a probe that transmits a radio frequency through the individual. The subject's body will then begin emitting radio waves (specific frequencies). The body becomes a "living antenna" transmitter. The energy produced by this " human antenna" is, in turn, received by a complex series of receiver-scanners located in an array behind the subject (the antenna grid—antenna receiver). Each probe has a unique receiver wired through a high speed multiplexer. This device converts information from the antenna grid to a computer where it is processed and displayed as electromagnetic energy (i.e., light and sound).

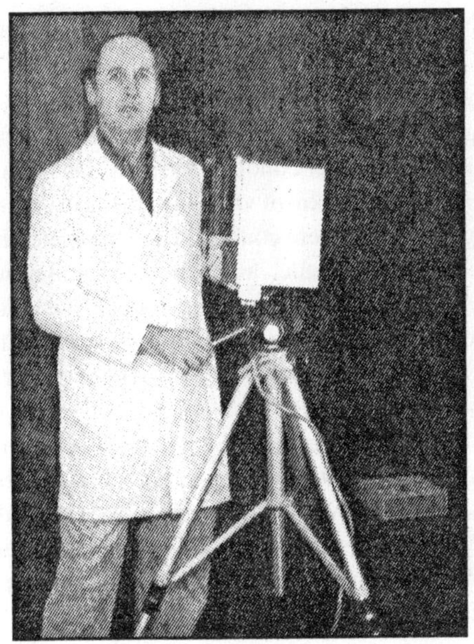

Guy Coggins,
inventor of the Aura Camera

Body and Machine

It has long been known that interstate (body energy) changes can produce physiological changes. These transformations include changes in a subject's skin: impedance, chemistry, dielectric constant, and the collection of free ions on the skin surface.

In Barbara Brennan's (1987) book, she explains some technological experiments validating the existence of the aura. A year later, in 1988, Richard Gerber states in *Vibrational Medicine* that the search for a scientific tool to prove auric existence must include research by Valerie Hunt, a professor at the University of California. Dr. Hunt devised a technique wherein standard EMG electrodes were used to study changes in bioelectrical energy in segments of the derma (skin) approximating chakra locations. Dr. Hunt found that color variations in the aura (i.e., red, green, orange, etc.), as observed by psychics, correspond with EMG recordings. Aura colors were associated with different wave designs registered at the chakra points. In this way, it was shown that the chakra and aura work together to influence the human organism.

According to Aura Imaging photographer, Susana Madden (1995):

> In 1988, "The Rolf Study," the most fascinating recent experiment to date using technology to prove the existence of auras and their importance in healing was conducted by . . . Dr. Hunt. . . . Electrodes were placed on the skin of various patients in order to transmit electronic signals which were conveyed and translated into varying wave frequencies with Fouier analysis and sonogram frequency analysis, while the patients were being rolfed. The different wave frequencies corresponded to different colors. For instance, a wave frequency, which was measured at 500-700 hertz, or cycles per second, was correlated to the color yellow. White, the fastest, was 1100-1200 hertz. What made this experiment exciting were the observations by clairvoyant aura reader Rev. Rosalyn Bruyere, . . . who . . . constantly observed and reported with her so called subjective "second sight" the same changing colors in the patient's aura that the electronic measuring system recorded with wave frequency/ color correlation.

Other scientific evidence substantiating the existence of the *Chakra-nadir* system (i.e., energy transformers) can be found in a series of tests conducted by Hiroshi Motoyama. Dr. Motoyama was able to measure the bioelectrical field of psychics, occultists, and others who had activated a specific chakra during meditation or spiritual enlightenment. The results were, according to Dr. Gerber (1988), that "the amplitude and frequency of the electric field over the chakra being concentrated upon [by the psychic] was significantly greater than the energy recorded from chakras of control subjects."

Whether in a still format (print), a video, or a finger or toe print using Kirlian technology, there are basically two methods used in observing these energy centers and auric emissions. The first one is the video method where an antennae grid (a sequential series of 100 x 100 radio receiving antennas, each capable of picking up signals closest to it) is placed behind the subject upon which energy is transmitted (Coggins 1994).

The second technique incorporates a procedure which simultaneously measures electromagnetic energy levels at various acupuncture points on the hands (using hand probes). These points correlate to different parts of the physical and auric bodies.

The Future

Although still experimental, Aura Imaging Technology has been widely used. As a parapsychological tool, the instrument seems to verify readings made by certain psychics and mediums. This technology is being used by many healers, therapists, biofeedback centers, meditation retreats, and private health and medical practices. Aura cameras provide practitioners one more tool for evaluating their client's physiological and psychological nature. The camera, as in Kirlian techniques, is also capable of recording interpersonal relationships (i.e., sexual attraction, hate, disinterest, and personalities). The scientific concept behind this technique is that when two people who like each other touch, their skin resistance drops. On the other hand, when people who have no emotional attraction touch, skin resistance increases and a barrier (an energy line, appearing as a bright section of light) is formed. An example of this technique was presented in an article on Kirlian photography appearing in the German magazine *Esotera* (Progen 1990). In this study, two subjects, male and female, were asked to place their fingers close together and have a picture taken by the Kirlian apparatus. This photograph was to be retaken during each of three consecutive weeks. The initial picture showed that the man was attracted to the woman (strong, bright red and blue corona). The female corona, however, revealed that the woman was disinterested. This fact was shown in the photograph by her corona's attempt to form an energy barrier between her electrical field and his. By the second week, the man's corona changed in shape and size (larger, more intense) showing his persistence. The barrier on the female's corona lessened and was beginning to show signs of red-orange (desire or pleasure), meaning that the woman was becoming more responsive to the man's advances. Finally, in the third week, the photograph showed two healthy, bright coronas, full of red, blue, and white—blending together. The article states that the couple are living together "happy ever after" (Progen 1990).

Using the aura camera, individuals may be photographed together, with the subjects kissing or touching. An alternative method is photographing the individuals separately while having them think of each other. The photographs are then compared.

According to Coggins (1994), the camera has also "show[n] comparative differences and improvements in a patient's energy field in 'before' and 'after' photos taken during healing and counseling sessions." The healing in these cases was performed by psychic or chakra healers. In this setting, a photograph was taken before the healing session and again after the psychic activated a specific chakra or energy center in the subject's body (one that, according to the practitioner, was causing the physical or emotional problem). When re-photographed, there appeared to be significant increases in amplitude and frequency of the electric field over the subject's chakra.

Full-body Imaging

Experimentation is also underway toward producing a full-body video image—an aura video. This system also combines traditional biofeedback measuring with high-voltage field imaging. The video displays the aura as colorful moving fields of light. With the video technique, the immediate effects of a healing treatment or therapy session can be seen in the energy field as the healing or therapy session progresses.

Coggins (1996) says the video system is based on the antenna grid design of his first aura camera. The subject places her hands on transmitting antennas. "The effect is as if you placed your hand on the antenna of your portable telephone," says Coggins. "The radio energy will flow through your body and be emitted in all directions. We scan our receiving antenna in such a way as to form an image. It's like an x-ray of your aura." Coggins believes this technology will be most effective for personal growth and self-discovery. "The visible aura will reflect a patient's emotional response in real time. The therapist and patient can see his emotions reflected in the colorful field. It effectively shows not only emotions but also energy blocks. Even physical maladies can be reflected in the field. The interactive computer talks through its speaker and can tell if there is a problem. The computers can also listen, so one can talk directly to a machine that appears to be very intuitive."

Interactive Aura Imaging

Coggins (1996) will use an interactive computer program that can walk a person through questions and give vocal feedback on the changes happening in the energy field. "The computer might take you through a relaxing exercise—it may ask you to tighten the muscles in your right arm, and you would see the colors change on your right side. After the computer asks you to relax, you see the corresponding cooling in color tones. You can see how tension and stress affect your energy field."

An interactive emotional feedback program might also ask specific questions about work or relationships. When one begins thinking about something that creates tension in his life, he might see the colors explode like Fourth of July fireworks. "Many of us fall into old patterns of saying 'Oh, it's just fine,' when we really have unresolved emotion about an issue," says Coggins (1996). "This technology can help bring those issues to the surface and deal with them in a gentle way."

Conclusion

The search for the aura continues. In small, one-man laboratories, psychic circles, healing sessions, and university parapsychological departments, scientists, psychics, and occultists are searching for the elusive aura. It is hoped that, within the near future, all individuals will be allowed, whether naturally or through some technological advance, to see, record, and study this inexplicable phenomenon.

CHAPTER FOUR

THE NEW PHYSICS[1]

Fritjof Capra, PhD

According to the Eastern mystics, the direct mystical experience of reality is a momentous event which shakes the very foundations of one's world view. D. T. Suzuki has called it 'the most startling event that could ever happen in the realm of human consciousness . . . upsetting every form of standardised experience', (Suzuki 1968, 7) and he has illustrated the shocking character of this experience with the words of a Zen master who described it as 'the bottom of a pail breaking through'.

Physicists, at the beginning of this century, felt much the same way when the foundations of their world view were shaken by the new experience of the atomic reality, and they described this experience in terms which were often very similar to those used by Suzuki's Zen master. Thus Heisenberg wrote:

> The violent reaction on the recent development of modern physics can only be understood when one realises that here the foundations of physics have started moving; and that this motion has caused the feeling that the ground would be cut from science. (Heisenberg 1958, 167)

Einstein experienced the same shock when he first came in contact with the new reality of atomic physics. He wrote in his autobiography:

> All my attempts to adapt the theoretical foundation of physics to this (new type of) knowledge failed completely. It was as if the ground

> had been pulled out from under one, with no firm foundation to be seen anywhere, upon which one could have built. (Schilpp 1949, 45)

The discoveries of modern physics necessitated profound changes of concepts like space, time, matter, object, cause and effect, etc., and since these concepts are so basic to our way of experiencing the world it is not surprising that the physicists who were forced to change them felt something of a shock. Out of these changes emerged a new and radically different world view, still in the process of formation by current scientific research.

It seems, then, that Eastern mystics and Western physicists went through similar revolutionary experiences which led them to completely new ways of seeing the world. In the following two passages, the European physicist Niels Bohr and the Indian mystic Sri Aurobindo both express the depth and the radical character of this experience.

> The great extension of our experience in recent years has brought to light the insufficiency of our simple mechanical conceptions and, as a consequence, has shaken the foundation on which the customary interpretation of observation was based.
>
> *Niels Bohr* (1934, 2)

> All things in fact begin to change their nature and appearance; one's whole experience of the world is radically different . . . There is a new vast and deep way of experiencing, seeing, knowing, contacting things.
>
> *Sri Aurobindo* (1958, 327)

This chapter will serve to sketch a preliminary picture of this new conception of the world against the contrasting background of classical physics; showing how the classical mechanistic world view had to be abandoned at the beginning of this century when quantum theory and relativity theory—the two basic theories of modern physics—forced us to adopt a much more subtle, holistic and 'organic' view of nature.

The world view which was changed by the discoveries of modern physics had been based on Newton's mechanical model of the universe. This model constituted the solid framework of classical physics. It was indeed a most formidable foundation supporting, like a mighty rock, all of science and providing a firm basis for natural philosophy for almost three centuries.

The stage of the Newtonian universe, on which all physical phenomena took place, was the three-dimensional space of classical Euclidean geometry. It was an absolute space, always at rest and unchangeable. In Newton's own words, 'Absolute space, in its own nature, without regard to anything external, remains always similar and immovable' (Capek 1961, 7). All changes in the physical world were described in terms of a separate dimension, called time, which again was absolute, having no connection with the material world and flowing smoothly from the past through the present to the future. 'Absolute, true, and mathematical time,' said Newton, 'of itself and by its own nature, flows uniformly, without regard to anything external' (Capek 1961, 36).

The elements of the Newtonian world which moved in this absolute space and absolute time were material particles. In the mathematical equations they were treated as 'mass points' and Newton saw them as small, solid, and indestructible objects out of which all matter was made. This model was quite similar to that of the Greek atomists. Both were based on the distinction between the full and the void, between matter and space, and in both models the particles remained always identical in their mass and shape. Matter was therefore always conserved and essentially passive. The important difference between the Democritean and Newtonian atomism is that the latter includes a precise description of the force acting between the material particles. This force is very simple, depending only on the masses and the mutual distances of the particles. It is the force of gravity, and it was seen by Newton as rigidly connected with the bodies it acted upon, and as acting instantaneously over a distance. Although this was a strange hypothesis, it was not investigated further. The particles and the forces between them were seen as created by God and thus were not subject to further analysis. In his *Opticks*, Newton gives us a clear picture of how he imagined God's creation of the material world:

> It seems probable to me that God in the beginning formed matter in solid, massy, hard, impenetrable, movable particles, of such sizes and figures, and with such other properties, and in such proportion to space, as most conduced to the end for which he formed them; and that these primitive particles being solids, are incomparably harder than any porous bodies compounded of them; even so very hard, as never to wear or break in pieces; no ordinary power being able to divide what God himself made one in the first creation. (Crosland 1971, 76)

All physical events are reduced, in Newtonian mechanics, to the motion of material points in space, caused by their mutual attraction, i.e. by the force of gravity. In order to put the effect of this force on a mass point into a precise mathematical form, Newton had to invent completely new concepts and mathematical techniques, those of differential calculus. This was a tremendous intellectual achievement and has been praised by Einstein as 'perhaps the greatest advance in thought that a single individual was every privileged to make'.

Newton's equations of motion are the basis of classical mechanics. They were considered to be fixed laws according to which material points move, and were thus thought to account for all changes observed in the physical world. In the Newtonian view, God had created, in the beginning, the material particles, the forces between them, and the fundamental laws of motion. In this way, the whole universe was set in motion and it has continued to run ever since, like a machine, governed by immutable laws.

The mechanistic view of nature is thus closely related to a rigorous determinism. The giant cosmic machine was seen as being completely causal and determinate. All that happened had a definite cause and gave rise to a definite effect, and the future of any part of the system could—in principle—be predicted with absolute certainty if its state at any time was known in all details. This belief found its clearest expression in the famous words of the French mathematician Pierre Simon Laplace:

> An intellect which at a given instant knew all the forces acting in nature, and the position of all things of which the world consists—supposing the said intellect were vast enough to subject these data to analysis—would embrace in the same formula the motions of the greatest bodies in the universe and those of the slightest atoms; nothing would be uncertain for it, and the future, like the past, would be present to its eyes. (Capek 1961, 122)

The philosophical basis of this rigorous determinism was the fundamental division between the I and the world introduced by Descartes. As a consequence of this division, it was believed that the world could be described objectively, i.e. without ever mentioning the human observer, and such an objective description of nature became the ideal of all science.

The eighteenth and nineteenth centuries witnessed a tremendous success of Newtonian mechanics. Newton himself applied his theory to the movement of the planets and was able to explain the basic features of the solar system. His planetary model was greatly simplified, however, neglecting, for example, the gravitational influence of the planets on each other, and thus he found that there were certain irregularities which he could not explain. He resolved this problem by assuming that God was always present in the universe to correct these irregularities.

Laplace, the great mathematician, set himself the ambitious task of refining and perfecting Newton's calculations in a book which should 'offer a complete solution of the great mechanical problem presented by the solar system, and bring theory to coincide so closely with observation that empirical equations would no longer find a place in astronomical tables' (Jeans 1951, 237). The result was a large work in five volumes, called *Mécanique Céleste* in which Laplace succeeded in explaining the motions of the planets, moons and comets down to the smallest details, as well as the flow of the tides and other phenomena related to gravity. He showed that the Newtonian laws of motion assured the stability of the solar system and treated the universe as a perfectly self-regulating machine. When Laplace presented the first edition of his work to Napoleon—so the story goes—Napoleon remarked, 'Monsieur Laplace, they tell me you have written this large book on the system of the universe, and have never even mentioned its Creator.' To this Laplace replied bluntly, 'I had no need for that hypothesis.'

Encouraged by the brilliant success of Newtonian mechanics in astronomy, physicists extended it to the continuous motion of fluids and to the vibrations of elastic bodies, and again it worked. Finally, even the theory of heat could be reduced to mechanics when it was realized that heat was the energy created by a complicated 'jiggling' motion of the molecules. When the temperature of, say, water is increased the motion of the water molecules increases until they overcome the forces holding them together and fly apart. In this way, water turns into steam. On the other hand, when the thermal motion is slowed down by cooling the water, the molecules finally lock into a new, more rigid pattern which is ice. In a similar way, many other thermal phenomena can be understood quite well from a purely mechanistic point of view.

The enormous success of the mechanistic model made physicists of the early nineteenth century believe that the universe was indeed a huge mechanical system running according to the Newtonian laws of motion. These laws were seen as the basic laws of nature and Newton's mechanics was considered to be the ultimate theory of natural phenomena. And

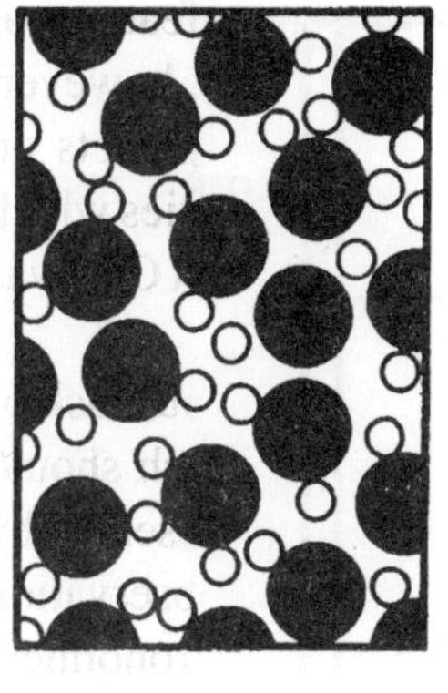

water

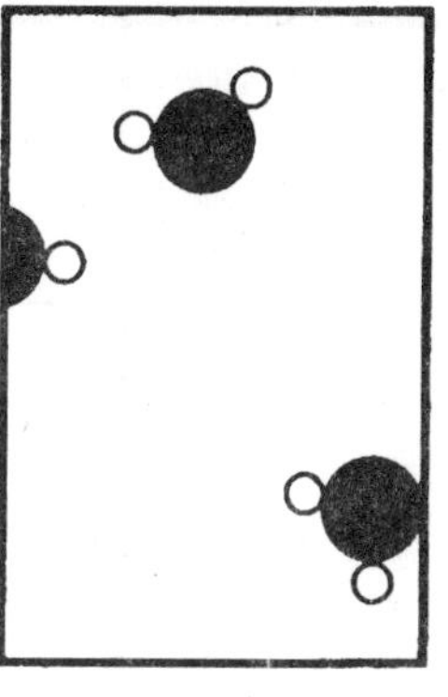

steam

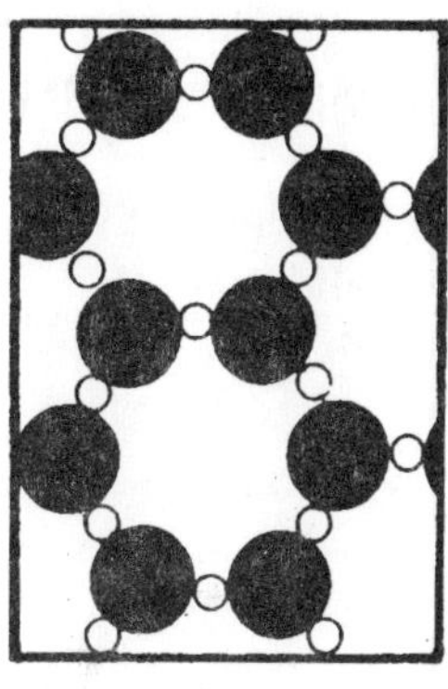

ice

yet, it was less than a hundred years later that a new physical reality was discovered which made the limitations of the Newtonian model apparent and showed that none of its features had absolute validity.

This realization did not come abruptly, but was initiated by developments that had already started in the nineteenth century and prepared the way for the scientific revolutions of our time. The first of these developments was the discovery and investigation of electric and magnetic phenomena which could not be described appropriately by the mechanistic model and involved a new type of force. The important step was made by Michael Faraday and Clerk Maxwell—the first, one of the greatest experimenters in the history of science, the second, a brilliant theorist. When Faraday produced an electric current in a coil of copper by moving a magnet near it, and thus converted the mechanical work of moving the magnet into electric energy, he brought science and technology to a turning point. His fundamental experiment gave birth, on the one hand, to the vast technology of electrical engineering; on the other hand, it formed the basis of his and Maxwell's theoretical speculations which, eventually, resulted in a complete theory of electromagnetism. Faraday and Maxwell did not only study the effects of the electric and magnetic forces, but made the forces themselves the primary object of their investigation. They replaced the concept of a force by that of a force field, and in doing so they were the first to go beyond Newtonian physics.

Instead of interpreting the interaction between a positive and a negative charge simply by saying that the two charges attract each other like two masses in Newtonian mechanics, Faraday and Maxwell found it more appropriate to say that each charge creates a 'disturbance', or a

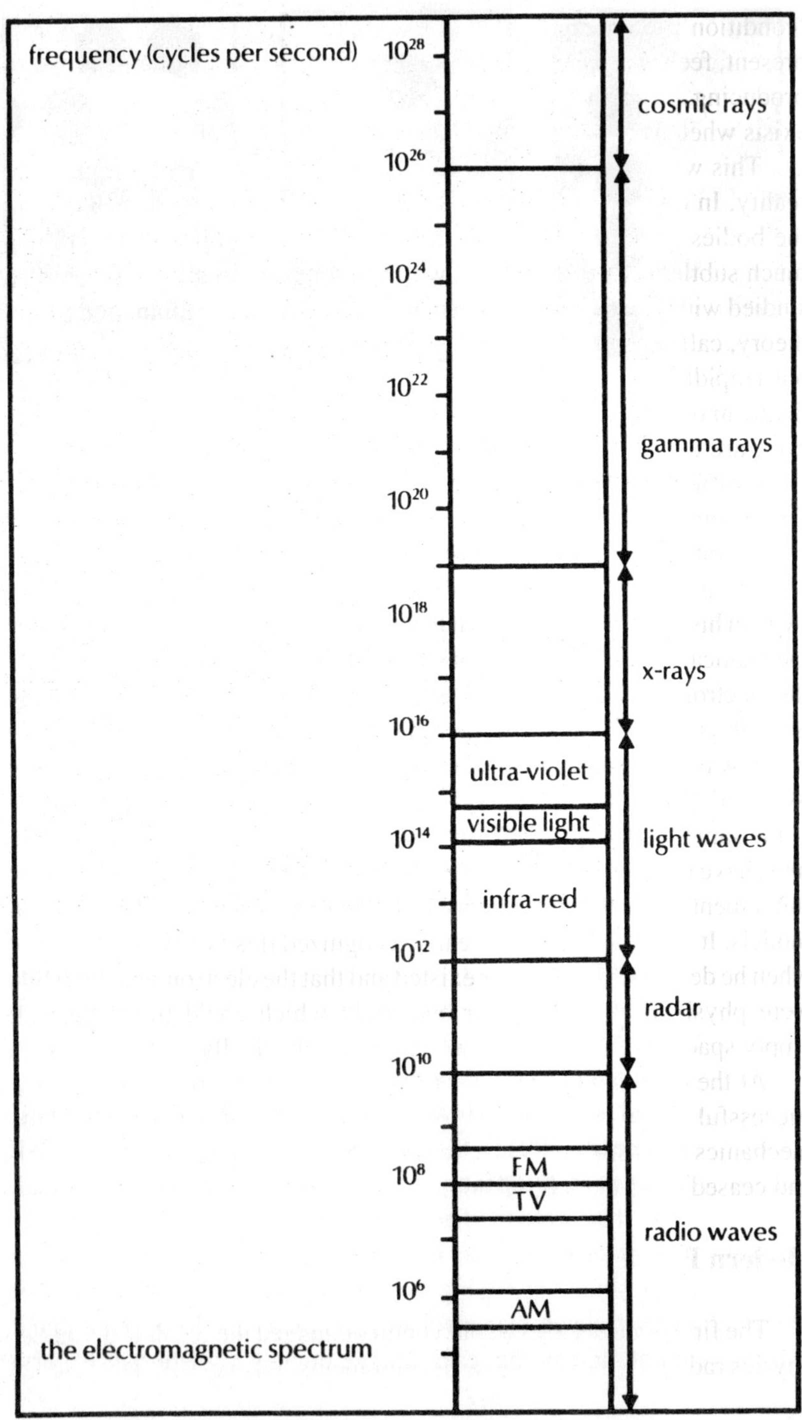
frequency (cycles per second)
10^{28}
10^{26}
10^{24}
10^{22}
10^{20}
10^{18}
10^{16}
10^{14}
10^{12}
10^{10}
10^{8}
10^{6}
cosmic rays
gamma rays
x-rays
ultra-violet
visible light
infra-red
light waves
radar
FM
TV
AM
radio waves
the electromagnetic spectrum

'condition', in the space around it so that the other charge, when it is present, feels a force. This condition in space which has the potential of producing a force is called a field. It is created by a single charge and it exists whether or not another charge is brought in to feel its effect.

This was a most profound change in man's conception of physical reality. In the Newtonian view, the forces were rigidly connected with the bodies they act upon. Now the force concept was replaced by the much subtler concept of a field which had its own reality and could be studied without any reference to material bodies. The culmination of this theory, called electrodynamics, was the realization that light is nothing but a rapidly alternating electromagnetic field travelling through space in the form of waves. Today we know that radio waves, light waves or X-rays, are all electromagnetic waves, oscillating electric and magnetic fields differing only in the frequency of their oscillation, and that visible light is only a tiny fraction of the electromagnetic spectrum.

In spite of these far-reaching changes, Newtonian mechanics at first held its position as the basis of all physics. Maxwell himself tried to explain his results in mechanical terms, interpreting the fields as states of mechanical stress in a very light space-filling medium, called ether, and the electromagnetic waves as elastic waves of this ether. This was only natural as waves are usually experienced as vibrations of something; water waves as vibrations of water, sound waves as vibrations of air. Maxwell, however, used several mechanical interpretations of his theory at the same time and apparently took none of them really seriously. He must have realized intuitively, even if he did not say so explicitly, that the fundamental entities in his theory were the fields and not the mechanical models. It was Einstein who clearly recognized this fact fifty years later when he declared that no ether existed and that the electromagnetic fields were physical entities in their own right which could travel through empty space and could not be explained mechanically.

At the beginning of the twentieth century, then, physicists had two successful theories which applied to different phenomena: Newton's mechanics and Maxwell's electrodynamics. Thus the Newtonian model had ceased to be the basis of all physics.

Modern Physics

The first three decades of our century changed the whole situation in physics radically. Two separate developments—that of relativity theory and of atomic physics—shattered all the principal concepts of the Newtonian world view: the notion of absolute space and time, the elementary solid particles, the strictly causal nature of physical phenomena, and the ideal of an objective description of nature. None of these concepts could be extended to the new domains into which physics was now penetrating.

At the beginning of modern physics stands the extraordinary intellectual feat of one man: Albert Einstein. In two articles, both published in 1905, Einstein initiated two revolutionary trends of thought. One was his special theory of relativity, the other was a new way of looking at electromagnetic radiation which was to become characteristic of quantum theory, the theory of atomic phenomena. The complete quantum theory was worked out twenty years later by a whole team of physicists. Relativity theory, however, was constructed in its complete form almost entirely by Einstein himself. Einstein's scientific papers stand at the beginning of the twentieth century as imposing intellectual monuments—the pyramids of modern civilization.

Einstein strongly believed in nature's inherent harmony and his deepest concern throughout his scientific life was to find a unified foundation of physics. He began to move towards this goal by constructing a common framework for electrodynamics and mechanics, the two separate theories of classical physics. This framework is known as the special theory of relativity. It unified and completed the structure of classical physics, but at the same time it involved drastic changes in the traditional concepts of space and time and undermined one of the foundations of the Newtonian world view.

According to relativity theory, space is not three-dimensional and time is not a separate entity. Both are intimately connected and form a four-dimensional continuum, 'space-time'. In relativity theory, therefore, we can never talk about space without talking about time and vice versa. Furthermore, there is no universal flow of time as in the Newtonian model. Different observers will order events differently in time if they move with different velocities relative to the observed events. In such a case, two events which are seen as occurring simultaneously by one observer may occur in different temporal sequences for other observers. All measurements involving space and time thus lose their absolute significance. In relativity theory, the Newtonian concept of an absolute space as the stage of physical phenomena is abandoned and so is the concept of an absolute time. Both space and time become merely elements of the language a particular observer used for his description of the phenomena.

The concepts of space and time are so basic for the description of natural phenomena that their modification entails a modification of the whole framework that we use to describe nature. The most important consequence of this modification is the realization that mass is nothing but a form of energy. Even an object at rest has energy stored in its mass, and the relation between the two is given by the famous equation $E=mc^2$, c being the speed of light.

This constant c, the speed of light, is of fundamental importance for the theory of relativity. Whenever we describe physical phenomena involving velocities which approach the speed of light, our description has to take relativity theory into account. This applies in particular to electromagnetic phenomena, of which light is just one example and which led Einstein to the formulation of his theory.

In 1915, Einstein proposed his general theory of relativity in which the framework of the special theory is extended to include gravity, i.e. the mutual attraction of all massive bodies. Whereas the special theory has been confirmed by innumerable experiments, the general theory has not yet been confirmed conclusively. However, it is so far the most accepted, consistent and elegant theory of gravity and is widely used in astrophysics and cosmology for the description of the universe at large.

The force of gravity, according to Einstein's theory, has the effect of 'curving' space and time. This means that ordinary Euclidean geometry is no longer valid in such a curved space, just as the two-dimensional geometry of a plane cannot be applied on the surface of a sphere. On a plane, we can draw, for example, a square by marking off one metre on a straight line, making a right angle and marking off another metre, then making another right angle and marking off another metre, and finally making a third right angle and marking off one metre again, after which we are back at the starting point and the square is completed. On a sphere, however, this procedure does not work because the rules of Euclidean geometry do not hold on curved surfaces. In the same way, we can define a three-dimensional curved space to be one in which Euclidean geometry is no longer valid. Einstein's theory, now, says that three-dimensional space is actually curved, and that the curvature is caused by the gravitational field of massive bodies.Wherever there is a massive object, e.g. a star or a planet, the space around it is curved and the degree of curvature depends on the mass of the object. And as space can never be separated

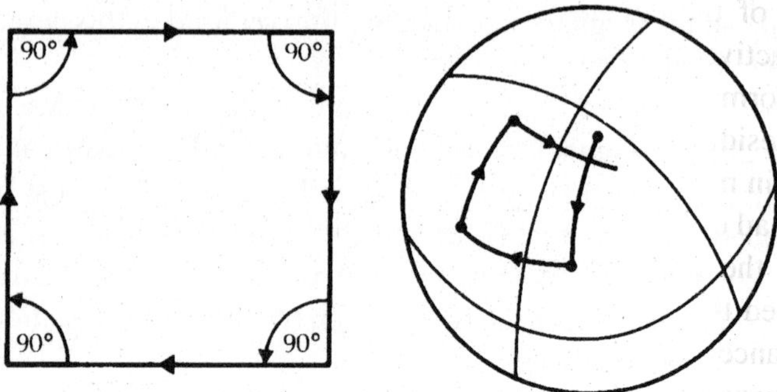

drawing a square on a plane and on a sphere

from time in relativity theory, time as well is affected by the presence of matter, flowing at different rates in different parts of the universe. Einstein's general theory of relativity thus completely abolishes the concepts of absolute space and time. Not only are all measurements involving space and time relative; the whole structure of space-time depends on the distribution of matter in the universe, and the concept of 'empty space' loses its meaning.

The mechanistic world view of classical physics was based on the notion of solid bodies moving in empty space. This notion is still valid in the region that has been called the 'zone of middle dimensions', that is, in the realm of our daily experience where classical physics continues to be a useful theory. Both concepts—that of empty space and that of solid material bodies—are deeply ingrained in our habits of thought, so it is extremely difficult for us to imagine a physical reality where they do not apply. And yet, this is precisely what modern physics forces us to do when we go beyond the middle dimensions. 'Empty space' has lost its meaning in astrophysics and cosmology, the sciences of the universe at large, and the concept of solid objects was shattered by atomic physics, the science of the infinitely small.

At the turn of the century, several phenomena connected with the structure of atoms and inexplicable in terms of classical physics were discovered. The first indication that atoms had some structure came from the discovery of X-rays; a new radiation which rapidly found its now well known application in medicine. X-rays, however, are not the only radiation emitted by atoms. Soon after their discovery, other kinds of radiation were discovered which are emitted by the atoms of so-called radioactive substances. The phenomenon of radioactivity gave definite proof of the composite nature of atoms, showing that the atoms of radioactive substances not only emit various types of radiation, but also transform themselves into atoms of completely different substances.

Besides being objects of intense study, these phenomena were also used, in most ingenious ways, as new tools to probe deeper into matter than had ever been possible before. Thus Max von Laue used X-rays to study the arrangements of atoms in crystals, and Ernest Rutherford realized that the so-called alpha particles emanating from radioactive substances were high-speed projectiles of subatomic size which could be used to explore the interior of the atom. They could be fired at atoms, and from the way they were deflected one could draw conclusions about the atoms' structure.

When Rutherford bombarded atoms with these alpha particles, he obtained sensational and totally unexpected results. Far from being the hard and solid particles they were believed to be since antiquity, the atoms turned out to consist of vast regions of space in which extremely small particles—the electrons—moved around the nucleus, bound to it by electric forces. It is not easy to get a feeling for the order of magnitude of atoms, so far is it removed from our macroscopic scale. The diameter of an atom is about one hundred millionth of a centimetre. In order to visualize this diminutive size, imagine an orange blown up to the size of the Earth. The atoms of the orange will then have the size of cherries. Myriads of cherries, tightly packed into a globe of the size of the Earth—that's a magnified picture of the atoms in an orange.

An atom, therefore, is extremely small compared to macroscopic objects, but it is huge compared to the nucleus in its centre. In our picture of cherry-sized atoms, the nucleus of an atom will be so small that we will not be able to see it. If we blew up the atom to the size of a football, or even to room size, the nucleus would still be too small to be seen by the naked eye. To see the nucleus, we would have to blow up the atom to the size of the biggest dome in the world, the dome of St Peter's Cathedral in Rome. In an atom of that size, the nucleus would have the size of a grain of salt! A grain of salt in the middle of the dome of St Peter's, and the specks of dust whirling around it in the vast space of the dome—this is how we can picture the nucleus and electrons of an atom.

Soon after the emergence of this 'planetary' model of the atom, it was discovered that the number of electrons in the atoms of an element determine the element's chemical properties, and today we know that the whole periodic table of elements can be built up by successively adding protons and neutrons to the nucleus of the lightest atom—hydrogen[2]—and the corresponding number of electrons to its atomic 'shell'. The interactions between the atoms give rise to the various chemical processes, so that all of chemistry can now in principle be understood on the basis of the laws of atomic physics.

These laws, however, were not easy to recognize. They were discovered in the 1920s by an international group of physicists including Niels Bohr from Denmark, Louis De Broglie from France, Erwin Schrödinger and Wolfgang Pauli from Austria, Werner Heisenberg from Germany, and Paul Dirac from England. These men joined their forces across all national borders and shaped one of the most exciting periods in modern science, which brought man, for the first time, into contact with the strange and unexpected reality of the subatomic world. Every time the physicists asked nature a question in an atomic experiment, nature answered with a paradox, and the more they tried to clarify the situation, the sharper the paradoxes became. It took them a long time to accept the fact that these paradoxes belong to the intrinsic structure of atomic physics, and to realize that they arise whenever one attempts to describe atomic events in the traditional terms of physics.

Once this was perceived, the physicists began to learn to ask the right questions and to avoid contradictions. In the words of Heisenberg, 'they somehow got into the spirit of the quantum theory', and finally they found the precise and consistent mathematical foımulation of this theory.

The concepts of quantum theory were not easy to accept even after their mathematical formulation had been completed. Their effect on the physicists' imaginations was truly shattering. Rutherford's experiments had shown that atoms, instead of being hard and indestructible, consisted of vast regions of space in which extremely small particles moved, and now quantum theory made it clear that even these particles were nothing like the solid objects of classical physics. The subatomic units of matter are very abstract entities which have a dual aspect. Depending on how we look at them, they appear sometimes as particles, sometimes as waves; and this dual nature is also exhibited by light which can take the form of electromagnetic waves or of particles.

a particle *a wave*

This property of matter and of light is very strange. It seems impossible to accept that something can be, at the same time, a particle—i.e., an entity confined to a very small volume—and a wave, which is spread out over a large region of space. This contradiction gave rise to most of the *koan*-like paradoxes which finally led to the formulation of quantum theory. The whole development started when Max Planck discovered that the energy of heat radiation is not emitted continuously, but appears in the form of 'energy packets'. Einstein called these energy packets 'quanta' and recognized them as a fundamental aspect of nature. He was bold enough to postulate that light and every other form of electromagnetic radiation can appear not only as electromagnetic waves, but also in the form of these quanta. The light quanta, which gave quantum theory its name, have since been accepted as bona fide particles and are now called photons. They are particles of a special kind, however, massless and always travelling with the speed of light.

The apparent contradiction between the particle and the wave picture was solved in a completely unexpected way which called in question the very foundation of the mechanistic world view—the concept of the reality of matter. At the subatomic level, matter does not exist with certainty at definite places, but rather shows 'tendencies to exist', and atomic events do not occur with certainty at definite times and in definite ways, but rather show 'tendencies to occur'. In the formalism of quantum theory, these tendencies are expressed as probabilities and are associated with mathematical quantities which take the form of waves. This is why particles can be waves at the same time. They are not 'real' three-dimensional waves like sound or water waves. They are 'probability waves', abstract mathematical quantities with all the characteristic properties of waves which are related to the probabilities of finding the particles at particular points in space and at particular times. All the laws of atomic physics are expressed in terms of these probabilities. We can never predict an atomic event with certainty; we can only say how likely it is to happen.

Quantum theory has thus demolished the classical concepts of solid objects and of strictly deterministic laws of nature. At the subatomic level, the solid material objects of classical physics dissolve into wave-like patterns of probabilities, and these patterns, ultimately, do not represent probabilities of things, but rather probabilities of interconnections. A careful analysis of the process of observation in atomic physics has shown that the subatomic particles have no meaning as isolated entities, but can only be understood as interconnections between the preparation of an experiment and the subsequent measurement. Quantum theory thus reveals a basic oneness of the universe. It shows that we cannot decompose the world into independently existing smallest units. As we penetrate into matter, nature does not show us any isolated 'basic building blocks', but rather appears as a complicated web of relations between the various parts of the whole. These relations always include the observer in an essential way. The human observer constitutes the final link in the chain of observational processes, and the properties of any atomic object can only be understood in terms of the object's interaction with the observer. This means that the classical ideal of an objective description of nature is no longer valid. The Cartesian partition between the I and the world, between the observer and the observed, cannot be made when dealing with atomic matter. In atomic physics, we can never speak about nature without, at the same time, speaking about ourselves.

The new atomic theory could immediately solve several puzzles which had arisen in connection with the structure of atoms and could not be explained by Rutherford's planetary model. First of all, Rutherford's experiments had shown that the atoms making up solid matter consist almost entirely of empty space, as far as the distribution of mass is concerned. But if all the objects around us, and we ourselves, consist mostly of empty space, why can't we walk through closed doors? In other words, what is it that gives matter its solid aspect?

A second puzzle was the extraordinary mechanical stability of atoms. In the air, for example, atoms collide millions of times every second and yet go back to their original form after each collision. No planetary system following the laws of classical mechanics would ever come out of these collisions unaltered. But an oxygen atom will always retain its characteristic configuration of electrons, no matter how often it collides with other atoms. This configuration, furthermore, is exactly the same in all atoms of a given kind. Two iron atoms, and consequently two pieces of pure iron, are completely identical, no matter where they come from or how they have been treated in the past.

Quantum theory has shown that all these astonishing properties of atoms arise from the wave nature of their electrons. To begin with, the solid aspect of matter is the consequence of a typical 'quantum effect' connected with the dual wave/particle aspect of matter, a feature of the subatomic world which has no macroscopic analogue. Whenever a particle is confined to a small region of space it reacts to this confinement by moving around, and the smaller the region of confinement is, the faster the particle moves around in it. In the atom, now, there are two competing forces. On the one hand, the electrons are bound to the nucleus by electric forces which try to keep them as close as possible. On the other hand, they respond to their confinement by whirling around, and the tighter they are bound to the nucleus, the higher their velocity will be; in fact, the confinement of electrons in an atom results in enormous velocities of about 600 miles per second! These high velocities make the atom appear as a rigid sphere, just as a fast rotating propeller appears as a disc. It is very difficult to compress atoms any further and thus they give matter its familiar solid aspect

In the atom, then, the electrons settle in orbits in such a way that there is an optimal balance between the attraction of the nucleus and their reluctance to be confined. The atomic orbits, however, are very different from those of the planets in the solar system, the difference arising from the wave nature of the electrons. An atom cannot be pictured as a small planetary system. Rather than particles circling around the nucleus, we have to imagine probability waves arranged in different orbits. Whenever we make a measurement, we will find the electrons somewhere in these orbits, but we cannot say that they are 'going around the nucleus' in the sense of classical mechanics.

In the orbits, the electron waves have to be arranged in such a way that 'their ends meet', i.e. that they form patterns known as 'standing waves'. These patterns appear whenever waves are confined to a finite region, like the waves in a vibrating guitar string, or in the air inside a flute (see diagram overleaf). It is well known from these examples that standing waves can assume only a limited number of well-defined shapes. In the case of the electron waves inside an atom, this means that they can exist only in certain atomic orbits with definite diameters. The electron of a hydrogen atom, for example, can only exist in a certain first, second or third orbit, etc., and nowhere in between. Under normal conditions, it will always be in its lowest orbit, called the 'ground state' of the atom. From there, the electron can jump to higher orbits if it receives the necessary amount of energy, and then the atom is said to be in an 'excited state' from which it will go back to its ground state after a while, the electron giving off the surplus energy in the form of a quantum of electromagnetic radiation, or photon. The states of an atom, i.e. the shapes and mutual distances of its electron orbits, are exactly the same for

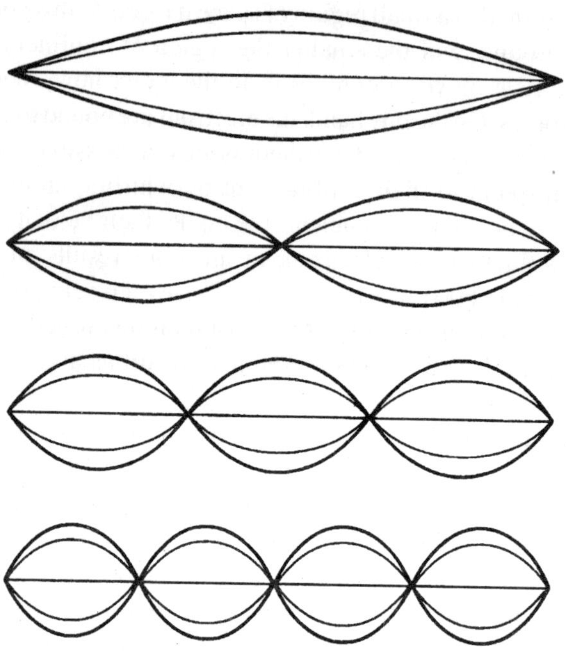

standing-wave patterns in a vibrating string

all atoms with the same number of electrons. This is why any two oxygen atoms, for example, will be completely identical. They may be in different excited states, perhaps due to collisions with other atoms in the air, but after a while they will invariably return to exactly the same ground state. The wave nature of the electrons accounts thus for the identity of atoms and for their great mechanical stability.

A further characteristic feature of atomic states is the fact that they can be completely specified by a set of integral numbers, called 'quantum numbers', which indicate the location and shape of the electron orbits. The first quantum number is the number of the orbit and determines the energy an electron must have to be in that orbit; two more numbers specify the detailed shape of the electron wave in the orbit and are related to the speed and orientation of the electron's rotation.[3] The fact that these details are expressed by integral numbers means that the electron cannot change its rotation continuously, but can only jump from one value to another, just as it can only jump from one orbit to another. Again the higher values represent excited states of the atom, the ground state being the one where all the electrons are in the lowest possible orbits and have the smallest possible amounts of rotation.

Tendencies to exist, particles reacting to confinement with motion, atoms switching suddenly from one 'quantum state' to another, and an essential interconnectedness of all phenomena—these are some of the unusual features of the atomic world. The basic force, on the other hand, which gives rise to all atomic phenomena is familiar and can be experienced in the macroscopic world. It is the force of electric attraction between the positively charged atomic nucleus and the negatively charged electrons. The interplay of this force with the electron waves gives rise to the tremendous variety of structures and phenomena in our environment. It is responsible for all chemical reactions, and for the formation of molecules, that is, of aggregates of several atoms bound to each other by mutual attraction. The interaction between electrons and atomic nuclei is thus the basis of all solids, liquids and gases, and also of all living organisms and of the biological processes associated with them.

In this immensely rich world of atomic phenomena, the nuclei play the role of extremely small, stable centres which constitute the source of the electric force and form the skeletons of the great variety of molecular structures. To understand these structures, and most of the natural phenomena around us, it is not necessary to know more about the nuclei than their charge and their mass. In order to understand the nature of matter, however, to know what matter is ultimately made of, one has to study the atomic nuclei which contain practically all of its mass. In the 1930s, after quantum theory had unraveled the world of atoms, it was therefore the main task of physicists to understand the structure of nuclei, their constituents and the forces which hold them together so tightly.

The first important step towards an understanding of nuclear structure was the discovery of the neutron as the second constituent of the nucleus, a particle which has roughly the same mass as the proton (the first nuclear constituent)—about two thousand times the mass of the electron—but does not carry an electric charge. This discovery not only explained how the nuclei of all chemical elements were built up from protons and neutrons, but also revealed that the nuclear force, which kept these particles so tightly bound within the nucleus, was a completely new phenomenon. It could not be of electromagnetic origin since the neutrons were electrically neutral. Physicists soon realized that they were here confronted with a new force of nature which does not manifest itself anywhere outside the nucleus.

An atomic nucleus is about one hundred thousand times smaller than the whole atom and yet it contains almost all of the atom's mass. This means that matter inside the nucleus must be extremely dense compared to the forms of matter we are used to. Indeed, if the whole human body were compressed to nuclear density it would not take up more space than a pinhead. This high density, however, is not the only unusual property of nuclear matter. Being of the same quantum nature as electrons, the 'nucleons'—as the protons and neutrons are often called—respond to their confinement with high velocities, and since they are squeezed into a much smaller volume their reaction is all the more violent. They race about in the nucleus with velocities of about 40,000 miles per second! Nuclear matter is thus a form of matter entirely different from anything we experience 'up here' in our macroscopic environment. We can, perhaps, picture it best as tiny drops of an extremely dense liquid which is boiling and bubbling most fiercely.

The essential new aspect of nuclear matter which accounts for all its unusual properties is the strong nuclear force, and the feature that makes this force so unique is its extremely short range. It acts only when the nucleons come very near to each other, that is, when their distance is about two to three times their diameter. At such a distance, the nuclear force is strongly attractive, but when the distance becomes less the force becomes strongly repulsive so that the nucleons cannot approach each other any closer. In this way, the nuclear force keeps the nucleus in an extremely stable, though extremely dynamic equilibrium.

The picture of matter which emerges from the study of atoms and nuclei shows that most of it is concentrated in tiny drops separated by huge distances. In the vast space between the massive and fiercely boiling nuclear drops move the electrons. These constitute only a tiny fraction of the total mass, but give matter its solid aspect and provide the links necessary to build up the molecular structures. They are also involved in the chemical reactions and are responsible for the chemical properties of matter. Nuclear reactions, on the other hand, generally do not occur naturally in this form of matter because the available energies are not high enough to disturb the nuclear equilibrium.

This form of matter, however, with its multitude of shapes and textures and its complicated molecular architecture, can exist only under very special conditions, when the temperature is not too high, so that the molecules do not jiggle too much. When the thermal energy increases about a hundredfold, as it does in most stars, all atomic and molecular structures are destroyed. Most of the matter in the universe exists, in fact, in a state which is very different from the one just described. In the centre of the stars exist large accumulations of nuclear matter, and nuclear processes which occur only very rarely on earth predominate there. They are essential for the great variety of stellar phenomena observed in astronomy, most of which arise from a combination of nuclear and gravitational effects. For our planet, the nuclear processes in the centre of the Sun are of particular importance because they furnish the energy which sustains our terrestrial environment. It has been one of the great triumphs of modern physics to discover that the constant energy flow from the Sun, our vital link with the world of the very large, is a result of nuclear reactions, of phenomena in the world of the infinitely small.

In the history of man's penetration into this submicroscopic world, a stage was reached in the early 1930s when scientists thought they had now finally discovered the 'basic building blocks' of matter. It was known that all matter consisted of atoms and that all atoms consisted of protons, neutrons and electrons. These so-called 'elementary particles' were seen as the ultimate indestructible units of matter: atoms in the Democritean sense. Although quantum theory implies, as mentioned previously, that we cannot decompose the world into independently existing smallest units, this was not generally perceived at that time. The classical habits of thought were still so persistent that most physicists tried to understand matter in terms of its 'basic building blocks', and this trend of thought is, in fact, quite strong even today.

Two further developments in modern physics have shown, however, that the notion of elementary particles as the primary units of matter has to be abandoned. One of these developments was experimental, the other theoretical, and both began in the 1930s. On the experimental side, new particles were discovered as physicists refined their experimental techniques and developed ingenious new devices for particle detection. Thus the number of particles increased from three to six by 1935, then to eighteen by 1955, and today we know over two hundred 'elementary' particles. . . . As more and more particles were discovered over the years, it became clear that not all of them could be called 'elementary', and today there is a widespread belief among physicists that none of them deserves this name.

This belief is enforced by the theoretical developments which paralleled the discovery of an ever-increasing number of particles. Soon after the formulation of quantum theory, it became clear that a complete theory of nuclear phenomena must not only be a quantum theory, but must also incorporate relativity theory. This is because the particles confined to dimensions of the size of nuclei often move so fast that their speed comes close to the speed of light. This fact is crucial for the description of their behaviour, because every description of natural phenomena involving velocities close to the speed of light has to take relativity theory into account. It has to be, as we say, a 'relativistic' description. What we need, therefore, for a full understanding of the nuclear world is a theory which incorporates both quantum theory and relativity theory. Such a theory has not yet been found, and therefore we have as yet been unable to formulate a complete theory of the nucleus. Although we know quite a lot about nuclear structure and about the interactions between nuclear particles, we do not yet understand the nature and complicated form of the nuclear force on a fundamental level. There is no complete theory of the nuclear particle world comparable to quantum theory for the atomic world. We do have several 'quantum-relativistic' models which describe some aspects of the world of particles very well, but the fusion of quantum and relativity theory into a complete theory of the particle world is still the central problem and great challenge of modern fundamental physics.

Relativity theory has had a profound influence on our picture of matter by forcing us to modify our concept of a particle in an essential way. In classical physics, the mass of an object had always been associated with an indestructible material substance, with some 'stuff' of which all things were thought to be made. Relativity theory showed that mass has nothing to do with any substance, but is a form of energy. Energy, however, is a dynamic quantity associated with activity, or with processes. The fact that the mass of a particle is equivalent to a certain amount of energy means that the particle can no longer be seen as a static object, but has to be conceived as a dynamic pattern, a process involving the energy which manifests itself as the particle's mass.

This new view of particles was initiated by Dirac when he formulated a relativistic equation describing the behaviour of electrons. Dirac's theory was not only extremely successful in accounting for the fine details of atomic structure, but also revealed a fundamental symmetry between matter and antimatter. It predicted the existence of an anti-electron with the same mass as the electron but with an opposite charge. This positively charged particle, now called the positron, was indeed discovered two years after Dirac had predicted it. The symmetry between matter and antimatter implies that for every particle there exists an antiparticle with equal mass and opposite charge. Pairs of particles and antiparticles can be created if enough energy is available and can be made to turn into pure energy in the reverse process of annihilation. These processes of particle creation and annihilation had been predicted from Dirac's theory before they were actually discovered in nature, and since then they have been observed millions of times.

The creation of material particles from pure energy is certainly the most spectacular effect of relativity theory, and it can only be understood in terms of the view of particles outlined above. Before relativistic particle physics, the constituents of matter had always been considered as being either elementary units which were indestructible and unchangeable, or as composite objects which could be broken up into their constituent parts; and the basic question was whether one could divide matter again and again, or whether one would finally arrive at some smallest indivisible units. After Dirac's discovery, the whole question of the division of matter appeared in a new light. When two particles collide with high energies, they generally break into pieces, but these pieces are not smaller than the original particles. They are again particles of the same kind and are created out of the energy of motion ('kinetic energy') involved in the collision process. The whole problem of dividing matter is thus resolved in an unexpected sense. The only way to divide subatomic particles further is to bang them together in collision processes involving high energies. This way, we can divide matter again and again, but we never obtain smaller pieces because we just create particles out of the energy involved in the process. The subatomic particles are thus destructible and indestructible at the same time.

This state of affairs is bound to remain paradoxical as long as we adopt the static view of composite 'objects' consisting of 'basic building blocks'. Only when the dynamic, relativistic view is adopted does the paradox disappear. The particles are then seen as dynamic patterns, or processes, which involve a certain amount of energy appearing to us as their mass. In a collision process, the energy of the two colliding particles is redistributed to form a new pattern, and if it has been increased by a sufficient amount of kinetic energy, this new pattern may involve additional particles.

High-energy collisions of subatomic particles are the principal method used by physicists to study the properties of these particles, and particle physics is therefore also called 'high-energy physics'. The kinetic energies required for the collision experiments are achieved by means of huge particle accelerators, enormous circular machines with circumferences of several miles in which protons are accelerated to velocities near the speed of light and are then made to collide with other protons or with neutrons. It is impressive that machines of that size are needed to study the world of the infinitely small. They are the supermicroscopes of our time.

Most of the particles created in these collisions live for only an extremely short time—much less than a millionth of a second—after which they disintegrate again into protons, neutrons and electrons. In spite of their exceedingly short lifetime, these particles can not only be detected and their properties measured but are actually made to leave tracks which can be photographed! These particle tracks are produced in so-called bubble chambers in a manner similar to the way a jet plane makes a trail in the sky. The actual particles are many orders of magnitude smaller than the bubbles making up the tracks, but from the thickness and curvature of a track physicists can identify the particle that caused it. . . . The points from which several tracks emanate are points of particle collisions, and the curves are caused by magnetic fields which the experimenters used to identify the particles. The collisions of particles are our main experimental method to study their properties and interactions, and the beautiful lines, spirals and curves traced by the particles in bubble chambers are thus of paramount importance for modern physics.

The high-energy scattering experiments of the past decades have shown us the dynamic and ever-changing nature of the particle world in the most striking way. Matter has appeared in these experiments as completely mutable. All particles can be transmuted into other particles; they can be created from energy and can vanish into energy. In this world, classical concepts like 'elementary particle', 'material substance' or 'isolated object', have lost their meaning; the whole universe appears as a dynamic web of inseparable energy patterns. So far, we have not yet found a complete theory to describe this world of subatomic particles, but we do have several theoretical models which describe certain aspects of it very well. None of these models is free from mathematical difficulties, and they all contradict each other in certain ways, but all of them reflect the basic unity and the intrinsically dynamic character of matter. They show that the properties of a particle can only be understood in terms of its activity—of its interaction with the surrounding environment—and that the particle, therefore cannot be seen as an isolated entity, but has to be understood as an integrated part of the whole.

Relativity theory has not only affected our conception of particles in a drastic way, but also our picture of the forces between these particles. In a relativistic description of particle interactions, the forces between the particles—that is their mutual attraction or repulsion—are pictured as the exchange of other particles. This concept is very difficult to visualize. It is a consequence of the four dimensional space-time character of the subatomic world and neither our intuition nor our language can deal with this image very well. Yet it is crucial for an understanding of subatomic phenomena. It links the forces between constituents of matter to the properties of other constituents of matter, and thus unifies the two concepts, force and matter, which had seemed to be so fundamentally different ever since the Greek atomists. Both force and matter are now seen to have their common origin in the dynamic patterns which we call particles.

The fact that particles interact through forces which manifest themselves as the exchange of other particles is yet another reason why the subatomic world cannot be decomposed into constituent parts. From the macroscopic level down to the nuclear level, the forces which hold things together are relatively weak and it is a good approximation to say that things consist of constituent parts. Thus a grain of salt can be said to consist of salt molecules, the salt molecules of two kinds of atoms, those atoms to consist of nuclei and electrons, and the nuclei of protons and neutrons. At the particle level, however, it is no longer possible to see things that way.

In recent years, there has been an increasing amount of evidence that the protons and neutrons, too, are composite objects; but the forces holding them together are so strong or—what amounts to the same—the velocities acquired by the components are so high, that the relativistic picture has to be applied, where the forces are also particles. Thus the distinction between the constituent particles and the particles making up the binding forces becomes blurred and the approximation of an object consisting of constituent parts breaks down. The particle world cannot be decomposed into elementary components.

In modern physics, the universe is thus experienced as a dynamic, inseparable whole which always includes the observer in an essential way. In this experience, the traditional concepts of space and time, of isolated objects, and of cause and effect, lose their meaning. Such an experience, however, is very similar to that of the Eastern mystics. The similarity becomes apparent in quantum and relativity theory, and becomes even stronger in the 'quantum-relativistic' models of subatomic physics where both these theories combine to produce the most striking parallels to Eastern mysticism. . . .

Notes

1. From *The Tao of Physics* by Fritjof Capra, © 1975, 1983, 1991. Reprinted by arrangement with Shambhala Publications, Inc., 300 Massachusetts Avenue, Boston, MA 02115.

2. The hydrogen atom consists of just one proton and one electron.

3. The 'rotation' of an electron in its orbit must not be understood in the classical sense; it is determined by the shape of the electron wave in terms of the probabilities for the particle's existence in certain parts of the orbit.

CHAPTER FIVE

DISCOVERY OF THE BIOFIELD
A Different Type of Magnetism?

Buryl Payne, PhD

THE CHINESE USE THE TERM *ch'i* or *Ki* to describe the energy that circulates along acupuncture meridians and provides the essential life force for the body. In the 1940s, Wilhelm Reich built what he called orgone accumulators, which collected an energy from space. Orgone was considered to be the vital energy of all living organisms and could be supplied to people who were ill by Reich's accumulators. It's easy enough to build an accumulator, and I made several but didn't find the results consistent and objectively measurable. Reich's devices and discoveries stimulated a lot of research which is continuing today.

Psychics who claim to see the human aura have always tantalized researchers to detect it with the latest and most sensitive instruments. However, measurements made with sensitive ultraviolet light detectors, electrostatic or radio wave detectors have found nothing except the typical infrared or heat radiation given off by a warm body, living or non-living.

On a cool, dry day, the body can pick up an electric charge, especially if synthetic clothing is worn, and this charge will spark to a metal surface as it is touched or to another person, if that person has less charge. This reaction comes and goes with the weather; the body does not generate an electric charge which can be detected beyond the skin.

There are small electric currents and voltages generated within the body that can be measured by placing electrodes directly on the skin or placing probes within the brain or heart. Brain waves are only about 10 millionths of a volt, and the largest muscle electrical signal is generated by the heart—one quarter of one thousandth of a volt. Other muscles produce voltages of only a few millionths of a volt.

Some people have written that the body has a magnetic aura. Although this statement has a tiny bit of truth, it is misleading and confusing. While it's correct that any moving electric charge generates a magnetic field, such fields are only a fraction of the strength of the electric fields. In order to make magnetic fields apparent, coils of wire with hundreds of turns must be used, with the current flowing in only one way. Blood flows out and back and has no net electrical charge, so it doesn't generate any external field, although a very small magnetic field is generated when nerve impulses propagate. To detect the tiny *electrical* signal produced by the heart muscle requires amplification of about 1,000 times with electrodes being placed directly on the body. The *magnetic* field generated by that tiny signal requires another thousand times as much amplification or a million times altogether. In other words, the magnetic field generated by the heart is only about one thousandth of the electric field. No compass would ever show such a small field. If the body had an appreciable magnetic aura, compasses would not work properly, and people would have been forced to rely on the sun and stars for navigation.

The SQUID

Within the last decade, a very sensitive instrument has been developed which can detect the very small magnetic fields around the heart and brain where busy neural activity also makes a tiny net magnetic field. The instrument used to detect these fields is called a SQUID, an acronym for superconducting quantum interference device. The SQUID usually is operated in special, magnetically shielded rooms. The SQUID itself, in early models, had to be cooled to liquid helium temperatures to reduce internal electrical noise. The measured magnetic fields from the head and heart are less than one millionth of a gauss (term used for magnetic field strength). While data from the SQUID is now providing information, to say that the body has a magnetic aura is like saying the body has a gravitational aura. We don't walk around attracting objects to our bodies, such as paper clips and rusty nails, by our magnetic fields. However, just because people don't have any appreciable magnetic field, does not mean that they are not affected by small magnetic fields.

Animal Magnetism

There is another type of field around the body that is not electric nor magnetic and is much larger than either of them. It is indirectly related to magnetism, and lacking a suitable term, people have often chosen to use the term "magnetic" to describe it. Mesmer apparently was one of the first people to connect this field with magnetism.

Mesmer believed there was a fluid-like energy around the human body that was highly charged in healthy people and weak or nearly absent in ill people. He recognized that this field of energy was somehow related to magnetism, and he thought that magnets could conduct it. He called this field "Animal Magnetism" to differentiate it from ordinary iron magnetism. He found that he could produce "magnetic-like" effects in his patients by stroking the space around them with magnets or his hands. His formulation was similar to what Reich later called orgone energy.

Detecting the Biofield

In 1978, the author discovered a simple device that can detect and measure an energy field around the body, which may be what Mesmer called animal magnetism. This field shows up as a spin or rotational force on a frame that is suspended over a person's head. *Figure 1* shows one form of the device used for this purpose. Although a pyramid frame was initially used, the force has no connection with so-called pyramid energy. The author was investigating the possible existence of pyramid energy when this other energy effect was accidentally discovered.

The frame can be of any material, wood, plastic, or metal, and any shape. It is suspended by a nylon filament (fishing line leader), and no components are critical. When a person sits under a hanging frame, it will rotate a few degrees. To measure the degree of rotation, a mirror is glued on the nylon filament. A wall-mounted spotlight will produce a reflected spot on an adjacent wall where a scale serves to provide accurate measurement of movement of the spot. A lady's compact mirror that slightly focuses the spot of light works better than a flat mirror. In the apparatus shown in *Figure 1*, ring magnets were placed such that their North poles point towards the apex.

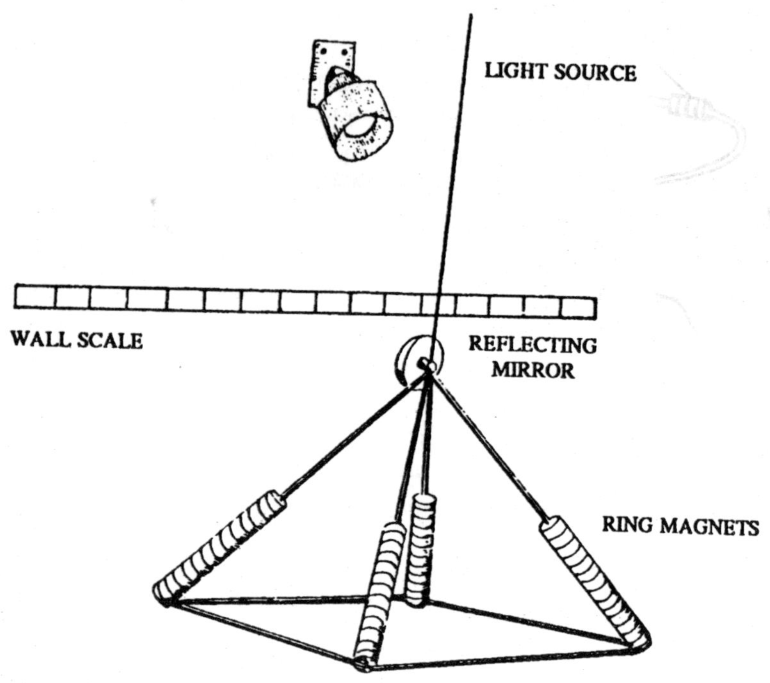

Figure 1. The Biofield Meter

Figure 2 shows a different version of the device, which uses a hanging scale. Other versions of the device have included a spiral helix fashioned from quarter-inch copper tubing, three-sided pyramidal forms, large rings, and pyramids hanging inside a bottle (*Figure 3*).

Devices have been made and tested with more, less, or no magnets. In general, the more magnets, the more movement, but biofield meters still rotate even when there are no magnets on them. The instruments are stable and rarely move when no one is near them. Over one thousand observations have been made.

Instruments suspended in bottles demonstrate that air currents and thermal currents could not be involved in their movement. Units placed in bottles or glass cases are caused to move by placing one's hands at the sides of the case. Electrical shielding or electrical grounding of the

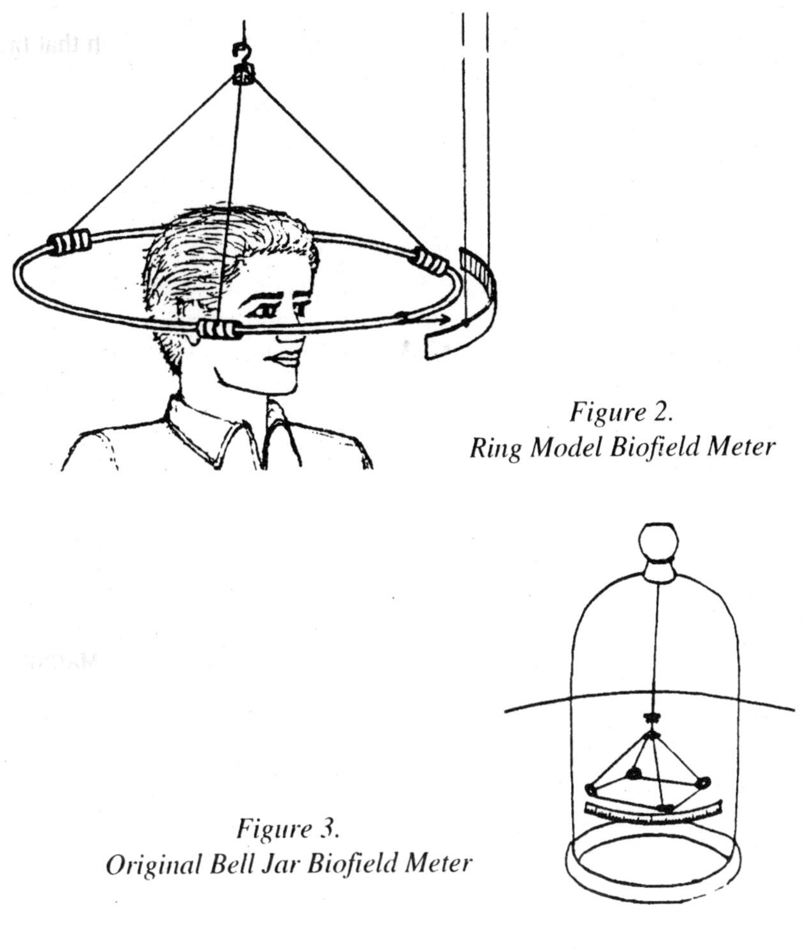

Figure 2.
Ring Model Biofield Meter

Figure 3.
Original Bell Jar Biofield Meter

operator made no difference; however, soft iron sheet metal wrapped around a bottle stopped the effect.

To test whether heat could be producing rotation of the larger frames, several observations were made using a hundred watt light bulb, a lighted candle, and a heat pack. No movement of the frames was observed when these heat sources were placed inside the frames. To insure that air currents produced by breathing were not affecting the movement, the breath was held as long as possible in a number of tests. The biofield meter always moved within five to fifteen seconds, so that factor too can be ruled out. The many observations made with units in sealed glass jars have repeatedly demonstrated that movement takes place when no air currents and only minimal heat transfer could be present. Devices in bottles have been observed to move at distances up to twelve feet from the observer during times of large magnetic storms.

Since the body's intrinsic magnetic field, measured in shielded rooms, is about one billionth of a gauss, this biofield could not be an ordinary magnetic field. The author has simply called it the Biofield, a contraction of biological energy field. Tesla, a contemporary of Edison and inventor of the alternating current motor and many other instruments, was reported to have spoken about a "higher octave" of magnetism that had not been recognized by traditional science.

Whatever we choose to call it—the aura, animal magnetism, orgone energy, *prana,* spin force, *ch'i,* or the biofield—this energy is quite large, over a hundred million times as large as the body's magnetic field! If it were magnetic, the biofield would be equivalent to several hundred gauss.

What is the biofield? It appears to be a genuine new force in science that manifests as a physical force clearly observed on all types of ordinary physical matter. As of this time (1989), it appears to be a force that produces movement at right angles around the human body. It does not push or pull like gravity or electrostatic forces. It appears to be in the form of a circle or spiral around the body. The origin of the force is not electrical, magnetic, heat, or gravitational. It is much too large to be produced by these forces. The author has chosen to call it simply the biofield and to call the instruments which serve to detect it, biofield meters. Descriptive equations will follow upon the development of additional and more refined instrumentation and further experimentation. New discoveries can probably be made by any reader of this book willing to construct a biofield meter and make careful observations.

After several months of observations, it was discovered that the amount of the initial rotational deflection of the biofield meter varied in association with the geomagnetic field. *Figures 4* and *5* show deflections of the meter over a forty-day period (daily measurements) and a three-day period (measurements made at three-hour intervals). The dashed line shows measurements made with the biofield meter, and the solid line shows data on Earth's magnetic activity provided by the National Bureau of Standards in Boulder, Colorado. At times of higher geomagnetic activity, the biofield also showed higher activity.

The second figure shows a similar relationship for the three-hour variations. There is a clear connection between the two measures, but it's not appropriate to do statistical correlations since there is definitely a component to the biofield data which varies with the emotional state or vitality of the person. When one meditates or is ill, their biofield is of lesser amplitude. When one is excited, either angry or happy, their field is larger.

Usually the direction of the initial rotation of the frame is to the right as seen from within the frame or clockwise as seen from above the person. At times of new or full moon or when there are large disturbances in Earth's magnetic field, the biofield often shows a change in the initial direction of rotation. Measurements of the biofield were made nearly every day.

Examination of the data for a two-year period showed that eighty-five percent of the time during a new or full moon (within thirty-six hours), the biofield showed a reversal in direction for a few hours. Such a reversal could have happened during the other fifteen percent of the time but escaped the author's notice if it happened to occur between observation times. Measurements made over a seven-year period on various forms of biofield meters showed consistent connections between their movements and solar/geomagnetic activity. This finding was so, even for those forms of the biofield meters that did not have magnets placed on them. It seems that the geomagnetic activity is the largest component of biofield activity.

The author detected biofields around a watermelon, a grapefruit, and several plants. Presumably all living organisms have such fields. A literature search uncovered reference to an article by Dr. Charles Ross published in the 1922 medical journal *Lancet.* He described an instrument that was set in motion by the proximity of the human body or by vision. In recent years, a German scientist, W. Peschka, appears to have discovered a similar effect. These men did not obtain numerical data on the amplitude of the field or notice its connection with the geomagnetic field.

Dr. Frank Brown was a pioneer in the study of interactions between magnetism and living organisms. He visited the author's laboratory in 1983 and observed the biofield meter with great interest. Among the 50 reprints of scientific papers he left me as a gift were several studies on bean seeds, magnetism, and spin. He found that when bean seeds were

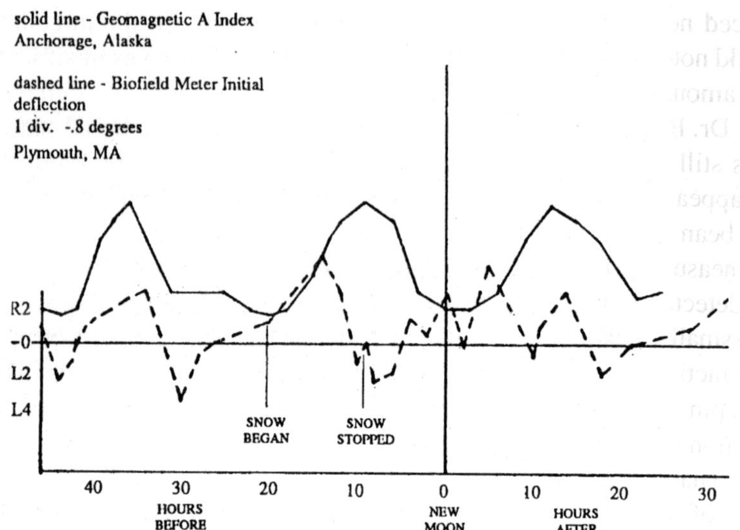

Figure 4. Geomagnetic Data and Biofield Meter deflections before, during, and after the New Moon, Feb. 13, 1983, four-day period

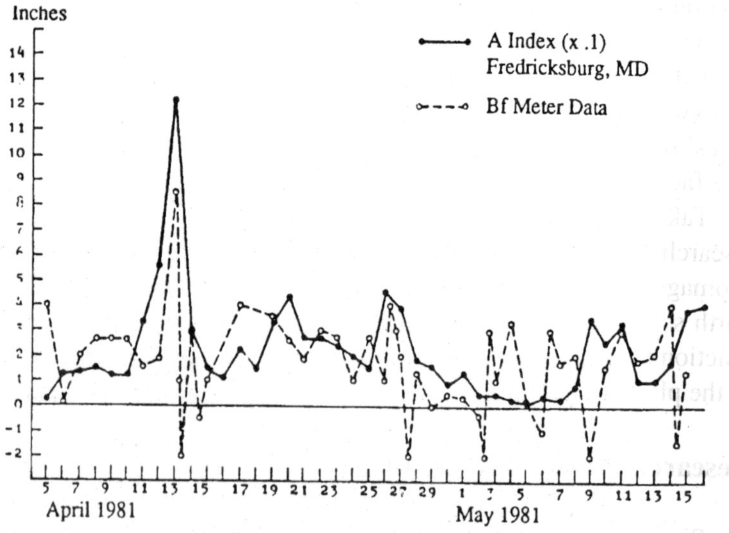

Figure 5. Geomagnetic Index (A) and Biofield Meter. Deflections one inch = .8 degrees. An index is divided by ten forty-day periods

placed near one another, there was an interaction between them that could not be explained. The effect was observed by carefully measuring the amount of water that the beans absorbed.

Dr. Brown thought the interaction was due to magnetism because it was still present when electrostatic shielding was in place but nearly disappeared when magnetic shielding was used. Although he believed the bean seeds had a magnetic field, he did not have the instrumentation to measure it. In fact, even if a magnetic field around a bean seed could be detected by ultra-sensitive SQUID apparatus, it would probably be far too small to account for the observed effects. It seems more likely that the interaction between the bean seeds was due to the presence of a biofield or spin force. The biofield around living organisms appears to be a million times larger than the magnetic field.

That the biofield was involved is supported by Dr. Brown's observation of a connection between rotation and bean seed interaction. He found that the beans interacted more strongly when they were rotated counterclockwise than when they were rotated clockwise.

In another series of experiments, he placed rotating magnets near the bean seeds and observed an interaction with the bean seeds. Brown and his associates also found interactions between geomagnetic activity and rotation of worms and other small life forms.

Brown also reported on the search of R. I. Jones, who reported in 1960 that plant growth could be altered by uniform daily rotation. Clockwise rotation depressed growth. No one has been able to explain Jones' findings, but the presence of a spin force around all plants might be a factor.

Taken together, the findings of Brown, Jones, the author, and other researchers all point to connections between living organisms, spin, and geomagnetic activity. All living organisms seem to be in resonance with Earth's dynamic magnetic area. Earth's magnetic field is in turn a function of solar activity and the positions of the moon and at least some of the planets.

Research Possibilities for the Biofield

Since the spin force has been observed around plants, a grapefruit, and a watermelon, presumably it is present around all living things. Therefore, it would be possible to suspend a biofield meter around a plant and continuously monitor the rotation. If no magnets were used on the biofield meter, there should be no magnetic perturbations, and the movement of the meter might accurately reflect the geomagnetic activity. In the case of human subjects, emotional states and vitality factors are more variable. Such an apparatus could be set up in a draft free environment, a Faraday cage, or a magnetically shielded room.[1] To make measurements of a human's field in a magnetically shielded room would be an excellent way to determine how much of the biofield was generated by the human and how much was induced by geomagnetic activity.

Biofield instruments in bottles have been taken to the pyramids of Egypt, the Grand Canyon, the ruins of Palenque, the mountains, and the seashore. Inside the great pyramid, there was no detectable biofield. On top of the pyramid, movement was as usual. Differences were observed at other locations as well. In general, the amplitude of initial rotation is less near the coast. Since the geomagnetic field strength varies minute by minute, thorough observations on place differences need to be made using standard instruments and simultaneous observation. Some careful experimental procedures would be necessary to make such tests.

Some other questions for research are: Does the strength of the biofield vary with altitude? Would it diminish in deep mines? Can it be detected in a steady, high flying aircraft? How much mass can actually be caused to move by this force? The heaviest device the author used weighed about nine pounds. However, this weight was not being lifted, only rotated, so very little physical force was actually required.

How do the biofields of individuals interact or combine? If a large ring is suspended over one person and a measurement made, then will two people crowded under the ring increase the amplitude of initial rotation by a factor of two?

Suppose a biofield meter is hung in the center of an empty room and people quietly come in and stand around it. If the mirror system is used, a spot of light can be reflected from the mirror on the biofield meter to a distant wall providing a very sensitive indicator of rotation. If people surround the instrument, moving slowly towards it, how close do they have to come before it rotates? Or will it rotate at all? How many people will be required to observe such a rotation?

How far does this force field extend around the body? How much interaction is there with the force fields of other humans? of plants? of animals? Although the field strength can vary from moment to moment, depending on the activity of Earth's magnetic field and on the emotional state of the human at a given moment, if these are held reasonably constant, how rapidly does it diminish? Gravitational, electrostatic, and magnetic forces have been found to diminish with the square of the distance. Does this force follow the same formula? There are so many parameters to uncover! It's as if we were back in the 1800s when electricity and magnetism were first discovered—an experimenter's paradise.

A most important question is: what is the direction of this force? Is it truly a spin force? The formal and informal experiments and observations I made, extending over many years, suggest that it is a spin force, but that could be disproved by another type of experiment. The devices I built never seemed to move in another manner except rotation, but that reaction may be because less energy is required to spin the rings or frames than move them in any other way. When a thirty-foot-long suspension line was used, spinning still occurred—not swinging. The pyramids hung in bottles rotated when hands were placed at the sides. Is there a spin force between one's hands? This is a puzzle. . . .

Ralph Stone, founder of Polarity Therapy, has illustrations showing a spin field around the body. One person who meditates reported to me that she experienced a spinning sensation during a meditation. If this force were a spin force, it would fit with other patterns found in nature. Laurence Badgley has found that a spiral vortex field appears around sites of injury on the body, which shows interaction with magnetic fields.

If the force were in a spin form, it would imply that, if we could place a small test object in space around a human, that object would start to spin. This experiment could not be done on Earth, but perhaps it could be done in space. If so, the spin force or life force is similar to magnetism, for it, too, is a spin force located in the space around a wire carrying an electric current.

Whereas magnetic forces only act on other magnets, this life force or biofield force apparently acts on all matter. Copper, iron, aluminum, plastic, and wood have been tried, but quantitative comparative measurements have not been made. If a material were found which did not show the effect, it would be a very important discovery.

Generalization of the Spin Force

Spin forces are not unique to living systems—they are omnipresent in the universe. Spin or angular momentum is associated with most subatomic particles such as electrons, protons, neutrons, etc. Apparently every body in the universe spins! Interstellar molecules spin. Stars, planets, satellites, even entire galaxies and clusters of galaxies all are known to spin. One astronomer maintains that the whole universe spins! A German scientist, Dr. D. Ashcoff, has invented an instrument known as a spin-tester for the cells of the body. The discovery of the biofield meter shows the existence of a spin force around the human body and other living organisms. Perhaps it is time to assume that spin be taken as a fundamental force in its own right along with gravity, electricity, and magnetism. Spin connects gravity and magnetism, for it is a more general type of magnetism, and, at the same time, it complements gravity. Spin forces, if they exist around suns and planets, would help to organize solar systems and satellite systems. The existence of spin as a force would account for why the universe has not come together in clumps, for spin forces operate at right angles to gravity forces.

The fastest spinning Pulsar was recently discovered (proof not yet definite) at the core of a supernova that was observed from the Southern Hemisphere two years ago. This fast spinning Pulsar was apparently formed as part of the supernova process and would be expected to start out spinning slowly and gradually increase in spin as more matter was drawn to the center. But it's measured spin rate is almost two thousand times per second, upsetting traditional theories. How this enormous object could spin so rapidly, apparently so soon after birth, is an unsolved mystery. However, it does lend additional support to the notion that spin should be considered a fundamental force present around all matter.

Assuming the existence of spin force as a force in its own right also would bring one aspect of aliveness into the equations of physics, something that is long overdue. Spin forces might be called "form forces" or "organizing forces," for they help form complex living organisms, which abound with spirals, helixes, and circles, over and over again in myriads of different ways, from double helices in DNA and RNA to whirling dervishes.

If we consider that spin be taken as a fundamental force along with gravity, electricity, and magnetism, Table 1 can be expanded. (Actually the more precise scientific term for spin is "torque," the product of force multiplied by distance from the center of the body, human, plant, animal, planet, or star.)

As previously mentioned, there are also two other forces now known to exist. Called the strong and weak nuclear forces, they operate within atomic nuclei to help keep nuclear particles from dispersing due to electrical forces.

TABLE 1 (Expanded)
THE FORCES OF THE UNIVERSE

FORCE	LEVEL OF OPERATION	EFFECTS
Gravitic	Operates between all matter.	Pulls matter together.
Electric	Only manifests between charged particles.	Pushes or pulls.
Magnetic	Manifests when charged particles move.	Pushes or pulls at right angles to the direction of motion. Only sensed by other charged particles. Causes charged particles to move in circles, spirals, or helixes.
Spin	Present around all bodies. Much larger around living organisms.	Causes all bodies to spin around one another. Counteracts gravity. Produces complex forms or structures.

More research on the biofield is urgently needed, and it's impossible for one person to do it, so it is the author's hope that many readers will take up the exciting challenge and enjoy the fun of exploring a whole new field.

Notes

1. The reader can easily make a biofield meter using simple household materials such as copper tubing, wood, or plastic rings for the frame; string or nylon fishing line for suspension, etc. Materials aren't critical. Apparently, the biofield acts on all matter. The use of magnets on the frame is optional. A standardized biofield meter is now available from Progen Co., 846-A Jefferson Avenue, Redwood City, CA 94063-1828, Tel: 1(800) 321-Aura

For a better understanding of body magnetism including magnetic healing, readers should read Buryl Payne. *The Body Magnetic.* Boulder, CO, fifth ed., 1991 (ISBN 0-9628569-9-1). This chapter is taken by permission from the author's book. Dr. Payne's business address is 4264 Topsail Ct., Soquel, CA 95073 — Tel: (408) 462-1588

CHAPTER SIX

NATURALLY INDUCED MAGNETIC ENERGY

C.E. Lindgren, DLitt
Ruby K. Corder

ACCORDING TO MANY EXPERTS, the human body and all other forms of life are surrounded by a field of energy. This etheric energy has been investigated, argued over, and experimented with for centuries. To understand the working of this higher subtle energy force, it is necessary to acquaint one's self with the more mundane physical workings of electricity and magnetism. Topics like the following: the harmonizing effects of these subtle fields in their relation to disease and wellness; the potentially healing or disharmonizing effects of magnetic radiation; and finally, the principles for applying magnetic forces, will be discussed in a general, yet in-depth manner, in an attempt to clarify their relation to auras.

In the nineteenth century, scientist and occultist Baron Karl von Reichenbach made the startling discovery that ill psychic subjects reacted to the introduction of magnetic fields (Beal 1974, 429). Later, research by Dr. Walter Kilner revealed that the density of the aura is influenced by magnetic force. Further, Kilner's research showed that "[the aura] is sensitive to electric currents to the extent of completely vanishing under a negative charge from a Wilmhurst machine and increasing to an additional fifty percent after the charge dissipates" (Shepard 1978, 71). Regarding the effect of magnetism on auric fields,

Patrick Alessandra, author of *Seeing Auras*, states that "A chaotic electromagnetic field (i.e., a power line) can completely devitalize the physical energy field (etheric aura), while a properly controlled one can actually bring about the regeneration of areas of the body."

Natural Magnetism

In the 1950s, children were intrigued by Mexican jumping beans, Hula Hoops, and magnets. Although the Hula Hoop and jumping beans are passé, kids of all ages are still mystified by magnets' secret powers. Old-fashioned, red horseshoe magnets, plastic alphabet magnets, and even "fridgies" have the power to attract metal, repel other magnets, and cause compass needles to spin. Often thought of as playthings, magnets have serious uses in industry, in science, and in medicine. While the most familiar medical application is diagnostic, Magnetic Resonance Imaging (MRI), magnetic therapy can heal bones, strengthen muscles, increase circulation, and alleviate pain.

History

The word magnetism, according to Sir David Brewster's *Treatise on Magnetism,* derives from the Greek and refers to properties of the loadstones or native iron magnets. Known for centuries, this ore was, according to legend, named for Magnes, a young shepherd who first observed the phenomena of magnetic attraction in the hills of Mount Ida. Historians, however, are inclined to believe that the word "magnet" came from Magnesia, a region in Lydia, where lodestone was discovered several centuries before Christ. Loadstone deposits, however, have been mined, studied, and used for their curative powers for millennia. The first known mining of magnetic ore was in Africa over 100,000 years ago.

Many theories have been postulated regarding the occult (secret) powers of loadstone deposits. Ancient philosophers, in Greece and elsewhere, speculated that the ore contained a soul (auric force) and that by combining the soul of the ore with man's body and soul, physical cures could be extracted. Therefore, for centuries, man has used magnets for alleviating muscle spasms, gout, scarring, pain, and illness. Magnets, used in conjunction with ointments, food preparations, and water, are reported by many as producing wondrous cures.

Magnetic Therapy and Research Through the Ages

One of the first major works on magnets and magnetic fields was written during the 16th century by William Gilbert (1540-1603). Gilbert's book, *De Magnete Magneticisque Corporibus* (1600), states that even the smallest piece of magnet or loadstone contains a magnetic field of positive and negative poles. His greatest discovery, however, was that the earth itself is a giant magnet with magnetic poles (North and South), axis, and equator. Over the next 300 years, other works would substantiate magnets' physical properties. It was not, however, until Franz Anton Mesmer (1733-1815) that an investigation of magnetism's use in healing was conducted. Mesmer, although later discredited by the French Academy of Science, believed that magnets (and later, animal magnetism) could cure diseased bodies. It seems, however, that many scientists who investigated Mesmer were biased and unwilling or unable to see the potentials of magnetic force.

Little scientific research was conducted until the twentieth century. During the 1930s, several physical and biological scientists became interested in magnets and their supposed healing qualities. In a 1934 article in *Arch. exper. Zellforschg*, Julia Lengyel states that when living tissue (plant or animal) is brought in contact with a magnetic field, there are marked increases in cell growth and proliferation. Lengyel also noted change in differentiation and in structural cell formation (atypical) resulting in irregular cells and, in some cases, gigantic multi-nuclear structures.

Research by Mario Lenzi, presented in the September 1940 journal *Radiology*, reported several preliminary findings relating to magnetic field intensity and variations in biological effects of alternating (pulsating) magnetic fields and constant ones. Lenzi also restates much of the research conducted by R. Balli, L. Hermann, L. Errera, T. Huzella, and J. Lengyel of the period. Lenzi's paper concerned the grafting of neoplastic material (tumors) on to healthy white mice. Using 1,500-1,700 gauss magnets (electromagnets of 120 v., 1.5-2 amp. DC), Lenzi found that, when using an alternating magnetic field, the grafted tumor material's growth was delayed and limited.

Since the 1930s, experiments have been conducted by Drs. N. Nakagawa and J. Arichi of Japan, Dr. W. D. Mühlbauer and Prof. M. F. Barnothy, A. R. Davis, W. C. Rawles, and Dr. A. Roy of America. These scientists and physicians have investigated magnetic healing and treated thousands of individuals for chronic back and shoulder pain, scars, wounds, burns, rheumatism, and arthritis.

Magnetism in Esoteric Literature

Much has been written regarding the mystical qualities of animal magnetism. Since ancient Egypt, the Essenes, till the time of Paracelsus, the concept of "mutual attraction between things of the same kind" (Lehmann 1924, 127) has been a part of esoteric literature. Paracelsus deemed anything that exerted an attraction to be a "magnet" (Schrodter 1954). Paracelsus and the later Rosicrucians adopted the concept of "as above, so below" (i.e., the interaction of the macrocosm and microcosm). This doctrine included the idea that magnetic force exists in man as it does throughout the Universe. This force, if correctly channeled, could produce wondrous healings. Later Mesmer utilized this doctrine in his work with animal or "personal" magnetism.

Equally as arcane was, and is, the teachings relating to natural magnetism (i.e., the use of lodestones). Although not as well recorded as animal magnetism, several occult and mystery societies since ancient Egypt have used magnets for healing not only physical dis-eases but also auric or energy dysfunctions.

With knowledge derived from the Far East, Rosicrucians (certain groups) utilized the power of magnets by placing them at right angles to auric fields and directly on energy centers (chakras) to pull out imperfections and clear the chakras. Former Rosicrucian Supreme Grand Master, Dr. Paschal B. Randolph (1825-1875), used magnets to increase psychic abilities and strengthen the auric field. In his work *The Guide To Clairvoyance, and Clairvoyant's Guide: A Practical Manual for Those Who Aim at Perfect Clear Seeing and Psychometry* . . . (1867), Randolph used horseshoe magnets and quartz crystals to increase clairvoyance. Other occult physicians, Rosicrucians, and scientists also attempted to use magnetic force to heal the mundane and spiritual layers.

Magnets in Alternative Medicine[1]

Today, many companies sell static-magnetic field devices (magnets), which range from simple stick-on magnetic patches, shoe insoles, necklaces, bracelets, and pillows, to entire body wraps. These items produce magnetic fields intensities between 1-100 mT. The Connecticut-based Body Magnetics™ also handles magnetic vests, magnetic hand exercise equipment, and multi-soft water magnets. Magnetic pads are also being used with continued frequency. According to a research project (1990) conducted in part by Dr. Kazuo Shimodaira, a physician of obstetrics and gynecology at Tokyo Communications Hospital, in a double blind test of 431 patients (i.e., 375 subjects using magnet pads, consisting of 104 magnets with a 750-950 gauss strength, and 56 without magnetic padding), more than seventy percent of the patients obtained positive results from using the magnetized pad.

As with similar devices manufactured in the 1800s, advertising claims range from relieving stiffness and arthritis, improving circulation and relieving pain, to eliminating scarring and healing muscle sprains. Several companies, including MagneSystems™ of Los Angeles, sell a headband that they suggest may help in alleviating stress. Such devices typically consist of an adhesive patch (either circular or square) holding a barium-ferrite magnet at its center. Other manufacturing groups made magnet beds which produce a pulsed magnetic field of 1-30 Hz. These magnetic beds, trendy during the Victorian Era, are once again in vogue.

Some foreign firms have developed more radical equipment. Among these are Magnet & Halso of Sweden, which has designed a full-body pulse coil magnetic field treatment center. This product is rather expensive and, at present, cannot be sold in the United States.

Deviating from the "traditional" mono-pole concept (positive on one side, negative on the other), MagneSystems™ has devised, after ten years of research and testing, a product they believe will help in eliminating minor aches and pains. Applied directly to the body, the magnet, sandwiched between two outer layers, is a barium ferrite material magnetized in a special, alternating bi-polar design. The inner layer is made of a soft cotton material. The outer layer is gold foil which deflects and distributes naturally occurring body heat back into the pain site. This configuration, according to its designers, increases localized heat a full four degrees Centigrade. According to the company's literature, evidence of heat increase and distribution was demonstrated in clinical thermographic test measurements.

Finding Magnetic North

Before beginning therapy, the therapist first determines the north and south (negative and positive) poles of the magnet he/she intends to use. Each pole of the magnet, according to magnetic therapists, produces a variety of physiological effects.

There are two ways of determining magnetic attraction. The first technique consists of bringing an unknown unipole magnet (differing from a horseshoe or bipolar magnet, the unipole magnet is positively polarized on one side while the other side is negative) in contact with a compass. The compass is placed on a non-metal table and allowed to freely point north. Since like poles repel and unlike attract, the south pole of the magnet always points toward the North Pole. Slowly, bring a magnet (bar or disc) in contact with the compass' north side (marked N). If the north side (- or negative) of the magnet is facing the compass, the magnetic point of the compass needle (the one pointing toward the North Pole) is attracted toward the magnet. If the magnet's pole is south (+ or positive), the compass needle's magnetic point will be repelled, pointing 180° in the opposite direction. The second method of determining a disc magnet's polarity is to suspend it from a string (non-magnet), allowing it to hang freely. The south side of the magnet will spin to face the North Pole.

Magnetic Therapy

As previously noted, different magnetic poles have different and opposing physiological effects. For infections caused by bacteria, parasites, fungi, and viruses, the north pole (negative -) of the magnet should always be used. The negative side of the magnet is helpful in reducing inflammation and swelling, stopping pain, increasing mental acuity, reducing fat deposits, and promoting cellular healing. More rarely used, the positive magnetic field (south pole) increases or promotes a variety of physiological effects including: bacteria and plant growth, wakefulness, inflammation, pain, infection, and changes in animal behavior.

Biomagnetic Handbook, by William H. Philpott, M.D. and Sharon Taplin (1990), reviews magnetic energy effects on living tissue. According to the authors, most human illness is positive or south pole induced. In fact, many physicians, including the late Dr. Randolph, stress the importance of sleeping with one's head aligned north. According to Randolph, pointing the head in this direction allows a greater degree of negative magnetism to be stored during the night. Accumulation of negative field particles aid in restoring auric, mental, and physical energy, reducing anxiety and depression, activating the pineal gland (third eye), and manufacturing of melatonin.

In his work *Magnetic Therapy*, Holger Hannemann (1990) states that a barium-ferrite magnet of about one-fourth inch in diameter with a magnet force of 600 gauss (a strength measurement used in conjunction with magnetic distance) can be used for treating pain. This magnet, which has a lift power of about two pounds, is held in place with a hypo-allergenic adhesive tape over the injury or painful area. The magnet is left on for several days, then removed for forty-eight hours and reapplied. The magnet can be left on during baths and showers, with an occasional reapplication of tape.

Magnets come in various sizes, shapes, and strengths (rated in gauss units). For use in healing, the therapist may use plastiform magnetic strips (available in craft stores), ceramic magnets, or the stronger neodymium magnet. As noted, some magnets can be applied using an adhesive. Other, more powerful, permanent magnets may be affixed as free-standing therapeutic instruments. These devices, producing 2000-10,000 of gauss power (a twenty-five-pound lift power magnet is rated at 2,000 gauss), need not come in direct contact with skin or test object. Magnets can be used or worn anytime of the day or night. They can be sewn into a piece of clothing, fixed in place by a bandage, or used in bedding.

According to the *Biomagnetic Handbook* (1990), magnetic force performs four essential services: heals, alkalinizes, oxygenates, and normalizes. Magnets, if used correctly, produce no side-effects. Perhaps the only precaution against using magnets relate to pregnancy and individuals using pacemakers. Magnets should not be used within five inches of a pacemaker, and while pregnant, women shouldn't use magnets on the abdomen. They should also avoid using any magnet over 600 gauss units.

Using Magnets

After having determined north and south polarity, gauss strength, and the correct polarity to use for the particular disorder, a person is now ready to use magnetic therapy. *The Biomagnetic Handbook* lists over one hundred disorders for which magnets may be useful. Although each case may differ, a general rule is that north pole (-) magnetic force increases oxygen, reduces infections, relieves pain, and reduces inflammation. Positive or southern (+) field produces wakefulness and, at times, stressful states. It can also, according to some researchers, increase pain, inflammation, reduce healing, and augment depression and anxiety.

Magnetic therapy should be used not as an alternative to traditional medicine but rather in conjunction with standard medical practice. For injury, the magnet should be placed directly on the site of the pain or soreness. If direct pressure of the magnet causes additional pain or swelling, it can be used adjacent to the site. Using more powerful magnets, requiring no direct contact, is an alternative procedure. Acupuncture points and chakra centers may also be stimulated by magnet forces. Magnetic therapy for other physiological and psychological conditions is similar to that which is utilized for injuries.[1] According to some researchers, for psychological conditions, magnets may be placed on the cranium or along the spinal region. Since strong magnets will penetrate into the muscular, glandular, circulatory, and bony areas, one type of general therapy works for most situations. Magnets start working immediately, yet their beneficial effects are not noticeable for several days. Generally, permanent magnets should be used for about twenty minutes, twice a day. Plastiform magnetic strips and ceramic magnets may be used for up to twelve hours a day. If, after a week, benefits are not obtained, magnetic treatments may not be the treatment of choice.

Conclusion

Magnets for treating a variety of illnesses and injuries have, in one form or another, been used for thousands of years. Their therapeutic value has been shown countless times in working with a variety of physiological conditions. As stated, each individual has his/her own unique psychological and physiological states. What works for one person may not be beneficial to another. The same holds true for an array of traditional medical techniques and drugs. It is, however, important that magnets be considered as an alternative or conjunctive treatment method.

Note

1. It should be noted that the writers are not physicians and are only providing information for general and research use.

CHAPTER SEVEN

THE CHAKRAS
A Key to Subtle Physiology

William T. McClellan, MAR, PhD (cand.)

THIS CHAPTER CONCEIVES of the *chakras* as a system of organs in the greater system of subtle human physiology. The intent is to be sympathetic to the mystical, parapsychological, and sometimes legendary material concerning human spiritual anatomy, while neither denigrating nor kowtowing to the assumption that no phenomenon is a fact that cannot be measured quantitatively on contemporary scientific instruments. In other words, the intent is to maintain a balance between spiritual and conventional scientific experience of the human body.

Chakra is a Sanskrit word that means generally "wheel, plexus, center" (Grimes 1989). Its meaning is also understood as "wheel of light" (Bruyere 1989, 40) or "whirling wheel" (Silburn 1988, 25). It refers to one of the seven discernible centers of activity that are arranged in regular hierarchical order along the spinal column, from the sacral region to the crown of the head. There are differences among the various Hindu and Buddhist traditions as to precisely how many main *chakras* there are—some say as few as five (Silburn 1988), some as many as ten (Svoboda 1993). Motoyama (1981) mentions a Tantric tradition that speaks of seven *chakras* for the gods, above and beyond the traditional seven. Lesser *chakras* are distributed throughout the body, in the center of the palm, and at the joints of the fingers and thumb (Bruyere 1989).

In recognition of the great number of distinct *chakras* that it is possible to analyze, Motoyama provides a principle by which to determine major *chakras* from minor: the possibility for a *chakra* to be awakened or activated in relative isolation from the others. Many, such as the *lalana*, "cannot be awakened independently of the related major chakra. For this reason, only the six major chakras, from muladhara to ajna, are called 'chakras of awakening'" (Motoyama 1981, 235).

The *chakras* are understood to function as major centers for the transformation and transmission of energy (Motoyama 1981). They are spoken of variously, depending on the specific instance, as blocked, dormant, activated, awakened, opened, pierced, etc. Transformation of consciousness is also involved because their energetic status correlates with attention that may be given to them, whether that attention is accidental or deliberate. Changes in the functioning of the *chakras* in an individual correspond to changes in the stability and scope of an individual's conscious self, as well to changes in physiological functioning.

Because the term *chakra* has references that are legendary as well as historical, and because it designates things (e.g., the lower *chakras*) that purportedly may be detected in every human being and yet only experienced (e.g., the awakened highest *chakras*) in the most advanced saint or adept, it is a term to approach with circumspection. The danger is to believe that one's little knowledge of the *chakras* is sufficient. The word "danger" is appropriate: the inadvertent arousal of a *chakra* may precipitate severe psychological and/or physiological crises (Brennan 1972; Grof 1988; Krishna 1967; Motoyama 1978; Scott 1983; Svoboda 1993).

To avert these dangers, this article approaches its topic with a plan designed for a high degree of systematic thoroughness. Where knowledge is lacking, or discussion must be abbreviated, the plan is to anticipate what is missing and to convey a sense of the odd combination of humility and boldness that this topic requires of the researcher.

An introductory definition of the *chakras* has already been given. Following this introduction will be a review of the sources of information and experience of the *chakras*, that is, a review of the *kinds of* legendary and historical accounts of the *chakras*, and of the *kinds of* contemporary sources of experience of the *chakras*.

An approximation of the cosmology of what might be called "the magical world-view" will come next. This cosmology is expressed in terms of the metaphysics assumed by the kinds of description and explanation employed in the traditional accounts of the *chakras*. Arguably, there are extensive and essential similarities among systems of

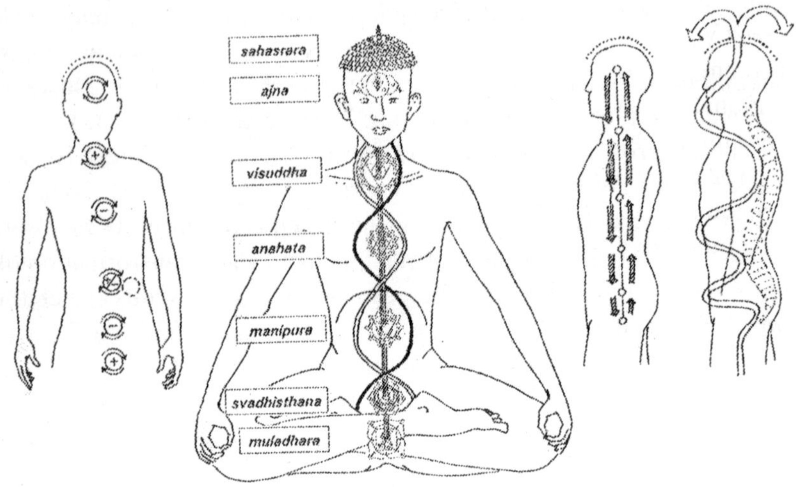

The central seated figure shows the most common way that traditional sources display the chakras *is relation to the human form. The central vertical straight line is the* sushumna; *the intersecting wavy lines are the* pingala *(golden, solar, hot, positive) and* ida *(silvery, lunar, cool, feminine). The tradition generally teaches that* kundalini *ascends at the back of the body and descends at the front, as shown by one of the profile figures. Roughly following Bruyere (1989), the profile figure at the far right shows* kundalini *in a wavy ascent from the legs (and from the earth below) through the top of the head. The motion of the waves toward or away from the vertical axis of the body correspond with the* chakras *on the figure at the far left, which are indicated as positive-expressive, negative-receptive, or mixed.*

Clockwise circular rotation is regarded as healthy; anything else is aberrant. Bruyere says that a chakra's *spin generates a unique electromagnetic field and that it is the combination of these fields, especially from the first* (muladhara), *third* (manipura), *and fifth* (visuddhi) chakras, *that produces primary field. The fields of all seven* chakras *combine to form the outer or "secondary auric field" (Bruyere 1989, 61).*

The mutability of the chakra-kundalini-nadi *system makes it difficult to study and to schematize. For instance, Bruyere notes that the* manipura chakra *is displaced to the left (indicated on figure at left) in many North Americans. Nonetheless, there are regularities to the phenomena, and there are many points of agreement among investigators.*

esoteric cosmology everywhere around the world, so that it makes sense in this case to speak—though cautiously—of a general magical world-view (Versluis 1986). Acknowledging and clarifying the very real differences in metaphysics between the magical world-view and conventional Western scientific world-view is necessary in preventing gross misunderstandings and to lead to fruitful research.

The cosmology section concludes with an overview of subtle human physiology. The *chakra* system is an important part, but only one part, of the human organism. Equally important are *kundalini*, the prime energy activating the *chakras*, and the *nadis* or channels connecting all parts of the subtle body. Therefore it is more accurate to speak of the *chakra-kundalini-nadi* system or theory. This theory is integral with the cosmology.

Finally, the stage is set to describe the seven *chakras* themselves. Each *chakra* will receive separate treatment, but various subgroupings of them will be mentioned. The intention is to convey a sense of the whole series of *chakras* as a unitary system. The theoretical basis of the unified system is suggested in this section on cosmology; in the descriptions of the *chakras* themselves, an effort is made to correlate traditional material with experiential and experimental findings.

The ideal of merging major accounts of the *chakras*—traditional, legendary, contemporary, and experimental—into a grand synthesis has animated this chapter but remains a distant goal. Toward this end, improved communication across academic specializations is needed. This chapter concludes with a suggestion to this end and with another suggestion for further research.

The Sources

This section of the chapter enumerates the possible sources of information concerning the *chakras*. It will become apparent that all five sources mentioned in the following are simply varieties of experience of the *chakras*. But pointing out the distinctions among these varieties of experience is exactly what may be helpful.

Sources: Myth and Legend

How early in the history of human cultural artifacts can be found what might refer to *chakras*? Finding a possible reference depends partly—as do all such finds in the rummage of history—on the interpretive determination and creativity of the seeker. However, it may well be that an ancient text or symbolic artifact indeed refers to centers of power that can be discerned by sensitives, or to stages of spiritual development, or to levels of being, arranged in a hierarchical sequence, and that details of these centers-stages-levels correspond extensively with details of the *chakras* as spelled out in texts that are dated much later than the earlier legend or artifact.

If the *chakras* are indeed universals of human and cosmic constitution, it would be remarkable if the *chakra* theory did *not* extensively correspond to depictions of the soul's place in and path through the cosmos that are found in the cultural materials of societies from every part of the planet at every point in history. The point is not to use history as a proof text, to claim that legendary material from Scandinavia (Dumézil 1973), the North American Southwest (Waters 1963), and Oceana proves the truth of the *chakra* theory. Such a strategy has no defense against the claim that, say, the *chakra* theory proves the truth of ancient Norse cosmological-physiological theories. The reality is much more complex.

> The most widely distributed variant of the symbolism of the Center is the Cosmic Tree, situated in the middle of the Universe, and upholding the three worlds as upon one axis. Vedic India, ancient China and the Germanic mythology, as well as the "primitive" religions, all held different versions of this Cosmic Tree, whose roots plunged down into Hell, and whose branches reached to Heaven. (Eliade 1961, 44)

Welcome to the philosophy of religions and to the often bewildering crafts of history of mythology and comparative mythology. If it is difficult to prove that one concept (say, the colors of the rainbow *Bilfrost,* that, conjunctly with the World Tree *Yggdrasil*, connect *Valhalla* to earth) does correspond to another (say, the colors attributed to the *chakras*) (Pollack 1988), it is harder to prove that there is *no* correspondence. The value of finding correspondences between systematic features of schemes that have little or no obvious cultural, historical, or geographical proximity is phenomenological corroboration of the kinds of experiences that contribute to and that are anticipated by such schemes.

This is not *less than* a knock-down scientific proof, and neither is it for this reason completely *other than* scientific proof. It is the discerning and articulating of *relevance*, an operation that precedes and lies at the foundation of the formulation of hypotheses that permit of the falsification that is the earmark of conventional experimental science.

Consider the similarities between the images in *Figure 2* (below). The vertical arrangement, the two channel/serpents intertwined about a third, the dual wings/petals . . . the correspondences are striking. At least two writers, Joseph Campbell (1986) and Ken Wilber (1983), say that the *caduceus* and the *chakra* scheme refer to the same reality; the identification was made also in the early 20th century by an acquaintance of Sir John Woodroffe (1919). There is a plausible geographical-cultural continuity between the Indus Valley civilization of 2300-1750 B.C.E. and the Sumer civilization of 2000 B.C.E. Alexander's empire embraced the Sumer and Indus regions by 323 B.C.E., deliberately assimilating many aspects of subjugated cultures. "From Hellenistic times forward, the theologies of the eastern Mediterranean were complicated by the tangle of correspondences between the traditional Greek

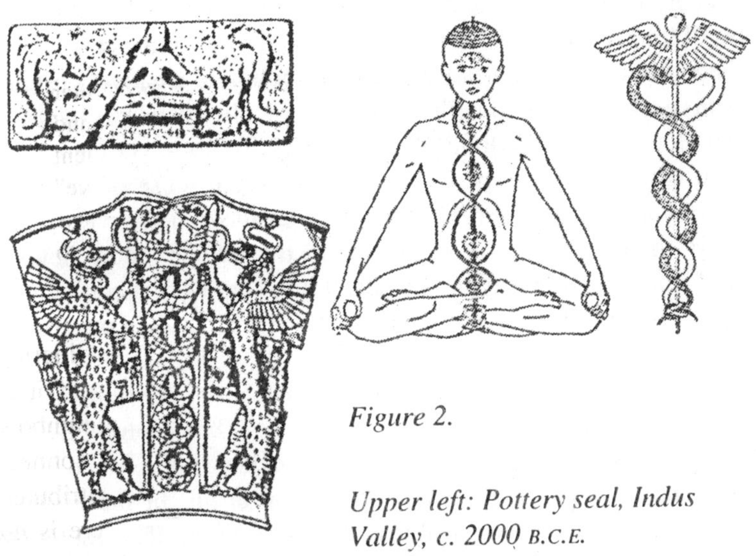

Figure 2.

Upper left: Pottery seal, Indus Valley, c. 2000 B.C.E.

Lower left: Design from libation cup of a Sumerian king, c. 2000 B.C.E.

Center: Figure with chakras *and* nadis; *the* ajna chakra *(second from the top) has two petals in the position of wings.*

Right: Caduceus, staff, and emblem of the Greco-Egyptian Hermes (Roman: Mercury).

pantheon and the newfound gods of nations subjugated by Alexander and later conquerors" (Copenhaver 1992, xxvi). An opinion suggests itself, namely, that the *caduceus* was handed to the Roman god Mercury by the Greek god Hermes who had received it possibly from Asiatic sources.

However, this judgment is too easy, too quick, and too shallow. It tacitly assumes that concepts are passed from one culture to another only by transmission of symbolic material that is already expressed in external form, i.e., oral, written, or artifactual symbolic material. If everything is assumed to depend upon transmission of articulated symbolic forms, the original emergence of the symbolic material is placed forever beyond reach. Yet the fact is, that symbols exist and must have emerged at some time or another. If a symbol emerged once in one culture, there is every reason to believe it may emerge independently in another culture, and all the more readily might it emerge to the extent that it pertained to issues and experiences of deep relevance to the life of the soul and the structure of the cosmos.

Accordingly, the existence of likely routes of transmission, even routes of transmission whose use is confirmed by exacting scholarship, need not and should not disallow the contribution of creatively original elements appearing in and with expressions of allied concepts by different but closely related individuals or cultures. To do so is to ignore the element of immediate experience and to lose the sense of the living reality of what is expressed. This issue of transmission-or-emergence is a version of the chicken-or-egg problem that divides most fields of cultural studies in one way or another. It turns out to be a battleground for deeper philosophical contests, often between varieties of materialism and other schools of thought.

Returning to the example of the *caduceus-chakra*, we find that even before Alexander, in the *Odyssey* of Homer (8th century B.C.E.), Hermes had a staff, a "golden wand" that can delude or awaken human beings, and awaken in the sense of eluding death. In the *Hymn to Hermes*, a staff that is recognizable as the *caduceus* itself is emblematic of Hermes' role as ambassador to Hades (Kerényi 1976). How early did he come by this office? "Hermes has the closest possible relation to the Kabeirean mysteries. It seems that one is led here beyond the classical tradition to an at least equally ancient mystical tradition" (Kerényi 1976, 43).

It should be remarked that any mystical tradition that is indicated here is of a period earlier than Homer and Hesiod, that is, before 800

B.C.E. The class of texts known as the *Corpus Hermeticum* was produced all but exclusively in Hellenistic Egypt, the Egypt that was a subjugated colony of Alexandrian Greece and of Rome through the Byzantine era (Copenhaver 1992). Certainly there are a wealth of correspondences between this Hellenistic Hermetic material and the *chakra* system, but the immediate issue is to focus on the irreducible and autonomous element of experience. For this, the protoHellenic material is more appropriate.

It should be possible to draw correspondences between other elements of ancient and classical material concerning Hermes and elements of the *chakra* system. The name Hermes is essentially identified with the number four and with square herms, or carved stones topped by a bust, but often by an erect phallus, monuments that were old even in Samothracian legend. The phallic theme is central to the story of Priapus, son of Hermes, in tales and cult in Thrace and Phrygia, which are nearby Samothrace (Kerényi 1976). The elements of fourness, stone, and squareness correspond especially to the *muladhara chakra*, which incorporates also a phallus; other chakras also employ phallic elements.

It is possible that prehistoric ancestors of the Hellenes adopted concepts from a conceptual scheme imported from the Indian subcontinent; this may always be admitted. The transmission of ideas both stimulates and is a response to what finally authenticates and naturalizes ideas in a given local immediate experience. And immediate experience, without influence from imported ideas, may produce forms of expression that are essentially the same as ideas imported at a later time. To query the myths and legends of the world's religions for insight into the *chakras* is to seek similarities in structure and detail of symbolic material on the hypothesis that where there are such similarities there are also similarities in experience.

How might *experience* of the presence of Hermes in the early Hellenic Hermetic material correspond to the way the *experience* of the *chakras* is expressed? It is difficult to imagine how fourness, squareness, or stoneness might be experienced, and the ithyphallic aspect, though decidedly experiential, is problematic for several reasons. But two other points of correspondence are ready to hand, decidedly experiential: bees with their honey or nectar or ambrosia, and inspired speech.

In the *Odyssey* (535-53), Apollo reserves for himself an insight into the private thinking of Zeus but allows Hermes to own the powers of bees. Originally three sisters with "swift wings" and "heads sprinkled with white barley flower" (pollen), they instruct in oracular practices.

"They, when they are full of the spirit of soothsaying, having eaten of the wan honey, delight to speak forth the truth. But if they be bereft of the sweet food divine, then lie they all confusedly." In classical antiquity bees convey the inspiration of the muses to gifted children and represent souls (Kerényi 1976). The experiential aspects of this apiarian intelligibility are: *a)* a bee-like presence, and *b)* a sweet nourishing liquid that *c)* is directly linked with inspired insight and speech.

Motoyama (1981, 118; 28) draws from classic texts and personal experience in telling us that "awakening the *muladhara chakra* will produce sounds that resemble the chirping of birds or the buzzing of bees." All sounds are produced by the cooperative interaction of the *muladhara* and *visuddhi chakras*. The *visuddhi* is located in the throat and is concerned with the sense of hearing; there are obvious implications for speech and understanding, the traditional province of Hermes-Mercury. A special function of the *visuddhi* is that its status as awakened or not affects the character of the divine nectar that comes from the *sahasrara chakra* and passes through the *visuddhi* on its way to the *manipura chakra*, where it is the prime subtle fuel for vital processes (Motoyama 1981).

This technical, rather anatomical and schematic approach is paralleled by devotional and instructional material with the same import. A Hatha Yoga text directs the aspirant to "contemplate that there is a sea of nectar in his heart; . . . there is an island . . . there are . . . trees laden with sweet flowers . . . and the fragrance of these flowers is spread all around, in every quarter. Insects are humming there and cuckoos are singing" (Muller-Ortega 1989, 76). The *Tantraloka* of Abhinavagupta, a classic text of non-dual Kashmir Saivism, describes the process of awakening the whole series of *chakras* as culminating in a "piercing" by "serpentine energy" such that "the penetration [resembles] that of the bumble bee;" the commentator clarifies: "its attendant sound is like the continuous and natural humming of the black bee" (Silburn 1988, 96-7). A completely contemporary adept tells us:

> Krishna's hair has been compared to a swarm of bees. What does a bee do with its time? All day long it moves from flower to flower, enjoying the nectar at each one. The flower longs for the bees to come and take its nectar; many flowers in fact exist only because of bees. . . .
>
> Bees are always buzzing, and the sound of Krishna's hair is likened by the Rishis to the murmuring drone that arises from

> innumerable intoxicated bees. That buzz is Nada [sound]. If you use this image to improve your concentration on Krishna you will begin to perceive this Nada when your concentration on Krishna becomes perfect. (Svoboda 1993, 196-97)

Examples could easily be multiplied. For instance, Hermes made a lyre from a tortoise found at the entrance of the cave where he, as a youth, was hiding and living. The lyre was traded to Apollo for a gold-tipped staff in a settlement over Hermes' return of stolen cattle (Kerényi 1976). The *Manipura chakra* "is sometimes called a 'tortoise' because it is said to look like a turtle, with large nadis appended at roughly the positions where the turtle's legs, head and tail would be" (Svoboda 1993, 230). Apollo represents the Sun and consciousness. He can play the lyre only because Hermes brought it to him, and Hermes receives in exchange a staff of authority and power.

The point is that mythological and legendary material from cultures of many times and places may contain elements that coordinate more or less closely with that of the *chakra* system. Sometimes the *chakra* system may illumine non-Asian material, and sometimes the outside material may provide insight into *chakra* theory.

The correspondences between *chakra* theory and myths and legends from around the world do at least three things that help understand the *chakra* system. First, they provide evidence for the universality of the phenomena of which the *chakra* theory is one of the most sophisticated expressions. Second, granting that there is some truth to the phenomena behind the *chakra* theory, the extra-Indian mythical material helps conceive of the developmental and evolutionary implications of the *chakra* theory. Third, for those who do not enjoy a background in Indian culture, these correspondences hint at continuities between the subtle experiences of Indian spirituality and subtle experience as mediated by images and conceptual frameworks of more familiar cultures.

Source: Classic Texts

Intimations of the *chakra-kundalini-nadi* theory are found early in Indian thought (see *Figure 2),* and a brief historical overview will provide a framework in which to locate the texts that are important for it.

Yoga is the cultivation of harmony of body and mind for the sake of self-realization, and it leads to experience of the subtle aspects of the self. *Chakra-kundalini-nadi* theory is the conceptual system of description and explanation used in accompaniment with the practice of yoga. There is evidence of wide-spread yogic practices in the Indus Valley's Mohenjo-daro civilization (Raju 1985), which declined as Aryan peoples made their way South. The Vedas are regarded as primarily an Aryan creation; thus *yoga* and its theoretical system predate the Vedas. "The history of Indian philosophy may be described as the story of the struggle for supremacy between these two systems" (Kalupahana 1976, 4).

The *chakra-kundalini-nadi* system grew out of a pre-Vedic strain of thought that came to be known as *sankhya*, meaning "enumerating" or "exact" knowledge. It emphasizes immediate irrefutable experience and exact description. It is not deductive, but empirical and intuitive in spirit. The pre-Vedic religion of the Jains played a part in exploring the subtle realms mapped in *sankhya* thought. *Sankhya* and *yoga* "are regarded in India as twins, the two aspects of a single discipline" (Zimmer 1951, 280). Together, they point "to a remote, aboriginal, non-Vedic, Indian antiquity. The fundamental ideas of *Sankhya* and Yoga, therefore, must be immensely old" (Zimmer 1951, 281). Elements of *sankhya* and *yoga* emerge in Vedic material only relatively late—in the later Upanisads—and illustrate "a long history of rigid resistance" on the part of the Aryan Brahmanic priesthood (Zimmer 1951, 281).

Radhakrishnan and Moore describe four major periods in Indian thought, starting with the arrival of the Aryans: the Vedic period, the epic period, the Sutra period, and the scholastic period.

During the Vedic period (circa 2500-600 B.C.E.), Aryan newcomers migrated into the Indian subcontinent and established themselves. This period produced the four Vedas (the word means simply knowledge or wisdom). Each Veda has four parts: *Mantras* (hymns), *Brahmanas* (prescriptions of rituals and duties), *Aranyakas* (instructions for individual practitioners), and *Upanisads* (philosophical commentaries). The *Mantras* are the earliest layer of recorded Indian thought; the *Brahmanas* are next. Both the *Aranyakas* and the *Upanisads*, but especially the *Upanisads*, criticize the *Brahmanas*, which expound a priestly conservatism. The *Upanisads* generally emphasize "spiritual monism" and the superiority of intuition over reason (Radhakrishnan & Moore 1957, xvii-xviii). Of the Vedic material, the *Upanisads*, and especially certain later *Upanisads*, have the most to say about the *chakra-kundalini-nadi* system.

The epic period (about 600 B.C.E. to 200 C.E.) gave birth to the great epics, the *Ramayana* and the *Mahabharata*, which includes the *Bhagavad Gita*. These works present philosophical teachings indirectly, through epic drama. The tales of the gods were elaborated, coordinated, and refined. In this period the main orthodox schools of Indian philosophy and religion emerged, although their systematic works appeared later. Buddhism was born, enjoyed its first schisms, and contended with the newer views (e.g., skepticism, naturalism, materialism) as well as with the older Jainism and with what would become known as orthodox Hinduism. One of the types of school that appeared during this period was *Tantric* (Radhakrishnan & Moore 1957).

The *Sutra* period (about 200-600 C.E.) produced systematic texts of aphorisms designed as key phrases to promote particular systems of philosophy, as well as self-conscious sustained criticisms of competing systems. *Yoga* emerged as a distinct and specific school during this period (Radhakrishnan & Moore 1957). The term *chakra* itself, used clearly in the sense in which it is now used in Hindu scholarship and New Age thought alike, may be found as early as the *Yoga Sutras* of Patanjali, from the third century C.E. Even more useful are certain of the latest *Upanishads* (about 600 C.E.) called *Yoga Upanisads*. These accounts give comparable attention to the *nadis* or channels and to the subtle body as a whole (Motoyama, 1981).

In the scholastic period (about 600-1700 C.E.), commentaries were written to explain the *Sutras*. "Without elaboration and explanation the *Sutras* are almost unintelligible. Not only were commentaries written upon the *sutras*, but also commentaries upon commentaries, and commentaries upon these, almost without limit." From this period the well-known writers Sankara (788-820? C.E.) and Ramanuja (11th century) styled themselves as commentators but in fact constructed elaborate and cohesive systems in their own right. In the sense the scholastic period continues, "but Indian philosophy lost its dynamic spirit about the sixteen century when India became the victim of . . . [f]irst the Muslims and then the British. . . ." (Radhakrishnan & Moore 1957, xx-xxi).

The web of Indian texts from the Vedic through the scholastic period is, if anything, more complex than the web of texts from the ancient Hellenic and Egyptian material through the Renaissance in Europe. This chapter cannot trace the development of *chakra-kundalini-nadi* theory through the literature from early Vedic times through the present. But later texts usually refer to earlier ones, so that the literature of a certain area of Indian thought illumines the lineage that leads up to it. Even the same Vedic text may be cited as authoritative by commentators with quite different—even opposed—positions, the lineage indicates similar interests. A text approved by an adept of the *chakra-kundalini-nadi* system, however technical it may be, in all likelihood, derives from and/ or instructs in the immediate personal experience of things—gods, structures, powers—described in *chakra-kundalini-nadi* theory.

No category of Indian thought pays more attention to *chakra-kundalini-nadi* theory than Shaivism, or the tradition of worship of *Siva*. This tradition can be found from the Mohenjo-daro religion onward. In Saivite doctrine, *Siva* is Godhead, Lord, and Ultimate Reality; the concept can be found in the *Rg Veda* where he is called *Rudrua*. The *Svetasvatara Upanisad* (5th-6th century B.C.E.), in prescribing yogic exercises leading to the knowledge of *Rudra-Siva* (the Supreme Being situated in the Heart of all creatures), articulates "a constant Shaivite theme: the yogic process should lead not just to an inner enlightenment, but also to a physiological transformation by which the body itself is led to enlightenment, to immortality" (Muller-Ortega 1989, 26-8).

Shaivism is associated with Tantrism. *Tantra* means rule, ritual, scripture, and connotes the systematization and disciplined practice of personal worship. "As religious treatises, they [the *tantras*] are usually in the form of a dialogue between *Siva* and *Sakti*. Sometimes they are referred to as the 'Fifth *Veda*.'" (Grimes 1989, 357). The *Tantras* have a practical orientation: their instructions may be applied to the development of powers for worldly gain as well as for spiritual development. Sorcerers as well as saints attend the lessons of the *Tantras*.

Siva and *Sakti* are the dynamic and static aspects, respectively, of one another. *Sakti* denotes power, energy, and potency. Theologically, *Sakti* is the Divine Mother, the latent power of *Siva* himself. As latent in human beings, it is called *kundalini-sakti*, coiled or serpentine *sakti*. *Siva* and *Sakti* long for one another, need one another, inspire one another, and enjoy ever more profound union with one another. The awakening and ascending of *kundalini* is *Sakti* herself coming to meet *Siva*.

The *Tantras* and Shaivism have no monopoly on *chakra-kundalini-nadi* theory, but Shaivist and Tantric traditions from Kashmir and North into Tibet, especially in texts from the first millennium C.E. and later, offer some of the richest of all material on the *chakra-kundalini-nadi* system. If required to select the best single text on the *chakras* and *nadis*, many informed students would choose the *Shat-chakra-nirupana*, "Descriptions of the Six Centers," a series of writings compiled in 1577 by Purananda, a guru originally from Bengal. This text is part six of Purananda's longer *Shri-tattva-cintamini* (Motoyama 1981).

Much is certainly to be found in *kundalini yoga*, *hatha yoga*, and elsewhere. Tibetan Buddhism concerns itself explicitly with *tantric yoga* (Cozort 1986). For the purposes of this article, when referring to "traditional" textual sources of information on the *chakras*, the reference may be to a text from the *Sankha*, *Tantra*, *Yoga*, or *Veda* category, including Buddhist literature.

Source: Experiences of Traditionally Trained Contemporary Experts

This category of information includes accounts by contemporary adepts who are trained in the traditional lore and techniques of experience with awakened kundalini. Unlike the traditional texts, works by these experts are written with an awareness of contemporary issues and often with some firsthand knowledge of other cultures and languages including contemporary slang. The sense of the text is usually very accessible, unlike many older works.

Dr. Hiroshi Motoyama (PhD, LittD) is an accomplished practitioner of *kundalini yoga* as well as a scientist. He interprets traditional techniques and literature with an eagerness to bring together, wherever possible, interesting *chakra-kundalini-nadi* phenomena and conventional scientific tools and theories (Motoyama 1978, 1981, 1990). Dr. Motoyama is founder and president of the California Institute for Human Science, a graduate school and research center in Encinitas, California.

Swami Sivananda Radha is an excellent expositor for Western readers (Sivananda Radha 1981, 1991). German by birth and a naturalized Canadian, she was sent to the West in 1956 by her teacher, Swami Sivananda Sarasvati. Her writing is notable for making connections between *kundalini yoga* and humanistic and transpersonal psychology. Swami Radha's teachings are available through the Yasodhara Ashram in Kootenay Bay, B.C., Canada, and through the Association for the Development of Human Potential in Spokane, Washington.

Svoboda's books have a contemporary voice, although his teacher, Vimalananda, was an older Indian gentleman, was idiosyncratic, and finally remains unidentified (Svoboda 1986, 1993).

These writers speak from experience, not simply from theory. Other contemporary experts with traditional lineages of instruction could be found. Any attempt to make a list of genuine practitioners would have to evaluate their experience, which would be rash. Living experts in the traditional practices are around and may be approached, even successfully, if one has a proper attitude.

Source: Experiences of Sensitives, Healers, and Psychics

An individual need not be trained in *chakra-kundalini-nadi* experience through a traditional guru-discipline relationship; one may simply have natural gifts for perceiving and/or affecting elements of the system. There is no reason to doubt the experience of someone who has never sat at a swami's knee. Experience is where you find it.

Experience with the exercise of natural psychic gifts may come by being the subject of the ministrations of the psychic, by observing the psychic ministering to others, or mediately, by watching video or by reading an account written by another.

By hypothesis, to the extent that the *chakra-kundalini-nadi* system is indeed universal for human beings, it will be the case that sensitives, healers, and psychics will have some regular elements of their psychic routines that coordinate with elements of the *chakra-kundalini-nadi* system. Finding this coordination and knowing what to make of it are formidable challenges, but it is theoretically likely that naturally gifted psychics demonstrate some elements of the system with a degree of regularity and accessibility.

Source: Observation and Measurement by Conventional Science

Western thought, especially most of its sciences, inherits a materialistic bias from 19th century Western physics and its triumphant applications in technology. With the shift to the 20th century's quantum physics, the conventional wisdom is that everything is not matter (particles, hard stuff) but is configurations of energy. This does not eliminate materialism but merely disguises it, if at the same time it is believed that the only criterion for the detection of energy is its effect upon material instruments of measurement. This is still materialism, for instruments (hard stuff) must be moved before the existence of energy (purportedly transmaterialistic) is admitted. The restrictive premise is that nothing *really* exists that does not register upon such instruments. In other words, if it doesn't move the needle (mark the film, trigger the photometer, etc.), it doesn't exist. This materialistic bias has a cohort.

A chain of circumstances from early Greek thought through Christian theology has produced a Western psychology that is generally biased in favor of cognitive operations and against sensory and intuitive operations. The unjustifiable character of this bias is documented by critics from within the field itself (Johnson 1987; Lazarus 1991; Varela, Thompson & Rosch 1991). Two important corollaries of this cognitive bias are: a) a distrust of immediate personal sources of knowing (i.e., sensation and intuition), and b) a reliance upon external authorities (e.g., the experts who manipulate the finest instruments of measurement). The problem is that these biases affect not only schools of thought within certain scientific specialties, but permeate the academic world, the educational system, and eventually the whole culture.

The cognitive (anti-sensory, anti-intuitive) bias of psychology, when combined with materialism, puts into effect the suppositions: a) that the only things to be known are the motions of material objects (e.g., the impact upon a photographic emulsion of a gamma particle or of a photon from a radioactive tag on a blood sugar), and b) that the only ways to know them are by proper experimental methods. This is a knowledge that requires sophisticated technology and experts; all else is not really knowledge.

Systematic philosophers call this bias a metaphysics, which in general means a set of premises (a nice word for assumptions) concerning that which is prior to (*meta-*) nature (*-physis*). Metaphysics is not something only for Greek philosophers, Medieval Christian theologians, or for that section in the book store where there is literature on astrology and mediumship. A metaphysics is revealed in the system—more or less cohesive—of premises that our behavior demonstrates that we actually believe, regardless of what we think we believe (which may be a different metaphysics!) This understanding of metaphysics can be found in William James, Alfred North Whitehead, and the contemporary writer David Ray Griffin, among others. There is no dispensing with metaphysics.

This materialistic cognitivism that apes and idolizes science is not what is commonly held by contemporary creative scientists themselves. It is more likely to be held by people farther from the cutting edge of a leading discipline. "For example, biology presupposes physics. It will usually be the case that these loans from one specialism to another really belong to the state of science thirty or forty years earlier" (Whitehead 1938, 131). The information explosion has not changed the habits of Western popular thought, which defer to experts of a bygone era. Increasing specialization has increased reliance upon experts even among academics. To call the unreflective, cognitive-materialistic bias of Western popular thought scientistic is not to denigrate science or scientists. Then again, a scientist or an academic may be the leading light in her or his specialty and still harbor a scientistic metaphysics.

Two important things left out of scientistic metaphysics are sensation and intuition, which exist strongly in science. All measurement finally depends upon a human being's sensory interaction with an instrument. In its design, manufacture, calibration, application, and final reading, there is sensory contact with the instrument. And intuition is essentially involved in the premise that the instrument might be designed and deployed in the first place, and in the intuition that the elements of the universe and of the instrument will remain constant enough for the results to be relevant.

> However far the testing of instruments is carried, finally all scientific interpretation is based upon the assumption of directly observed unchangeability of some instruments for seconds, for hours, for months, for years. When we test this assumption we can only use another instrument; and there cannot be an infinite regress of instruments. (Whitehead 1978 [1929], 127)

Intuition is essentially involved in the formulation of hypotheses. The much-analyzed scientific method of repeated experiments describes only the follow-up work to successful demonstrations of creative hypotheses. Much creative work is required before reliable repetitions of experiments occur. Far from being excluded from science, immediate personal experience is essential to science.

It is false to imagine that scientific measurements can offer a purely objective assessment of the *chakras*, while other sources of information can offer only subjective hints and approximations. This attitude reveals a cognitive-materialistic bias. Each kind of source of information offers experiences, each experience can offer a combination of the presence of something real and of personal perspectives.

Conventional Western science was not a factor in the development of the *chakra-kundalini-nadi* system nor in conveying it to adepts who use it in their spiritual discipline. It is widely remarked that the *chakra-kundalini-nadi* system is known purely by personal intuitive experience and not by public demonstrations of things available to the external senses (Motoyama 1981; Scott 1983; Svoboda 1993). Accordingly, one might wonder if the instruments of conventional science could reveal anything at all about the *chakras*.

However, descriptions of the *chakras* in classic texts locate them in the human body at specific places (e.g., a few finger-widths below or above the navel, or between the eyebrows). Although the chakras do not correspond in a one-to-one manner with any visible organs or tissues, they are explicitly mapped onto the human form as it is known to the external senses. The student on the mystical path is instructed to imagine the *chakras* in these places. This leads to the expectation that there is a direct relationship between a given *chakra* and the part of the body where that *chakra* is located. For instance, the *Muladhara chakra* (perineal region) is linked with the element (*tattva*) earth, and Western culture considers that part of the body as earthy on several counts. Again, the *Ajna chakra* (eyebrows) is linked with mind, and this is as it should be also in cerebrocentric Western physiological thought. But along with obvious correlations, there also are jarring incongruities, e.g., the *Muladhara*, the *chakra* the farthest from the nose, is linked with the sense of smell, and sight is linked with the *Manipura chakra* (navel).

This points to the need to bring together the most complete possible understanding of the *chakra-kundalini-nadi* system with a good understanding of the spectrum of contemporary techniques of experimental measurement. The former is addressed in the next section. The latter is addressed here, with a glance at what measurements have been tried and what measurements might yet be tried, especially pertaining to chakras. This glance is neither all-encompassing nor penetrating, but it mentions some of the tools and terms of the trade.

In the mid-1930s attempts were made to measure oxygen consumption and heart rate in subjects in yogic meditation. By 1957 electroencephalogram (EEG) measurements were being taken, revealing distinct brain wave patterns. Blood pressure and galvanic skin response (GSR) were also measured (Wulff 1991). The experiments were not specific to particular *chakras*. These—with the exception of measuring oxygen consumption—are basic operations of the lie detector, whose proper name is "polygraph," denoting the many records it makes, i.e., of heart rate, EEG, GSR, etc.

With the advent of instruments for measuring extremely minute energies in specific locations, research into the activities of the *chakras* that may actually register upon scientific instruments becomes possible. It is possible now to measure extremely small changes in GSR, in radioactivity, in magnetic field strength, and in electromagnetic radiation output (Krippner 1979). Payne (1988) is an authority on magnetism and GSR instrumentation, among other things. Bruyere (1989) reports regular correlations between wave forms (on oscilloscopes) from electromyelogram (EMG) skin contact measurements at *chakra* sites and colors she perceived at those *chakras* in her healing ministrations; her instrumentation and method is specified in detail.

Motoyama (1978) has developed a computer-assisted "Apparatus for Measuring the Function of the Meridians and Corresponding Internal Organs" that he calls the AMI. Its twenty-eight electrodes attach to acupuncture meridian endpoints on the fingers and toes and measure GSR before and after application of a small DC charge. Acupuncture meridians from all over the body converge into close proximity in the fingers and toes. Motoyama claims that the AMI can diagnose distress anywhere in the body within minutes. If he is correct that acupuncture meridians basically correspond directly with the *nadi* system (1981), then the implications for measurement of *chakra* activity are obvious.

The techniques mentioned above are fairly gentle on the subject, requiring only skin contact for electrodes. Also, the equipment is within the financial reach of relatively small institutions. More invasive and much more expensive is positron emission tomography (PET), in which radioactively tagged sugar or water is injected into the blood. The decay of the radioactive material registers an accurate picture of where the blood carried this material at a chosen time. Magnetic resonance imaging (MRI) does not require injection, has a higher resolution of detail, and can complete a picture in a shorter time span that PET. MRI registers changes made in the magnetic fields of spinning hydrogen protons already in the body, by radio pulses produced by the apparatus. It seems that either of these machines could be applied to *chakra-kundalini-nadi* research.

Many interpreters of *chakra-kundalini-nadi* theory believe that the *chakras* have a direct link with endocrine function. A scientific instrument that could measure the production of hormones and hormone predecessors quickly, non-invasively, and inexpensively, would be a boon to researchers of subtle physiology.

At no level, so far, have Western medical researchers found phenomena that demand to be explained by a theory such as that of a subtle body comprising a hierarchical system of *chakras*. This remains merely an irrelevant suggestion, from the viewpoint of Western medicine. Accordingly, it is difficult to bring the more expensive scientific equipment to bear upon subtle body research. And it is difficult to bring adepts who may truly know the *chakras* to the scientific equipment. "[T]he yogis who have experienced *samadhi* are likely to view the scientist's efforts as trivial and futile, if not also sacrilegious. When practitioners are willing to serve as subjects in scientific research, it is difficult to estimate the degree to which their practice is genuine. . . ." (Wulff 1991, 176). In the best of cases, in the presence of the researcher the instruments may be disturbing. Further, researchers have not yet agreed upon a standard for what measurements to take and for the conditions under which to take them (Wulff 1991, 176-77).

There are semantic issues and issues of plain fact to be cleared up about what it is to perceive the *chakras*. Svoboda's teacher Vimalananda tells us, "The chakras exist only in the subtle body and are perceptible only to the enlightened mind. . . ." (Svoboda 1993, 66). Two things are said here: that *chakras* exist *only* in the subtle body and that *only* the enlightened mind perceives them. Both things are true in a sense and, in the sense that they are exaggerations, are not true. "Only" is a tricky word to use to describe relations within a complex system, because it is absolutely exclusive: something is excluded from a given category in every way, in every degree, in every regard. *Chakras* may exist *primarily* in the subtle body but not *only* in the subtle body. Unnecessarily exclusive distinctions are a common source of intellectual problems.

Regarding the location of the *chakras*, it is wrong to say "only in the subtle body," because there are senses which exist also in the physical body. This idea is suggested by the very notion of mapping them onto the human form, carried out graphically, and in instructions to students. According to general magical theory, the physical body results from a confluence of factors, which produces all layers of the greater human individual from the most subtle to the most dense layer, which is the physical body itself. The *chakra-kundalini-nadi* system is essential to the very plan of the whole and exists within the whole and within each of its parts. Although the *chakras* have primary origination from and dependence upon the more subtle layers (in this sense the existence of *chakras* is primarily subtle), the physical body provides essential things for the greater human individual. This greater individual (the *jivatman*) is like a tree rooted *in* the soil, which is the physical body.

Regarding the perception of the *chakras*, it is wrong to say "perceptible only to the enlightened mind," because other than enlightened people perceive them. Enlightenment may be necessary for regular daily perception of all the *chakras*, but there are people who are not enlightened but who, at least occasionally, perceive *chakras* up through the *Sahasrara*. Of course, the definition of perception is not restricted to the five external senses. Bruyere reports interacting with others *chakra*-to-*chakra*: ". . . if the person I am trying to heal has a heart problem, I can channel from my own heart *chakra*" (Bruyere 1989, 95). Her verbal reports of interactions with the *chakras* are paralleled by EMG data from electrodes on a subject's body at *chakra* sites. It is not an ordinary matter to perceive *chakras*, but it is not a skill restricted in every circumstance to the enlightened.

Svoboda's (1986 & 1993) accounts of his teacher Vimalananda are unique, well-written, and immensely valuable. They are analytical and critical in their own way, but they are also casual and anecdotal, and deliberately and properly so. The above reflections took a remark by Vimalananda out of context for the purpose of illustrating a kind of semantic wrangle that needs further interdisciplinary negotiation.

While good experiments have been done in many areas of psychic research, which is an appropriate place to categorize subtle body research, the experiments stand as metaphysical orphans on the scientific landscape. Cognitive-materialistic scientism is fighting a turf war of grand proportions, and psychic researchers must operate in something of a guerilla manner for funding, laboratory space, and academic presence. Part of this underdog status may be rectified by continuing to develop metaphysical paradigms that synthesize the considerable truths of cognitive materialism into a more inclusive viewpoint. Part of the difficulty in doing this is articulating a cosmology that is true to the more psychic aspects of the world's religions: their esoteric teachings. And for this cosmology it is necessary to clarify the metaphysics behind the magical world-view.

Cosmology: The Magical World-View

The metaphysics behind the *chakra-kundalini-nadi* system is a version of the magical world-view. There are brief expositions of Hindu thought bearing on *yoga* that use Sanskrit terms. Eliade starts from four main concepts: *karma* (causality), *maya* (illusion), *nirvana* (liberative assimilation into ultimate reality), and *yoga* (means for attaining this liberation). "A coherent history of Indian thought could be written starting from any one of these concepts," he tells us; "the other three would inevitably have to be discussed" (Eliade 1969, 3). Woodroffe's discussion (1919) is relatively brief but dense with unfamiliar Sanskrit terms.

There are advantages to characterizing the magical world-view in familiar English terms as a generic type that is instantiated in particular historical and cultural traditions, always with particular variations and emphases. One advantage is accessibility of exposition to those who don't know Sanskrit terms. This allows economy of expression and brief systematic completeness. Another advantage is that the characterization of the magical world-view can be articulated so as to show its differences from, yet compatibilities with, scientism more clearly than might be the case were the more—what, exotic?—world-view of Hindu thought itself portrayed. Again, there are assurances from scholars of magic that systems of magic from around the world are essentially congruent with one another.

When launching into a description of a complete metaphysical system, the choice of starting-point reduces easily to a handful of concepts, but to choose the single starting concept is relatively arbitrary, for the other concepts are immediately required to make sense of whichever is expounded first. With this caution, we attempt to state all our first-order principles at once, in the following interpretation of the relations of the One and the Many: everything is part of the whole or the One, emerges from the unity of the whole, derives its purpose from the unity of the whole, and returns to the unity of the whole. This whole or One is not just a principle of systematic cohesion but is full of and is the source of life, power, and desire; this has rich implications for consciousness and eros, which are never divorced from one another as they are in scientistic thought.

The story of the One's differentiation into the Many is cosmogony, usually told in terms of deities, their interactions, and motives. A parallel account of cosmogony usually is articulated in terms of the qualities and elements. Western thought preserves Anaximander's (6th century B.C.E.) arrangement of the qualities into

> two pairs of opposed qualities, Hot/Cold and Dry/Moist, . . . one hundred years before Empedocles introduced the four elements, . . . [and two] hundred years before Aristotle's systematic analysis of the elements in terms of qualities. He explains that the Earth is Dry and Cold, Water is Cold and Moist, Air is Moist and Hot, and Fire is Hot and Dry.

> . . . [E]ach element comprises two qualities, one from each opposition. (Opsopaus 1995, 3)

The elements spoken of here are not the earth in which beans grow, not the water we drink, not the air we breath, and not the fire in the barbecue. The qualities may be understood as the potential for certain kinds of operations.The elements are possible ways in which the poles of the qualities may be conjoined. For example, Coldness is centripetal, slowing things down so that they compact together regardless of their own inclinations. Dryness emphasizes the rigid structure and static situation of things. In Earth (Cold + Dry) things mix together, retaining their own forms regardless of their own purposes and of purposes around them (Opsopaus 1995).

There is a high degree of compatibility among the elements in esoteric systems of thought around the world. The fact that Oriental systems employ a fifth element (e.g., ether or spirit) does not indicate incongruity. Western systems also have a fifth element (e.g., ether or spirit), and both Eastern and Western systems agree that the first four elements dominate the denser planes of existence. Chapter X of Lawlor's excellent *Sacred Geometry* (1982) shows how the four-element system is included within a five-element system that is compatible with both Eastern and Western schemes.

The differentiation of the elements from the One can be read from the finer elements to the more dense (i.e., from Ether through Fire to Earth) as an emanation into the gross elements (perhaps the subatomic particles formed in the cooling microseconds after the Big Bang) from which our cosmos has evolved. This is a rhythmic process of breathing out; after sufficient differentiation is achieved, a complementary process of involution occurs, in which the integration of experience proceeds in the direction of assimilation of the more dense elements to the finer (i.e., from Earth through Fire to Spirit). This rhythmic pulsation and interweaving of patterns of emanation and return are characteristic of the magical world-view. The awakening of *kundalini* in the *muladhara chakra* and its ascent through the higher chakras is, of course, exactly this kind of return to the One. *Yoga* connotes unification in exactly this sense.

At this point it is easy to see how the *chakra-kundalini-nadi* physiological theory implies the liberation of the individual soul, called *jivatman*. But the theory is no guarantee of this intention, for black magicians as well as saints employ it; the system is value-neutral in the

chakra	**muladhara**	**svadisthana**	**manipura**	**anahata**	**visuddha**	**ajna**	**sahasrara**
place	perineal	genitals	navel	heart	throat	eyebrows	crown
glands, organs	ovaries gonads	spleen adrenals	liver pancreas	thymus heart, lungs	thyroid parathyroid	pituitary	pineal
spinal contact	4th sacral vertebra	1st lumbar vertebra	8th thoracic vertebra	1st thoracic vertebra	3rd cervical vertebra	1st cervical vertebra	none
element	earth	water	fire	air	ether (akasa)	ether (akasa)	
sense	smell	taste	sight	touch	hearing	mind	
petals	4	6	10	12	16	2	1,000 (972)
sound	birds, bees	tinkling bells	gong, explosion	mellow flute	drum, AUM mantra		
note	C	E	E	F#	G	A	B
colors	red	orange	yellow	green	sky blue	indigo	violet
area of life	physical & sexual energy, passion	feelings, urges, appetites	vitality, nervous energy, emotions	compassion healing	communication, creativity	perception, intuition, insight	love, bliss oneness
psychic powers	pain control, esp. over earth (metals)	control over bodily fluids (blood)	power over heat (fire)	invisibility, telempathy	telepathy, omniscience		

These are some of the commonly noted correspondences, every one of which has qualifications. They may be extended to planets, scents, gems, herbs, angels, spirits, vowels, geometric figures, and other things, and this may be accomplished in the associated traditions of most of the major systems of occult cosmology.

sense that it describes regularities that are—with some qualifications—at the disposal of whoever uses the system.

All the elements, principles, operations, and potentialities of the greater cosmos are recapitulated in miniature in the individual human being. The human being comprises mineral, vegetable, animal, and spiritual operations and is capable of embodying the consciousness of the One itself. This line of thought is summed up in the principle of the correspondence of macrocosm and the microcosm. It is said that activities above the *Anahata* level are transpersonal and involve the whole cosmos. The unity of the adept with the purposes of the One may transform the adept's very body and confer psychic powers.

This is a good place to introduce what is perhaps the most famous maxim of Western magic, "As above, so below." The saying is a quotation from the Emerald Table of Hermes, a collection of sayings preserved through late antique world Greco-Egyptian magical papyri. It is a reminder that what manifests on the level of external senses (the level "below") is a reflection of what manifests on the level of the more refined senses and the higher powers ("above"). The most efficient place to invest attention and energy for external results, therefore, is internal.

Other principles follow from the ones mentioned so far. The principle of like attracts like means that concentration upon a symbolic form, an anticipation of a certain event, a habitual expectation, brings about the expected event. Magic—indeed, prayer in faith—is a simply passionate and disciplined employment of this principle. Icons, *mantras*, and *yantras* employ this principle. The Western doctrine of signatures is connected with the concept that holy scripture (the Bible) is paralleled by a Book of Nature, which is also written by God and can be read by those with the gift for it; the concept is prominent in Paracelsus and Jakob Boehme. This doctrine of signatures may correlate to the Indian understanding that everything not only has but is a *mantra*.

A reminder is useful about the importance of sacred mathematics, which holds that everything is, finally, mathematical pattern. It takes a shifting of metaphysical gears to understand this. The integer one (1), for instance, is not just a label and a place-holder for arithmetic operations but a living actual entity, the prime instance and omnipresent possibility of cohesion and unity Itself.

Once, One was the beginning of everything. "Ancient geometry begins with *One*, while modern mathematics and geometry begin with *Zero*" (Lawlor 1982, 16). The symbol for zero traces to India, eighth

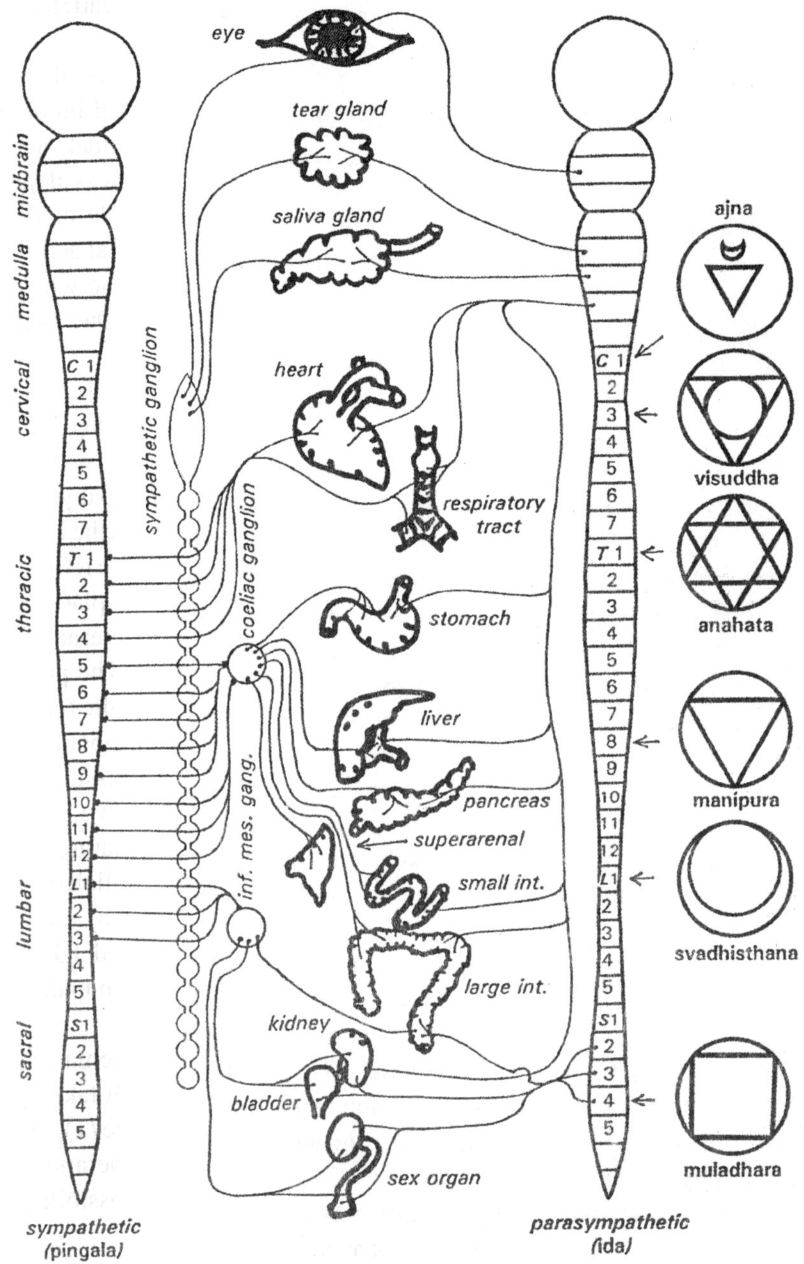

Tradition registers the chakras to the spine as shown. For the sake of schematic clarity, the spinal cord appears twice.

century C.E.; it quickly entered the Arabic world but came into Europe only with the translation of Al-Gorisma (thus algorithm) into Latin in the twelfth century. Merchants gladly adopted the zero for practical ease of calculation. When, in the late sixteenth century, the zero came to be placed *in front of* the integer *one*, the concept of negative numbers could emerge. This method effected a break between ancient and modern mathematics (Lawlor 1982).

The great metaphor for the application of mathematics is music: everything is sounding and vibrating. It bears precisely on this point to say: the sense of hearing is attributed to the *visuddha chakra* (5th), while sight belongs to the *manipura* (3rd); the implication is that sight and seeing is less profound than hearing and being heard. Pythagoras is certainly the most widely-known representative of sacred mathematics and sacred music theory in the West. It is just as important in Indian thought. Working closely with traditional materials, Dyczkowski shows how essential a doctrine of vibration is to Kashmir Shaivism: "Every activity in the universe, as well as every perception, notion, sensation or emotion in the microcosm, ebbs and flows as part of the universal rhythm of the one reality, which is Siva, the one God Who is the pure conscious agent and perceiver" (Dyczkowski 1987, 21). In light of all this, it makes sense that a *mantra* (a chant, a spell, or a prayer) is best not just said but intoned. It is resonated, sounded, vibrated. Its message and effect are not delivered only by its semantic-intellectual content but at least as importantly by its vibrational-physiological presence.

Chakras have their musical-mathematical attributes and may be understood as sounding nodes on a continuum of variable pitch. Sounding out in the respective spheres of influence, the nodes establish subharmonics and cyclical rhythms of their own. They turn, they wheel about, while remaining related to one another as peaks in a larger pattern of standing waves. The major *chakras* can be seen as seven peaks in the standing wave that is a human individual. The progressive concretion of more and more dense embodiments at the loci of these nodes produces the several layers of the human body, of which the most dense is the familiar physical body.

In this view, it may be that the most important relations between the *chakras* and specific parts and functions of the physical body may be resonances. Bruyere (1989) has done work specifically correlating healing and measurement of vibrational rates and wave forms. To study this method systematically, a profile of the various types of physiological resonances (acoustic, electrical, elastic, magnetic, etc.) of the various physical tissues, organs, and systems should be correlated with information as to the resonances of the *chakra-kundalini-nadi* system. A problem may be that this profile of the physiological resonances does not exist. Some such information is available, for instance concerning electrochemical patterns in heart activity (Winfree 1987). Other information, especially on the endocrine system, may need to be established. Some of this information would be in answer to simple questions, e.g., what acoustic (electric, magnetic, etc.) wave forms cause the typical pancreas (thymus, pituitary, etc.) to vibrate in what kind of distinct ways? What are the tissues' normal rhythms, how can they be altered, and to what effects?

At a finer level of physical analysis, the same question may be asked of the harmonic periodicities involved in the interaction of various forms of energy and several endorphins. This thinking is speculative, but the hunch is as follows: a) endorphins are chemical products of the endocrine glands and seem to be chemical correlates of the emotions (Goldberg 1989); b) it is possible to extrapolate this to the notion of a chemistry of values, including beauty, in a way that respects physical science and also major classical positions in the humanities (i.e., in philosophy and theology) (Turner 1985 & 1991); c) the frequent references to nectar and soma, especially as being enjoyed at the higher chakras, and the emphasis upon physiological transformation generally, lead the student of *chakra-kundalini-nadi* theory to expect some concrete mind-body links, to put it in traditional Western language; d) if such links do exist, they might be demonstrable through the induction of vibrations of the proper form of energy, of the proper frequency and waveform, in the products of the endocrine glands, the endorphins.

A final remark about the magical world-view is that it implies a path of salvation. It is not value-free, as Western physiological theory is assumed to be, but while *chakra-kundalini-nadi* theory teaches its esoteric view of subtle physiology, it is also instructing all comers to look within and find liberation. Someone acquainted with comparative religion may want to point out that the concept of salvation can be contrasted with the concepts of liberation and of enlightenment. Salvation is conventionally linked with Judaism, Christianity, and Islam; liberation and enlightenment with the religions of the East. However, forms of piety exist in the West (the magical world-view, for instance) for which the rhetoric of liberation and enlightenment is more natural, and forms of piety exist in the East for which the rhetoric of salvation is more natural. Motoyama (1990) slips into it; so do other writers.

In theology, this overarching topic is called soteriology. The conventional Western attitude is that soteriology has been relegated to churches and that science has nothing to do with it. The sciences deal with facts; the religions deal with values. Where one locates the humanities on this fact-value spectrum depends upon the hardness of the nose of the one doing the locating. However, many hold that value and fact are not split apart in such a facile manner and that this view, in fact, is a naive assumption of established cognitive-materialist paradigm. As a myth, this assumption serves to perpetuate this paradigm's dominance in Western culture. And it could be argued that Western physiology has a soteriological message of its own: that continued physical life (first) and continued health (second) are the benefits of salvation, and following the advice of your AMA-approved doctor (priest or priestess) is the straight and narrow path. You may have your specialty and may even have more degrees than your doctor, but life and health are the province of your doctor.

This caricature, admittedly, is a crude one. The general principle is that *any* cosmology implies a theology, and *any* theology implies a cosmology. Part of a theology will be a doctrine of soteriology; part of a cosmology will be the description of what it is that is a candidate for salvation-liberation-enlightenment. Wildiers (1982) traces the history of the peculiar interaction of cosmology and theology in the West that has led to the standoff between theology and the natural sciences in 20th century. It is hard to overstate the importance of a sensitivity for metaphysical differences in thinking that attempts to bridge cultures and disciplines.

The available depictions and descriptions of the *chakra-kundalini-nadi* system vary from the literal-phenomenological to the iconic to the mantric, mathematical, and musical. There may be other types of representations of *chakras*, but there are at least these types.

The term literal-phenomenological means simply that the intention is to describe what the phenomenon feels like in ordinary literal language, without getting fancy about it and without introducing theoretical interpretations into the description. Bruyere (1989), Gardner (1990), and

Scott (1983) present this kind of description of *chakras* along with other approaches. When a healer describes working with a *chakra*, the literal-phenomenological mode of discourse is often used. There is literal-phenomenological description of the experience of the *chakras* in traditional literature as well; e.g., particular sounds, colors, vibrations, smells, etc. may be associated with particular *chakras*.

When traditional texts offer pictures of the *chakras*, they are what could be called iconic or mandalic depictions: designs of the *chakras* that are not the *chakras* themselves but that are so true to them that meditation upon these designs, like meditation upon an icon of the Orthodox Church, may occasion a degree of direct experience of what they represent. At the beginning of each of the discussions of the *chakras* (to follow) is its illustration.

A glance at these pictures shows that they each have elements that are obviously representational, geometrical, and verbal. Each one includes small pictures of one or more deities, and in each picture the deity has two or more arms holding implements or making gestures of specific meaning for that deity and *chakra*. These small pictures of the gods and goddesses evoke tales and legends in the ancient texts. More than mere mnemonic devices, these deities are regarded as presiding over that *chakra*, and complete mastery of that *chakra* is possible only in proper relationship with these deities. Each illustration (except for the *Ajna*) includes an animal, characterizing the kind of habits and impulses that must be controlled in that *chakra*. At the center and in the petals of each illustration are Sanskrit letters for the syllables of the *mantra* for each *chakra*, so these *yantras* are mantric. Each illustration includes mathematical elements in two ways—in the central geometrical shape and in the number of petals. Finally, the illustrations are not independent things that only arise and come together by haphazard circumstance; the system emerges as a whole, and the ordering within the system is as important as the individual content. It is misleading to regard these illustrations as wholly icons and as not including also, say, mantric and mathematical aspects.

A *mantra* is a sacred word or phrase that, when repeated, leads to increasing unity with its meaning. Each *chakra* also has *mantras* associated with it, each an outgrowth of the *bija* or "seed" sound of the particular *chakra*. Swami Radha (1978 & 1993) lists the *bijas* for the six main *chakras*. In light of the general principles of magic, one can understand why Vimalananda says that not only does every existing thing *have* a *mantra* but that every existing thing *is* a *mantra*, and can be controlled by its *mantra* if one but knew it and articulated it properly (Svoboda 1993). This teacher also says that only a few adepts specialize in *mantras* to such a degree. In practice, the *mantras* given to students by their teachers are tailored to individual situations, and it may be worse than useless to swap them around like gossip.

With the notion of the *bija* or seed sound of each *chakra*, the topic comes close to the notion that each *chakra* has a fundamental vibration or periodic frequency, represented mathematically. Indeed there is a tradition of sacred mathematics in Indian thought. Lawlor (1982) mentions mathematical aspects of ancient Indian principles of temple design, music, and dance forms. McClain's (1976) interpolative reconstruction of the mathematical-musical aspect of the *Rg Veda* has awesome implications; his work has found neither an expositor to let more of us understand it nor a critic to prove it wrong. In India as elsewhere, sacred mathematics is closely related to astrology and alchemy, and it has its application to human physiology. From the standpoint of sacred mathematics, it makes more sense to say that a *chakra* actually *is* a certain number, than that it is something else that merely corresponds to a certain number.

Using musical tone is another way of articulating the *chakras* in a way that may at first impression seem symbolic. Gardner (1990) and others have taken music therapy in both clinical and theoretical directions, including a study of the relation of particular musical tones to the *chakras*. Stewart (1987) works in terms of Western magical traditions but shows how correspondences between tones and cosmological elements (i.e., earth, water, fire, air) work. These elements are a kind of Rosetta Stone for registering one esoteric system of thought to another. It should be remarked that magical theories of music tend to be more concerned with scales and tones than with attack, rapid articulation, and harmonic movement in the Western sense, and esoteric music theory generally sticks to just or natural scales rather than to the tempered scale that has dominated Western music since the time of Bach. In Gardner's work, the proper tone stimulates the corresponding *chakra*.

The existence of a profound and systematic esoteric Indian theory of music, with specific applications to the human body, can be surmised from the tantalizing remarks of de Nicolás in his translation of and commentary upon the *Bhagavad Gita*:

> Most of the statements of the *Gita* . . . will remain lost if we are not able to account for the model upon which the emancipation of the body is made possible. . . . [T]he model on which the body moves . . . is that of music. It is on a mimesis of sound and number, musical tuning or some kind of *mantra-yantra*, that the movements of the *Gita* with its corresponding statements may be understood.
>
> Every action in the *Bhagavad Gita* is to be understood as modeled on a sound-point, or tone. As sound-point every action is both a limit and an origin of manifestation—the "male" principle symbolized by an integer "cutting" the undifferentiated pitch continuum, thus opening space itself, the "female" principle, to further differentiation. Much of the "mystery" of Hindu thought and practice could be erased, especially in the later Tantric tradition, if these musical and mathematical ideas and presuppositions would be thoroughly examined. (de Nicolás 1976, 330-31)

This section of the chapter has served as kind of a second introduction. The first introduction enumerated and discussed the possible sources of information on the *chakras*. This second introduction has enumerated and discussed some of the ways that each of these sources may present its information. Each source may present its information in more than one way. For instance, a traditional source may offer material that is literal as well as iconic.

Do the mantric, mathematical, or musical methods *depict* (represent) or do they *evoke* (make present) a *chakra*? It would seem their intention is to do the latter. Graphic illustration occupies a middle ground. It inevitably represents *chakras*, since there are labels, if nothing else, to tell us inexperienced people which *chakra* is being depicted. The drawings in Swami Radha's book (1978 & 1993) are available in larger size and in full color; Kul (1974) includes glossy full-color plates of simplified iconic *chakra* designs specifically intended for meditation. Presumably, in meditating upon a well-executed icon of a *chakra*, neither a label nor instructions as to bodily location would be needed for the expected effect to occur.

But the very abstractness of mathematics and music relieve them of any tinge of representation. They are free to do whatever they will do. In the abstract freedom they are, ironically, the most concrete forms of articulation of all, for their result is the immediate presence of what is intended.

An Overview of the *Chakra-Kundalini-Nadi* System

From one point of view, the *chakras* are distinct things, connected by channels called *nadi* through which flows an invigorating energy called *kundalini*. It is probably the natural inclination of Western common sense to think of the *chakras* this way. They are presented as locations in the body, and even if they do not exist in the physical body the same way as do other organs and tissues, it is reasonable to think that the *chakras* exist in a more subtle body with a distinction comparable to that between, say, the liver and the brain. But this way of thinking of the *chakras* is limited and remains within the metaphysical assumptions of the West.

From an Indian (Shaivist) point of view, "The supreme Kundalini, being the very heart of Siva, cannot be experienced and thus remains unknown" (Silburn 1988, 63). Siva is the ultimate reality, and *kundalini* is his essence and his omnipresence. The very forms of the cosmos, from the elements to the most complex living forms, emerge as regular and enduring patterns in the dynamics of *kundalini*. The *nadis* are routes established by repeated transmission of forms of *kundalini* as it is transmuted somewhat metabolically on one level of operations, to pass—both up and down—to other levels. The *chakras* are protocols of transmutation maintained by and in terms of *kundalini* itself.

From a physical point of view, the *chakras* can be represented on a two-dimensional line drawing of the human form and are implied to be three-dimensional things, but from a more general understanding of dimensionality, their status as sites should probably be understood as centers of coordination of authority. Their authority is in embodying the protocols of transmutation of power into and out of their respective domains. A domain would be a sphere of dominant influence of a given element (i.e., earth, water, fire, air, ether). The dimensionality of a given *chakra* would be informed mainly by the character of the element with which it is linked. Presumably it would become less feasible to imagine the dimensionality of *chakras* as one progressed to the higher centers. But this fact, presumably, would remain: that a *chakra* is the cohesion (thus a center of coordination and thus a locus, a site) of the protocols for transmutation into and out from a given domain.

This interpretation does not try to stick to Indian terminology, but it does try to be true to a magical conceptuality that may resonate with the Indian. The present account uses contemporary abstract Western language in order to shake up the Western common-sense view by inverting the metaphysics behind it. For an account of the underlying metaphysics that is true to the terms of Indian Tantrism and also is very brief and systematically complete, Woodroffe's (1919, 22-4) ranks among the best. Hopefully, the importance of understanding the *chakra-kundalini-nadi* system as a whole has been indicated.

The Nadis

"*Nad*" (motion) is the root of the word *nadi*; it is not a channel in the sense that a ditch or a wire can exist apart from the movement of water or electricity. A *nadi* exists as a distinct thing, the way a distinct current can be discerned in the ocean (Scott 1983). One thinks of convection currents around a candle, sometimes made visible by traces of smoke. In this analogy, the physical body is the candlestick, the wick being the central *nadi*.

The Upanishads mention that there are up to 350,000 *nadis*; 72,000 is the number most commonly given as the exhaustive total count. "Of these, ten, fourteen or fifteen—depending on the text—are deemed most important" (Motoyama 1981, 135). Motoyama finds such great similarity in function, mapping, and number ("vast numbers of minor meridians") between the *nadis* and the meridians of the Chinese acupuncture system (1981, 141) that he conducts a systematic investigation of 19 *nadis*. There are some differences among the kinds of energy transmitted, but these can be attributed to differences in cultural interests; for instance the acupuncture system is more specifically oriented to medical purposes than is the *chakra-kundalini-nadi* system.

Of all the *nadis*, the three largest and most important are the *sushumna*, the *ida*, and the *pingala*. The *sushumna* is the central channel aligned with the spine. It connects with the *muladhara chakra* at the base of the spine and with "the small twelve-petalled 'lotus' which lies just under the Sahasrara [chakra] and forms part of its field" (Scott 1983, 146).

The *ida* and *pingala nadis* also start at the *muladhara* and move upward like the *sushumna*, but outside and to either side of the spinal column. The *ida* starts to the left of the *muladhara* and the *pingala* to the right; they connect with the *sahasrara chakra*. They either pass through the nostrils on their way to the *sahasrara*, or they terminate at the nostrils after connecting with the *sahasrara* (Motoyama 1981, Scott 1983). The importance of breath control in many yogic techniques is implied. The *ida* carries a feminine and lunar power; the *pingala* a masculine and solar power. The connection of *pingala* with the sun, heat, and activity (*"ha"*), and of *ida* with the moon, coolness, and receptivity (*"tha"*) is what is intended in *hatha yoga*: the interaction and balancing of the two (Radha 1978 & 1993).

Gopi Krishna suffered greatly from excess heat via the *pingala* in his spontaneous *kundalini* experience; relief was sought and found in the cooling energy of the *ida*. He describes the energy of the *pingala* in these terms: "fiery stream . . . ruddy blast . . . red-hot pins coursing through my body . . . flying sparks"; the energy of the *ida* he describes as: "a silvery streak passed through the spinal cord, exactly like the sinuous movement of a white serpent in rapid flight, . . . filling my head with a blissful lustre in place of the flame. . . ." (Krishna 1967, 63-66).

The exact routes of the *ida* and *pingala* from the *muladhara* to the *sahasrara* are a matter of debate and conjecture. It is possible that there is some truth in all accounts and that these channels simply resist being represented in two or three dimensions (Scott 1983). Motoyama (1981), who has some personal experience of *kundalini*, concludes partly from coincidences with acupuncture meridians that the *ida* and *pingala* are straight and do not cross the *sushumna* or one another. The most familiar iconographic map of the *chakras* upon the human form shows the *sushumna* as a straight vertical course, with the *ida* and the *pingala* as a pair of intertwining paths.

Swami Radha (1978 & 1993) and Svoboda's teacher indicate that the six lower *chakras* each connect with both the *ida* and the *pingala*. One way to understand this idea is by imagining pre-established and stable routes of connection, but another way is to emphasize the authority of the major *chakras* as centers of mutual adjustment of all *nadis*, including specifically the central three. At the major *chakras*, there is an availability of the protocols for transmutation and interchange, even between ascending and descending energies, whether in *ida* or *pingala* or both. Energy may be blocked, shunted, and squandered, as well as employed in more beneficial ways.

The central *sushumna* has within it two other *nadis*, concentric with it. Next innermost is the *vajra*, which carries an active, arousing, and forceful energy. The innermost of all is the *chitrini*, which carries a balancing and compensating energy that tends toward consciousness (Scott 1983). It may be that a path termed the *Brahma-nadi* is internal to the *chitrini* (Motoyama 1981), but Scott says that the *Brahma-nadi* is simply what the *chitrini* may be called when awakened *kundalini* flows in the *sushumna*. The *sushumna* itself, apart from its included *nadis*, is a current of inertia of rest and of habituation tending to unconsciousness.

"It is upon the Chitrini that the five intermediate Chakras between the Muladhara and the Sahasrara are strung like jewels on a thread" (Scott 1983, 148). Woodroffe's (1919) translation of Purananda's *Shat-chakra-nirupana* (Descriptions of the Six Centers) is sometimes daunting; Motoyama's adaptation of Woodroffe is more accessible:

> verse 2
> Inside the Vajra is the Chitrini, shining with the lustre of Om. She is as subtle as a spider's thread, and pierces all the Lotuses [chakras] which are placed within the backbone. She is pure intelligence. Inside the Chitrini is the Brahma-nadi, which extends from the orifice at the top of the Linga (the symbol of the phallus, also representing the astral body) in the Muladhara chakra to the Bindu (spot or knot) in the pericarp of the Sahasrara.
>
> verse 3
> The Chitrini is beautiful like a chain of lightning and fine like a lotus fiber, and shines in the minds of sages. She is extremely subtle; the awakener of pure knowledge and the embodiment of all bliss, her true nature is pure consciousness. The Brahman gate shines in her mouth. This place is the entrance to the region sprinkled by ambrosia, and is called the Knot; it is the mouth of the Sushumna. (Motoyama 1981, 164-65)

The "wheels and triangles" in the designs for the *chakras* are illustrations, finally, of "[t]he yogin's experiences." It should be remembered that the argument of this chapter is that this is comparable to the best scientific expressions which are, finally, illustrations of the experiences of scientists. There are further elements common to the anatomy of the *chakras:*

1) A periphery of "*kala*, subtle energies to which correspond . . . the . . . letters . . . of the sanskrit alphabet." These can be seen in the letters in the "petals" around each *chakra* (Silburn 1988, 31-2). They denote—and potentially evoke and express—the energies of that *chakra*'s proper domain (principle, element, dimensionality). A *chakra*'s domain may be thought of as a horizontally extendable plane with a characteristic dimensional thickness; the *chakra* itself is the central point of (vertical) transmission and transformation by which there is access to other comparable domains.

2) ". . . [R]ays that are the *nada*, vibrant resonances, radiating from the center to the periphery or from the periphery to the center, depending on whether the energy is directed outward or . . . inward" (Silburn 1988, 32). Each *chakra* has a distinct number of rays that are directly related to the element (Radha 1978 & 1993) and thus to the dimensional characteristics of the subtle environment or domain of that *chakra*. These rays inhere in the very center of the *chakra* and thus express that *chakra*'s place as a node in the greater *chakra-kundalini-nadi* system. The *kala* or subtle energies of a *chakra*'s own domain (described in 1 above) presumably may be thought of as subharmonics and overtones proper to the activity of the central *nada*. The *nada* of a *chakra* is represented by the central Sanskrit letter that is the point through which the *sushumna* passes.

3) "[A]t the center of each wheel, the *bindu*, extensionless point, dwells in the *sushumna* or median way" (Silburn 1988, 32). The extensionlessness of this point is continuous with the very subtlety of the *chitrini* at the center of *sushumna*. In the ontological core of each component of the *chakra-kundalini-nadi* system is the absolute One, where union of components becomes an identity that makes dimension irrelevant; extensionlessness rules; all is One. This concept explains the abrupt way that the *sushumna* is depicted, in the illustrations of the *chakras*, as coming up from beneath each wheel and simply appearing in the top center and moving on. It is as true to say that the *sushumna* pierces the *chakras* as to say that the *chakras* emerge from the *bindus* along the primordial *nadis* of *kundalini*.

Bruyere (1989) says that the first, third, fifth, and seventh *chakras* tend to be masculine or positive in the sense that they push energy out. The second, fourth, and sixth *chakras* tend to be feminine or negative in that they pull energy in. The *chakras* of one polarity tend to work together on a given issue. For a subtler analysis, she offers this breakdown of the chakras: first (*muladhara*) masculine; second (*svadhisthana*) feminine; third (*manipura*) androgynous; fourth (*anahata*) feminine; fifth (*visuddha*) masculine; sixth (*ajna*) androgynous; seventh (*sahasrara*) exogenous.

Bruyere's scheme may originate in her hands-on experience, but it does not seem to fit with the kind of energy Swami Radha (1978 & 1993, 39, 41) attributes to the *muladhara*: "The male aspect of energy unmanifest" (Child Brahma) and "The female aspect of energy manifest" (Dakini). But Silburn (1988) says that centripetal (Bruyere: feminine, negative) energy is associated with the ascension of *kundalini*. If so, the quiescence (energy unmanifest) of all the gods and the active status (energy manifest) of all the goddesses in Swami Radha's account is correct for a practitioner of *kundalini yoga*. The possibility of each *chakra* expressing centrifugal or centripetal energy is confirmed by Silburn (1988). Malfunction of the *chakras* is often described as a reversal of spin or charge, and the correction is considered a healing.

There are several ways that two or more *chakras* form subsystems with particular functions not shared so directly by other *chakras* not in that subsystem. Some subsystems will be mentioned by way of example.

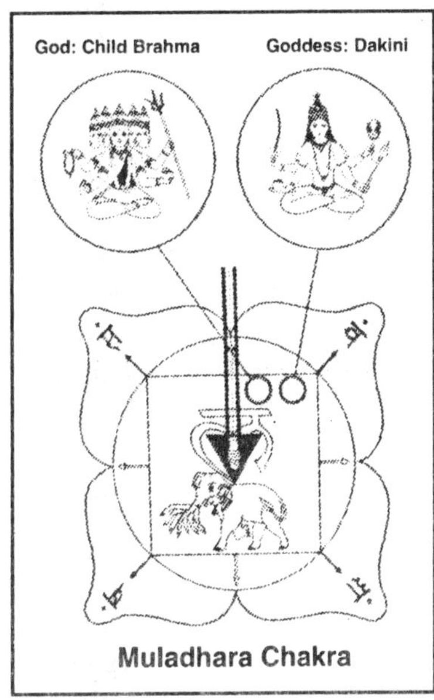

Muladhara Chakra

The Muladhara Chakra

The *kanda* (bulb or knot) is the "root of all the Nadis" (Woodroffe 1919, 320). It is at once "the mouth of the Sushumna," the opening at the top of the phallus, and the opening at the top of the astral body. Representations are telescoped and nested together in the triangle-serpent-phallus icon at the heart of the *muladhara* illustration. The highest and lowest exist together in actuality, with the suggestion that this actuality has the potential for full conscious realization. For this, *Chit* (consciousness, subjectivity, the root of the word *chitrini*), uncoils *kundalini* and becomes itself an integral being, a dominant factor, uniting cosmic, subtle, and physical aspects of the human self.

Dychtwald (1977, 87) delineates the psychological issues of the *muladhara* as "grand human potential, primitive energy, and basic survival needs." The varieties of malfunction of this *chakra* show up as a restriction of emotional expression in anxiety of either losing or not acquiring the basic needs of life, i.e., status in occupation, self-esteem (one's evaluation of oneself as to fulfillment of one's potential).

The elephant here is young—note the perky head, foot, and tail, and the proportion of the head to the body. It is active, clumsy, impulsive, and powerful. The seven trunks correspond to the seven strongest virtues and the seven strongest temptations (Radha 1978 & 1993), also to the seven minerals needed for physical nourishment (Motoyama 1981). Common to both these interpretations is that the trunks smell and respond to basic social and physical desires. The association of this *chakra* with smell but its placement so far from the nose makes sense in light of the routing of *ida* and *pingala* through or to the nostrils. A long nose, the length of a human spinal column, is proportional to the length of an elephant's trunk in relation to its spinal column.

Scott (1983, 164-65) provides a fascinating speculation on the ontogenesis of the fetus. From fertilized egg through the blastula stage, all cells are totipotential or unspecialized. Then placental cells multiply rapidly to form an environment for the embryo, and only a few cells remain totipotentiality. The caudal or tail end—the *muladhara* end—of the embryo retains its totipotentiality longest. Ontogenetically as well as in *chakra-kundalini-nadi* theory, the *muladhara* region has the greatest experience with undifferentiated desires, a capacity to be attracted to all potentialities.

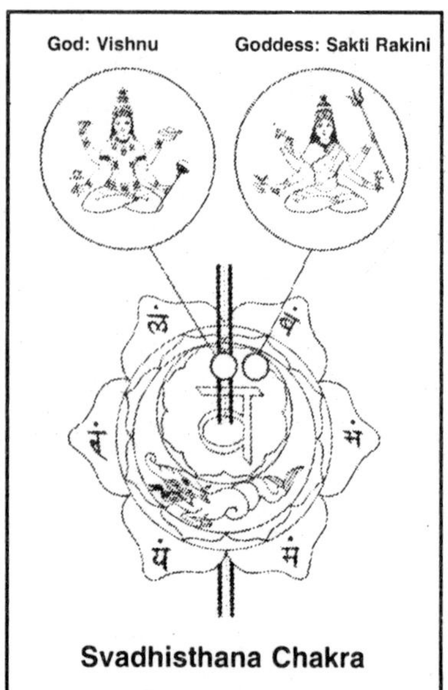

Svadhisthana Chakra

The creature is a combination of alligator and fish, representing an appetite which "swallows up everything without discrimination. This *chakra* governs imagination which creates desire leading to gratification, particularly of pleasure" (Radha 1978 & 1993, 81). Female alligators are famous for ferociously guarding their eggs while they hatch. This level of appetite, though primitive, has some admirable traits. The simple urge to mate, to enjoy the obvious pleasures of sexual action, creates an issue in this chakra: "'You must conquer lust, the instinctual drive to procreate, before you can move beyond the Svadhishthana'" (Svoboda 1993, 73).

The two lowest *chakras* are particularly close together in the human form and function in intimate correspondence (Motoyama 1981), almost as if one should speak of the *muladhara*-and-*svadhisthana* complex. Smell and taste are first cousins, one implying the other. In the *svadhisthana* there may be a watery merging with and tasting of (reception of) earthy elements only smelled in the *muladhara*.

Motoyama calls attention to the interpretation of *svadhisthana* by Satyananda, a modern yogi. This *chakra* functions as the individual's connection with "the collective unconscious." (The reference must be to Jungian psychology.) The *svadhisthana* "houses not only the karma of the individual's past lives, but all the experiences and associated karma which have contributed to the process of human evolution." The involvement of the unconscious is depicted in the two circles, one with petals outward and the other, with petals inward, pressing on the back of the creature: it is "the phantom-like existence of the unconscious" (Motoyama 1981, 220, 222)

Awakening this *chakra* can lead to terrors from contents normally unconscious and transpersonal. Accordingly, the goddess Sakti Rakini (manifest female energy) has a fierce aspect. Rakini rules the vegetable kingdom; her ferocity may be partly a reflection of irreconciliation with a carnivorous diet, a mirrored projection of the fear associated with killing animals for food.

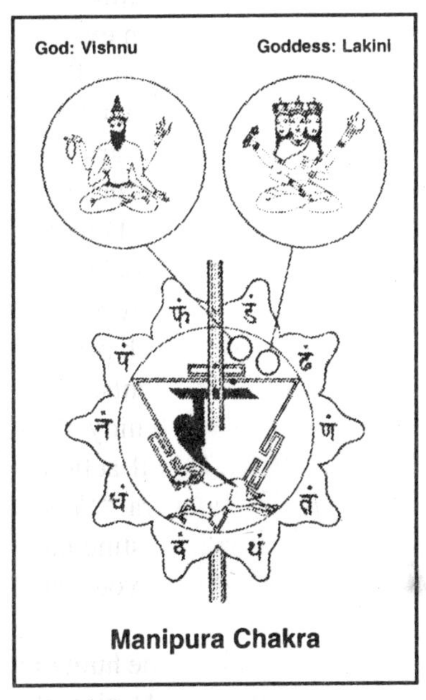

Manipura Chakra

"'From the Svadhishthana Chakra, Kundalini moves up to the Manipura Chakra, the seat of the Fire Element, where metabolism takes place.' . . . The Manipura Chakra is really crucial. There you learn the difference between . . ." *bhuta agni*, the "fire of life" or etheric fire, and *jathara agni*, the "fire of the belly" or digestive fire (Svoboda 1993, 73). Both kinds of fire digest; *bhuta agni* is mental digestion of ideas, and *jathara agni* is physiological digestion of food. An active *pingala* (solar, masculine) may inflame the digestive processes. The digestion of food and the assimilation of ideas are inversely related: when one is strong, the other is weak.

The problem is more than just an emphasis upon food and a dulling of the mind. "When you try to take in too much energy before your Bhuta

Agni becomes strong, much of that undigested energy gets converted into anger, the emotion that is characteristic of the Fire Element" (Svoboda 1993, 73). There is a danger that excitement of the *manipura* can hasten physical death.

> This is because the activated fire of this chakra burns up the life-supporting nectar which is said to be generated in the bindu—the psychic center at the back of the head, represented by a cool, crescent moon. Normally this Nectar descends to a gland deep in the throat (closely associated with the vishuddhi chakra) and is stored there. However, the fire in the manipura draws and consumes the nectar, causing accelerated decay of the body. (Motoyama 1981, 225-26)

The ram in the emblem of this *chakra* indicates the stubbornest of strong emotions that cloud the vision. Strength in this case is not necessarily vehement, it is simply unthinking, habitual, and compulsive. The contrasting quality is spontaneity.

The awakening of the *manipura* is considered a milestone on the spiritual journey. It is usually a step from which there is no turning back. The unconsciousness of basic biological needs (*muladhara*) has been passed, the collective unconscious of the human species (*svadhisthana*) has been tamed, and in the *manipura,* the aspirant begins to experience "the consciousness of Jiva, the personal soul" (Motoyama 1981, 224).

The lower three *chakras* are grouped together in several ways. They are elaborations of elements that have a visible aspect (i.e., earth, water, fire); higher chakras are elaborations of elements that have no visible aspects (i.e. air, ether). The three lower *chakras* are mapped onto the human form from the diaphragm down; the other *chakras* operate from the diaphragm up. The lower three *chakras* represent the worlds of mineral, vegetable, and animal life, and that aspect of human life that is animal in character. Motoyama (1981, 229) puts it this way: "At the lower levels, the individual soul merely accepts what is presented by karmic circumstance, but, at the anahata, it can exercise its free will."

Like the other *chakras* before it, the *anahata* is also pierced by the central tripartite *sushumna*, right through a sounding syllable (a Sanskrit letter) that forms the center of the *chakra*. The animal is the black antelope: shy, fast, and graceful, implying spiritual experiences that cannot be grasped by the slower ego-centered self. It cannot be possessed

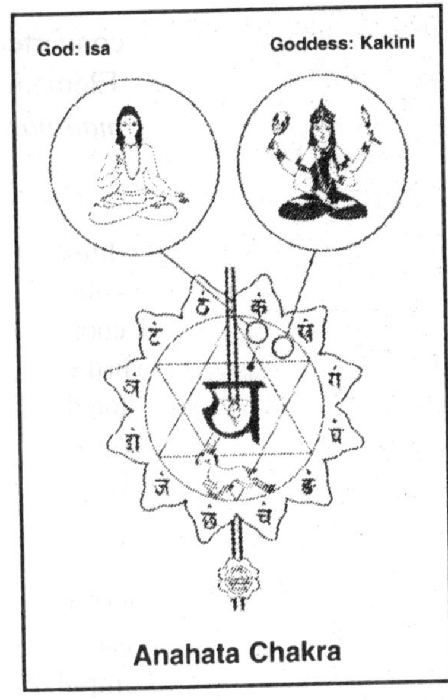

Anahata Chakra

and owned but only enjoyed in comparable speed, grace, and innocent spontaneity.

The small center below is the *anandakanda* lotus, the venue of "mental worship" (Radha 1978 & 1993, 165) where even unspoken and unconscious desires are granted. Within the lotus is the "'*Wishing-tree*' . . . the tree in Heaven which grants all one asks; . . . it bestows more than is desired (Woodroffe 1919, 372).

The "sound which comes without the striking of any two things together" can be heard here; it is "the Pulse of Life" (Woodroffe 1919, 120). There are two things here: two triangles—but they do not conflict with one another.

Filling the whole wheel and concentric with it are the two intersecting equilateral triangles, the female pointing downward, the male pointing upward. A triangle implies the dynamism of the number three, sustained by actualization in a functioning trinity of some kind. The dynamism projects to any of the points of the triangle and can be determined only by the orientation and context of the figure. These triangles each provide a context for the other, intersecting in a balanced way, the downward-tending harmonizing with the upward-tending. The essential theme is spontaneous balance and harmony; coercion is not possible (Tyson 1987).

In another context, this, of course, is the Star of David. In Tantric usage, it is "the *satkona*, with the *bindu* as its center, the unique spot for the spontaneous coincidence of Siva and his energy" (Silburn 1988, 33). In the *anahata,* Siva and Saki begin to find themselves. The *anahata* is three-and-a-half *chakras* from the *muladhara*, where *kundalini* lies dormant, coiled three-and-a-half turns around the central *linga*. The *bindu* of the *anahata* coincides with the "minute orifice" at the tip of the central *linga*. "The Linga itself is not pierced [by *sushumna*], but it carries the Bindu, which has an empty space (Sunya) within its circle (Woodroffe 1919, 378).

Touch, the sense proper to this *chakra*, must be made subtle to the extreme, so as not to startle the antelope and so as to realize a coincidence of triangles without touching anything (without striking together anything) but the dimensionless *bindu* at the center. This touch is so subtle that its proper element is air. It is possible for two people to touch one another this way: by singing harmonies together, by the mutual entrainment of sound and breathing.

With breath we generate words and tones of voice that touch one another. The breath in the lungs is heated by the fire below the diaphragm and expresses things in ways that sooth or anger others. The *anahata*'s god Isa is called Lord of Speech. Dychtwald (1977, 141), with extensive experience in body-oriented psychotherapy, believes

> that the diaphragm is the gateway through which the feelings generated in the lower three chakra segments pass as they move to the upper portions of the bodymind. When this region is open and unblocked, energy flows freely and the bodymind experiences health and pleasure. When this region is tight or restricted, the result is a limitation of feelings, breathing potential, and energetic flow. Frequently, people armor this region as a personal defense against unwanted feelings. By holding these muscles tight and rigidifying the diaphragm itself, they temporarily stifle the emotions.

In her healing work, Bruyere perceives a common pattern of displacement of *chakras* in which fluidity is lost from the waist down. ". . . [A]ll the chakras are displaced upward by two steps: the first chakra sits where the third should be, the second where the fourth should be, and so on" (Bruyere 1989, 86). The earth of *muladhara* displaces the water of *manipura*, so that the diaphragm rests on rigid stone instead of responsive water. The fire of *svadhisthana* carries digestive fire into the airy space of the *anahata* and consumes the nectar intended for etheric fire. The heart becomes a compulsive, consuming, and raging beast, while the emotions are surprisingly cold and stoney at the same time.

Scott devotes a chapter to the group of *chakras* that include a *linga* in their emblems. These are: the *muladhara* (perineal or coccyx), where the physical body is anchored; the *anahata* (heart), where the vital body is anchored; and the *anahata* (brow), where the mental body is anchored. "The importance of the Linga Chakras is that they are vital meeting places of Shiva (Linga) and Shakti (Trikona) forces, and are mechanisms for enhancing the scope of their interactions in the spheres of body (Muladhara), life (Anahata) and mind (Ajna)" (Scott 1983, 199). The *linga chakras* are also the *chakras* containing *granthis*, or knots. As such, these *chakras* "are of special importance. Only when they are awakened and the knots are loosened can the *kundalini* rise to further the process of spiritual evolution" (Motoyama 1981, 232).

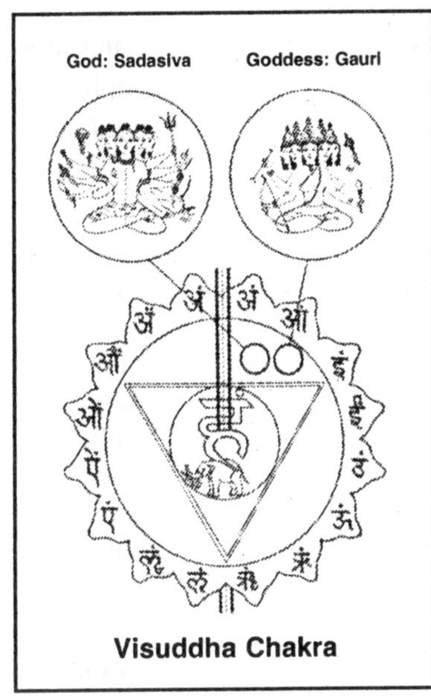

Visuddha Chakra

The *visuddha chakra* concerns purification. *Shuddhi* means *to purify*, which is a chief function of the *chakra*. One of the things that is purified, in the sense of refined, is speech and hearing. Mental chatter is quieted in the awakened *anahata*. This is a main meaning of the gestures of the deities there (e.g., Kakini's skull on a wand=empty mind). In the *visuddha,* the deities offer many implements for the cultivation of the mind.

These implements are needed because each of the lower *chakras* has at least a chance to test the integration into a higher *chakras*. An upsurge of fiery emotion from the *manipura* may require all the equipment that the deities can supply. The ego will struggle to the end; when aiming to skewer it with Guari's arrow, it can subtly distort the aim (Radha 1978 & 1993). The goal is the refinement of balance in all areas.

Sound—and hearing and speaking—are more important than conventional Western opinion supposes. According to magical principles, sound is more properly a vehicle for meaning than light. The evolutionary emergence of elements, from the primordial differentiations of the One to the return of conscious beings to the One, moves through the hierarchy of elements from etheric levels downward to earth and back again. The movement through the hierarchy of senses reaches first mind (*ajna*), then hearing (*visuddha*). On the route to physical manifestation, the other external senses are posterior to hearing. On the route from physical existence to unification with the One, hearing (hearing-and-sounding) is the most refined of the external senses.

Another thing the *visuddha* purifies is poison. In light of its proximity to the thyroid gland, and in light of this gland's important role in the immune system, this function of the *visuddha* has a certain plausibility. In legend, Siva's throat is blue because he drank poison. This tale is linked with a cosmogony, a creation story. The effect of the interactions of elements below the *visuddha* is the cycle of births and deaths, or *samsara*. At one time this might have destroyed the world, which Siva loved. To save the world, he drank the poison of *samsara*. He holds it above his *visuddha,* and it does not affect him, but in iconography, Siva is represented as blue (Svoboda 1993). Not incidentally, blue is the color traditionally attributed to the *visuddha*.

An active *visuddha* will enable the nectar produced in the *sahasrara* to be stored in a reservoir in the head, at the top of throat. Stored and purified by the *visuddha*, it rejuvenates and invigorates the physical body. An inactive *visuddha* permits it to remain poisonous, descend, and be improperly assimilated (Motoyama 1981). This sounds like the discussions of Svoboda's teacher about the importance of the balanced metabolization, *bhuta agni*, fire of life or etheric fire, and *jathara agni*, fire of the belly or digestive fire.

The *visuddha* is linked with the *muladhara* in the task of generation of sound (Motoyama 1981, 234). A link with the *muladhara* might be expected from the reappearance of the elephant, a bit older this time. The elephant is specialized for hearing and memory, without which sound is irrelevant. In the *muladhara,* the elephant is in a square in a circle, with a triangle on its back. In the *visuddha,* the elephant is in a circle which is in a triangle. It carries no geometrical form on its back, only the central letter. In the petals of the *visuddha*'s *mandala* are the sixteen vowels of the Sanskrit alphabet. Vowels, of course, are essential to language and begin in the throat, unlike consonants.

In doing auric readings coordinated with electronically measured and recorded data in a clinical setting, Bruyere (1989, 221-22) found, among other things:

> 2. Chakras frequently carried the color stated in metaphysical literature, such as red kundalini [*muladhara*], orange hypogastric or emotional body [*svadhisthana*], yellow spleen [*manipura*], green heart [*anahata*], blue throat [*visuddha*], violet third eye [*ajna*], and white crown [*sahasrara*], although this was not always the case. . . .

3. Certain chakras seemed to be directly related. Increased activity of the kundalini, red [*muladhara*], triggered the throat chakra [*visuddha*], blue, while activation of the hypogastric or emotional body [*svadhisthana*], orange, showed linkage with the third eye [*ajna*], violet.

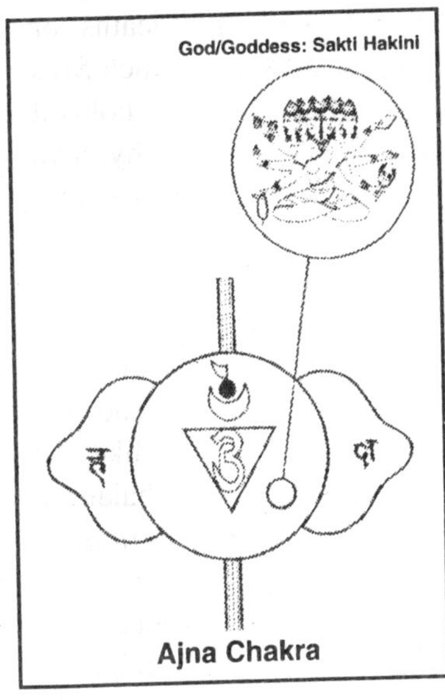

Ajna Chakra

Again, as with the other *linga chakras*, there is a *linga*, a *bija* letter (seed-sound), and a triangle, but in the *ajna* they are arranged differently than below. In the lower two *linga chakras*, the *linga* is enclosed in the triangle, and the triangle is enclosed within or surrounded by the *bija*. In the *ajna*, the *bija* is in the triangle with the *linga* and coincides with the *linga*. This implies an identity of triangle, *bija*, and *linga* that does not obtain in *anahata* and *muladhara*.

The letters in the design produce the syllable AUM (commonly Om). Above the triangle is a crescent moon, the symbol of Shiva. Above that is a *bindu*, a dimensionless point, but now represented as remarkably prominent. Above that is *Nada* (sound in general, but in this context an unheard sound), intended to be brighter than the moon below it (Woodroffe 1919, 403).

Why the *Nada*—a sound, and an unheard one—has this graphic shape and color has to do with experiential aspects. Also, together with the *bindu* and the lunar crescent, these elements help spell AUM; there is a typographical pun going on.

Om immediately connotes Shiva, from whom this unheard sound endlessly propagates.

> The Absolute Itself is silent; It has no qualities whatsoever, which is why there is no Bija Mantra for Lord Shiva. Shiva has no melody to Him; He is pure rhythm, the father of music. . . . The sound "Om" is the first sound to arise when creation begins, and it is the last sound to disappear at the time of the Pralaya [dissolution of the universe].

> But even after the melody—the manifested universe—has totally disappeared, its rhythm lingers on, first as anusvara and then as bindu. (Svoboda 1993, 189)

The last line refers to the typographical pun, which has a dignified profundity to it. *Anusvara* is the name for the nasal "m" at the end of Sanskrit words such as *Om*. Its typographical shape is a half moon with the points up. This sound lingers after what is manifested has disappeared. Finally, this rhythm also disappears, and nothing but a dimensionless point, a *bindu*, is left. In a metaphysical context, *bindu* means dimensionless point and implies the sound associated therewith, but it is also a term with typographical application. The typographical *bindu* is often coupled with *anusvara*.

At the *ajna* level, the student is urged to withdraw the senses, and enjoy this dissolution of the universe.

Sahasrara *and Other Chakras*

There seems to be no traditional *mandala* for the *sahasrara*, although it is represented from the outside as a skull cap of petals. This "Lotus of a thousand petals . . . has its head turned downward." Purananda tells us, "It charms. . . . [I]t is the absolute bliss" (Motoyama 1981, 179).

The nectar-producing function of the *sahasrara* seems to be delegated to the *bindu visargha*, located close to the top of the brain, to the rear. Motoyama (1981) speaks of it with considerable physiological precision. Its relations to the *lalana* and *visuddha chakras* have already been discussed.

It is arguable that the *sahasrara* is "not really a *chakra* because there is no plexus of nadis there; there is only one nadi, which connects the Sahasrara with the Anja Chakra" (Svoboda 1993, 69).

Inconclusive Postlude

This chapter has tried to introduce *chakra-kundalini-nadi* theory in a way that is sympathetic to experienced practitioners and those who want to push the tools and techniques of conventional quantitative science as far as possible into the unknown. The intention has been to stimulate interest and to set an example of systematic approach even where the ability to accomplish the full task was lacking. To this end, the architecture and bibliography of this chapter are possibly of as much (or more) use than the actual text.

Hopefully, the importance of a systematic critique of the metaphysics of both Tantric and conventional scientific thought has been presented persuasively. Magical thought is a topic that deserves a major systematic analysis.

The lack of philosophical—and specifically metaphysical—sophistication even at the graduate school level—in the sciences, the humanities, theology—is deplorable. Specialization of thought (e.g., methods, technical language) that improves the penetration of initiates into their subject matter is laudable. Beyond this purpose, the best to be said about specialization is that it is silly. Too often it serves to prevent communication across disciplines and plays into power games (e.g., who gets the money). In these cases, "silly" is too nice a word for it.

Metaphysics is the field of philosophy that embraces fundamental generalization about what exists (ontology) and about how it may be known or experienced (epistemology). When every special field of knowledge defends its institutional (i.e., financial) turf by claiming it has its own special objects (the ontological claim) to be studied by its own special methods (the epistemological claim), common sense seeks common language, a way to translate from one speciality to another. Thinkers with a bent for systematic synthesis sometimes propose overarching conceptual schemes or metalanguages for interdisciplinary communication. Systems theory produces these with some regularity, and some have real contributions to make. Any new scheme, however, that is not integrated with philosophical metaphysics will inevitably reinvent the wheel many times over. Metaphysics is out of favor in contemporary academic philosophy, especially in Anglo-American culture, but the facts remain that any philosophical position implies fundamental ontology and epistemology. This is a plea for basic education in metaphysics.

One can think of other projects that may help bridge gaps between the humanities and the sciences. It has been suggested that physiologists assemble data on the periodicities of resonance of natural physiological substances, tissues, and organs.

There is work to be done in the humanities as well. A project that would help researchers is a well-indexed collection of the more important texts on *chakra-kundalini-nadi* theory. The texts should be edited in parallel. The index should include common anatomical names (e.g., mouth, fingernail, hair) so that one could look up, say under "mouth," the *nadis* that extend to the mouth as well as legendary incidents and traditional postures in which the mouth is important. Kinds of psychic experience should be indexed and referred to instances in classical literature. This presupposes a critical classification of kinds of psychic experience such as has been started by Dychtwald (1977) and many others. Such a project would help correlate classic instances of experience with contemporary physiological experiences occurring under persuasively authoritative conditions of observation.

CHAPTER EIGHT

THE SEVEN ENERGY CENTERS

Professor Arnold Keyserling, University of Vienna, Austria, and Ralph Losey, JD

SELF-OBSERVATION CONFIRMS the traditional esoteric knowledge of all cultures that there are seven layers of human energy—seven Chakras. These are the main centers of the human aura. Three other "higher" energy centers are also known to exist, for a total of ten, but they will not be discussed in any detail here. The three "higher chakras" do not exist as personal energies—the aura with which most people are familiar—but only as impersonal historical forces. The seven different energies that dominate the aura of most people correspond with the seven consciousness functions, their organic points of gravity, and seven areas of potential:

1. Sensing. Sensation relates to the data of the senses: colors, smells, tastes, sounds and tones, and observation of the sense of touch. The point of gravity is in the organs of generation and excretion. It is the base of all energies and is present in most people as sexual energy. Its basic potential is for creative imagination, revelations. Its vocation, how it's applied in society, is that of a "Worker" who has confidence, trust, intuition, and an ability to heal. This energy feels like a force emitted from yourself in order to do something. Its direction is the East, and it partakes of the "Power of Fire."

2. Thinking. Breathing relates to Thinking. Its point of gravity is, however, found near the sacrum near the tip of the spine, which is also the point of gravity of bodily movement. All thinking is based on language, which is heard by the vibrations of air. Its basic potential is to discern and affirm the differences and the similarities between all things. Its vocation is that of a "Designer" who adapts and conceives new things, including a unique style of life and a creative understanding. This energy feels like experiencing movement from out of the center. Its direction is the West, and its Power is the Minerals.

3. Feeling. The function of Feeling has as its contents the impulses, the point of gravity lying in nourishment, in the digestion, and in deposination metabolism. Its basic potential is for creativity and inner growth in the synthesis of new forms of understanding and learning. Its vocation is that of the "Helper" who heals through understanding, personal growth, and cognition of the underlying archetypes. This energy feels like awakening. Its direction is the South, and its Power is the plants and water.

4. Willing. The Will means the capacity to decide yes and no on the basis of the inner void, the force of attention. One has to get behind the rhythms of the heart, of the circulation, and get to them from being. Its potential is self-affirmation, finding your unique "medicine," in the Native American sense, that puts the Ego into a healthy, positive relationship with the greater Self. Its vocation is that of the "Leader," with affirmative energies, strategies, and imagination. This energy feels like finding your role. Its direction is North, and its Power is the Animals and nature. The contents of thinking, feeling, and sensing are conscious. Willing puts them together in being. Their continuity, their putting together, changes the data of the functions into data of consciousness ordered in the three spheres: Body—Soul—Spirit.

5. Body. The Body continuity, steered by the genetic code, has its point of gravity in the spinal cord and in the central nervous system, which is activated from the brain stem and cerebellum just above the neck. This point is the basis of material experience; movement activities are stored in the memory so that the force of attention can remain free. Its potential is to start new things and become more human, responsible, and discerning. Its vocation is the "Friend," who assists in projects and helps others to see the world and themselves more clearly. This energy feels like becoming an expression. Its direction is the center, and its Power is the Sacred Earth.

6. Soul. The continuity of the Soul, which puts Man into family in its farthest sense by endogen engrams, conditioned and unconditioned reflexes, has its point of gravity in the limbic system. All personal relations and memories, as well as those of Man and our whole evolution, are stored there and unite Man with the animal realm. The potential is to heal and to synthesize opposing forces into a larger whole through communication and discussion. The vocation is the "Teacher" who helps set priorities and values and who has strong communication skills. This energy feels like partaking of an abundance. Its direction is the South East, and Power is the Ancestors.

7. Spirit. The highest Spirit field of the cerebrum or neocortex, with its two hemispheres, shows the capacity of mental representation of knowledge in its largest meaning—from language up to opinion and world conception. The basic potential is for responsiveness to take the lead in reacting to the environment. Its vocation is the "Facilitator" who takes action, questions, cajoles, even fights, so that everyone can find their unique potential and resolve conflicts. This energy feels like becoming aware of the physical totality. Its direction is South West, and Power is the Nature Spirits.

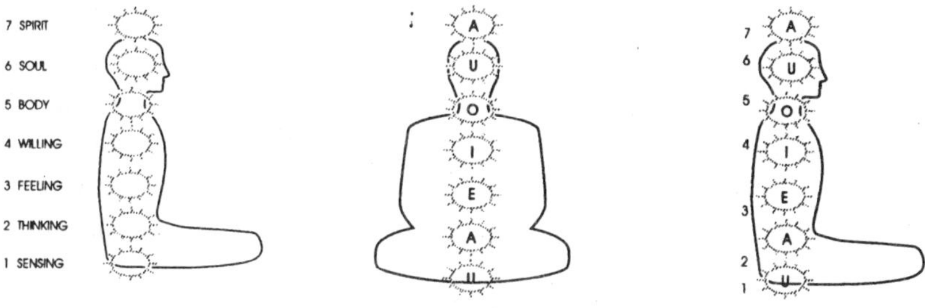

SUMMARY OF KNOWLEDGE OF THE SEVEN ENERGY CENTERS

7	Spirit	Knowledge	Cerebrum	Responsibility
6	Soul	Instinctual	Cerebellum and Limbic System	Healing
5	Body	Conditioned	Spinal Cord	Initiative
4	Willing	Attention	Blood Circulation	Essence/ AWARENESS
3	Feeling	Impulses	Metabolism	Creativity
2	Thinking	Language	Breathing	Discernment
1	Sensing	Sense Data	Sex & Excretion	Imagination

Each of these points of gravity correspond to one of the centers of vibration of the human energy field and are activated in a certain way. All function at once, but consciousness can only refer to one or another. This concept can be understood by means of the flageolet tone: in a vibrating string, not only the first tone, but a whole series of harmonics are resounding according to the law of whole numbers. If the vibration is regular, after the first impulse, the vibration returns from the ends of the string and forms string vibration nodes. This fact can be visualized in an example. If one takes a circular pond and throws a stone into the middle, the point of impact will dive in and up. From this point, waves go out to the periphery, they reflect back, and, where they meet, the newly emerging waves will be a proliferation of water, a node.

WITHIN A STRING ONLY THE LOOPS ARE
RESOUNDING,THE NODES REMAIN SILENT

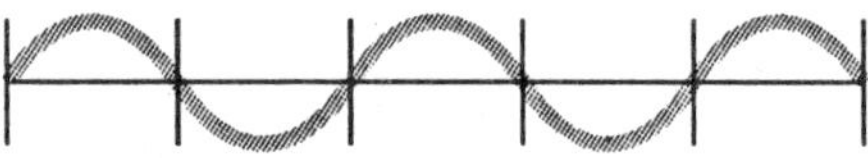

If one touches a string instrument at one of these places, s/he will hear only the corresponding partial tone as a flageolet tone (on the guitar there are points to mark these places), and the other overtones will remain silent. In the above example, with each fifth, only the great major third will resound.

With the fundamental tone C, it would be E.
1 2 3 4 5 6 7 8 9 10
c c g c **e** g x c d e

Our energies are tuned to the seventh even though our ears are not. The difference arises from the fact that bioplasma is not made up of material vibrations but of energetical vibrations which keep bodies together, move them, and make them ripe for functions. The pulsating bioplasmic energy of the human aura is unlike a string which has a potentially infinite number of vibrations. The bioplasmic field has exactly seven points of gravity or vortices of energy and should be steered from those. These seven energy centers exist along the spinal cord.

The existence of these micro-vibrations, the aura, was well known to the ancient traditions. The Chinese found their points of gravity and their relation to medicine in acupuncture, an art of healing that can prognosticate illnesses out of the disturbances in the relation between Yin and Yang bio-energies. These energy centers have been referred to in the East for thousands of years as the "chakras." Chakra is a Sanskrit word which means simply "vortex of energy."

European scientists have tried to identify the chakras with endocrine glands or with different plexus of nerves, but chakras are a completely different kind of energy. They are wave fields without particles; pure potential with no content. They are like the other side of Black Holes where the energy is streaming out, not in. They can be initially located and identified as void spaces, pure energy fields. Cosmic energy of immeasurable power, called by the Indians *Prạna* and by the Chinese *Chi*, can flow through the chakras. Technically speaking, the chakras are the fields through which the energies flow, not the cosmic energies themselves. They are like doors, and the PrimaSounds (Chakra tones) can rattle them open a crack.

"Chakra tones" work by using resonance and attention in the element of Energy. Our center of attention normally exists in another element, called Consciousness. (There are four fundamental elements or fundamental principals: Matter, Energy, Consciousness, and Self-Organization). As shown before, Consciousness has seven basic components: the four functions—Sensing, Thinking, Feeling, and Willing; and the three realms—Body, Soul, and Spirit. These seven functions have a natural internal relationship whereby Sensing corresponds with Body, Thinking with Soul, and Feeling with Mind. Willing stands on its own in the center, connected with Attention and Awareness.

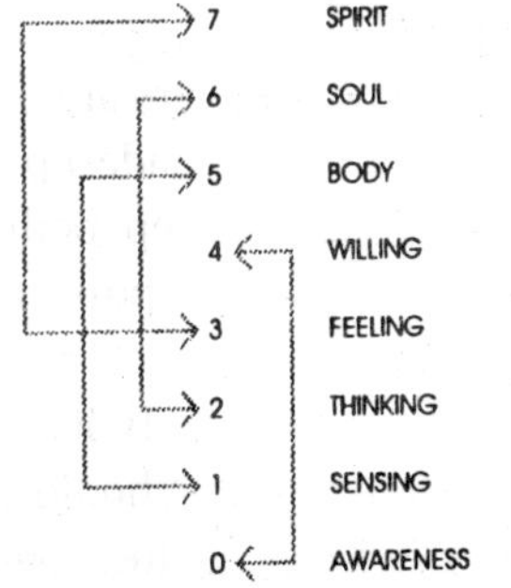

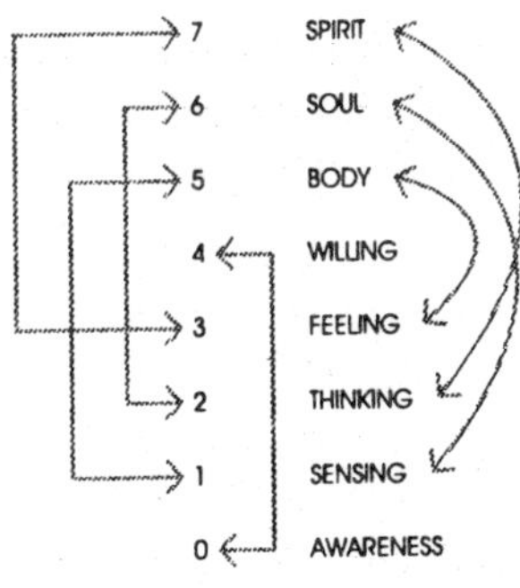

For example, the senses are sharpest when perceiving the physical world, as opposed to sensing other people (soul) or an idea (spirit). Conversely, the Body is most directly apprehended by sensing. Thinking is most acute when in dialogue with other people, as opposed to pure abstract thinking. Conversely, the Soul is understood best by thinking. Feeling and its twin sister imagination are at home in the Spirit where free reign is given to it. Feeling in the body or soul is more limited and often negative. Conversely, the Spirit is most easily accessed by the Feelings. Thinking about the Spirit frequently leads to erudite nonsense. Spirit must first be felt before it can be seen or put into words.

When these seven components are moved from the scale of Consciousness to the scale of Energy, there is a fractal variation in the internal alignment. In the world of Energy—the domain of the aura—Chakra tones vibrate in accord with the seven energy centers, or chakras, in a new and different alignment of the original seven. Now, Sensing corresponds with Soul, not Body, and Thinking corresponds with Spirit, not Soul. Feeling acts on Body, instead of Spirit, with Willing remaining the same in the center, related to Awareness, the dynamic Nothingness outside of and underlying the seven. As a consequence of this fractal variation, Chakra tones should be listened to by Feeling the effects of the vibrations on the body, Sensing the energy of soul stimulation, and thinking of the Spirit, of abstract ideas, or no-thinking.

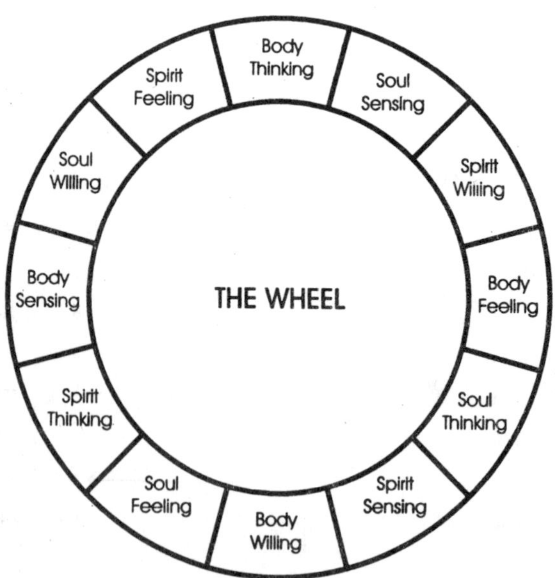

This new alignment has been demonstrated with PrimaSounds for years and is the key to "hearing" the aura. As researchers continue work on the aura with other tools such as aura imaging cameras, knowledge of this alignment may also prove helpful.

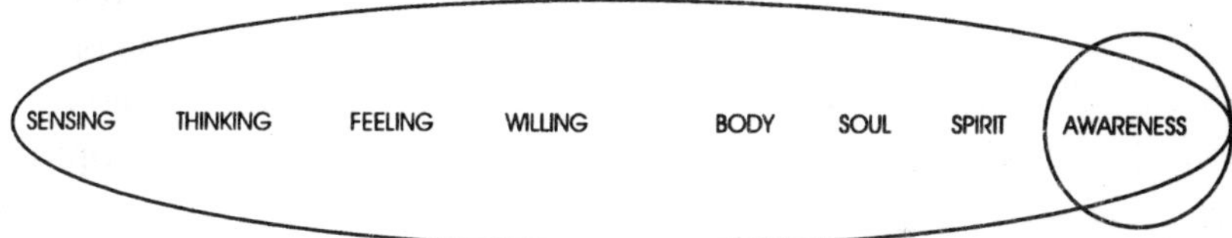

SECTION II:

EFFECT OF SOUNDS AND MUSIC ON CHAKRAS AND AURIC FORMATIONS

CHAPTER NINE

THE IMPACT ON THE AURA OF MUSIC, SOUND, AND PRIMASOUNDS

Ralph Losey, JD

THE HUMAN AURA, the energy system which surrounds the body, can be affected, indirectly, by music and sounds. The aura can also be affected directly by the resonance of certain, select vibrations in tune with the seven energy centers of the aura—the chakras. The sound vibrations in tune with the chakras are referred to as "Chakra tones" or "PrimaSounds." They are the primal tones of the human aura. The Chakra tones provide a powerful method to directly impact and influence the aura. Music and sounds are now used by many people who work with auras, such as music therapists, healers, and certain new age musicians. PrimaSounds, by contrast, are still little known and frequently misunderstood, as are the mechanics of the process by which sounds can impact the aura and the distinction between music, sounds, and Chakra tones. This chapter will briefly discuss how sound and music effect the aura, but will focus on PrimaSounds, the subject I know best.

PrimaSound

Until recently, the existence of certain tones in tune with the aura—PrimaSounds—was almost completely unknown in the West. A few initiates in the East and in some aboriginal cultures in the Americas,

Africa, and the Far East still knew of and used Chakra tones, but they were bound by traditions of secrecy. Rumors of the existence of these primal tones persisted in the West in various myths and legends of the "lost chords" such as the horns of Jericho or the music of Orpheus, but there was no exact knowledge.

In 1971, Professor Arnold Keyserling of the Academy of Art, University of Vienna, Austria, who had long been intrigued by such legends, rediscovered this knowledge based on his research of esoteric traditions, music, and math. Arnold Keyserling had been a student of the esoteric philosopher George Gurdjieff in Paris after the War. He also studied with the famous composer and mystic, Joseph Hauer, in Vienna, and was influenced by Ramana Maharashi and others in India where he lived for five years.

I was studying with Professor Keyserling in Vienna in 1971 at the University and at his private, the School of Wisdom, when he made his discovery. He mathematically calculated the exact frequencies of the chakras—the seven energy centers which drive the aura. The chakras are the doorway, or source, of auric energies—the places where the energy concentrates. Professor Keyserling mathematically calculated the frequencies of the seven chakras and found that these seven frequencies were in a musical relationship with each other. With only slight temperament, they formed a pentatonic (five tone) scale. This was a completely new type of pentatonic scale, unlike any other five-tone scales known in Western music, such as the black scales of the piano, or the equal five-tone octave of much folk and aboriginal music.

A five-tone scale was formed by the seven tones of the chakras because there is an octave relationship between the first and the sixth, and the second and seventh chakras. In other words, the first and second notes of the new pentatonic scale repeat to match the seven chakras. This previously unknown relationship between the seven and five allowed us to see an underlying unity between the two major energy systems of the world—the systems coming from India, which work with the seven chakras, and the systems of China, which work with the five kinds of Ch'i. Both systems were right. There are five kinds of energy, but the first and second types repeat to form seven centers of energy.

The musical scale created by PrimaSounds has five tones with frequencies, intervals (the distances between the notes), and harmonics totally different from the seven- or twelve-tone scales normally used in Western music. The scale is based on the seventh harmonic, the natural seventh (7/4). This harmonic is usually excluded in Western music because it sounds "sour" or dissonant to our ears when compared to all of the other harmonics, such as the third or the fifth. The one harmonic which sounds out of place with the others turns out to be the doorway to the special sounds in tune with the aura—the Chakra tones.

I was naturally excited by this discovery and have been working with PrimaSounds and Professor Keyserling ever since. We have slowly crafted Chakra tones into a new type of meditation music experience designed to directly impact and effect the human aura. The full story of Professor Keyserling's thirty-year quest for the "once lost tones," and how my life became involved with that quest, is told elsewhere *In Search of the Lost Chord* (Ralph Losey 1994, School of Wisdom; available on the Internet at http://ddi.digital.net/~prima/lostchrd.html).

We have found that PrimaSounds listening can accelerate the realization of full potential, in all sides of the brain, in three important ways: (1) stress reduction and relaxation; (2) enhanced concentration and energy; and, (3) by serving as a gateway and "push" into peak experiences.

Stress Reduction. The resonance properties of Chakra tones relieve stress and facilitate relaxation when listened to in the right environment. It puts listeners into a calm, meditative state, where they are able to let go of stress and anxiety.

Aura Energization. After the relaxation stage, the second use of PrimaSounds is possible as you become aware of your bio-energies. Then you can begin to stimulate, open up, and balance your energies. It a kind of massage of the aura. The meditation music allows you to strengthen and tune your aura to the primal vibrations of life—the natural frequencies of the chakras. For most people, success in the second level requires some training or at least a strong background in related disciplines, but it is not overly demanding or impossible.

Peak Experiences. With even more training and practice, PrimaSounds can also be used to induce profound inner experiences such as: a deep state of spiritual contemplation; visions and voices from the Higher Self, collective unconscious, and beyond; and even a Cosmic experience of union with the fundamental tone of the Universe.

Once the peak experience stage is attained, PrimaSounds can begin to fulfill its highest potential. It can serve as a tool to help in the full integration of consciousness, a process we call Life Tuning. Here the aura itself is refined, tuned, and balanced. Profound understanding develops, and ever stronger energies are released and absorbed as you find and begin to fulfill your meaning in life.

Chakra tone music works directly on our aura by resonance. Resonance is natural amplification effect which occurs when one energy vibrates at the same frequency as another. These tones move at the same rate, the same frequency, as the centers of the aura, the chakras. This movement stimulates them, opens them. It amplifies the chakras and the entire auric field, making the aura far easier to sense. An explanation will follow later, detailing exactly how the movement of sound energy can have any resonance effect on the aura, even though the aura is a completely different type of energy than sound.

For those who have never heard this new type of meditation music, it is important to understand how different it is from all other music. It is a completely introversive experience. This concept contrasts with most other types of music, which are extroversive and serve to bring people together. Unlike any other type of music, PrimaSounds has no melody and no rhythms. It sounds chaotic on the surface, with no formal structure or easily recognizable structures or patterns. Finally, the harmonics of the Chakra tones, based on the natural seventh, are completely different from all other forms of music where the natural seventh harmonic is avoided.

The net result is that PrimaSounds do not necessarily produce any emotional effect upon the listener at all. This music is not even designed to be listened to in the normal manner. Rather, it is to be felt by the entire body, by the inside of the head, and by the aura itself—where a strong tingling sensation is common when Chakra tones are played. The sounds in the ears themselves are secondary. Any emotive effects of PrimaSounds on the listener are also purely secondary, a by-product of the stimulation of certain aspects and locations of the aura. This result is the complete opposite of how all other types of music and sounds affect the aura.

Indirect Impact of Music and Sound on the Aura

Most music, excluding Chakra tones, primarily influences our emotions, moves us in some way, or affects our mind—appealing to a mental esthetic. Emotions and other conscious states produced by the music affects our aura. For instance, an uplifting symphony makes us feel good, which in turn strengthens and brightens our aura.

How we feel, what kind of emotional state we are in, obviously has a direct bearing on our energies. Harmonious music puts us in a kind of state where we are balanced, centered. Again, this in turn affects our aura. Conversely, dissonant, disturbing music, music which makes us agitated and imbalanced, will have a negative impact on our energies. Other music, like some rock and roll for instance, is oriented to our sexual drives. That stimulant, in turn, will amplify our sexual energies. Other music is more cerebral, intellectual, like the music of Bach. That kind of mood tends to amplify the auric fields around the head. Thus, all music has the potential to affect our aura indirectly by its emotive effects. Music affects our mood and consciousness in many ways. Our aura, our energies, are in turn influenced by our conscious state.

Music is composed of rhythms, melodies, and harmonics. Certain rhythms produce changes on our consciousness, and they can put us into an altered state. This reaction is well known by shamans around the world who use the drum and rattle to induce shamanic voyages and expanded states of consciousness. When this happens, the aura is naturally affected. This state of mind is an indirect effect induced by the change in consciousness. Melody, lyrics, and harmony also influence our consciousness, our state of mind—impacting our state of being. As we are moved, as our body and mind are affected by a piece of music, our energies are changed too.

The music itself is not directly influencing the energies. The influence is only indirect through the conscious state the music engenders. For that reason, two people can listen to the exact same piece of music and have their auras effected in completely different ways. One person may like the music, but another may hate it. This subjective response to the music controls what impact it will have on the aura.

Sounds can have the same kind of indirect affect on the aura. Loud noises, like jet engines, agitate and disturb most people; that, in turn, agitates the aura. For some people, however, like baggage handlers, the sounds of the jets are commonplace and don't annoy them in the least. For these people, such sounds will also have no effect on their aura. Other sounds are tranquil and soothing, such as most of the sounds of nature—bird calls, surf, crickets, frogs, wind. We have positive associations with these sounds. Listening to these sounds can influence us, lead us to a calm peaceful center, and our aura will then be affected as well. For others, some sounds of nature may invoke fear and anxiety. The clap of thunder scares many and exhilarates a few. The hoot of an owl may please some and annoy others. It may well depend upon what mood one happens to be in when one hears the sound. Again, the subjective response to the sounds is what changes the aura. The sounds of nature themselves have no affect on our aura, only our response to these sounds.

Sound is used as part of many meditation techniques to achieve a heightened awareness and euphoric feeling. An example is Toning, when you sing a tone (the frequency of which is not that important) and focus on it, or mantras, when you repeat a word or sound over and over again. In both techniques, you are using the sounds to quiet the mind, focus the attention, and achieve a contemplative state. Some think that, in this case, the sounds themselves are affecting the aura. Certainly these sound exercises alter your aura, but it is mostly an indirect, subjective influence, although some talented people may naturally begin to tone or chant in a seventh harmonic. They may intuitively tune into the Chakra tones. But aside from this, the emotive, consciousness effects provide the link between most sound meditations and the aura. The sounds themselves, unless they happen to be in tune, do not directly modify the aura. The sounds are instead a focal point for attention and only secondarily, if at all, a stimulant of energies, which explains why exact frequency intonation is not required for most mantras and toning to work.

Chakra tone meditation music is different from other sound work, such as toning and mantras, because with PrimaSounds only select frequencies are used. PrimaSounds employ a very narrow spectrum of sound energies and require very precise reproduction of particular frequencies. Although the subjective, emotive effects of Chakra music may still be present, it is to a lesser and secondary degree. The primary impact of PrimaSounds on the aura is direct through the resonance effect of the sounds themselves.

How PrimaSounds Directly Impact the Aura

This section will provide some speculations in physics as to how and why PrimaSounds work and how they are able to directly impact the aura. If, like some people, you dislike physics or anything too technical, you might want to skip to the next section. Still, I'll try to keep it simple, and I promise—no math. If you know the terrain of physics and acoustics, this concept will be familiar territory, but these theories are novel and will certainly provide you with new insights. If you are unfamiliar with these subjects, it may take some effort to follow, but the insights should make it worthwhile. There may well be other applications to these theories that only you can provide.

All sound energy is longitudinal, whereas all electromagnetic energy is transversal. The energy of the aura is electromagnetic in nature and has transversal characteristics, not longitudinal. As will be explained, this is the fundamental reason certain frequencies of sound have a far stronger impact on the aura than others. Thus, an understanding of how Chakra tones impact the aura requires an exact knowledge of the meaning of longitudinal and transversal energies, and the differences between them.

Longitudinal energy is the "back-and-forth" movement of matter, such as sound vibrations in air. The air, on a molecular level, is compressed and expanded or rarified, resulting in a back-and-forth movement of the air molecules in the same direction as the sound wave. The energy particles move parallel to the propagation of the energy wave. Transversal energy is the "up-and-down" movement of energy fields, perpendicular to the direction of travel of the wave. This type of energy is the wave form one normally see on an oscilloscope or on water. All electromagnetic energy is transversal. Here the energy particles move perpendicular to the propagation of the energy wave.

LONGITUDINAL SOUND WAVES

TRANSVERSAL ELECTRO-MAGNETIC WAVES

The scientific dogma of the day is that it is physically impossible for sound energy to have a **direct impact** upon electromagnetic energy. There is good reason for this skepticism because longitudinal and transversal energies are fundamentally different. The subject is "direct impact" resonance, not indirect, mechanically mediated relations between the two kinds of energy, such as when a microphone translates longitudinal sound energy into transversal electrical energy, or when a speaker does the reverse. There is a natural "common sense" expectation that there will be no significant direct resonant interplay between the two forms of energy and that they will be like two ships passing in the night, one never touching or even seeing the other. One is energy with a vertical based movement, while the other is matter with a horizontal movement.

This concept is shown by the following diagram of the adult pushing a child on a swing. When the adult pushes in the direction of the child's movement and does so at the right time, in resonance with the back-and-forth movement of the swing, the adult gives the child a boost. If the timing of the adult is not right, and he pushes against the child's direction, the adult is not in resonance, and the swinging is hindered instead of helped. It is obvious that the adult cannot push the child by moving his arms up and down like a transversal wave. It does not even make sense to talk in terms of resonance of the two movements. The adult has to push back and forth—longitudinally, not up and down, to attain resonance with the child and push her forward.

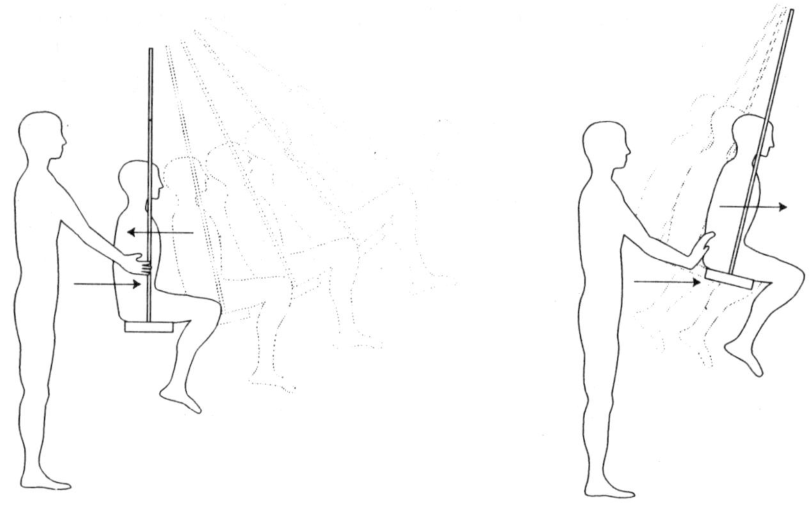

A third alternative to pushing back and forth (longitudinal) or up and down (transversal) is energy moving in a circle or rotational energy. This is the key to PrimaSounds. It may well be the key to understanding many other inexplicable phenomena associated with the aura. The circle is the bridge between the horizontal and the vertical. It is the one form that combines both directions in an even flow. The circular form of the energy thus appears to be the reason that sound waves can have a resonance effect upon the chakras, the energy centers of the aura. Otherwise, longitudinal sound waves would have no direct effect upon transversal energies at all.

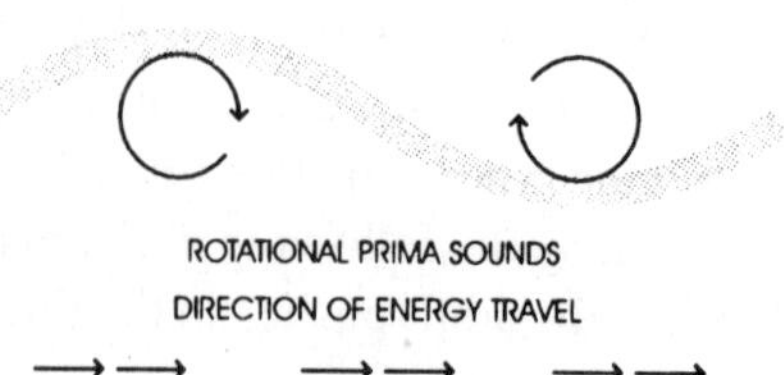

This movement can be better understood by remembering again the child on the swing. If the adult moves his arms in a circular fashion, and the movement is in resonance with the child on the swing, the horizontal energy in the circular movements of the adult's arms will push the child forward. Admittedly, the push will not be as effective as a simple horizontal movement, but it will have a direct positive impact and make the swing go faster than before.

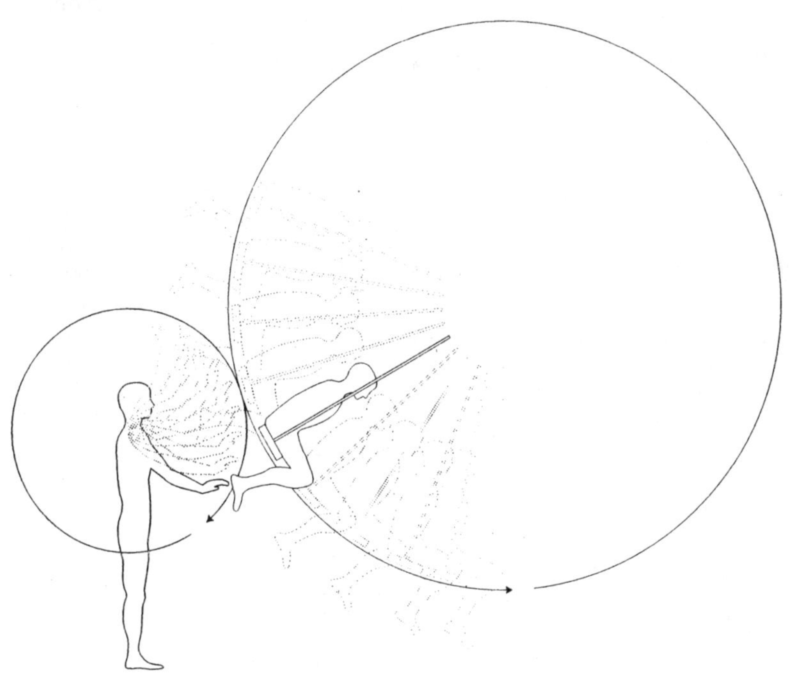

At least one example in nature is where circular energy results as an interaction between longitudinal and transversal energy, and the one form or energy has a direct impact upon the other. It is the movement of longitudinal energy on the surface of water: the waves at sea. The vertical and horizontal energy movements of transversal and longitudinal energies interact with each other to produce a circular movement, an energy vortex. Such rotational movement is also found in whirlpools or tornados.

In the ancient language of Sanskrit, an "energy vortex" is called a "chakra" (see Chapter Seven). In all traditions, the centers of the energy fields surrounding the human body are described as emanating from vortexes of energies. By understanding the phenomena of a wave at sea where horizontal and vertical energies directly impact each other, you can grasp how the resonance effects of PrimaSound waves (a horizontal longitudinal energy) can have an effect on the chakras (a vertical transversal energy). The explanation requires a little more knowledge of the physics of longitudinal and transversal waves.

Longitudinal waves are all matter-based and cannot be conducted through a vacuum. For this reason, there can be no sound on the moon, or as the movies put it, "in outer space no one can hear you scream." Transversal waves can be both matter-based and pure energy, such as electromagnetic energy. Energy-based transversal waves, such as light, can travel through the vacuum of space, which is why we can see the sun but cannot hear it.

Longitudinal waves can be conducted through air, liquids, and solids. (Non-electromagnetic transversal waves, in other words, matter-based transversal waves, can only be conducted through solids.) They cannot pass through gasses and liquids because a matter-based transversal wave requires one section of a body to move sideways with respect to another and then reverse that motion. This movement requires a type of force called a "shear." It requires a countervailing force to bring the portions of the body back into line. Such shearing force is present in solids which have strong cohesive forces between molecules. But in liquids, and especially in gases, the cohesive forces are very weak and are not strong enough for shearing. If a portion of water or air is shifted sideways with respect to a neighboring portion, additional water or air simply flows in to fill the region left "empty" by the shifting portion.

Why does it look as if there are transversal waves on the surface of the ocean? The ocean is certainly a liquid. Here is the key. Although it appears as if transverse waves are traveling on the horizonal upper surface of a liquid, this transversal wave movement is produced by circular movements of the water particles. The water takes a circular path to create a transversal energy on the surface. A duck sitting on the surface of the ocean makes this movement apparent.

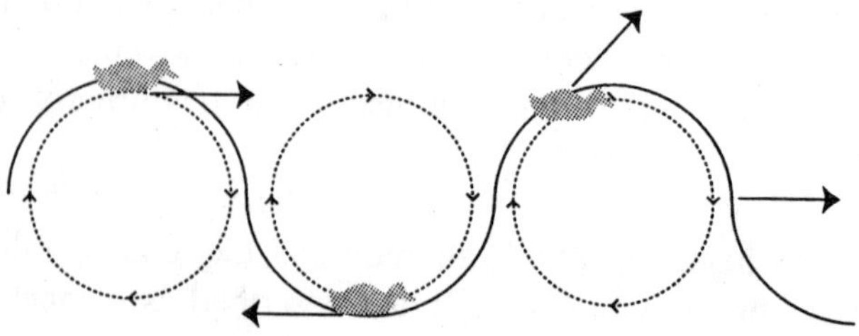

The vortex on the surface between the two states of matter, gas and liquid, and the two kinds of energy is caused by the interaction of longitudinal waves with another energy force. In this case it is the force of gravity. This other energy force then transforms the longitudinal water waves from a horizontal movement into a circular movement, a vortex. These rotational energies can exist only on the surface. Below the surface, the circular vortex waves disappear. They are impossible there, and there are only longitudinal waves, called currents.

The outside force, in this case gravity, resists the up and down shear. Under the surface, within the body of the liquid, gravity does not do this because each fragment of water is buoyed up by the surrounding water. Since the density of each bit of water is equal to the density of the surrounding water, each bit of water has a weight of zero. Under water, gravity is effectively neutralized, making transversal waves impossible. If a portion of water under the surface is raised by a shear, it remains in the new position in spite of gravity. On the surface of a liquid where the buoyancy effect does not exist, gravity can interact to counteract a shear and cause the water to move back again into its old position. However, since longitudinal energy waves are below the surface, that is, horizontal "back and forth" movement, its old position when it goes down is now forward to where it used to be. Then, as it goes up again, the position horizontally goes back to where it started. The influence of an outside force has transformed longitudinal energy into circular energy, a vortex, and in the process, has created a transversal wave.

PrimaSounds work in an analogous manner to waves on the surface of water. It appears that when the frequency of the horizontal (back and forth) sound waves matches that of the transversal (up and down) waves, an outside force or energy is released which causes the sound waves to move in a circular manner. These particular frequencies appear to be analogous to the surface between two forms of matter, liquid and gaseous. They may well be a kind of gate between two worlds, or a doorway to a higher dimension. At this surface point, an outside force causes the longitudinal to move up and down, thus creating circular sound waves which create transversal energy. The outside force might be gravity, or perhaps it is the so called "strong" or "weak" nuclear forces that make up the four forms of energy now known to science (electro-magnetic, gravitational, weak nuclear force, strong nuclear force). We are unsure about this conjecture. We have found that a person's gravitational alignment and sensitivity will frequently have a significant impact upon the experiences invoked by Chakra tones. Still, another force altogether might be involved, one not yet named by science, a force linked with a higher dimension or a unified field of all energies. We suspect that may be the case because traditional wisdom refers to the chakras as possessing a kind of cosmic energy of immeasurable power, called by the Indians *Prana* and by the Chinese *Ch'i*.

The evidence that initially led to this "vortex sound wave theory" was the discovery made by Professor Keyserling when he first played the Chakra tones, that an unusual number of "standing waves" were created in the room. In fact, all Chakra tones appear to be standing waves. For normal longitudinal sound waves, this feat would not be possible. A standing wave is one which remains in place, with clear position and form. A few, and only a few, such standing waves are always created with longitudinal waves in any enclosed room. Which particular frequencies of longitudinal sound will become standing waves is based on the size of the room. If the room is fifteen feet long, then the sound wave, which has a frequency that makes it fifteen feet long will be reinforced by the room itself. The sound wave ends at the wall and bounces back to the other wall, touching the wall just when it is reversing direction. Waves one half the size, one quarter, and so forth, will do the same. A person can walk around a room and hear where they are resounding. They have a definite location, and, since they are reinforced by the structure of the room itself, they play or resound longer. These are natural, acoustically produced standing waves. They cannot exist outdoors, except in natural caverns or mountain wall echo effects.

Many investigators have reported that when PrimaSounds are played, many more standing waves can be heard in a room than when other sound frequencies are played. (Moreover, some investigators report hearing standing waves outside, but this result is more problematical due to the interference of many other factors, such as wind, other sounds, etc., and is more difficult to detect outside.) It appears as if Chakra tones produce standing waves—a wall of sound effect—that is not tied into the acoustics of the room itself. It produces standing waves that must have an origin completely different from that of acoustically produced standing waves, and the rotational phenomena enters in again. If the sound waves were circular, they would naturally create more standing waves. In fact, that would be their inherent nature. The air molecules would be rotational and would reinforce themselves. The circular movements would tend to disrupt each other less than normal longitudinal waves.

The Chakra tone standing wave form pattern can be easily verified by anyone listening to Chakra music. Play the music, walk around the room, and hear the definite "pockets" of sound, the places where it is unnaturally loud or quiet. In a little more subtle experiment, but still an obvious one, try just turning or moving your head a few inches when listening. The music will suddenly change, and one standing wave pattern will be emphasized over another. With a good sound system and depending on your location in the room, the effects of these standing wave effects can sometimes be very dramatic. Beyond experimental verification of my representations here, try the subtle head movements as a way to enhance your listening experience.

The Effects of Chakra Tones on the Aura

PrimaSounds stimulate the energy centers of the aura and make it easier for one to detect the aura through the other senses. For instance, it is much easier to see an aura or to touch it, as in Ch'i Kung, when PrimaSounds are playing or just afterwards. Chakra tones also serve to tune the aura somewhat by amplifying the frequencies of the chakras over other frequencies. The heightened, auric resonance effects are present while the sounds are played and remain for some time after it stops. One can feel what a stronger, healthier aura is like. Although the amplification and tuning effects eventually wear off, with practice, the artificial effects can be extended.

By amplifying the aura with Chakra tones, one can much more easily tune into the vortex centers in the aura, the chakras. One can then learn by direct experience which are the strongest and weakest energies. Thereafter a person can use the Chakra tone vibrations to focus on and amplify the weaker energies to try and achieve a balanced whole and bring the aura as a whole into tune. All traditions teach that the goal is to balance the chakras and produce an even flow of the aura. An aura which is out of balance, not evenly distributed, dissonant, or stagnant and blocked in certain areas is unhealthy and can lead to numerous adverse physical ailments. By activating, tuning, and balancing all of the energies, a person will achieve greater wellness on all levels—physical, psychological, and spiritual.

Another way to use Chakra tones is to listen to one tone at a time, facilitating the tuning of the chakras and overall energy field (see Resources Chapter). The single tones can help one to focus on the different energies, to tune into each energy. This procedure can be particularly helpful for initial orientation to the energies, differentiating the existing energies, and awakening the weaker ones. Later, the individual tones can be selectively used to work on your weakest energies and bring them all into tune and balance.

Over time, by observation of these energies from out of a deep inner silence—a pure, content-free Awareness—one will learn which of the chakras are strong and in tune and which are weak and dissonant. This awareness can happen while listening to the music, just after, or at other times during the day when you spontaneously awaken, particularly in times of crises. This kind of basic knowledge of the strengths and weaknesses of one's aura is very important. A person needs to know himself well enough to know which energies need the most work. With this knowledge of one's aura, a person can use his time accordingly.

Fast progress can be made with PrimaSounds in the tuning and balance of your aura. But remember, even though Chakra tones can facilitate this process, the attainment of a fully tuned, open, and balanced aura takes years of work and mature patience. There is no substitute for effort and attention. Beware of the temptations of the lazy ego that would delude you with visions of false progress or easy enlightenment. This condition not only stops all progress, it invites disaster. Life will usually wake one up in a rude fashion, with illnesses and crises of all types, to show bluntly that one still has a long way to go. This technique is no cure all; it is just a tool to help one help oneself along the way.

Although a basic intellectual understanding of PrimaSounds and the aura can be provided in a book, the techniques and methods for using Chakra tones can only be effectively transmitted as part of a living wisdom tradition, with direct personal contact from teacher to student. Repeated practice and exposure to Chakra sounds is also indispensable for these ideas to be beneficial.

The Ultimate Meaning of PrimaSounds and the Development of the Aura

PrimaSounds provide an easy access for many people to have a direct experience of the aura, but this is only the first step. Chakra tones can take one further along the journey of life when it is used as a tool for human development in the context of a Wisdom Tradition. Then the sometimes astounding effects of PrimaSounds on our aura can facilitate and accelerate all types of meditation and open up many previously undreamed potentials and realizations.

This sound technology can take the trained listener to the threshold of other worlds, the Shaman's gate. The chords create a musical doorway for anyone to penetrate to their fundamental vibration, their deepest, center tone. From this inner core of silence—pure Awareness—a new harmony with the Universe can be attained. With training and practice, Chakra tones music can be used to help you fall into a state of expanded Awareness, a state of Wisdom. It can come as a vision, a dedication, an experience of Love, Communion, Spirit, a state of Samadhi or Satori, Enlightenment, communion with Nature, etc. There are many forms and names to an experience which is essentially formless, nameless—the source of all forms and names. Each person, potentially at least, has their own special idea of the infinite, just as they have their own bliss to follow, their own destiny.

Once this final peak experience is attained, Chakra tones can begin to fulfill its highest potential. It can serve as a tool of Wisdom to help in a process of "life tuning." With perseverance and a little help from friends, coherence in the midst of chaos becomes possible. A person begins to understand what life is all about—why he was born. The aura is tuned further and intensified as an individual applies this new understanding and fulfills the meaning in life. Through creative activity in tune with one's depths, ever more profound understanding results. Even stronger energies are then released and absorbed. A person naturally become more loving and light, and his life becomes ever more creative, vibrant, meaningful, and energetic. One joins in the joyful dance of life and engages in the world flow of activity that fulfills one's meaning and destiny. An individual becomes a part of history, an essential voice in the larger harmony of the planet. Old age then comes as a joyful time of wisdom realization. The body weakens, but the aura remains strong—it sings with harmony, intensity, and color. One is then able to face his end on this planet—"death"—with knowledge and love, ready for the next step. Why else are we all here?

SECTION III:

AURIC COLORS

CHAPTER TEN

THE INTERPRETATION OF AURIC COLORS USING AURA IMAGING PHOTOGRAPHY

Guy Coggins and Susana Madden

THE PURPOSE OF THIS CHAPTER is to provide the practitioner or researcher the opportunity of understanding the various colors and their meanings as interpreted by the Aura Imaging Camera. The same color analysis can also be used by psychics and healers in viewing the various aspects of the human aura.

It should be emphasized that the color analysis forms a "blueprint" of how the various colors can and, in most cases, should be viewed. However, with any medical problem, the individual in question should seek trained medical help. This help comes from many avenues, including family and general physicians, physical therapists, surgeons, gynecologists, orthopedists, other traditional medical practitioners, or alternative health and medical care providers. It is, therefore, not the purpose of this color analysis to replace therapeutic (mental, physical, or emotional) analysis.

Auric colors provide us with an alternative in understanding our emotions, consciousness, energy processes and centers, and the inner Self. In obtaining a color analysis, one should always seek the assistance of a trained and experienced Aura Imaging therapist (healer) or counselor.

Following is a description of what the main colors represent in aura imaging photography. You will find that each color has several explanations. This is because each aura photo can be divided into many parts, each with relevance to a different part of ourselves. Please read on.

Center (Experience)

The color seen over your head is what you experience for yourself now. It's the color that would best describe you. If the color is high, it could mean aspirations or what you wish to be.

Ultraviolet center: This color may mean one of several things: you may be experiencing a time of stress, illness, or most likely, are being inspired by startling and profound visions. You have "genius," meaning you are able now to think thoughts that have never been thought. Your psychic abilities are phenomenal. You may wish to channel what you see into a new and unique art form or some amazing new invention, or who knows? Your highest goal is to manifest into the world what you see in your mind's eye.

Violet center: You are the fairy or leprechaun person of the color spectrum. "Magical" would best describe your life and your way of operating in the world at this point. You would rather talk about miracles, magic, and pots of gold at the end of the rainbow than anything ordinary or mundane. You would rather focus on the ethereal and the sublime. The beautiful world of the imagination is where you feel safest and happiest. You create a magical environment to live in. Your psychic abilities are also strong and fine-tuned now.

Light violet center: At the present time you may be experiencing a profoundly magical spiritual awakening. White, a mix of all the colors of the rainbow spectrum, represents intense healing, while violet symbolizes vision and clairvoyance. The mix of these two shades indicates that you are going through a supercharged, magically synchronistic healing period. The energy of those around you may be instantaneously raised just by your mere presence.

Lavender center: You sparkle and glow with a mysterious inner light. Not only are you a magical, elfin/fairy-like creature, seemingly of another world, you can think and feel very intuitively and seem to just have an inner knowing by which you can direct your life. Remember you are very privileged to have these gifts.

White center: You are a natural, clear conduit for spiritual healing energy. In your present balanced state, you channel pure, divine, white light and heal others with just your mere presence. You have a need for quiet, harmony, and peace in your life, allowing plenty of time for rest, reflection, and meditation. Your primary focus in life at this point is spiritual. Every day matters hold little importance compared with your spiritual and meditative activities.

Blue/white center: "Peaceful, loving, and healing" best describe your focus in life now. You are a natural, clear conduit for spiritual healing energy for others as well as yourself. This light-colored blue indicates you are in a regenerative, restful phase. If you do not work in the healing arts, you may find yourself gently encouraging and nurturing others with just your mere presence. Presently, your highest goals are to achieve complete inner peace and to develop your relationship with the creator.

Light blue center: Spiritual, sensitive, peaceful, loving, and healing best describe your focus in life now. This light-colored blue indicates that you are in a regenerative, restful phase, but at the same time, you are channeling the divine white light, which indicates you are acting as a clear, spiritual healing conduit for others as well as yourself. If you do not work in the healing arts, you may find yourself gently encouraging and nurturing others with just your mere presence.

Blue center: At this point in time, you are experiencing deep inner peace and tranquility in your life. Above all, you want to create harmony and ease in your environment. You may be on vacation or just experiencing a "time out" to relax and gather your energies. If you meditate, you may be able to easily access blissful states of consciousness. Your spirituality, rest, and peace are your main focus now.

Aquamarine center: You have a compassionate, sensitive, and peaceful nature, yet you know how to focus yourself in order to accomplish your goals. You are a natural teacher, counselor, health worker, and parent.

You know how to help, encourage, and nurture others with equal amounts of firmness and affection. People respond to your sensitivity and caring and naturally want to confide in you. You may find yourself presently in a period of transition and change.

Turquoise center: You have a compassionate, sensitive, yet practical nature. You are a natural teacher, counselor, health worker, and parent. You know how to help, encourage, and nurture others with equal amounts of firmness and affection. Presently, you may find yourself in a "healing" phase, needing time to be alone, rest, and recuperate. Self-healing and nurturing is essential for people who are constantly giving to others.

Green center: "Hard at work" would best describe you now. You have serious goals, and you live your life in an organized, deliberate, and economical fashion. You are ambitious and desire prestige, notoriety, and power. You are also full of compassion and can be just as generous as you are demanding. You may be an excellent teacher, counselor, health worker, or business owner. You are full of gentle strength.

Yellow/green center: Compassion, idealism, healing, and teaching mixed with a sense of joy would best describe your present focus in life. You have serious goals and ideals and have natural compassion towards all of humanity, yet you wish to enjoy yourself while you work. You have a bright and quick intellect, always curious for new ideas. You may be a voracious reader, gobbling up every book you can get your hands on when you encounter a new subject that interests you.

Green/yellow center: Compassion and idealism mixed with a sense of fun would best describe your present attitude toward life. You have serious goals and ideals and have natural compassion towards all of humanity, yet you wish to enjoy yourself while you work. Just because you're serious about accomplishing something doesn't mean you live your life seriously. You're fun to be around, and you inspire others with your happy, hopeful attitude.

Yellow center: Joy and happiness surround you now. Your excitement is contagious, life is your playground, and you make everything fun. Even the most tedious of household tasks becomes a game when you do them because you infuse everything with a sense of playfulness. At heart you are a happy, laughing child. You also have a bright and curious intellect, hungry for new and exciting ideas.

Gold center: Prosperity is yours now just for the asking. Luck, abundance, and joy surround you. You inspire others with your warm, optimistic, and happy attitude. Your goodwill toward everyone you encounter triggers a chain reaction of love, acceptance, and friendship. Your whole being radiates like sunshine, and others look to you to lift their spirits.

Golden orange center: Joy and creativity are what you wish to focus on at this point in time. Friendship, socializing, having fun, and being yourself are present goals most important to you now. You make your work and chores a pleasure and strive to enjoy every moment. You have a great sense of humor and laugh easily. Your life is a fun, creative project.

Orange center: You can't help expressing yourself creatively! You are an artist at heart and march to the beat of a different drummer. Right now, you are feeling powerful. You have the energy, enthusiasm, confidence, and will to accomplish anything you desire. This is a time to "go for it." If you have any original ideas or creative projects in mind, you need to begin them now! Orange is also the color of originality and independence.

Red/orange center: Right now you are driven to express yourself! You want to bring out and promote your creative ideas and inspiration. You now have the confidence and certainty to stand on your own and show the world who you are. "Creative" and "dynamic" would best describe you. You are a lively and entertaining companion and usually find yourself the center of attention in most social situations. You may be an inspired entertainer or artist or perhaps an entrepreneur with an original product. Whatever you do, people are entranced by your charisma and originality.

Orange/red center: It looks like the direction for you right now is forward. What you may have been afraid of in the past, you can now achieve. Until today you may have held yourself back, but now you are able to prove that your own strength and determination will get you what you want most from life. Passions are aroused. By staying focused, you will achieve a huge amount and may even surprise yourself with your rapid progress.

Red center: At this time, you are experiencing a time of challenge, with an action-packed schedule, barely leaving you time to breathe, let alone sleep. You have a lot to do, and you have the energy and power to move mountains at this point in your life. You may find yourself acting as a dynamic leader or find yourself in the lime light. You are definitely being noticed. You have so much energy, you sometimes don't know what to do with it. You may exhaust the people around you with your incredible enthusiasm.

Infrared center: You may be experiencing one of several things: you may be feeling stressed, ill, or most likely you are experiencing a time of intense activity, feeling powerful emotions to the extreme. You may be feeling so ambitious and full of energy that you may even forget to sleep. Your entire being is a volcano of passionate life force energy exploding in many directions. Your social life and career thrill and inspire you at the present time. You aspire to have many exciting, adventurous, and passionate experiences.

Right Side (Expression)

The color on the right side of an aura photo (in other words, your left side) is traditionally the energy being expressed. It is the vibrational frequency most likely seen or felt by others around you. Many times, your friends will think this is the energy of which you are made. However, it is what you are putting out to the world.

Ultraviolet right: This color may mean one of several things: you may have been feeling ill or stressed or, most likely, have been experiencing a profoundly magical period in your life. People probably see you as mystical and magical. You put the highest vibrational frequency out into the world. What you want comes to you as if by magic. You seem to effortlessly receive all that you need. Your third eye is open and active, enabling your clairvoyant abilities to blossom. You desire a mystical union with the divine and have a high degree of sensitivity, leading to complete fusion between you and what you put your attention on.

Violet right: The world cannot help but notice your glorious inner light. Your aura shines and radiates outward towards others with loving, healing energy. You put a high vibrational frequency out into the world. Violet symbolizes magic, mysticism, and visionary capacity. It also indicates a person who is profoundly insightful and keenly aware of their spiritual path. You have the ability to be a charismatic spiritual leader.

Light violet right: You show a magical, fairy/leprechaun-like face to the world. People see you as someone living in a somewhat different dimension or realm, not the everyday, harsh, concrete reality-oriented world where most of us live. Through your imagination and spiritual life, you are able to transcend physical reality and live in a more magical and peaceful place.

Lavender right: You put out high vibrational frequencies into the world. White represents spirituality and intense healing while violet symbolizes magic, mysticism, and visionary capacity. A combination of these two colors indicates a person who is profoundly magical and keenly aware of their spiritual path. You have the ability to be a charismatic spiritual leader.

White right: You have a healing effect on all those you encounter. White is actually a mixture of all the colors, so it contains qualities of all the colors within it. Although white tends to be highly unstable, like a supernova, it is the color of intense healing. You have the ability to be a spiritual leader.

Blue/white right: You have a generally quiet and contemplative nature which has a pacifying effect on others. Unification and a sense of belonging is important to you. You have the ability to communicate on a deep and meaningful level. Your sensitive nature sometimes feels overwhelmed by the harshness of the world, but once you are able to spend quiet time alone, you are able to easily rebalance yourself.

Light blue right: You glow with a mysterious inner light, and people respond to your powerful healing presence. Others know that you have tapped into something profound and divine. The world sees you as calm and peaceful. You have a generally quiet and contemplative nature which has a pacifying effect on others. Unification and a sense of belonging is important to you, and you have the ability to communicate on a deep and meaningful level.

Blue right: The world sees you as calm and peaceful. You have a generally quiet and contemplative nature which has a pacifying effect on others. Unification and a sense of belonging are important to you. Blue represents loyalty, depth of feeling, relaxed sensitivity, empathy, and an artistic nature. People see you as the calm of the untroubled sea.

Aquamarine right: People instantly recognize you as their friend and comfort. You are so nonjudgmental and compassionate that you may find yourself attracting many people to you, asking for your help and guidance. You are a natural healer, counselor, and teacher. Blue is the color of harmony, communication, and generosity towards others, while green is the color of healing, growth, and dedication. The combination of these colors, blue/green or aquamarine, shows that you are a person of great depth and compassion.

Turquoise right: The world sees you as a peaceful healer. Blue is the color of harmony, communication, and generosity towards others, while green is the color of healing, growth, and dedication. The combination of these colors, blue/green, shows that you are a person of great depth and compassion. You would save the world if you could. You are expressing healing energy. You are generous towards others and have a great deal of patience. You may be a wonderful teacher, health care worker, healer, or parent.

Green right: You are expressing healing energy. The world sees you as someone with high self-esteem, who is goal oriented, hard working, and dedicated to achieving chosen goals. You are willing to persevere to attain wealth in terms of educational, monetary, cultural, or physical achievements. You are also generous towards others and have a great deal of patience. You may be a wonderful teacher, health care worker, healer, or parent.

Yellow/green right: The world sees you as confident, hard-working, ambitious, and, at the same time, cheerful and optimistic. Yellow is the color of sunshine, warmth, and intellectual capability, while green is the color of healing, self-confidence, and discipline. Yellow/green, a blending of these two colors, indicates an optimistic, generous, and thoughtful attitude. You may often find yourself the center of attention or in a leadership role. In any case, you radiate success and command respect.

Green/yellow right: The world sees you as cheerful, happy, and confident. Yellow is the color of sunshine, warmth, and intellectual capability, while green is the color of healing, self confidence, and discipline. A blending of these two colors indicates an optimistic, generous, and thoughtful attitude. You may often find yourself the center of attention or in a leadership role.

Yellow right: The world sees you as cheerful, happy, playful, carefree, and lucky. Yellow is the color of sunshine and warmth, and your personality is definitely outgoing, and optimistic. Others see you as radiant and self-expressive. Yellow represents relaxation and a release from burdens, problems, harassment, and restriction. Your energy shines like the warmth of the sun, giving happiness and joy to all those who stand in the radiance of your smile.

Gold right: You glow with a radiance that lights up any environment you enter. Your warmth, optimism, humor, and natural joy inspire all those who encounter you. The personality you show the world is hopeful and confident, enabling you to be a great comfort and inspiration to others. Your mere presence uplifts the spirits of those around you.

Golden orange right: You express cheerful, outgoing, warm, and creative energy to the world. Your natural radiance allows you to attract friends easily. You are a charming and entertaining companion. You may enjoy expressing yourself in the performing arts, and those watching your efforts may be amazed at your talents. Popularity reigns.

Orange right: The world sees you as a warm and innovative individual. You are constantly expending energy outward. Orange is a mixture of red, which symbolizes passion and force of will, and yellow, which represents cheerfulness and intellectual capability and expression. People see you as an upbeat, happy, capable, and free person. You like to get out, have fun, and just be yourself.

Red/orange right: A couch potato you will never be. There is too much out there in the world for you to accomplish and do. The personality you show the world is powerfully creative, full of passion and lust for adventure. You have freedom in your heart and tend to be an independent spirit. You want to test the limits of your physical as well as creative nature. People know you as an adventurous, unique, risk-taking, and fun-loving individual.

Orange/red right: Other people can't help but notice your drive and will to live well and succeed. You express yourself as a go-getter, and you probably are. Not being one to follow, you are seen as one happy to lead others or at least find your own way through the wonderful and challenging experience you call life.

Red right: You work extremely hard at whatever you do, and you want intensity of experience and fullness of living. You dive head first into whatever it is you're doing. Passion could be your middle name because you long for adventure, yet at the same time, you are down to earth and practical.

Infrared right: Everybody's wondering where you get all your energy. You don't walk, you fly! You probably have a tendency to want to do everything all at once in a great big hurry, not wanting to spend any time quietly alone or pleasantly idle. Be careful to look both ways before you leap, because you have a tendency now to throw all caution to the wind. These are the qualities you put out to the world!

Left Side (Future)

The color on the left side of an aura photo (your right side) is normally the vibration coming into your being. The closer it is to you, the sooner it will be felt. It may be felt in a few moments, hours, or as long as a few months.

Ultraviolet left: This color may mean one of several things: you may be entering a period of introversion and emotional upset, or, most likely, will be experiencing profound visions. You are truly a "child of the new age." Shortly, you will probably be coming into your power as a spiritual beacon, visionary, and guiding light, communicating to people a new way of living, thinking, and being in the world. Spiritual evolution is in store for you. Ultraviolet, then, on the left side of your aura indicates a time in your life in which you will be able to attain unlimited spiritual knowledge. You will encounter the rays of benevolent guide energies, and you will, in turn, share your enlightenment with others.

Violet left: Spiritual evolution is in store for you. Violet is a mix of blue, a color which symbolizes unlimited knowledge, and red, which represents activity and power. Violet, then, on the left side of your aura, shows that you have the opportunity for great spiritual growth. You may encounter the rays of guides, and the highest vibrational energies will be bestowed upon you.

Light violet left: There can be enchantment and deep spiritual understanding in your future. Violet symbolizes magic, whimsy, and clairvoyance, while white represents highly charged spiritual and healing energy. A whitish violet, then, signifies that a deeply spiritual and magical time in your life shortly awaits you. Be prepared for your psychic abilities to awaken if they haven't already. You will begin to understand how synchronicity works in your life.

Lavender left: You may be entering a time of magic and heightened spirituality. White signifies oneness with the divine. Violet represents power of the imagination and magic. A healing is coming for you and those around you. You are not a novice in the workings of the spiritual dimension. You know the beauty of white light attracts all beings at every level of existence. You are entering a time to assist others in transition or to make transitions yourself.

White left: A supercharged time of miraculous spiritual healing is ahead of you. You can have a healing effect on all those around you. White is a mixture of all the colors; therefore, it is the most powerful. It indicates a healing experience. White give you the ability to choose from all of the energies, so life will be fully open to you.

Blue/white left: Blue is the color of peace, meditation, intuition, and tranquility, and white is the color of spirituality. You are entering a time now in your life of intense beauty, inner peace, and oneness with the divine. A beautiful healing time is coming to you and those around you.

You will be able to act as a clear conduit for spiritual healing energy to flow through you to heal yourself and others. You may be working on developing a close connection with the Creator.

Light blue left: Since white is the color of spirituality, and blue is the color of communication, calmness, and depth of feeling, you are entering a time when your own doubts and insecurities may leave you, a time when you love and trust yourself more, a time when you will make use of your inner knowing and feelings more and more.

Blue left: Blue is the "communication" color, which indicates that you are a sensitive and intuitive listener, able to transform and heal others through your loving listening. You may be coming upon a good time for learning, since you are in a particularly receptive state. Trust your intuition, because it will lead you to learn about things which are important for your soul's evolution and growth. Peaceful times are in your future.

Aquamarine left: A time of peace and healing is ahead of you. Prepare to relax and contemplate the clouds for a period of time. Your vacation has been long past due, and you need some time now to recharge your batteries. Blue is the color of tranquility, and green is the color of healing. It's probably a time then to kick off your shoes and replenish your energy.

Turquoise left: Blue is the color of communication and intuition while green is the color of change. Blue-green indicates new learning. Blue also signifies the ability to listen and receive information. Expect to be entering a time of peaceful receptivity when you will be able to learn many new things.

Green left: Green is the color of growth and renewal. It brings to mind the season of spring. A period of transformation and new beginnings is in store for you. Like the new grass popping out of the dark soil and small leaves sprouting from the barren branch ends as the last days of winter slumber fade, your life will be similarly "springing forth." You are bringing new healing energy into your life.

Yellow/green left: Your future is full of change and bright ideas. Yellow is the color of the intellect, and green is the color of growth, transformation, and renewal. A yellowish-green, then, indicates that your attitudes and ideas about certain subjects and life in general will be expanding in exciting, new directions. The thought of change in your life does not scare you. On the contrary, it inspires you and rejuvenates your spirit.

Green/yellow left: Your future is bound to be packed with new thoughts, because yellow is the color of the mind, and green is the color of growth and change. A greenish-yellow hue, therefore, indicates that your beliefs will be changing, perhaps in many areas. You are entering a growing time in which your outlook and attitudes will be going through a transformational process.

Yellow left: Your future is bound to be thought provoking. Like the rising sun, yellow brings forth warmth and light, and yellows are representative of the intellect. Each shade or tint of yellow expresses a type of function, ability, or expression of the intellect, from the craftiness of a mustard yellow to the high, intellectual thought of a golden yellow. You approach your future with a sense of excitement and joy.

Gold left: In the near future, you will have opportunities to be an inspiration to many people. You glow with a beautiful inner light to which people instantly respond. You are full of hope, inspiration, utopian ideals, and zeal. You easily inspire others with your optimism and excitement for new ideas. You have a quick, curious mind, always happy and hungry for new learning. You are happy to be just who you are, and you feel the confidence to accomplish anything you want.

Golden orange left: Your future is bound to be thought provoking as well as highly creative. Activity-generating energy is coming into your field. This shade of golden orange is a mixture of active red and intellectual yellow, a color which indicates, in this position of your auric field, that a very creative and intellectually stimulating future lies in store for you. Inspired ideas are already unfolding within you, and you will also have opportunities to enjoy the sensual pleasures and live life as you wish to.

Orange left: Activity-generating energy is coming into your field. Orange is a mixture of active red and intellectual yellow, a color which indicates, in this position of your auric field, that a very free thinking future lies in store for you. Activity, wakefulness, and inspiration are unfolding in your being. You will have opportunities to direct your life yourself without hindrance. Orange is known to give way to green, which signifies healing and growth after the balancing period is over. Now is a time to help yourself.

Red/orange left: A dynamic and exciting future is ahead of you. Red is the color of power, high energy, and leadership. Orange is a mixture of active red and intellectual yellow, a color which indicates originality and independence. Red/orange, then, indicates powerful self-expression. Be prepared for an inspired time in your life in which you dive head first into your creative activities and endeavors. You will feel the confidence and personal power to begin and complete projects which interest you.

Orange/red left: Your future looks very bright. You will most probably not only see the way out of any troubles, you will also leave them behind you as you race forward and onward. This is really a great time of achievement and progress. Know what you want, and it will almost certainly be there for you. This can be a most fulfilling time in your life.

Red left: "Stop lights," "warning lights," "pushing the limits"—may have something to do with your future. You will be living life in the "fast lane" and be able to experience life to the fullest. Your future is full of stimulating activity, high energy, intense activity, and accomplishment, a great time to begin and complete projects. Fun is in store for you.

Infrared left: This color can denote more than one thing: you may be entering a time of indecision with so many choices, or, most likely, you have an eventful, exciting, action-packed future ahead of you. You will have a tendency to want to do everything all at once in a hurry, not wanting to spend any time idle. You may even forget to sleep. Be careful not to take on too many challenges. If you stay with one or two, success is virtually guaranteed.

Throat (Communication)

The color on the throat is traditionally the energy being verbally expressed. If the energy is flowing well in this area, you can easily express how you feel and what you think.

Ultraviolet throat: Most likely you have an intense desire to communicate your startling, incredible visions. You could best be described as a true visionary. You see worlds beyond what is thought possible by the majority of people. You may be a gifted psychic, artist, writer, inventor, or scientist. Your ideas are so original that people see you as a magician or modern-day alchemist.

Violet throat: You may find yourself in a position of power or visibility, deeply affecting the lives of many people, for you are a genuine myth-maker, presenting to the world a different and altogether unique reality. You speak of miracles, magic, and pots of gold at the end of the rainbow. You'd rather discuss the ethereal, the sublime, and metaphysical rather than anything ordinary and mundane. The perfect world of your imagination is where you feel most at home.

Violet throat: This color is a peaceful and low physical energy hue. It possesses little contact with the earth and mundane things and more with the fantastic potential relating to psychical ability, incredible dreams, and esoteric abilities. As with the ultraviolet, you are a true visionary and a mystic in your abilities, able to connect with the divine. Reaching beyond the physical plane, you perform miracles, healing, magic, and possess inner peace and power. There are many sides to this color including great mental powers, kindness, idealism, justice, and leadership.

Light violet throat: You speak of miracles, magic, and oneness with the divine. You radiate an other worldly and magical inner peace. People are magnetically drawn to your mysterious serenity. They know there's something uniquely wonderful about you because you naturally express your spirituality and imagination.

Lavender throat: You radiate a mysterious and magical inner peace, and people are magnetically drawn to your mysteriously ethereal and deeply serene personality. They know there is something wonderfully different about you. You naturally express your spirituality and powerful healing abilities, and you trust your inner knowing and follow your intuition. People sense your intuition and inner knowing and recognize that this is what you can rely on in your daily life.

White throat: You radiate an inner peace, and people are magnetically drawn to your ethereal and deeply serene personality. You naturally express your spirituality and powerful healing abilities. You trust your inner knowing and follow your intuition. Guided by your sixth sense rather than by logic, you have a certainty about which direction to take in life. You speak of the importance of faith and the ever present energy of the divine. Being an articulate communicator, you have the ability to be a spiritual leader.

Blue/white throat: What you wish and desire to communicate in your life now are messages of peace, harmony, beauty and spirituality. Expression of a higher order is what you most want to put out into the world. Every encounter is dealt with patiently, calmly, and with compassion.

Light blue throat: Sensitive by nature, you most desire to express yourself in harmonious, peaceful, and beautiful ways. Much of the time you are more comfortable in your imaginary or spiritual world. You may wish to express yourself artistically or spiritually and have the ability to articulate your deepest feelings. You experience bliss, wholeness, and connection with the divine through meditation. You may need to spend a great deal of time alone in order to communicate with your inner self.

Blue throat: Your ability to communicate with love and compassion is heard by all around you. Your voice can calm and soothe others who may be in a state of flux. You also have the ability to let others communicate more with themselves, leading to their greater peace of mind.

Aquamarine throat: You wish to achieve inner peace and create harmony in the world. Not only must you feel peaceful, but you also feel the need to teach, foster, and nurture peace in others. You may wish to change the world by helping others to achieve well-being or perhaps through creating beauty in the environment through the arts. You are practical and diligent as well as spiritual and sensitive.

Turquoise throat: You are peaceful by nature and wish to express yourself in a calm and serene manner. You want to create harmony and reduce discord. A natural diplomat, teacher, and healer, you are constantly nurturing, teaching, consoling, and inspiring others with your loving, kind words. You see the good in everyone and are patient and compassionate when expressing your feelings. Always temperate, logical, and understanding, you take the time to think before you speak.

Green throat: People sense from you an ability to heal and teach. Your words are seen as reassuring, and you have a special way of helping others without even trying. There is no doubt that doors open for you due to your kindness and trust. Life just seems to come naturally to you.

Yellow/green throat: You can easily express yourself to others, and this ability can bring a lot of joy to them. Because you can speak so freely, you also know how to make friends easily. You are very entertaining, and your sense of humor will take you places.

Green/yellow throat: Compassion and inspiration is what you're all about. In order to be happy, you need to be excited and inspired about what you're doing and know that you are helping others. You communicate a sense of joy and warmth as well as understanding to those around you. Your good sense of humor is infectious. Always hopeful, you enjoy planning and discussing a bright and prosperous future for yourself and everyone else. You want to save the world and have fun while doing it.

Yellow throat: Fun is your main concern. In order to be content, you need to be excited, inspired, and happy about what you're doing. You communicate a sense of joy and warmth to those around you, and your good sense of humor is infectious. Always hopeful, you enjoy planning and discussing a bright and prosperous future.

Gold throat: You express yourself joyfully. Your excitement is contagious and inspiring. You communicate a sense of warmth and happiness to those around you. Naturally curious, new ideas excite you. With such a great sense of humor, you are a natural entertainer and comedian.

Golden orange throat: You can't help expressing yourself joyfully and creatively. Happiness, excitement, and humor is what you most desire in your life. You spread sunshine wherever you go. Your voice is your instrument, and you may enjoy singing, acting, telling jokes and stories, or just chatting with friends. People find you a pleasurable, lively, and entertaining companion. You are warm, outgoing, and sociable.

Orange throat: You love to speak out, and you are willing to be different. Your creativity and originality give you the edge in conversation. You celebrate your uniqueness and freedom of expression, and you know that you don't have to follow others because there are so many new and fresh ideas in your head.

Red/orange throat: People are naturally drawn to your charismatic personality, and you can't help energetically and dynamically expressing yourself. You are a natural entertainer and enjoy basking in the limelight. People find you a fascinating, lively companion and are instantly drawn to you. Friendship comes easily. You are the life of the party.

Orange/red throat: You wish to express yourself creatively, and you have an extremely powerful desire to talk about what's on your mind. This is a time of inspired communication, a time to express your strong emotions and ideas. You feel confident to speak freely and honestly with conviction.

Red throat: You have an extremely powerful desire to talk about what is on your mind. This may be a time of heated conversations when you will speak frankly and truthfully. Remember that when you are honest with yourself, you will go far.

Infrared throat: This color may mean one of two things: you may have a sore throat, or, most likely, this is the time for speaking your mind. It will be hard for others to avoid hearing you at the moment because you feel that something must be said. A brownish color could mean physical or emotional stress.

Heart (Empathy)

The color on the heart represents the energy of your feeling for yourself and others, and the heart is the center of compassion, love, sensitivity, and connection with the universe.

Ultraviolet heart: You are opening up your visionary capabilities. You probably have profound insights and the ability to see into the multidimensional layers of reality. You are a true "child of the new age," able to grasp the true meaning of universal love. You understand humankind's role in the grand plan of the cosmos. You have qualities that may enable you to be a leader of some sort in the "New Age." You have psychic abilities and appear to live your life according to some magical laws that the majority of people on this planet have yet to learn and understand. You are ahead of your time, yet you are in the right place at the right time. Your heart is full of unconditional love.

Violet heart: "Magical" and "visionary" would best describe you. You have a deep belief in magic, the other worldly, and the metaphysical. You have psychic abilities and are not afraid to demonstrate or use them. The occult also attracts you. You have the vivid imagination to write best selling novels or create new forms of art. What you desire most is to manifest the magic you are able to so clearly visualize and feel.

Light violet heart: Like an angel, you express yourself magically. You glow with a mysterious inner light and are an inspiration to others as you prove anything is possible. You may be a talented clairvoyant, artist, or visionary. Your thoughts and dreams are of another world. The spiritual, the metaphysical, and the divine are what hold your attention. The everyday and the mundane are a bore to you, as well as harsh and ugly. You prefer to shift your attention and desires into a higher dimension.

Lavender heart: There is something different and other worldly about you. You have a "sixth sense." You live by faith and believe in miracles. You are magically guided by a higher power. You work to heal yourself and others. Always seeing the bigger picture and yourself reflected in the cosmos, the mundane details of life often bore you. Paying the bills seems far less important than your daily meditation or writing down your visions from dreams or pondering your favorite current fantasy. You exist in another world far more beautiful and humane than the one everyone else lives in.

White heart: You glow with a mysterious inner light and desire a strong connection with the divine. The world around you knows that you think of more than just yourself. You may be spiritually motivated, environmentally conscious, or just have a feeling for your community. Your selflessness is noticed by all and respected by many.

Blue/white heart: Your need to know the truth is strong. Your heart is probably making more decisions than your head at the present time. You are an inspiration to those around you. You also have a profoundly sensitive and imaginative nature and may wish to express yourself through the arts or spiritual rituals. You desire deep and meaningful communication with others and feel lonely and isolated by superficiality.

Light blue heart: You are a deeply spiritual and peaceful person, desiring harmony and quiet, time to be alone, to rest, to meditate, or to simply daydream. At this time you wish to recoup and gather your energies. Your whole being is hungry for a vacation, relaxation, or deep meditation. Inner peace is your goal at this point in time. You expend a great deal of energy healing and inspiring others, which can be draining and depleting. Quiet time spent alone nurturing yourself is essential to your well being and ability to continue healing others.

Blue heart: Because your heart plays a vital part in your life, this can be a time to reflect, to rest, and reconsider how you have been using your heart's energies.

Aquamarine heart: You desire peace and quiet, time to be alone and rest, yet you also desire to save the world and will work extremely hard, using all your resources, to promote or to fight for a worthwhile cause. You are a humanitarian, empathetic to the needs and plight of others. You may be an excellent counselor, teacher, healer, or artist. You are sensitive and imaginative as well as practical and pragmatic. You need to find a balance between the time you give to others and the time you give to nurturing your own inner and spiritual life.

Turquoise heart: You are a natural healer, counselor, and teacher with a balanced, compassionate nature, yet you also have a rich spiritual life. You work hard to achieve position and authority in life because you have a proud heart and desire to be looked up to, yet you also need to make time for rest and introspection since you are also very sensitive. You take your responsibilities very seriously and sometimes place obligations and the needs of others before your own. You have a quiet, patient strength and generous heart. Your quiet time spent reading, praying, meditating, or simply daydreaming is essential to your happiness.

Green heart: Your natural gifts shine from your heart. You have great ability to heal and teach others and can be a great negotiator because of your innate ability to see both sides of an event. Your patience and your harmony are very beneficial to you, and when you respect these qualities, you are in great balance.

Yellow/green heart: You are a balanced, compassionate, caring individual desiring the best for everyone. You work hard to achieve position and authority in life because you have a proud heart and desire to be looked up to. Although you take your responsibilities very seriously, you still want to enjoy yourself and have fun in your life. Your optimism is contagious. You are a charming, humorous individual with a powerful and commanding presence.

Green/yellow heart: What you most desire in life is to heal and nurture others with your humor and optimism. You are fun loving and carefree, yet you feel a responsibility and desire to counsel and help people with their problems and challenges. You have deep insight and empathy into what others are experiencing, but you have the unique ability to remain centered and amused when all else is falling into chaos around you. Your humor is often your strength and saving grace.

Yellow heart: You are a happy, fun loving, innocent child at heart and want to enjoy yourself no matter what you do. Everything must be a pleasure even if it's just going to the grocery store or working around the house. You have a way of making everything seem fun. You have many friends and acquaintances since you are such a pleasure to be around. Almost always excited and optimistic, you breeze through life with the certainty that every cloud has a silver lining.

Gold heart: You desire joy, spontaneity, amusement, and ecstasy. You are also confident, have self-respect, and a strong sense of personal power. You have discovered your personal gift in life, and there is a strong desire to share it with others. You spread light, hope, and happiness wherever you go. Your child-like innocence makes others feel at ease and happy around you. Your humor helps to heal and lift the spirits of everyone you meet. Your creative, fun-loving approach to life opens up many doors and possibilities.

Golden orange heart: What you desire most in life is fun, adventure, spontaneity, and self expression. You are an original thinker, a fun loving non-conformist, a "happy go lucky" risk taker and must live life on your terms in order to be content. You are care-free, imaginative, and ready for adventure. You may be inspired and excited about a new creative project or endeavor. Basically happy and optimistic, you feel free to experiment and have fun with new ideas.

Orange heart: What you desire most in life is self-expression, autonomy, independence, and freedom. Your freedom of thought and expression allow you to be yourself. Even when a feeling of restriction is around you, there is little doubt that your own optimism will get you through with flying colors.

Red/orange heart: You need to fly and move unfettered, able to follow any whim that may flame in your heart. Your passion is deep and intense, yet you need the freedom to live life on your own terms, beholden to nothing and no one, or else you may feel trapped and listless. Your happiness and boundless energy depend on your being able to maintain an abundance of freedom and excitement in your life.

Orange/red heart: Having a creative and whole-hearted attitude towards life would best describe you. Full of energy, drive, and unique ideas, you do nothing half way, diving head first, full throttle, into projects and relationships that interest you. You feel strongly about expressing your own ideas, either completely for or against, without ambivalence or apathy. Most of all, you desire your presence to be known, seen, and heard. Being curious, fearless, and ambitious, you want to enjoy and experience all that life has to offer, and you are a natural leader and trendsetter.

Red heart: You like life and what it can offer you. Almost certainly your heart is moving you forward and onward to new challenges—to new experiences. You have the ability and self-confidence to override all of your fears. You relish and embrace life with gusto and sensuality.

Infrared heart: Your heart is full of passion, burning desire, and emotion. Your moods may be erratic, with periods of ecstatic highs as well as plummeting lows. You experience life on a roller coaster of powerful, changing emotions, creating and attracting dramatic scenes. This is a time of great experiences.

Solar Plexus

The color on the solar plexus is normally the central vibration of your being. The solar plexus is associated with power and money and is called the "money pot" by the Hindus. This is the center of self-esteem and ego.

Ultraviolet solar plexus: Spiritual enlightenment, personal growth, following your own path or quest—whichever way you may look at it, your power center is looking for more than just physical or material gain. This feeling may be very subtle, so give yourself a moment to look within. You will know yourself better.

Violet solar plexus: You may be experiencing the mysteries of spiritual fulfillment. Violet is a mixture of blue, a color which symbolizes unlimited knowledge, and red, which represents activity and power. Violet in the solar plexus area indicates a time in your life in which you may be able to experience unlimited spiritual knowledge. You may be enjoying new and gentle yet profound energies, and the highest vibrational attunement harmonizes in the center of your being.

Light violet solar plexus: Magic, enchantment, and deep spiritual bliss are resonating in the center of your being. Violet symbolizes magic and the psychic, while white represents highly charged spiritual and healing energy. A whitish violet in the solar plexus area signifies divine transformation unfolding in the deepest part of your soul. Don't be shocked as your psychic abilities are awakened. You probably are feeling and understanding how Synchronicity works in your life.

Lavender solar plexus: You are probably experiencing feelings of magic and heightened spirituality. White signifies oneness with the divine, and violet represents power of the imagination and magic. A healing is transforming your being at the very center of your soul. You may be "floating on air" as you immerse your ego and personality in the spiritual dimension.

White solar plexus: The very center of your soul is supercharged with miraculous, spiritual, healing energy. You will have a positive and transforming effect on all those around you. White is a mixture of all the colors; therefore, it is the most powerful. Miracle energy spirals out from your center. Use this white power for your own benefit. This is a time when you have the choice to use any energy.

Blue/white solar plexus: Blue is the communication color, and white is holistic. You have the energy within you to fulfill your desire to grow more holistically. Your center of power just needs the command from your conscious self. Then you can receive even greater healing and spiritual energy. All that you have been seeking will now seem to fall into place.

Light blue solar plexus: You are able to use your energies to further remove your own doubts and insecurities. A graceful healing spiral is felt by others around you. It is emanating from your solar plexus center. With a little rest, you are able to rebuild and even increase the level of energy you have. Your own faith in yourself can grow. Just listen to yourself and your trust rises.

Blue solar plexus: You have the power to communicate more with yourself. This need not be done by force—that won't achieve anything. Listen to yourself., to your inner voice. The answers to your questions are all there. Try it! Look calmly and peacefully within yourself. You have the strength to do this. A solitary and peaceful time can be of great benefit now.

Aquamarine solar plexus: From the center of your soul, you feel as if a time of peace and healing is at hand. You may be experiencing spiritual fulfillment and a mysterious "oneness" or "connection" with all other living beings. You may feel a calm satisfaction with life, and you may wish to relax and contemplate the clouds for a period of time.

Turquoise solar plexus: What you are probably experiencing now is a great learning time—a time when you are teaching yourself to learn about yourself and about what is around you. You can now move into your power center with confidence. Be more generous to yourself. You have very strong abilities to heal yourself and loved ones around you.

This gift is probably coming naturally to you. Allow the energy to flow. Relax. You will find that not only others will benefit, you will too.

Green solar plexus: Green is the color of balance, harmony, healing, and teaching. The solar plexus is your power center. What you are probably feeling from your power center now is the energy to put yourself into greater balance. You have the innate ability to help yourself and heal any problems you may be hanging on to. You may be working on changing yourself or healing some aspect of your life. You have the hope and the courage to quit smoking, to start that diet, or join a support group and to make improvements.

Yellow/green solar plexus: Yellow is the color of the intellect, and green is the color of growth, harmony, and renewal. A yellow/green color, then, shows that your thoughts and beliefs are branching out, allowing you to see your life and your energies with a bright, new perspective. Oh, how you now are able to progress, to see, hear, know, and feel the direction you are to take in your life.

Green/yellow solar plexus: Your fine, fresh thoughts are a bonus to you. You know that now is the time to let go of all those stagnant, old attitudes, as you have the power to let go of the old and invite the new. Now you can combine balance and joy! You feel the courage to feel joyful and hopeful about all the wonderful "newness" surrounding you.

Yellow solar plexus: Yellow is the color of joy, fun, variety, and change. Joy and spontaneity are almost always around you. It is time to use these wonderful gifts more and more. You can have a lot of good friends. Your sense of humor is more finely tuned than usual, and this lets you entertain yourself at a whim. You probably feel happy and confident as you have discovered your life's work. You have the confidence to accomplish anything you desire to do. You laugh easily and are amused by life.

Gold solar plexus: You have such a well of joy and beauty inside yourself. You have the ability to let others help themselves, in spite of themselves. Your mind is a huge asset and no doubt is always looking for more to learn and do. Just be yourself. Gold is the purest color of all. Coming from your solar plexus, you have no restrictions.

Golden orange solar plexus: Activity-generating energy is bursting from the center of your being. This shade of golden orange, a mixture of active red and intellectual yellow, indicates that you have a very creative and intellectually stimulating personality. You may be the center of attention in many circles, and inspired ideas are already unfolding within you. You also may be creating opportunities to enjoy the sensual pleasures and enjoy life.

Orange solar plexus: You attract activity-generating energy into your field. Now you feel the courage, power, and inspiration to accomplish anything you want! This is the time of high achievement that you have been waiting for. Know that with orange in your solar plexus, your time for manifestation is now. Creativity is heightened.

Red/orange solar plexus: Your solar plexus is packed with energy at the present time. You may even find that your mind is racing ahead of you. From the very center of your being, power and dynamism burst forth. You awe others with your intense energy, often wearing them out in the process. You are inspired to dive head first into your creative activities and endeavors. You feel the confidence and personal power to begin and complete projects which interest you.

Orange/red solar plexus: Your power center is probably bursting with energy and creativity right now. This is when you can move forward faster than you have ever progressed before. Keep yourself under control so you don't burn out. Know what you want; set your goals, and you will have what you have been seeking. You will probably be amazed at your own strength.

Red solar plexus: Red is the first color of the visible spectrum and so this can be a wonderful time to begin things, to challenge yourself, to do what you want to do, but may have been afraid of doing. Accomplishment is probably looking you in the face.

Infrared solar plexus: Your energy center is probably really energized now. Try to direct this energy into something positive. This is a time to move forward. You may be holding onto some anger or experiencing some emotional turmoil. You may have a tendency to want to do everything all at once in a hurry, not wanting to waste even a minute.

Sex

This energy center of the body is about creativity, sociability, one's emotional life, and sexuality. Sex is a profound source of creativity, joy, and pleasure, which is nurturing, healing, and bonding. It is often considered sinful by most manipulative religions and, from this aspect, can be a source of guilt, fear, and shame. When the energy in this area is balanced, the person will probably have a healthy positive attitude toward basic love. The sexual center is the position from which one reaches out, expands, and relates to others.

Ultraviolet sex: You are being inspired to take some time out for yourself and relieve yourself of social burdens. Your psychic abilities are also likely to be awakened at this time. You may find yourself "knowing" things and not knowing why. Your "gut level" intuition is strong, and you may shock your partners with your incredible insights and clairvoyant abilities.

Violet sex: "Magical" would best describe your life and your way of operating in the world at this point. You want to share your miraculous visions with others. The beautiful world of fantasy and art is where you feel at home. In your relationship it is likely that the use of fantasy is important too.

Light violet sex: You may be involved in a deep and karmic love affair or may be opening yourself up to the loving energy of the universe, letting it flow through you. Violet blending with white creates a gentle and holistic mix, allowing you to experience physical pleasure in a way like no other. You can create that special ambiance with a touch of mystery and intrigue.

Lavender sex: You express your deep love and affection for others in a gently ethereal and mystical manner. Your active imagination plays a vital role in your sex life. Romantic and erotic literature has great appeal. You have a need for quiet, harmony, and peace in your life, allowing plenty of time for rest, reflection, and meditation.

White sex: White gives you a special strength to move toward the holistic and the divine. A relationship can mean so many different things to you.

You have the ability to explore all aspects, but probably most relevant to you is that which is not only physical but also is beyond words. You can enjoy the full spectrum of a love affair.

Blue/white sex: "Peaceful, loving, and healing" best describe how you relate to others at this point in your life. You are a natural, clear conduit for spiritual healing energy. This light blue indicates you may be taking "time out" from sexual and romantic liaisons. If you are in a relationship, this period is probably a time when you are both focusing on friendship, companionship, and spiritual growth. You may find yourself gently encouraging and nurturing others. Presently, your highest goals are to develop harmonious communication with others. You are definitely a "giver."

Light blue sex: A calmness and gentleness is around you, and others can sense it. Your partner will often be relaxed in your company, and the quality and level of communication is probably great. You can give a lot of trust and sensitivity to your intimate moments. What you want most in your relationships with others is clear, honest, heartfelt, deep, and intimate communication.

Blue sex: Right now you probably have a lot of calmness and peace within yourself. This can be due to your surroundings, or you have created this all by yourself. This energy can be channelled into meditation or arise in your trust and self-confidence. The last thing you want or need is romantic drama and emotionally charged encounters. You are mature and wise as to what love really is. You allow yourself and others the freedom "to be."

Aquamarine sex: You have a placid and calming nature and are able to bring balance and harmony to your relationships. You can be trusted and expect the same in return. Even though there is a lot of pleasure from physical intimacy, most likely you look for more than that in your life. Your parenting qualities are noticed by many, and you are very likely to spend much of your life in a stable relationship.

Turquoise sex: You can be a compassionate person who is willing to respect, nurture, and guide your partner to greater heights in many pursuits in life. You may give a lot of yourself and, understandably, will appreciate the same in return. In a love relationship you need a partner who can be equally as generous with you as you are with him/her.

Green sex: When you are with a partner, there is usually a greater feeling of stability in your life, although you may be quite demanding. Therefore, you need a partner equally as strong and ambitious in order for there to be balance and harmony. You are full of gentle strength. Others feel and respond to your "big heartedness."

Yellow/green sex: Healing and teaching energies within you, enable you to be seen as harmonious in your relationships. For happiness in love, you probably require a partner equally as fun-loving, generous, and goal-oriented as yourself. This time may also be a transition stage for you in your relationship, or you might be preparing yourself for a new one.

Green/yellow sex: You like to laugh and no doubt desire joy, fun, and laughter with your loves. Just because you're serious about accomplishing something doesn't mean that you live your life seriously. You're fun to be around, and you inspire others with your happy, hopeful attitude. In love, you may be spontaneous and playful, yet very caring toward your partner.

Yellow sex: Others are attracted to your outrageous sense of humor. Life is your playground. You find love easily, and you make everything fun. "Life just wasn't made for boredom" could be your motto. You like to have fun and that certainly includes fun with a partner. Having a great sense of humor is probably a prerequisite for you.

Gold sex: You are in a state of "havingness." You have healthy self-esteem, and others respect you for it. You inspire people with your warm, optimistic, and happy attitude. A partnership for you most likely will be very mutually beneficial and stimulating. You are probably a natural clown and enjoy a busy social life.

Golden orange sex: Friendship, socializing, having fun, and being yourself are the priorities on which you wish to focus. You make your work and chores a pleasure and strive to enjoy every moment. You have a great sense of humor and laugh easily. Your life is a fun, creative project. You have a healthy attitude toward sex and probably enjoy an active and exciting love life. You are able to relate to others in a warm, open, and friendly way.

Orange sex: You are the lover of the rainbow spectrum and enjoy romance and an active social life. Right now you are feeling powerful. You have the energy, enthusiasm, confidence, and will to accomplish anything you wish. You have the energy and ability to reach out, express yourself, and satisfy your desires.

Red/orange sex: You have the confidence and certainty to stand on your own and show the world who you are. Others may find you extremely desirable. You probably enjoy sex very much and relish a satisfying and active love life. People are entranced by your charisma, originality, and animal magnetism.

Orange/red sex: You may be an inspired entertainer or artist or perhaps an entrepreneur with an original product. You are charged with animal magnetism and sensuality and may channel that energy into creative projects or an active sex and love life.

Red sex: You have a lot to do, and you have the energy and power to move mountains at this point in your life. You may find yourself acting as a dynamic leader or entertainer basking in the lime light. You are definitely being noticed. You have so much energy you sometimes don't know what to do with it. You probably have a great sexual appetite and may find yourself surrounded by many smitten admirers. You tend to exhaust the people around you with your incredible energy and enthusiasm.

Infrared sex: You can be a most passionate person. Just remember to consider another person's feelings in a relationship. Go for life. People can see that you are a doer—not one to sit around and complain for too long. Throughout your life you may have many partners. When someone suitable comes along, treat that person with respect and you will be given respect in return.

Root

The color of the root area is traditionally the energy of the physical plane and material reality. People with strong energy in this center usually have a red color here and have good survival skills. This is also the center of manifestation. If you are trying to succeed in the world, either by making more money, establishing a business, or accumulating possessions, you will be focusing your energy here. This is also the place from which passion flows, the source of power and ego development.

Ultraviolet root: Most likely, you have been experiencing a profoundly synchronistic period in your life as things seem to mysteriously come to you and fall into place almost automatically. People probably see you as mystical and magical. What you want comes to you as if by magic. You seem to effortlessly receive all that you need.

Violet root: Your aura shines and radiates outward towards others with loving, healing energy. You put a high vibrational frequency out into the world. Violet symbolizes magic, mysticism, and visionary capacity. At this point in your life, things are probably flowing easily. You do not put out unnecessary effort. You are efficient and relaxed in your worldly dealings. This stage is probably a time of ease rather than of struggle. You have taken care of the most practical aspects of your life and now can concentrate on your spirituality, creativity, and artistic pursuits.

Light violet root: Your desires can be surprisingly varied now. It is almost as if your body can sense what is right for you now. Somehow you get everything you need without effort or struggle. People may be in awe or jealous of how easily and happily you can live without worry or perhaps without much money. Somehow, you have mastered the material plane and now can move onto more spiritual pursuits.

Lavender root: People sense your high energy. There is no doubt that the deep and the as yet unknown are important to you and your self-satisfaction. Somehow, you have managed to transcend the physical plane, in a sense, because you easily negotiate your worldly affairs without worry, stress, or effort. Others wonder how you accomplish things so easily. You just let everything flow, and everything gets done.

White root: White, being a combination of all colors, signifies an affinity with the holistic, the spiritual, and the non-physical. Practical matters probably hold little importance to you. You do not live for money, material wealth, or prestige. Your spirituality, your relationship with the Creator, and healing service to others are your most important concerns.

Blue/white root: The world sees you as a spiritual healer whether you consciously know it or not. You glow with a mysterious inner light. Others know that you are tapped into something profound and divine. You probably are not the most ambitious person in the world and are more concerned with having a pleasant day than amassing great amounts of capital or possessions.

Light blue root: People respond to your powerful healing presence. The world sees you as serene, calm, and peaceful. You have a generally quiet and contemplative nature that has a pacifying effect on others. You move in the world with ease and, above all, great patience. You create calmness and tranquility wherever you go. Even the angriest, most irrational, and irate people act like gentle puppy dogs when they are around you.

Blue root: The calmness of blue gives you a nature that is willing to stop and think and contemplate others. Your own sense of self benefits from your ability to communicate with yourself. You have extraordinary patience and are able to solve the most chaotic of situations peacefully and quickly. You are a natural diplomat and generous to a tee.

Aquamarine root: The combination of green and blue now allows you to dedicate yourself more to your being. Balance and harmony are almost all you need for a fulfilling life. Your trust in yourself can be very strong now. There is not a competitive bone in your body, and you run your professional life according to your spiritual ideals.

Turquoise root: You can be generous to yourself, and that doesn't necessarily mean materially. By rewarding yourself, doubts and inhibitions fade away. Just remember not to give too much energy away to others. By striking the balance, you can find great happiness within and without.

Green root: Your ability to heal yourself and to share that energy with others is outstanding. Your generosity is a strength of your character. Although you are ambitious, sometimes your big heart can get in the way and prevent you from attaining your professional goals. You may make a million dollars, but watch yourself—you may just give it all away.

Yellow/green root: Success is in store for you, and the world is your oyster. You feel prosperous, and you manifest prosperity out in the world. You are hard-working and do not necessarily expect something for nothing. You are alert for new opportunities and fun in your life, which in turn can bring you greater fulfillment and joy.

Green/yellow root: Be prepared to have the life you always wanted. You've been preparing for success, and now you're about to enter into it. The world sees you as cheerful, happy, and confident. Yellow is the color of sunshine, warmth, and intellectual capability, while green is the color of healing, change, self-confidence, and discipline. A transition for the better is more than likely taking place.

Yellow root: Fun is what you want to concentrate on now. No matter what you do, it needs to be an enjoyable experience. You may be successful in your business or career if it is fun and creative for you. You probably do not like strict routines and enjoy a changing environment. You may often find yourself the center of attention, because others see you as radiant and self-expressive.

Gold root: This is a special time for you. Believe it. If you have any doubts, let them go now and you will know you are very important. You're a shining star. You feel it, know it, and people recognize you as someone special. You are a natural entertainer or spiritual leader. Worldly success is inevitable.

Golden orange root: You are a fountain of creativity, joy, and inspiration. You express cheerfulness, friendliness, and warmth to the world. You may enjoy expressing yourself in many different ways. You are ready to do what you want to do, no matter what it is. This is your time. Success is at hand!

Orange root: You are a fountain of creative energy! This period is your time to do all the things you've ever wanted to do. What have been your most outrageous, outlandish goals? These things are the ones you are ready to do now! Orange represents creativity, and doing things in your own way with your own style can develop your individuality. Your ability to think for yourself is enhanced.

Red/orange root: You are a dynamo of creative, powerful energy. You may wear people out with your enthusiasm! There's too much out there in the world for you to accomplish and do! Your personality is powerfully creative and full of passion. You have freedom in your heart and tend to be an independent spirit. You want to test the limits of your physical as well as creative nature. People know you as an adventurous, unique, risk-taking, and fun-loving individual. You also have a practical side and take care of things on the material level quite efficiently. Money, possessions, financial stability, and security are all important to you.

Orange/red root: Material success and adventure are in store for you, and you are probably feeling powerful and confident of your abilities. You are aware of what your unique gifts are. The personality you show to the world is dynamically creative and full of passion. You have freedom in your heart and tend to be an independent spirit. You want to test the limits of your physical as well as creative nature. People know you as an adventurous, unique, risk-taking, and fun-loving individual.

Red root: You are bound to be successful. You have the drive and energy to run a successful business or enterprise. Material comfort and wealth are probably quite important to you. Your confidence and desire for life open doors for you. Because you are willing to put yourself forward, you get what you need.

Infrared root: Your drive and will to succeed are exceptional. As long as you concentrate on what is most important, success is achieved with lightning speed. Remember that exercise, rest, and a balanced diet will keep the fire burning longer inside of you.

CHAPTER ELEVEN

COLOR AND THE AURIC ENERGY FIELD

Experiments in Auric Colors

Chip Weston, BA

WHEN I WAS VERY LITTLE, I lived in a "soft" world populated by luminous eggs of all different shapes and sizes. From my crib, I could see the objects in my room as enticing cocoons of light with shapes inside. Colors themselves glowed with their own penetrating energy aura . . . so for me, I saw energy-field upon energy-field, all with objects "trapped" inside. The objects were secondary to the more interesting light that surrounded them. When the sun would shine through the shades and cast shadows on the wall, still more diverse waves of energy would stream forth . . . even the shadows had their own presence; seeing was a continuous show. I remember that my senses were more an amalgam of a continuous spectrum of energy waves. Seeing was connected to smelling which was connected to taste and touch. Hearing penetrated all four of the other senses. Each glow had its own sound; when all was quiet, the room would hum with a "silent" symphony that seemed to beat with my heart and flow with my breath.

When another person would enter the field of energy that was my room, a great change would take place. The once extremely calm and subtle energies would shudder like shaking Jell-O, loud sounds would rip through the peaceful sound field; strong smells would disrupt the atmosphere of odors that had been stratified and ordered a moment before. Bursts of dancing sparklets of energy would fly from the calm, shimmering fields and commingle or fly away and merge with others or disappear completely. My soft environment would split, as a strong and powerful force would surf through from the doorway, usually directly toward me. I became aware of another energy force that was an intense emotional force projected out directly toward me. This force was an underlying intent, projecting from deep within a more visible field, that carried its own special colors, smell, and especially heat. Although intense, it was not usually scary.

Slowly, I learned to separate the different energies into distinct patterns of different textured energy "glows." Although these glowing energy fields remained attached and influenced each other, they had their own rhythm, vibration. I also realized that the other people who came into my room were very interested in the objects inside the energy fields and paid no attention to the fields themselves. Gradually, I learned to see the objects more distinctly. I remained very aware of the intentions projected by other people and continued to see intent as a force projected from either the middle of the body or the head. It was real obvious that my mom and dad had different intentions toward me. They were each moving universes of different swirling stars and planets, clouds and sprites. Their colors and light intensities were different. Mom was attentive and comforting, and Dad was more playful and happy. Mom was more focused, and Dad was more expansive. Their joy at being around me quickly overcame the often intense smells and other lurking energies they also possessed. Other people had very different energy auras, which were often not projected at me but were swirling around within themselves, distracted, like masks with a lot of activity behind them. I was very leery of these people because I intuited that they were more like a thunderstorm in the usually calm, warm air of my room. I did not like for most people to touch me or pick me up because they were a cacophony of strong and bad smells, and a swirl of different energies that disrupted my energy field when they got too close. If someone was sick, they really smelled bad and they had deep pockets of darkness. I really wanted to avoid them and didn't even like them to come into the room because it took a long time for their energy to go away and the room to come back to normal . . . in a sense, I was my whole room because the energy that was me was merged with the room.

Seeing Auras

In meditation class, I ask my students what they want to achieve by learning meditation techniques and try to demonstrate procedures to facilitate their particular intent. For many, meditation is an ethereal affair because the experience is not navigated by a clear road map. Our culture does not have a consensus vocabulary and symbolic language by which we can codify our inner experience to ourselves and to each other. When I ask a student to articulate the change before and after their meditation, it is often difficult, and typically a new student will simply say they feel great, more relaxed, more aware. For this reason alone, it is of considerable benefit to teach techniques that enable students to see the auras around themselves and others. Seeing auras reinforces the meditative experience and allows a student to progress at a rapid pace. What the student eventually does with the new information is critical to the continued ability to perceive auras. The premise is that seeing auras is an atrophied ability that needs to be awakened. Once reactivated, then the student needs to learn what to do with the information that they now have become aware of. A good analogy can be made using the 3-D stereo noise images that are popular in posters and calendars (such as the *Hidden Dimension* by Dan Dyckman). By looking at these images correctly, you can begin to discover three-dimensional images that pop out from the background of undifferentiated noise. Do these images have more than entertainment value or can they contain useful information? Do auras have more than entertainment value? Do we need to develop a consensus on how to interpret auras? Do we need to learn how not to project our own filters on the auras so that they can convey more germane information about their source? These questions and their answers can be developed elsewhere and are of little relevance unless a person can see an aura. The following are four techniques that are helpful in learning to perceive auras.

Remembering . . .

Many people can remember seeing auras when they were young children. Guided meditations specifically designed to stimulate these memories are beneficial in helping a person remember how to see auras. Typically, a memory is rekindled in which a person was able to sense an aura, and the meditation facilitator tries to expand the memory, temporally, spatially, and emotionally. The person is asked to describe the experience in detail. After the meditation, the person is asked to write down the event and think about what the most memorable object was in the experience. That object becomes the key to reentering the experience at will. In the next meditation, the student is asked to remember that object-key. The person is quickly brought into the experience in which they have seen auras, and then a "bridge" is constructed to their present reality by helping them be in both places at once. A student who is able to remember seeing auras will often be able to translate part of that memory into a temporary ability in their present moment. Remembering the object from their past forms an association that hastens the memory and the subsequent ability to see auras. A student can also be instructed to try to see the object-key in their dreams. Some people are able to see auras in their dreams even though they cannot see them in their waking state. Once a student is able to see or "feel" an energy field, with the guidance of a meditation facilitator, they usually can progress to noticing more detail in the auric field. Different people sense auras differently. Some can hear an aura, some feel it emotionally, some perceive it as fluctuations in temperature, etc. It is important for the instructor to start with whatever perceptive strengths the student has and build on those; the heart of the Remembering Technique is to create an integration of consciousness between the otherwise dissociated states. The premise of Remembering is that our ability to see auras has atrophied in the consensus reality we share with society. We all perceive auras at some level, but we just do not remember the experience in our waking consciousness.

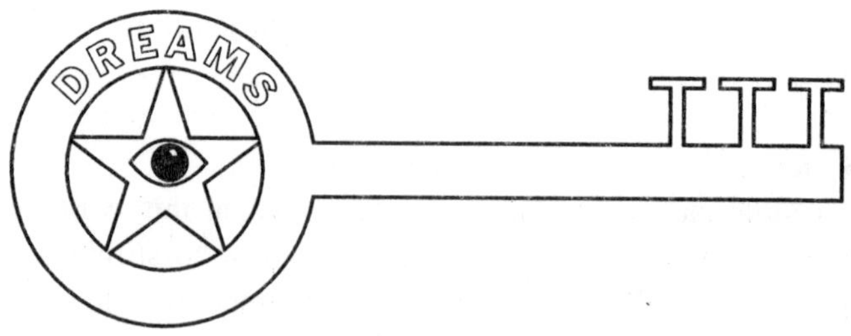

Daydreams

For the purpose of this discussion, let us postulate that there is a difference between Imagination and Fantasy. Imagination is a way to "pre-create" that which can become real, and Fantasy is the creation of an ethereal world that cannot become part of the consensus reality shared with other souls. Grounded imagination can become a powerful tool. By using a person's ability to imagine or daydream and by creating the proper environment for this to take place, a facilitator can quickly help a person to perceive auras. When you watch elite athletes, eyes closed before an event, imagining the perfect way they intend to move their bodies, you see that this imaginative-visualization practice has become an accepted and successful technique. A facilitator can use a similar technique by guiding a person to their imaginary self and asking that "I self" to tell them what they see. A person will often be surprised to find that their imaginary self is quite adept at seeing and describing auras. When a person is empowered by their imaginary self to see auras in their waking existence, it is important to integrate these two states of consciousness. It is crucial to learn to "hand off" the knowledge gained from the perceptions of the imagination to the waking personality. By the consistent use of the imagination and the conscious dialogue between the ego and the imagination, integration can quickly be achieved with spectacular results. It is important to remember that a good facilitator never suggests what a person should see but listens intently to what the person says they do see. The facilitator should always use techniques that keep a person grounded. Fantasy will not lead to success, and Imagination should lead to Reality.

Although often a gradual process, meditation builds upon itself and creates a vocabulary and a compilation of symbols by which an individual can recreate a heightened sensory ability. When the basics are successfully embodied, more advanced techniques can lead to the detailed perception of the auras in waking consciousness. The prerequisite to advanced meditation and its attribute of the detailed perception of auras is "stopping the world."

Stopping the World

Typically, an advanced meditation student will learn a technique that focuses their conscious attention in the mid-point between the two hemispheres of their brain. Preliminary techniques that have increased the energy stored in their bodies and stretching "asanas" help to empower, align, and relax the student. Proper posture helps to sustain the experience. A quiet environment eliminates distraction, and the facilitator's occasional vocal instruction keeps the focus.

A great disassociation with the external world is achieved by closing your eyes and going inside to a specific point. To help a student achieve this solitude, a meditation instructor may say something similar to this: "Watch your breath; sit straight; feel the beating of your heart; go within. Now, inhale and feel the energy moving up your back, and bring it up to your head; bring the energy into the midpoint between the two hemispheres; go four inches deep, exactly between the eyebrows. Exactly between the ears find the spot of light, sound, and vibration that resides deep within. Now, exhale and bring the energy back down. Continue to feel the infinite energy of the Universe rising with your breath and falling with your exhalation." A few minutes pass as the instructor looks for signs that the student has achieved a first level of withdrawal from the external world. Now the instructor says, "Pinpoint your attention in the center of the pituitary gland; look for sound, light, and vibration; be calm, be still." The meditation instructor can easily perceive when a student enters the profound state of calmness. The person almost floats, as though lifted by a force just over their head which pulls them up. Their breathing becomes almost imperceptible; their face glows. When this state is achieved and maintained for a few minutes, the instructor begins to guide them back into the consensus reality. The trick is to allow the student to remain in the calm, meditative state and yet be able to open their eyes. "Slowly open your eyes without focusing on anything," or "Tilt your head up and open your eyes . . . don't focus, just look through the wall where the ceiling and the wall come together." These instructions allow the student to maintain their meditative state. It is in this part of the meditation that an instructor can help a person to notice auras. Instructors who are able to project vast amounts of energy can ask the student to look at a spot a few inches over the instructor's head. "Relax your eyes, don't focus . . . just look above my head." The student is asked to describe what they see. It is usually easy for the instructor to tell the difference between fantasy and actual discernment. It is also imperative that the instructor not use suggestion. Only actual perceptions by the student can become the real foundation for seeing auras.

Any other apprehensions will only add to the world of delusion that many people already find a hindrance to their potential to become enlightened beings. Eventually, students can keep their world still while speaking and seeing their instructor. Instructors are able to alter their own auras and ask the students what they see and, thus, evaluate a student's progress. It is often at this stage that an advanced student can really begin to distinguish layers and colors of auras and the interconnected threads of luminosity that form the subliminal web of creation.

Difficulty Seeing Auras

In my experience, many people are able to remember seeing auras at some time in their lives. I have worked with many artists and musicians. They will often remember seeing auras when they are "in the flow," "participating in the great, ongoing event," "in the grove," etc. Why don't these artists see auras all of the time? What takes us away from our ability to see more deeply into the roots of reality?

We live in a material consensus reality. We quickly become conditioned by society to quantifiable consensus—a hierarchy of things, "who ever dies with the most toys!" Behavioral scientists, building on the work of Pavlov, time and again are able to explain consensus reality in terms of repetition and conditioning. The same behavioral modification techniques that can be used to break habits can also be used to break through the encrusted filters on the doors of our perception. But it is the integration of the diverse states of human consciousness that must be bridged in order for the wisdom of the enlightened states of consciousness to impact favorably on our daily lives. The quality that musicians experience when they play Bach in a small chapel before a transfixed assembly is too ethereal to fit into the average quantified reality. Their epiphany is relegated to its own separate dimension and finds a difficult time integrating into the musician's daily life. The glow of the musical performance fades as the musician fights the traffic on the way home and experiences the demands and desires of the family and friends who have not had the same experience. The "holy" vibration is quickly devoured by the contending noise of consensus reality.

"Primitive" societies used rituals to map out the directions to a richer reality, and often whole societies were able to perceive the energy which surrounds and attaches all things. They would spend days and nights after the ritual trying to understand and integrate the experience into the daily existence. But for us, the avenues to these perceptions are barricaded by material and social desire, association, conditioning, and superstition. Our very beliefs are often the primary barrier to a "greater seeing." Exercises which temporarily suspend belief are often the prerequisite to helping one to rekindle the ability to see auras. When we are babies, we have no beliefs and see the world through only the filters of our genetic limitations. As we get older, we put filter after filter between our raw perception and physical reality. Although necessary to function in society, these filters are often impediments to "real seeing." Learning to temporarily remove specific filters gains us the vantage of a much larger spectrum of vibration.

Trees and Stars

One of my favorite exercises centers around learning to see the auras of trees at night. When all else fails, this simple exercise usually brings quick success. All you need is a quiet place where you can stand undisturbed for about ten minutes. Hopefully, there will be few distractions, e.g., temperature, insects, cars, other people, etc. Stand so that you can see a bright star through or slightly above the silhouettes of trees. It works best if the trees are at least one hundred feet away so that you can take in the entire shape of the tree(s). Stand comfortably, tall and straight. Feel that you are part of the Earth and that gravity is pulling you straight down. Feel that you have grown roots into the ground and have become like a tree. Now look intently at the star. Try to see the star from a place about four inches deep, straight in from the center point between your eyebrows. Now, keep your eyes open wide, but don't strain. Try to look within the star, and let your eyes relax enough so that the star splits into two stars. Now, your eyes relax even more. Keep your attention directed at the star on your left if you are right-handed, vice versa if you are left-handed. Your mind may tell you that there is only one star and that your

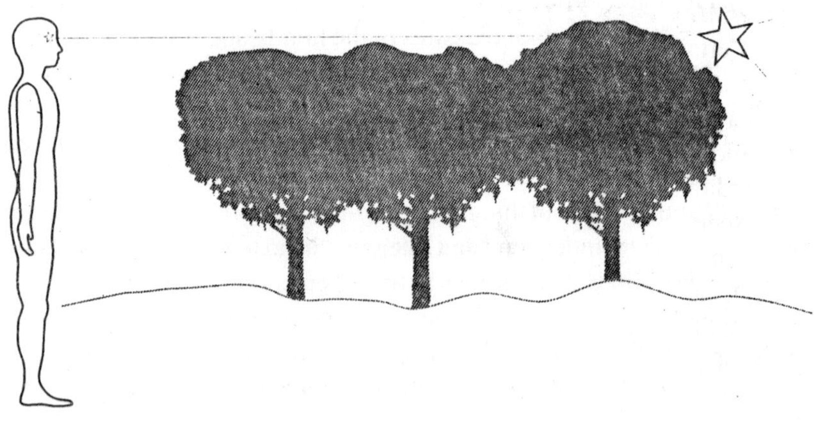

eyes are out of focus, but just relax more and go with the experience. You may become very calm, aware of your breath, of your heart beat. Just relax and keep looking from the center point. You may notice that your stomach muscles relax and your lungs expand. Now, without moving your gaze, notice your peripheral vision. See if something has changed, as if all of a sudden you are able to take in more light from the corners of your eyes. If you notice a change, that things have become brighter, then pay attention to the dark silhouettes of the tree tops. See what happens. If you are prone to suggestion, you may choose not to read the next paragraph until you have tried this experiment.

Often, within three or four minutes of beginning this exercise, people will shift their perception. One second they are seeing the star, and the next they have noticed that the trees have "caught on fire" and glow with bright colors. If they pay more attention, they will often notice that the trees are connected to each other. Soon the trees seem to be swaying, even dancing on a subliminal breeze. By doing this exercise over and over in the same spot, a relationship may be formed with the trees. When this experience happens, a person may be able to perceive the consciousness of the trees. At this point, a whole new type of reality emerges where one is able to see both into and out of the aura. Often, people describe seeing threads of glowing light or lines of force which seem to connect everything together. This profound vision seems to mirror the quantum theories because, from this vantage, our every thought, movement, and emotion run out along these fibers and alter all of reality in all directions. From this place of perception, we can see ourselves creating our own reality.

Other Methods

Certain colors and sounds also tend to amplify the experience, as do the practices of different arts, Ch'i Kung, and intense endurance sports. PrimaSounds, mentioned elsewhere in this book, combined with other techniques, help to amplify the soft glow that most people are able to see around other people. Spending quality time with people who see auras also seems to help. If you can remember to recall your dreams, then you can remember to see auras. It is a similar process based on desire and intent, emotion and will. While drugs, hypnotic suggestion, and early life or past life regressions also work to allow people to experience auras, the lack of integration between these states of amplified sensing and the person's everyday reality are often so great that the person remains unable to perceive auras in their daily life. If an aura is worth seeing, then a person should be willing to make gradual but persistent progress. Trying too hard for ego sake alone can lead to fantasy that, at best, leads nowhere. But trying to truthfully remember "who am I" and "why am I here . . . what did I come into this life to achieve or experience" are most helpful to place a person in the right frame of mind to see auras. These almost magical questions seem to loosen our focus of perception from its everyday location and help us to relocate it in a place more conducive to letting in the vast amount of electromagnetic vibration that is normally filtered out. Realizing how useful it is to see auras is a great stimulus and necessity is the mother of invention. If you have to move to Spain, you had better learn Spanish. When you grasp how useful it is to perceive a person's intent and emotional characteristics, you should be motivated to learn to see auras. When you realize that a glimpse of a person's aura is a direct picture of their soul at a particular place and time, you begin to realize that seeing auras holds profound responsibility. When you stand in front of a full length mirror and look at your own aura, you see the reality of who you are. This is not a practice for the faint of heart. Accepting yourself as you are and remembering your mission in life brings a clarity of perception that opens you to a greater reality. Self-awareness and self-realization lead to love. Being profoundly in love is perhaps the best way to move our point of perception to a location where we see the beautiful auras of our friends, the Earth, and the Universe.

CHAPTER TWELVE

AURIC AND EMOTIONAL STABILITY BASED ON COLOR TECHNIQUES

Margo von Phul, BFA

THE AURA IS THE SPIRITUAL RESULT of contact between the physical and nonphysical worlds. From all levels of our auric field, we pick up sensory data that we call our intuition. Our intuition is a channel for using the knowledge of the spirit to direct physical life. Intuition passes information back and forth between the physical and nonphysical worlds. Much of the intuitive process is not performed on a conscious level. Intuition is more like a television antenna picking up data as needed. Sometimes these frequencies overlap, and questions or unclear messages are created.

The auric field is actually a distinct rainbow each person is given. By our very existence, we become a rainbow. The colors of the rainbow also reside within our bodies. Diverse colors are in our skin tones, hair follicles, eyes, lips, blood, and bone. Each one is a part of a very subtle rainbow of colors and energy. Our rainbows define who we are without needing words. Our individual rainbows are unique and far more amazing than any rainbow we could see in the sky.

The aura is far more complex and dense than the beautiful color bands some people perceive. It appears as a delicate colored mist; however, it is really an extremely strong energy field. The auric field acts as a protective layer, offering a shield from the potentially deadly rays of the sun. The ozone layer is earth's protective aura, but that alone cannot offer us full protection. The aura provides additional protection, giving us the ability to survive on this planet. The auric energy field is tough yet flexible, much like an incredible, space-age material. Thus far there is no material quite like it found in the physical world.

Color Organization of Auric Bands

The auric bands are organized into seven different color regions of the body. The colors create balance between the physical, mental, emotional, and spiritual aspects of a person. The aura is a perfect energy system that guides and controls all aspects of our existence. It is the higher electromagnetic information we gave ourselves before we were born and acts as our light. Through development of intuition, we can learn about the colors of our auric bodies. This knowledge is valuable to us in the areas of health. Understanding the basic characteristics of the seven colors is the first step toward developing intuitive ability to perceive the aura.

Red is the first color in the aura and in ancient symbolism represents the body and the earth. Due to being the warmest of all colors, it stimulates the body. Red helps increase circulation and can be an invigorating tonic to those who need it. Red is stimulating and exciting. It is the fire element, concerned with strength, endurance, human affection, willpower, justice, progress, evolution, and new ventures. It creates an impulse to win and a drive to achieve. Red vitalizes the physical body and the nervous system. Red foods, i.e., apples, tomatoes, wearing red, have been recommended to people experiencing inertia, physical exhaustion, worry, and fear.

Orange is the color of the sun. It represents joy and positive construction. Orange is a vital, good color generally indicating consideration for others as well as thoughtfulness and peacemaking. This color can strengthen the lungs, pancreas, and spleen. Orange symbolizes understanding, tolerance, wisdom, concrete thoughts, and mental stimulation. It is related to new ideas, all forms of leadership, and self-discipline. Orange stimulates physical vitality and mental attitude, while combining both to enliven emotions. It produces a feeling of well-being. Orange foods help bring in some of the aspects mentioned. Natural sunshine also has a positive effect as an orange vibration.

Yellow is the second primary color. It indicates health, well-being, intellect, and thought. Yellow cleanses, stimulates, and increases activity. It also enhances one's artistic and creative abilities. Yellow represents unity, spirituality, self-control, balance, optimism, original ideas, and inspiration. It operates on many levels, bringing in intelligence, wisdom, logic, balance, optimism, and an overall harmonious attitude toward life. Yellow radiates an optimistic and joyous energy that affects the nervous system and stimulates the mind. The color yellow has been recommended for depression, mental lethargy, nervous exhaustion, and some skin troubles. Yellow foods and sunshine counteract these conditions.

Green is the color of balance. When a little bit of blue is added, it also has great restorative healing properties. It is the color of doctors and nurses and symbolizes youthfulness and fertility. Green is a helpful, strong, and friendly color, while representing balance and self-control. Abundance, growth, hope, newness, and peace are also associated with green. It represents the physical home and harmony. It prevents complacency of thought and is one of nature's best tonics to relieve tension. Green is the bridge between personality and spirit. Green's energy both relaxes the body and stimulates the nervous system. It has been recommended for muscle tension, sleeplessness, headaches, and nervous irritability. Eating green foods, taking nature walks, and wearing green can provide a welcome change from the hectic pace of life.

Blue is the color of faith and aspiration. The selfless love spirit, the symbol of contemplation, prayer, and devotion, is associated with blue. It is a soothing color representing inspiration and high spiritual ideals. It can represent life dedicated to unselfish causes such as science, art, or social service. There are wonderful characteristics attributed to this color such as loyalty, femininity, illumination, tenderness, unity, and emotional contentment. Sensory perception, hope, and serenity, associated with blue, have a calming effect on the nervous system and mental attitude. Blue foods and blue clothing have been recommended for sore eyes, earaches, sore throats, hoarseness, and nausea.

Indigo is the color of practical idealism. It is life's intuitive faculty that provides energy to relieve fears, frustrations, and inhibitions. It is the philosopher and adjuster of problems. It is attuned to the reality of living. Indigo enhances the understanding of the self and helps transmit understanding to others. Indigo has the ability to idealize and reform and broaden the horizons of the mind. Indigo helps us show noble compassion. This color has been recommended for eyes, ears, nose, throat, lungs, and stomach. Indigo can be ingested through foods or worn as clothing.

Violet's energy represents intuitiveness. Its energy purifies the blood, calms the nerves, and inspires the brain with mental and spiritual uplifts. The color represents a transition in life from turbulence to the higher realms of faith. Violet is associated with divine love, honesty, humility, and kingship. It offers a true understanding of life for those seeking its meaning. It attracts spiritual power, honor, and is a self-ruler, with understanding of the abstract nature of power. Violet foods have been recommended for insomnia, eye troubles, diseases of the scalp, and dandruff.

The aura can be compared to a computer, with colors likened to different software programs. Each one can have different files or macros within the main program. There are different tasks for each color or band of color. Through development of intuition, we can learn about our auric bodies. Our aura guides us through physical obstacles, letting us know which direction is right for us. It guides us through the myriad of emotions by making us aware of what we need or don't need from others. The aura acts as our guide through the spiritual realm, giving us clues along the way. These clues can guide us through events to avoid serious accidents or alert us by causing the hair on our arm to stand on end.

Color Vibrations and Proper Living

The seven basic color vibrations of the aura enhance learning processes. The vibrations related to specific colors can also push us through these processes when we are reluctant to go any further. Each of the seven color vibrations can be measured on a scale where the greatest intensity would be 100. Each intensity along this scale would relate to the manner the color manifests itself within the individual. For example, strong red bands in the range of 90-95 would give quite a bit of energy for considerable physical perseverance. This type of intensity of red would be found in athletes, public speakers, and people involved in outdoor work. Less intense red values of 50 or less would still give quite a bit of energy but not necessarily in the athletic or physical aspects. If there is a need for this energy from red, red-colored food can fuel our physical being. In a like manner, we seek the visual color red to satisfy our need for love, caring, and compassion for others. If the color red, or any one color for that matter, is lacking or weak, problems associated with that color will occur.

Operating without all your colors is like functioning without all the necessary nutrients and vitamins needed to maintain good health. You may function for a while, but over time the deficiencies will cause problems in health and well-being. The auric colors also reflect what is happening inside the body. In addition to foods, vitamins have a profound effect on the aura. The right combination of foods and vitamins translate through the body to the aura to maintain its balance.

The individual can keep the auric body balanced in many other ways as well. Exercise is an excellent method of organizing the color bands and giving each one more definition. The aura is a reflection of what is occurring internally. Maintaining a balanced, organized aura keeps the body in a state of health. Meditation is another excellent way of giving the body rest. The silence and focus of meditation allow the colors of the aura to rearrange themselves into the appropriate channels.

Depleting Mental and Emotional Energies

There are situations that deplete mental and emotional energies, leaving the aura depleted of vibrant colors. Letting go of these stressful situations and feelings allows the colors of the aura to regroup naturally into their appropriate bands. When there is a deficiency created by stress, a gentle auric repairing needs to be performed. Through gentle exercise, rest, meditations, and kind thoughts performed slowly and steadily, colors can be restored.

While the physical body may be healed with traditional medicine, surgery, laser, and the like, nothing is done to the aura, an important part of overall health. The aura is not affected by traditional medical methods, therefore, often the illness returns. Mostly technology and physical medicine have pushed the limit on physical recovery. The near future will be a combination of already tested and true physical medicine and an enhancement of information from the auric field. The recovery from illness will include traditional methods along with some aura healing ones still virtually unstudied.

The existence of an aura can explain the phantom pain effect when a limb is removed. It is like a loose connection or exposed or missing wire or a tear in the auric field. When the aura is not realigned along with the physical treatment, it is like having a front end car accident and not getting the car realigned. Sure, it will run, but not with the same efficiency as before it was hit.

Conclusion

The future will bring new programs and methods that a person can integrate into their auric field for maintenance, much like adding computer programs to enhance the capability of your computer. Methods for wellness, genetic selection, mental awareness, and spiritual understanding will be uncovered. There are two ways the human aura can be balanced. One is by healers and people trained in the intuitive field of energetic healing. Another will be the use of new machines and methods to be developed in the future. Increased awareness of spirituality will lead to greater understanding of what the aura colors represent and how to use them to heal the body.

With the physical environment being so polluted, the addition of more and more toxic materials, and the use of certain medicines and procedures, humanity is being weakened. The aura, being connected to the larger universal energy field, can rehabilitate itself quicker than the physical body. This is simply because the vibration is different. The aura acts as an energetic surge protector for many pollutants. The aura colors have a quick recovery time; however, the body's ability to benefit from them is impaired if the condition of the body is compromised. Usually this process works very well, except when the body has been stressed through drug or alcohol use or factors affecting the mental or physical well-being. Given the amount of pressure these factors apply to the aura, it is nothing short of a miracle that it continues to survive. The ability of the auric field to adjust to negative factors illustrates just how strong it is. The aura keeps the body whole even though the renewal of the physical body is impaired. The aura field allows the alcoholic or drug addict to live for many years before the toxins accumulate and overdose finally results.

We may wish to attract specific colors for our well-being or just for fun. We can wear colors to overcome things or just because we feel better in them. We can dress intuitively, knowing what colors we need on given days. We can mentally assign each day to a different hue and color. And we can do the same with people, situations, and the outside environment. If we learn to trust our intuition, it will guide us as to what colors we need to balance our lives and ourselves.

SECTION IV:

MENTAL, PHYSICAL, AND SPIRITUAL HEALING

CHAPTER THIRTEEN

PSYCHOPHYSICS
A Holistic Approach to Energy or Auric Healing

Julia Melges Jablonski, BA

SKEPTICISM REGARDING AURAS has been centered mainly in the West. In the late 1800s, there was great interest and research into life energy and the use of electrical and magnetic devices for healing in the United States. There were no national safeguards at this time, and some of these treatments may have been dangerous or harmful. In 1909, the U.S. government sponsored the *Flexner Report* with the aim of upgrading and standardizing medical care and education nationally. This report made electromagnetic healing treatments illegal and ruled that electromagnetic energy was in no way involved in physiology or medicine. Research in bio-energy was deemed preposterous and quickly fell into disrepute (Eidelman 1995).

In Eastern and other cultures, treatment of illness through the aura is an ancient and continuing practice. Mystics and "seers" have traditionally held highly respected positions in these cultures as shamans, healers, and medicine people. Western academia, by contrast, has rejected and derided intuitive knowledge during the last century. Recent developments, however, negate the possibility of true objectivity in research and demand the integration of subjective experience with scientific methodology.

Research in the twentieth century has led to the development of sensitive technology that has proven the existence of luminescent energy fields surrounding living organisms (see Chapters Two & Five). And, through modern technology, we can now observe, measure, and explain the energetic basis for auric healing (Alvino 1966).

Psychophysics: The Wave of the Future

In approaching the human aura or electromagnetic energy field from a scientific perspective, one must expand on the traditional scientific approach. The traditional focus of science is on the mechanical processes involved in the physical or mechanical realm. While this approach yields a great deal of knowledge about the physical world, to adequately observe psi phenomena one must expand the traditional mechanical model to include the non-physical. Psi phenomena such as auric fields, extra-sensory perception, and spiritual healing, contradict physical laws and transcend space and time. It is little wonder scientists often conclude that psi phenomenon do not exist. They are trying to study five-dimensional phenomena in a three-dimensional model (the fourth dimension being time).

Traditional science typically stands at the edge of the known world and tries to move into new territory using "maps" of the already-conquered territory as guides. This scientific approach tends to blind them to the potential scope of the vast unknown territory ahead. Non-traditional researchers, inventors, and thinkers, on the other hand, tend to use a "plane" to fly into the wilderness and then work their way back, and in the process, they create the maps for the less daring to follow after them.

Some of the greatest thinkers and inventors in history were such pioneer researchers, and they often faced the same scorn from the establishment that psychic phenomena researchers face today. A study of people historically recognized for their creative and innovative work led to the development of a six-step model of the creative process based upon the works of these individuals. The study concluded that a person must possess a "capacity to see things without prejudice for the conventional" (Schwartz 1990). Relatively few people possess such a capacity, creating the basis for the perceived chasm between "science" and "spiritual" understanding. While there is much work to be done in integrating these two spheres of thought, there is in actuality no true conflict between them.

What does this concept have to do with auras? Despite the skeptical reaction of many well-educated individuals to the existence of the aura, electromagnetic fields have been proven to exist around all living things. An abundance of research data exists that illustrates the nature of all life and matter to be empty space with patterns of energy running through it and demonstrates the effects of the interactions of these subtle energy fields (see Chapter One).

Scientific Research Supporting Life Energy Fields

Until recent times, conscious perception of these auric energy fields was the province of clairvoyants, healers, and sensitives. With the development of ever more sensitive technology, however, we are now able to objectively measure these energy fields and interactions. That all living organisms are surrounded by electromagnetic fields is not disputed today (Eidelman 1995; see Payne's Chapter Five). The electrostatic field surrounding the human body can be easily measured by a static meter (Bentov 1988). These fields have been measured and even photographed in experiments with humans, animals, and plants.

For example, EKGs measure the electrical impulses of the heart, and EEGs measure the magnetic fields around our heads resulting from the tiny electrical currents in the brain. Polygraph tests measure the human body's electrical potential, and fluctuations in this energy provide feedback in response to the subject's thoughts and emotions. Aura Imaging Photography using hand-shaped plate sensors measure the "electromagnetic field, based upon the Ayurvedic (acupressure points on the hand) system of meridians" (Hurkos 1996). Finally, Kirlian photography, as detailed in Chapter Two, captures a representation of electromagnetic fields on film, transferring the aura of the subject to film by placing the subject of the photograph (such as a leaf or a human hand) directly onto the photographic plate and passing high-frequency electrical currents through it.

Semyon Kirlian, the co-developer of this photography, was asked in 1950 to photograph the energy radiations of two nearly identical leaves presented to him by a stranger. He and his wife stayed up late into the night, but despite their efforts, one leaf revealed strong energy flares on film while the other barely registered even weak luminescence. When they showed their dismal results to the stranger the next day, he became very excited, for despite their identical appearance, the leaf that had revealed strong energy had been plucked from a healthy plant, and the leaf that had registered little energy had been plucked from a diseased plant. Subsequent Kirlian research has shown that the energy photographed around plants is indeed related to its vitality or life, for if a leaf is injured or allowed to die, the energy will gradually diminish and then disappear (Tompkins & Bird 1973).

Interaction of Electromagnetic Fields

Research into the energetic aura surrounding plants and humans has found that non-biological electromagnetic waves have a strong impact on the energy fields of other living organisms and even that the electromagnetic fields of living organisms interact with and affect each other. All living beings appear to be in constant communication with and affect each other, even down to the cellular level.

Not only do the energy fields of people and plants affect each other, but highly sophisticated measurements reveal that the tiniest change in any system in the body affects all other systems of the body in some manner (Bentov 1988). How is it that these systems affect each other? The answer to this question provides the mechanisms behind psi phenomena, such as extrasensory perception, telepathy, and auric healing.

Everything, everyone, every action, every thought, every feeling—ALL is energy. Physicists have established that all life, indeed all matter, is empty space with matrices of oscillating energy fields running through it. These waves radiate out at the velocity of light into the farthest reaches of the cosmos and interact with all other radiating waves, as detailed in Chapter One. These energy fields interlock with neighboring fields as they radiate out into the cosmos. By our bodies' very nature, as transmitters of energy, they are also receivers of energy. Therefore, life is constantly communicating and interacting with everything else in the universe on subtle or imperceptible energy levels. This common basis of all things as interconnected energy is reminiscent of the "Oneness" of existence central to many spiritual philosophies (Bentov 1988).

The Underlying Mechanisms in Energy Healing — Thoughts Are Energy

The nervous system is a conductor of electrical impulses that order our biological rhythms from breath, heart beat, and movement to the functioning of our immune system and beyond. As science has established, all electric currents radiate electromagnetic fields.

Observable physical phenomenon is one manifestation of energy, and thoughts and emotions are another; they just don't share the same range of frequencies. Thought is simply energy that causes the neurons in the brain to fire in a certain pattern which produces currents in the brain that can be measured through electrodes. We know that no energy is lost in a closed system, so, if this energy can be measured outside of the head, it means that the thought energy radiates out, as electromagnetic waves at the velocity of light, into the environment and eventually into the cosmos (Bentov 1988).

Just as light energy can be focused in a laser, thought energy can be focused on a target. Unfocused light energy spreads out in waves, much like the soft light given off by a lamp. Focusing light with a laser sends the light out in even, coherent waves that can be directed in a narrow beam over great distances. Consider thought energy like a force affecting the surface of water. If we drop a stone in water, it radiates out in ever-weakening ripples or waves, but by pushing the water forcefully with a hand, we can manipulate its flow into a much narrower direction. It is within the electromagnetic spectrum, and perhaps even more subtle levels, that thought and emotional energy can affect other fields of energy, such as those of the body. Conscious awareness and manipulation of this subtle energy is the basis for auric and energy healing.

Thought Energy: Brain vs. Mind

If the body and brain are just conductors of energy, then where does thought originate? Clearly, consciousness is separate from the physical body and brain. Our language is rich with the understanding of the nature of mind as separate from the physical. Phrases such as "passed out," "out of your mind," "out of touch," and "out like a light" reflect at least a subconscious understanding that it is possible to be separate from the brain or body.

For example, if one is "knocked out" (literally, knocked out of the body), then the physical body will continue to function. But the consciousness can be experiencing nothing or experiencing "altered realities" or "dreams" or "out of body experiences" in no way involving the physical body. Many models of consciousness portray the body as the subconscious, the mind as the conscious, and the soul or spirit as beyond these.

In dreams, a car is often a symbol for our bodies. A driver can get out of a car and leave it running, but in order for it to move in a purposeful manner, a higher consciousness (the driver) is needed. The driver is the mind and the source of thought (Bentov 1988). As this driver exists independently of the physical body, it may be said to correlate with ideas of a "soul" or "spirit." The spiritual source of the soul is believed by many to be "God" or the ultimate creative force of the universe. As science is now attempting to rationalize and validate some aspects of metaphysical beliefs, including the measurement of auric life energy, perhaps one day people will be also able to somehow observe and measure "God." For now, the origins of the mind are beyond the scope of intellectual knowledge.

Extrasensory Perception: The Product of Extra-Sensitive Nervous Systems

Fascinating work with plants reveals much about the interaction of subtle energy between living systems. Of particular interest are findings related to the subjective interference of experimenters and discrepancies in results achieved by different observers.

By hooking plants up to polygraph, ECG, and EEG equipment, Clive Backster and other researchers discovered that not only do plants respond to experiences in their environment, but they respond to the "intentions" of people in their environment. They appear able to pick up on people's thoughts and emotions. The strongest readings obtained were in reaction to the destruction of living cells, whether they were plant, animal, or human cells. The death or "threat" of death to living cells caused intense electromagnetic reactions in the plants tested.

While many of the amazing results of experiments with plant energy or auric fields have been reproduced over and over, the sum of the experiments has revealed that some people are better able to affect and monitor these energy reactions in plants. This result may be because the energy of some individuals interacts more powerfully with the experiment. It is likely, however, that sensitive people are better able to attune themselves and establish "communication" (note Moss' "green thumb" and "brown thumb" experiments in Chapter Two) or energy interaction with plants (Tompkins & Bird 1973).

Altered States of Consciousness and Extrasensory Perception

If everything is empty space with patterns of energy running through it, then it is these patterns, or the wavelengths or vibrations of these patterns, that determine whether something is a car, a person, or a thought, etc. Differences in these frequencies determine the exact form of the field in its every detail. There is a range of vibrations that compose ordinary human consciousness and its manifestation on the physical plane. For example, our eyes perceive light frequencies between red and violet. We know, as dealt with in Chapter One, that infrared and ultraviolet rays exist but are beyond our visible range of perception. Human ears perceive sound waves between 20 and 20,000 Hz. Dogs can hear sounds that are much higher and imperceptible to us humans. Just because we can't hear it, doesn't mean the sound doesn't exist. We can't perceive x-rays or microwaves with our senses, but we have developed technology that is more sensitive than our physical senses, capable of measuring these waves. Vibrations existing outside of the range of the five human senses normally escape our conscious perception.

Clairvoyants and healers either come programmed with an expanded range of perception or can alter the state or frequency of their consciousness with an act of will, in order to perceive energy vibrations outside of the normal human range of perception (Bentov 1988). Through altered states of consciousness one can expand the range of perception to perceive these higher frequencies.

In *Stalking the Wild Pendulum*, Itzhak Bentov created a strong metaphor to demonstrate the relationship of altered states of consciousness to "extrasensory perception." He compares consciousness to listening to a radio. When listening to a radio, the closest local station we have the radio tuned in to is the one we hear best. But there are many other radio stations broadcasting on that "same" frequency that we don't hear, because of the noise of the one to which we are listening. If we can selectively "tune out" the noise of that station (or our physical consciousness) and turn up the volume of other stations broadcasting on the same frequency, we can hear all the other stations that generally go unnoticed.

People with exceptional hearing (sensitives) may pick up signals from the weaker stations, despite the noise of the local one, but anyone who turns down that loud station should be able to perceive these signals as well. This is how one can develop auric vision through meditation or learn how to quiet the consciousness. It is interesting to note that many "normal" people report paranormal experiences through dreams or during sleep-states, for at these times one's consciousness is naturally more quiet than during waking hours (Bentov 1988).

Recall the analogy of thought to the movement of water, in which dropping a pebble in the water produces waves that spread out and diminish in all directions, but pushing the water with one's hand allows one to direct the flow. If the surface of the water is choppy and full of waves because it's constantly being bombarded with thought-boulders, it is unlikely that one will notice the ripples of any pebbles. But by calming the surface of the water (quieting the consciousness), we can perceive the finest ripples.

Healers: Receivers, Transmitters, and Directors of Energy

Experiments have demonstrated that not only are those adept at quieting their consciousness better receivers of information, via electromagnetic waves, but they are also better generators or channels of this energy.

A study of electrostatic charge on electrically-isolated meditators revealed that exceptional meditators can produce large surges in bodily electrostatic energy. The experiment compared ten average meditators with nine "exceptional" meditators (professional healers) in a Copper Wall Lab designed to electrically isolate the subjects from the ground. To detect electrostatic potential, each meditator's body and the walls were "floated" on single-ended electrometer inputs. In forty-five-minute sessions, no body-potential surges reached 4 volts in the regular meditators, but in sessions with the healers, surges ranged from 4 volts to 221 volts (with a median of 8.3 volts). When measuring the body-potential surges of the healers during a healing session, surges were recorded ranging from 4 volts to 190 volts. At the high end of this spectrum the surges are 105 times greater than EKG voltages and 106 times larger than EEG voltages, a phenomenon that can not be accounted for by any presently known biological processes (Green *et al.* 1991).

A person adept at altering their state of consciousness can learn how to consciously receive and interpret energy or information from other living systems, to generate powerful energy surges themselves, and to direct the flow of this energy. These skills are the foundation of energy healing and healing through the auric field.

Disease and Healing: Harmonizing Energy for Health

The tiniest disturbance in one energy field disturbs the others around it, and these spread out to, ultimately, the farthest reaches of the cosmos. Whenever a disturbance in these fields drives the fields out of harmonious rhythm, this discordant pattern of energy radiates outward and disturbs the surrounding fields it encounters. Once this original discordant energy is re-balanced or harmonized, all of the energy effected by the original disturbance will return to order. At the same time, if one introduces strong harmonizing energy to a matrix of discordant energy fields, this harmonizing energy may "entrain" the discordant elements of the system, or bring them into order and harmony (Bentov 1988). When discordant energy is introduced to the human energy system, the unbalancing may produce dis-ease. By introducing strong harmonizing energy to a discordant or "dis-eased" system, one can bring the system back into balance, or "heal" it.

Every organ, tissue, and cell of a living being has its own unique frequency; measurement of its energy indicates a consistent vibration or resonance. Cells are essentially organic electromagnetic transceivers that emit and absorb high-frequency waves. Extensive research has shown that disruptions or imbalances in these frequencies correlate with dis-ease, infection, and injury (Townsend 1996).

Several alternative treatments directly aim to alter or balance electrical currents in the body through the use of technology. Transcranial electro-therapy is used to treat alcoholism, drug addiction, stress, and pain. Its aim is to stabilize the neuroelectric environment by transmitting electrical currents through the skin. An electroacuscope measures and corrects areas of altered electrical activity in the body. With disease or injury, the movement of ions between cells is blocked, causing detectable physical changes in the body. By restoring electrical balance to the body, medical doctors have used these devices to successfully treat pain, injury, and disease (Janiger & Goldberg 1993).

"As Above, So Below"

Another avenue for healing through energy involves affecting the frequencies of the energy field surrounding the body. Clairvoyants and mystics maintain that the human body is the physical core of several layers of non-physical bodies, which correspond to successively higher frequencies of non-physical life. The first layer beyond the physical is called the etheric body, and the etheric is said to be the template or pre-form for the physical body. Because it is a template of the ideal physical, when a limb is amputated, sensitives claim that the missing limb will continue to show up on the etheric level. This phenomenon has been photographed through Kirlian photography (see Chapter Two) on a plant which shows the energetic outline of a whole leaf despite part of the leaf having been cut away.

The widely held spiritual belief that manifestation begins in the non-physical dimension and then manifests in the physical is supported by other research as well. Marcel Vogel discovered, in microscopic research of magnified liquid crystal, that through an "inner vision" or non-physical perception he was able to perceive activity not usually revealed by the microscopic field. He then developed methods of bringing these phenomena into the range of visual perception. He concluded from this research that crystals manifest from "pre-forms, or ghost images of pure energy which anticipate the solids" (Tompkins & Bird 1973).

If manifestation begins in the non-physical planes, and if one can affect the non-physical energy or "pre-form," one can influence the physical manifestation. This example is one probable mechanism underlying psycho-somatic illness and energy or spiritual healing.

Beyond Theory and Energy Healing

Many studies have been conducted that have verified the power of healing energy. In fact, in researching this phenomenon, I was struck by how many universities have elaborate facilities for conducting such research. These experiments rule out the power of suggestion and placebo affects by objectively measuring various aspects of the electromagnetic fields in healing situations. Kirlian observation of healing sessions has revealed that the observable energy of healers is smaller after a healing session, while the patient's energy is enhanced, indicating a transfer of energy (Tompkins & Bird 1973).

One experiment by Daniel P. Wirth, MS, JD, demonstrated that subjects who received five minutes of exposure to a Non-contact Therapeutic Touch Practitioner (aura healer) experienced a significant acceleration in the healing rate of identical wounds as compared with control subjects who either received no such exposure or exposure to a "fake" aura healer (Wirth 1990).

A thirteen-year series of experiments demonstrated the human ability to mentally influence biological systems. This ability was active regardless of distance or isolation of the subjects from all conventional and energetic influences. Many controls were implemented to rule out error or extraneous influences. Through intention, focused attention, and visualization of desired outcomes, subjects were able to influence another person's "electrodermal activity, blood pressure, and muscular activity; the spatial orientation of fish; the locomotor activity of small mammals; and the rate of hemolysis of human red blood cells." The experiments have been considered laboratory analogs of mental healing (Braud & Schlitz 1991).

In an experiment by Dr. Valerie Hunt and colleagues at UCLA in which a sensitive or clairvoyant relayed her observations of the color, size, and energy movements of the chakras and auras of a healer and patient, it was found that the measured and mathematically analyzed energy patterns of the healer and patient corresponded to the auric colors observed by the clairvoyant. The location of the colors and time of occurrence also corresponded with the quantitative data. Seven other clairvoyants also achieved similar results (Alvino 1996). At last the observations of technology are approaching the depth of those of mystics throughout history!

Tachyon Energy, the Creative Force of the Universe

While study of the electromagnetic interaction of all life may seem revolutionary, quantum physics has gone even farther. Experiments showing the reaction of plants to mental influences suggest there are forces beyond the electromagnetic spectrum responsible for these interactions; for plants responded even when placed in a Faraday cage that blocked penetration of electromagnetic waves (Tompkins & Bird 1973).

Quantum physicists speculating on this response call the force beyond the electromagnetic spectrum, "Tachyon energy." The following two photographs, taken by the Aura Imaging camera, shows before and after pictures of Tachyon energy through the use of a Takionic® belt around the subject's neck.

Before

After

Tachyons are the theoretical source of subatomic particles, and the expansion of the tachyon field is speculated to be the creative force of the universe. Tachyon theory explains the instantaneous nature of psi phenomenon, which transcend Einstein's relativity theory that restricted the movement of energy in the universe to the speed of light. Tachyon theory postulates that there are actually two universes involved in creation: the visible, sub-light speed universe we are conscious of and an invisible, faster-than-light universe. This tachyon energy is omnipresent, or exists holographically and simultaneously everywhere, because it travels much faster than light and hence takes no time to travel through space (Takionic Products 1996).

Tachyon energy is speculated, by some, to be the creative and sustaining force of all life, requiring a balance of energies to sustain itself. When a life form requires life energy, a vacuum or energy demand is created and tachyon energy rushes in to answer this demand. The nervous system is viewed as a conductor for the absorption and processing of this energy. Energy healers are, perhaps, simply individuals whose sensitive or developed nervous systems make them more adept at manipulating or processing this energy (Takionic Products 1996).

Conclusion

Recent technological developments have, at last, intellectually confirmed much of the ancient metaphysical knowledge: that life is essentially energy and that this life energy is observable in the auras emitted by all living organisms. Scientific research into the nature of this energy and the interactions between electromagnetic fields has produced results that mirror the observations and views of mystics, sensitives, and healers. This research has provided evidence not only of the existence of auras, but also of the mechanisms behind auric healing.

Perhaps future research into the nature of life and consciousness will also benefit from the serious contemplation of esoteric knowledge and the incorporation of spiritual philosophy into scientific exploration. With recent observations that "objective research" can be self-contradictory—given that the mind of the observer can affect the results of an experiment—then clearly the thin line between objective scientific methodology and subjective experience has collapsed.

Open-mindedness or the ability to approach the unknown without prejudice for conventional thought has led to the greatest innovations in history and continues to hold the most promise for future progress into the vast territory of the unknown.

CHAPTER FOURTEEN

TOUCHING THE QI

Janice Dye[1]

Introduction

"The ancient Chinese perceived human beings as a microcosm of the universe that surrounded them, suffused with the same primeval forces that motivated the macrocosm. They imagined themselves as part of one unbroken wholeness, called *Tao*, a singular relational continuum within and without.

"The concept of *Qi* (chee) is absolutely at the heart of Chinese medicine. Life is defined by *Qi* even though it is insensible to grasp, measure, quantify, see, or isolate.

"Matter is *Qi* taking shape—mountains forming, forests growing, rivers streaming . . . etc. In the human being, all functions of the body and mind are manifestations of *Qi*: sensing, feeling, digesting, etc. . . . *Qi* begets movement and heat. It is the fundamental mystery and miracle. Life cannot be separated from the way it manifests. When the heart beats and the breath is warm, it is understood that life exists within the body.

"The ancient knowledge of Kundalini brings back the wisdom of the primordial consciousness of the Indian civilization and of the energy centers called the chakras.

"The chakras work to vitalize the etheric shell around the physical by providing the nourishment of the life force energy. As a wheel of energy, the chakras rotate and either bring in energy or expel it outward. They work as energy centers inside the auric shell and also designate a type of physical, emotional, and psychological consciousness.

"It is important to know and understand the interactions of negative and positive energies and the elaborate philosophy of energy and healing. In courses of esoteric and occult healing, there is a continuous focus on the need for purification and neutralization of energies. The aspirant is engrossed with the problem of purifying the bodies in which the centers are found, which are primarily the astral, etheric, and physical bodies.

"Matter or form is becoming recognized as a magnetic interplay of energy. Science defines magnetism by positive and negative charges but has not offered meaning to its intrinsic and pervasive nature. The energetic movement of the electron current (wave) from the negative pole to the positive pole sets up the magnetic and electromagnetic field. This relationship is always at a ninety degree angle to one another and forms the geometric relationships of intelligence behind the forces.

"Each part of life is bound by its own vibrations into a geometric form, a form which changed in type and quality as the vibrations changed. Modern science has found that no cell, no molecule, whether animal, vegetable, or mineral, escapes geometric form.

"This concept is just the beginning point of the introduction of human aura into the scheme of relationships that will enable a world view in wider perspective. The scientific vantage point from the basis of the unified field of energy and quantum science has great importance in developing evidence, validation, and integration into a new theoretical acceptance for further research into the nature of the human aura and energy body.

"There are other theories from quantum physics that could be addressed, but the foundation is laid in the form of an intelligent mind behind the creation of action, changing, adjusting, and responding to all possibilities. The basics of the human aura and unseen energies of the chakras are being understood at a deeper level, without the former mysticism"

The Universal Energy

The aura is the manifestation of *Qi*, *ch'i*, or Universal energy. It is otherwise known as the light or rainbow field, flowing from within and radiating outward, through the body's chakras (energy centers). The human body is entirely made up of energy, with layers of density and manifestation. The further out the radiation, the higher the vibration and the subtler the layer. In order to consciously perceive subtle layers, one must increase one's vibration to that level's vibration by bringing more light into oneself.

Although not all people are aware of their aura-seeing ability, all of us sense auras through a combination of perceptions at a subconscious, instinctual level. We are all part of the infinite and therefore exist well beyond the boundaries of our three-dimensional physical form. One does not have to touch a person to feel the heat of the energy emitted through his field. It has been my experience that the block or inability to see this energy comes strictly from fear. Realizing, or even beginning to understand, that the physical body is merely energy vibrating at a low frequency is realizing and understanding that man is not solid. Accepting this truth brings release from the boundaries of the limited reality of three-dimensional experience.

Accepting the expansiveness beyond the known reality of the self is release of the ego. Ego can only perceive from a three-dimensional viewpoint, with the concept of "I exist, as I believe I exist." Aura vision threatens the ego's concept of self (existing only within the physical form) and, therefore, cannot be achieved unless fear of the unknown is abandoned through releasing the concept of self.

Intuitively, we begin feeling that there is "more to us than meets the eye." There is energy that is dense and physical, and energy that is higher in vibration and not visible. As energy is stimulated with more energy, the energy increases its vibration. I put a pot of water on the stove. I utilize the magic of electricity and direct concentration of energy to the pot of water by turning on the element under the pot. The energy from the element begins stimulating and increasing the vibration of the water energy. The water energy begins dancing, vibrating, and bubbling before your very eyes. This water energy seems to change as it rises up and transforms into steam. It continues evaporating until it is no longer visible. The energy is not gone, but the concept of "water in the pot" is no longer present.

If I put this same pot of water on the stove and did not focus intensified energy from the burner, it would still increase vibration and transform during evaporation, only at a much slower rate. Universal energy in its expansive nature is constantly working to effect change, and the transformation of the water is inevitable. It evaporates into the ethers and then showers down again to the earth in droplets of rain in a cyclical experience of eternal abundance of water. If enough energy was given to the pot of water, the pot as well as the water would also transform. So, applying the same metaphor to yourself: your body is the pot (dense container). The universe is constantly pouring fluid energy into this container, and, as the container overflows, it is radiated back out to the universe through your chakras.

The Energy of Love and Light

What is energy? Energy is Love and Light and Consciousness. How do I increase my own energy? Increase Love . . . turn on the element and direct your Consciousness inwardly.

***Exercises*:**

Before commencing, place yourself in a fully relaxed state of consciousness. Although some of these exercises may seem detailed and require a great deal of concentration, it is quite the opposite, and the eyes, as well as the body and mind, must remain relaxed as if in a posture of calm serenity. Therefore, it is suggested that you close your eyes and take a few deep relaxing breaths, releasing all tension on each exhalation (a more general set of exercises may be found in Evelyn Monahan and Terry Bakken's *Put Your Psychic Powers to Work,* 1973).

Opening and utilizing the third eye or brow center is necessary for seeing the auric field. This energy center is located in the middle of the forehead, just above and between the eyes. Direct stimulation of this center should be practiced before attempting to gaze into the auric field. This stimulation is a mental exercise which can easily be done by focusing awareness on this center and imagining opening it, as opening an eyelid. Combine this mental exercise with a focus of energy, internally stimulating the third eye chakra with a clockwise circling motion from the inside. This exercise is purely a mental one, so no muscular movement is necessary, and a completely relaxed state should be maintained. Do not focus vision directly on the object whose energy field you are intending to view. Instead, focus on nothing, gazing just beyond and to the side of that object.

The auric field will not be viewed with direct focus but rather with peripheral vision. While setting your optical gaze, continue mentally stimulating the third eye. The "gaze" referred to here is the very same necessary when viewing a 3D picture. It is required to shift focus slightly before seeing the image appear out of the tiny dots. While doing this, the eyes physically relax into a different position. Usually, one eye will turn in slightly, and one may find oneself struggling with the pull into cross-eyed vision. This slight adjustment of focus, once found, can be easily recaptured during the next viewing. Some people struggle for weeks to see a 3D picture. Once the focus has been attained, however, the ability to see 3D images is almost immediate from that point onward. When viewing an aura, the eyes must be released from focus and allowed to relax into a blind stare gaze as if shifting into daydream mode. This occurs naturally if concentration is on stimulation of the brow center. This naturally brings about a state of double vision of sorts, the internal intuitive brow chakra opening, and, with eyes opened, merging with the external optical vision. Although one eye tends to fall into a state of laziness (usually the right eye), the eyes do not cross to double the external vision. It may be beneficial to make a conscious note of this eye focus adjustment with an intentional shift into daydream mode.

The Candle Flame

1. Sit in a dark room, preferably without any light whatsoever. Take a few deep breaths. Relax, releasing the tension from the body. When staring into the darkness, what do you see? Is it complete blackness, nothingness, or is there something there?

While gently relaxing into the rhythmic flow of breathing, look deeply into the darkness. Particles of light energy, dancing and swirling in the dark, will soon become apparent. Continue staring, noticing patterns of energy as they take form and shape-shift into different images.

2. After spending a leisurely time enjoying the cosmic dance of energy in the dark, light a candle and sit in front of it. Either sit cross-legged, in a lotus position, or in a straight back chair with feet touching the ground. Keep the spine straight, as this allows energy to move freely through the body. Relaxation is paramount, so choose a position that is comfortable while taking relaxing deep breaths to release any tension.

3. Relax; focus just beyond and to the side of the flame. With every exhale extend energy (consciousness) outward to the flame. Notice how easy it is to see the aura of the flame, the glow from the candle's light as it expands as a halo of light. Continue moving consciousness outward, noticing that the halo expands. Keeping eyes relaxed in gaze, take in the peripherals.

Without shifting focus, notice the space between yourself and the flame. See the energy going from you to the flame, and see the energy coming back. The more you relax and open, the more the aura will expand and engulf the room.

At this point, one might want to close the eyes and look into the internal darkness. With internal sight, see the candle once again burning and glowing, yet this time envision it within the heart. Move consciousness into the center of the flame in the heart and feel the LOVE ENERGY constantly radiating from within. Allow yourself this luxury and BE in LOVE. (Note: This exercise with the candle can be intensified and increased when practiced with another person. As you both concentrate your focus on the candle, you will notice that the flame grows higher and the aura brighter very rapidly.)

Auras in Nature

If everything is made up of energy, then all must have an aura. The easiest and most natural way of identifying the energy field is to go out into nature. Animals, rocks, trees and vegetation are wonderfully open and receptive to attention. Sit in a comfortable spot and take in the light of the forest.

Gazing into the daylight sky (not in direct sunlight of course) can also be an interesting exercise for opening awareness to the dance of energy. Slipping into focus and becoming open, one notices particles of energy swirling and zipping around, looking much like little flying bugs. After noticing this energy, it is almost impossible not to see it everywhere. Next, gaze between two trees and watch what is happening between them. The energy will move from one to the other, and there is a clear relationship and pattern in the flow. Remember: for most of life, man has been reprogrammed to see only the very dense energy. One looks at the solid objects rather than the spaces between objects. Let the gaze fall on the space between objects and notice what is really going on. There is always so much going on in the gap between matter. Slip into that space and explore.

The Human Aura

Before attempting to gaze upon the human aura, much practice and comfort should be attained with inanimate objects, plant life, and animal life. When viewing the human aura, we once again have to learn to shift focus away from the natural tendency to look directly at the dense physical energy and actually focus on the space surrounding the physical body. This way of thinking can be very difficult. The mind tends to grasp for a solid object to fix the gaze upon. Self-imposed pressures shut down the relaxed consciousness state necessary for aura vision. It is much easier to practice this procedure alone first, without limitations of self-consciousness on your part or the part of the subject.

Experiencing one's own auric field is the primary stage before experiencing the field of others. Placing hands together as if in prayer, move them slightly apart, very slowly, and keep gazing on the space between the hands. Often the energy will appear as threads between the hands. When seeing the energy clearly, rub the hands together, creating heat and friction, and then repeat the exercise, noticing the difference of the energy movement. Taking a position in front of a mirror (a white or neutral background behind you works best), gaze just off to the side of your ear and behind it. If this focus seems like a struggle, you are not doing it correctly. It is really important to relax first, and then relax the eyes, shifting into the "blank stare" vision. This exercise is not one that is done with time limit expectations. It is something that you do when you are willing to honor yourself with your time and attention without expectation. Remember at all times to stimulate the brow center mentally.

The first thing you might notice is a thin white or yellow layer of light close to the head. This layer is the first one in the auric field, and it is known as the ethereal layer. As you continue radiating energy with each exhale, watch as the energy expands. The energy is moving and changing form and is often seen swirling, as smoke does as it rises. When this energy first becomes apparent, there is a tendency to shift the eyes back to regular focus to follow the energy. This shifting will break the awareness, and visually, the energy will seem to vanish again. Continued practice will help maintain the peripheral vision, which is the only way of seeing the auric field. When you can maintain the gaze posture, it is possible to move focus around, encompassing other people or objects. With practice, you will begin identifying colors. A healthy human energy field is radiant and lively with color.

Often people will report unusual experiences during this mirror meditation. Facial features might begin changing or look unfamiliar. This change should not be alarming or frightening. As energy and light are increased, the body will be less dense, and you may become aware of subtle changes in form (matter). Allowing yourself to move beyond your concept of self is a very exciting experience. Many people report that this mirror exercise brings about a feeling that the person in this reflection is amazingly unfamiliar, yet, at the same time, a chord of ancient familiarity is recognized.

When attempting to see another's aura, I suggest you find a partner with whom you are very comfortable. If the two of you are looking into each other's energy field, you will be able to fully relax and take your time as you let the energy flow and expand. You will not be able to identify the auric field if you are self-conscious or afraid of invading someone else's privacy or space. Clothing will affect the aura and alter the color. Therefore, unless the skin is exposed, the aura is most visible around the head. Using all the techniques previously mentioned, a simple way of viewing another's aura would be placing them in a chair situated in a dark room and placing a candle behind them. While gazing upon the aura, allow intuition and inner guidance to offer messages.

Sensing Auras

It is important to state that the ego must be honored, and one must not become frustrated by an inability to SEE the auric field. Very few people have this particular ability, yet we all perceive auras and sense them in a variety of ways. The subconscious is constantly at work, reading and identifying energy resonating from another being. The easiest way to become more conscious of this energy is first trusting that it exists and, secondly, being open to all the senses and alert to the sense through which you most easily identify the energy. For some, the sense of feeling is primary, and visual reception distracts attention. The same could hold true for an auditory perception or other senses. In this case, it may be a good idea to practice sensing auras by depriving the visual connection until the distraction is under control and the senses combined efficiently. You can practice alone or with a partner. Close your eyes, or blindfold yourself if necessary. Position hands about three feet above your partner's body. Very slowly, move your hands lower, keeping alert to the subtle changes of heat and vibration you may start experiencing through your hands. Tingling may occur, and you may perceive an actual pattern in the flow, moving through your hands and into your body up through your arms. When you first notice the energy changes, stop and take note and have your partner register the approximate distance between your hands and his/her body. The more you practice and develop your alertness of attention, the more you will sense the energy at greater distances.

Once you have found a comfortable place where you have identified the auric field, move your hands around, still hovering over the body. You will notice energy shifts in direction and in temperature. If you are having any difficulty perceiving the energy through your sense of touch, I suggest reversing this practice and start by laying your hands on the person (relaxed, fingers together, and palms slightly cupped) and feeling the energy move from them into your hands. Again, as you move your hands around the body, you will sense differences in the energy from position to position.

Since external vision is disconnected, it is likely that one will perceive color and imagery internally. Stimulation of the third eye increases the flow of this inner vision. Be open and receptive to this internal vision for it has been stimulated by the reception of the other person's auric field and therefore, is a means of interpreting the energy. Emotions or intuitive insights may also be sensed while in this state of receptivity. You will be feeling through your own senses, and the feeling will be similar to your own emotions and thoughts. Yet, if your intent is to receive, and you have opened yourself to the energy of another, you should trust that this change of energy within you is simply your way of reading the rainbow field of another.

Using Crystals

Crystals are very powerful conductors. They each carry their own pattern and power, and each has the ability to hold and transmit energy. The way that energy naturally flows through the body suggests that the body's right side is the side of expression, and the left is the side of reception. Holding a crystal in the palm of the right hand and focusing attention on charging the crystal will load a crystal with energy. Holding the crystal in the left hand, focusing on listening and feeling and receiving the energy with full alert attention, will allow one to sense the vibration of the crystal and accept it into one's being.

Each crystal has its own unique vibration and power. Some crystals will feel static and hyper-charged. Others will feel like wave vibrations rippling through the arms and into the body, often finding a resting place where the energy is most needed. If the internal and external space is quiet enough, the sound frequency of energy can also be perceived. When using crystals in meditation, many people often comment on the music that the crystals seem to resonate, as if the stones are singing. Visually, crystals often project an intense stream of energy which can especially be seen on a crystal with a point. Holding the point to the palm of the left hand, move the crystal slowly back from the palm, looking at the space between the crystal and the palm. Although the human aura is much more dazzling, one soon learns through examination of the auric field of crystals and other gifts of nature that there is a beautiful field of energy radiating from everything. Crystals, trees, plants, and rocks can become friends and teachers, speaking to us, merging with us, in a relationship of ever-flowing light energy.

Healing Through the Aura

The human aura is not stagnant. It changes color. Patterns fluctuate with changes in the physical, emotional, and mental states. When the ability to consciously read the human aura is established, great work can be done towards healing the body, mind, and spirit. Physical illness does not usually start in the body. It starts as a concept in the ethereal that, either through lack of attention or understanding, becomes increasingly more dense, eventually manifesting as a physical illness. This unaddressed issue or injury will move itself into the vibrational level of consciousness (whatever the density) in order to grasp the attention and be dealt with and healed. The "being" is a fully integrated system, so anything affecting one aspect of that system affects the whole.

A friend once discussed the topic of not being able to see auras with her spiritual guru. He responded by questioning her on why she wanted to see this energy so greatly and asked her if she expected to see all rainbows and light. When she replied in affirmation, he simply told her that this was not usually true. Often human auras were murky, cloudy, or dark. This type of aura is, in fact, common in people, since most auras require healing and mending of body, mind, and spirit. Healing at an auric level can help alleviate illness before it manifests as physical symptoms.

Our aura and our energy body are parallel to our immune system and our physical body. Disease collects in the aura, and the energy of the aura works to break down the disease or issue. Just as the immune system focuses and concentrates on a particular area of the body undergoing attack, so will the rainbow field work on the energy body in balancing the system. Several conditions and internal states have direct effect on the aura's integrity.

Unresolved emotional issues as well as negative or limiting belief systems cause weakness, breaks, and holes in the aura. Drugs (legal and illegal), alcohol, poor diet, and lack of sleep are a few examples of the many factors that could contribute to the vulnerability of the aura. Just as one would not want weakness, holes, or blocks in the immune system, one does not want the breakdown of the auric system. So not only is it important to clear emotional and self-esteem issues for the health of our mind, it is also clearly important for the ongoing health of the energy body.

As a natural energy healer, my work involves the clearing and healing of damaged auric fields. I am a Reiki practitioner, and my approach to auras is primarily through touch in a hands-on session. Reiki is an ancient hands-on healing art wherein the practitioner simply allows the *Qi* to flow through him/her to the client receiving treatment. The practitioner is simply a vessel for this universal energy; however, the intuition often provides guidance.

There are at least seven major chakras (energy centers) on the body. Each has its own vibration and frequency of energy, moving out and into one another and radiating outward into the aura. From the base of the spine to the crown of the head, each chakra has its own color. When healthy, all are spinning in perfect rainbow harmony. However, usually there are blockages, holes, or over-active chakras disturbing the balance. I am inspired to visualize a particular color or pattern of energy when placing my hands in different positions around the body.

Sometimes, when I see a blow out of one particular color in someone's aura, I am inspired to tone it down by sending an opposite color (e.g., green to red). At other times, there will be a deficiency of a certain color, and I am guided to send a concentrated focus of energy in the color that is lacking using mental imagery. Understanding and fully experiencing the auric field has become more than a mild curiosity in the last couple of decades. The development of Kirlian photography and Aura Imaging cameras were significant scientific breakthroughs in bringing a wider understanding and acceptance of these normally unseen forces. As more of us tune our vibration and become conscious of our ability to perceive and understand the auric field, our concepts of relationship will change dramatically. We can learn so much about each other from our energy, which is much more revealing and truthful than our limited physical concepts. The intrigue with the aura is simple. In understanding its existence, we also may come to understand that we are much more than our physical bodies and in no way separate or detached from the rest of the universe. Hence, no one is alone. We are all connected through our auric field as part of a greater whole. Follow your heart as it leads you to the truth.

Note

1. Introduction, in quotation marks, by **Richard Bernard Wigley**, author of Chapter One.

CHAPTER FIFTEEN

ACUPUNCTURE THERAPY AND ITS POTENTIAL RELATIONSHIP TO AURIC ENERGY

Rosalee Elizabeth McCurdy, RN, AP, MSc, DOM

THUS FAR, LITTLE HAS BEEN WRITTEN regarding the relationship between acupuncture and the human aura. Although the origins of acupuncture theory and practice date back more than five thousand years, there is no such analog in Western medicine. Research into the effectiveness of acupuncture as a method of healing is in its infancy in the United States; much of the clinical data comes from China or Japan.

Recently, however, the Food and Drug Administration declared acupuncture needles safe and effective as a medical device. This recognition is an important first step in acknowledging acupuncture's therapeutic value. Likewise the concept of the human aura or energy field has existed for eons. Clairvoyants, mystics, healers, ancient and modern, have spoken of the aura. "Pythagoras, the Greek philosopher and mathematician (500 B.C.), perceived a luminous body that produced cures which he called vital energy" (Brennan 1993, 16). People have observed colors of light around the body and the intact image of an entire leaf after it was cut away, all due to the method of photography known as Kirlian photography. I have observed varying degrees of light around inanimate objects, as it were, jumping around these objects in clockwise, then counterclockwise motion.

The idea that matter and energy are the same, that we live in a four-dimensional reality of time/space continuum, that energy functions both as particle and wave, and that all parts of the universe are intimately and deeply connected and ordered at the most fundamental level is the commonly accepted view among scientists today. David Bohm, Professor of Physics at the University of London, calls this "unbroken wholeness" (Zukav 1979), a philosophy long held by Buddhism and other Eastern religions. Recent developments in science have made it possible to measure the electromagnetic characteristics of acupuncture points and meridians, giving some credibility to the concept of *Qi* (note Janice Dye's Chapter Fourteen) as the energy circulating in the body via the meridian pathways. There is also striking evidence that the acupuncture points are sites of lowered electrical resistance relative to the surrounding skin (Matsumoto & Birch 1988).

Some evidence further suggests that the meridians and acupuncture points retain their electrical characteristics for some time after death. Brugh Joy, MD (1979), in his book *Joy's Way,* states that he was able to feel the aura of patients who had been dead for several hours, if their physical body was still intact. My most profound personal experience of the interconnectedness of the aura and acupuncture occurred a few years ago at a healing conference held by Barbara Brennan, author of *Hands of Light* and *Light Emerging*. In the closing moments of the conference, the participants were being led through a channeled meditation. With clairvoyant vision, I saw, as it were, thousands of small, oval (bell) shaped particles of light pop out in my aura. It was as if a rosebud had opened instantly into a flower. My entire aura suddenly became full of multicolored light which radiated six feet in front of me. These bell-shaped particles of light produced a musical melody, and simultaneously, it seemed as if my consciousness lifted out of my body and floated across the room facing my physical body, which was still sitting in the chair. This consciousness took the form of a golden Buddha sitting in the lotus position. At that moment I recognized that these bell-shaped particles were minor chakras and the same as the acupuncture points.

It is therefore no mystery that when one maps the electrical conductivity of the skin at a acupuncture point, it appears as a funnel from the surface of the skin, with a connecting path beneath the skin and soft tissue. A great deal of the information that I will present here comes from my own clinical experience in my acupuncture practice in Miami at the

Center for Radiant Health. I have developed a system using the pendulum as a tool in assessing the flow of energy within the chakras and the aura. I assess the flow of energy within the chakras on all seven layers of the aura. This gives me a clear picture of the energy configuration within the patient. I correlate these findings with the patient's complaints or presenting problem, assessment of the tongue and pulses, and then develop a plan of treatment together with the patient, using acupuncture and therapeutic healing touch techniques. Herbal remedies, breathing, and other exercises are often prescribed when necessary to support the healing process.

A Western Approach to the Seven Layers of the Human Aura

The literature, although some contradictions exist, supports the theory of seven basic levels or layers of the human aura (note McClellan's excellent introduction to the Eastern explanation of the auric layers—Chapter Seven). The first level and closest to the body is the *etheric level.* To clairvoyant vision this is composed of tiny blue lines that form a web-like structure within and around the physical body and can be palpated up to two inches from the physical body.

The second level, known as the *emotional level,* corresponds to the emotional and/or psychological nature of the person. To clairvoyant vision it appears as clouds of colored light in motion that can be palpated up to five inches from the physical body. These colors change according to the emotional state of the person and are infused into the first layer of the aura.

The third level is called the *mental level* and is described by Brennan (1987) as having a yellow color. It is very structured and may extend up to eight inches from the physical body in persons with a highly developed mental field. In my clinical experience, I observed this field in many patients with the same characteristic pattern. To my clairvoyant vision, it appears as long strands or bands of matter extending outward from the central vertical plane of the body. These strands appear to be two to three inches wide and are interwoven with a texture and feel similar to linen or cotton fabric. In most patients these woven strands are often tangled and knotted and seem to take on the predominant colors of the emotional level. When un-knotted after energy work on this level of the aura, they appear a luminous amber color glowing with multicolored specks of light.

The fourth level of the aura is commonly referred to as the *astral level* and is believed to be associated with the heart chakra. All the levels of the aura are connected to a corresponding chakra, which extends through all seven layers. A rose color has been ascribed to this level, which is less structured than the third level. To my clairvoyant vision, it appears as a clear sort of mercurial gel-like substance that flows over the other layers. I believe that it also reflects the colors that are predominant at the emotional level, because I have seen it with a different color from person to person but with the same distinct texture. This level can be palpated up to twelve inches from the physical body.

The fifth level, called the *etheric template level,* appears to clairvoyant vision as a negative of a photograph and contains all the components of the physical body in negative space. It can be detected up to fourteen inches from the body.

The sixth level, also known as the *celestial level,* may extend beyond the body several feet. This is where universal consciousness or universal mind resides. It imbues us with the understanding of our connection to the "whole" and that all life is sacred and touched with divine spark. To experience this level is to know what it means to "trust spirit." It appears in clairvoyant vision as multicolored light mingled with gold and silver threads.

The seventh or *ketheric level* appears to my clairvoyant vision as an opaque white color in the shape of an egg that surrounds all the other layers. It appears to have a protective function. It is very solid to touch, with a definite boundary. In people with very strong boundaries and who do not like to be touched, this layer feels very hard. In others, whose boundaries are less defined, this egg is discontinuous and soft. When this level is healthy, it communicates and interfaces with the sixth level of universal mind via the hara. This line runs through the central core of the body, extending several feet beyond the body, causing the person to become open to giving and receiving. This level, in my opinion, is where true transformation of consciousness takes place. I have actually experienced this egg opening in a healing session.

There is little mention in the literature that other levels of the aura exist above the seventh level. However, the eighth, ninth, and tenth levels of the aura, which I refer to as the *transdimensional levels,* come from my clinical experience. I have grouped these levels together because when they first appeared to me in clairvoyant vision, they seemed to be connected to each other, as the layers of the skin are connected to the soft tissue beneath it. The eighth level appeared above the intact egg of the seventh layer as a diffuse yet coherent vapor-like substance, which I believe to be colorless but which appeared to be smoky. This substance emanated from a dense black crust approximately three inches thick. This was the ninth level. The tenth level appeared as a very fine, white, granular, crystalline substance of extremely high vibration, above the more porous crusty crumb-like ninth layer.

These layers are the only strata that conform to the description of "layer." They literally appeared layered and horizontal to the egg of the seventh layer and seemed to continue infinitely. I experienced this layer in a actual healing session with a client. At the moment I experienced this, I simultaneously experienced myself as a different physical form in another physical dimension. I also experienced my patient in the other dimension. I discussed this with the patient, who substantiated that what I had experienced in relation to her had meaning in her frame of reference and to events in her present life. These layers of the aura, I believe, hold the history of our existence through the time/space continuum. It is important to note that these levels of the aura are relative levels and vary from person to person, depending on their state of wellness.

Basic Principles of Chinese Medicine

To understand the relationship of acupuncture to the human aura, it is important to understand some basic principles of Chinese Medicine of which acupuncture is only one aspect. The ancient Chinese believed that the energy existing in the universe also resided in the human body. This energy was the primordial life force which they called *Qi*. It is difficult to define *Qi* because it assumes different manifestations and expressions. *Qi* is both physical and spiritual, is in a constant state of flux, and changes with locality and function. It represents, ". . . the infinite variety of phenomena in the universe, and is the result of the continuous coming together and dispersion, to form phenomena of varying degrees of materialization of life" (Maciocia 1989, 36). *Qi* is that rarefied material that comprises the aura and infuses the meridians and the acupuncture points.

Another important concept is that of yin and yang. This concept developed in China more than five thousand years ago and is based on the observations and interpretation of natural phenomena operating in the universe. The material world appeared to have an inherent dual nature that was reflected in all phenomenon. Certain characteristics of this duality were identified. They sometimes appeared as opposing each other as well as transforming into each other. For example day (yang) is opposite to night (yin) and eventually transforms to night and vice versa. Another important characteristic is that yin contains yang and yang contains yin. For example, day (yang) can be divided into morning (yang within yang) and afternoon (yin within yang). Likewise night follows the same pattern. Therefore, yin and yang are said to be infinitely connected and interdependent, in continuous transformation one into the other. This concept brings us to the current world view based on Einstein's general theory of relativity—that time and space are not separate but interwoven—as opposed to the Newtonian construct where time and space were viewed as separate from each other. The theory of yin and yang can be applied to the characteristics of the aura and the physical body.

HUMAN AURA (yang)	**HUMAN BODY (yin)**
energy	matter
rarefied	solid
immaterial	material
produces energy	**produces form**

The human aura and the body are in a state of dynamic balance to maintain wellness, and acupuncture affects the aura in three specific ways: 1) Opening, 2) Stimulating/Activating, and 3) Balancing /Harmonizing.

It does so via the *Qi* energy that flows through the twelve main meridians and the eight extraordinary meridians, also called extraordinary vessels. *Qi* has both yin and yang manifestations and is capable of circulation and movement as well as stagnation. It lifts and descends, can be dispersed or accumulated, clear or turbid. It has the function of warming and cooling, nourishing and protecting the entire body energetic system. The twelve regular meridians primarily affect the first four levels of the aura that correlate with the physical functions, while the extraordinary vessels have a powerful effect on levels four through seven and correlate with mental/spiritual awareness.

THE TWELVE REGULAR MERIDIANS AS PAIRED VESSELS (yin/yang)

Yin	Yang
Lung (LU)	Large Intestine (LI)
Heart (HT)	Small Intestine (SI)
Spleen (SP)	Stomach (ST)
Kidney (KI)	Urinary Bladder (UB)
Pericardium(PC)	Triple Warmer (TW)
Liver (LV)	Gallbladder (GB)

THE EIGHT EXTRAORDINARY MERIDANS (yin/yang)

Yin	Yang
Ren Mai	Du Mai
Chong Mai	Dai
Yinqiao	Yangqiao
Yinwei	Yangwei

In general, the eight extraordinary meridians are different from the twelve regular meridians because they do not function as paired meridians nor do they pertain to the organs of body. However, they do share their acupoints with the regular meridians, with the exception of the Du Mai and Ren Mai, which have their own acupoints. In this respect they are also able to influence the organs as well as the aura. The extraordinary vessels are so named because little is understood about how they work, but because the effects of their action on the body produce therapeutic results when all other techniques have failed, they have been called the

"Miraculous Meridians" by the French acupuncturists. In China they are called *Qi Jing Ba Mai,* which when translated means, "odd and mysterious vessels." They are also refered to in some of the literature as the "psychic channels" because the acupoints (confluent points) associated with these meridians produce strong psychic and psychological responses in a person. They are also the reservoirs for *Qi,* while the regular meridians constitute the rivers of the *Qi.*

The aura is part of the defensive *Qi* system of the body; when there is a breakdown in this defensive system, disease results. The pathogenic influence or disease-causing factor enters through the auric field and invades the body system. When the aura is healthy and strong, it is said to be as "smooth as glass," able to deflect invading pathogenic influences from the external environment. This defensive *Qi* floats beneath and above the level of the skin and around the orifices of the body, protecting them from pathogenic invasion. When there is obstruction in the energy/body system, acupuncture is useful in opening the bi-directional flow of defensive *Qi,* thus promoting communication between the physical body and the aura. From clinical practice, I have discovered several points that open the flow of energy into the body from the aura. These points, which open into the major chakras, are different from the points where one meridian opens into another.

Opening Points

Du 20 — This point is located on the top of the head, at the mid-point of the line connecting the two auricles of the ear at the epi-center of the crown chakra. Needling, massaging, or directing energy throughout this point with intentionality results in a flow of energy between the layers of the aura, with resultant positive and therapeutic changes in the body. This point is very effective in treating vortex headaches.

Du 16 — Located one inch above the posterior hairline in the depression between both sides of the trapezius muscle, it corresponds to the posterior chakra of the third eye. In acupuncture this point is indicated in the treatment of mental disorders, vision problems, and headaches.

Yintang — Is located midway between the medial end of the two eyebrows. Coupled with Du 16, these points open the chakra of the third eye, influencing our willingness to see and experience reality in multidimensional ways. It opens the flow of energy bi-directionally between the aura and the physical body as well as between the levels of the aura via the chakras located in the auric field.

Du 14 — Located just below the spinous process of the seventh cervical vertebra at the base of the neck, at the epicenter of the yang portion of the throat chakra. Directing energy throughout this center, by acupuncture, acupressure opens the energy flow to the aura, thus affecting the avenues of expression.

Ren 22 — Located at the center of the suprasternal fossa, at the epicenter of the throat chakra, this point, coupled with Du 14, opens the throat chakra front and back. It thus promotes free exchange with the levels of the aura, resulting in the opening of the expressive and receptive center for clear verbal communication.

Du 11 — This point opens into the yang aspect of the heart chakra and can be located at the mid-point of the back, below the spinous process of the fifth thoracic vertebra. The posterior ramus of the fifth thoracic nerve enervates this point, as well as the medial branch of the fifth intercostal artery. Blocks or disturbances in the heart and lung energetic system can be felt in this area when one hand is placed over Du 11 and the other over Ren 17. When there is good communication between these points and the aura, the chest feels light, breathing is easy and effortless. The emotions flow appropriately. The ability to give and receive love and affection is enhanced, and the aura on the fourth level glows bright and crystal clear.

Ren 17 — Located in the center of the chest midway between the nipples. This point is said to "open the chest" and is the yin aspect of the heart chakra, governing a person's ability to receive love and affection.

Ren 12 — A major influential point of the organs of the abdominal cavity, it opens into the yin aspect of the solar plexus chakra and governs all the functions relating to the organs and chakras on all seven levels of the aura. It can be located approximately four inches above the umbilicus in the mid-line of the abdomen.

Du 8 — Coupled with Ren 12, these two acupuncture points open the solar plexus chakra so that the energy flows bi-directionally front and back between the chakras, thereby opening the flow to and from the auric levels. When the aura communicates through these acupoints appropriately, the person experiences positive feelings about themselves. The ego is balanced and in harmony with the psyche. Du 8 is located below the spinous process of the ninth thoracic vertebra.

Du 4 — This acupoint is called "life gate" and is located just below the spinous process of the fourth lumbar vertebra. It is responsible for warming the *yang qi* of the body and is the epicenter of the posterior sacral chakra.

Ren 4 — Located on the front of the body, three inches below the umbilicus, it is the epicenter of the yin or receptive aspect of the sacral chakra. Together with Du 4, they open the bi-directional flow of energy to the aura. Physical problems can develop in a person when the energy flow within these acupoints is obstructed. The person may experience diminished libido, lack of creativity, depression, and physical pain in the low back. Uterine fibroids can develop in females and prostate problems in males.

Du 1 — Located between the tip of the coccyx and the anus, Ren 1 is located between the root of the sacrum in males and in females between the anus and the posterior labial commissure. These are the major opening points for the flow of *Qi* energy from the earth via the root chakra, up the spinal column, and through the crown chakra, forming the kundalini energy of the Chong Mai, affecting the aura through the root and crown chakras. When energy is blocked between the root and crown, there is dissociation between the lower levels of the aura and the upper levels, and the person experiences suicidal tendencies, despair, and no desire to live.

There are secondary opening points located in the palms of the hands (PC 8) and the soles of the feet (KI 1), also at the top of the shoulders (GB 21), and finally the opening of the "four gates"(Li 4) on the hand between the first and second metacarpal bones, and (LV 3) on the top of the foot distal to the first and second metatarsal bones. These open to the lower three levels of the aura, which are closest to the physical body and are not related to the effects of the extraordinary vessels.

Secondly, acupuncture can stimulate and activate the levels of the aura once the opening gateways are clear and unobstructed to the flow of *Qi* energy. Often in my practice, I see patients who have come to me as a last resort, because all other interventions have failed or all their diagnostic tests are negative, yet they continue to experience symptoms that limit their functioning. Energy disharmony manifests itself in several ways. A person may experience a depletion (low energy), stagnation (blocked energy), or excessive accumulation in one area and depletion in another. Depletion of energy can result from damage to the aura by trauma, emotional or physical. I have observed energy leaks in the aura from surgical interventions and from traumatic childbirthing, as well as holes in the aura that occur as a result of exposure to toxic chemicals and/or radiation treatments. Overwork, severe emotional stress, worry, and over-indulgence of all sorts can weaken the aura. The following will illustrate damage to the aura from childbirth.

Case

A thirty-five-year-old female with complaints of general fatigue, who stays at home full-time caring for her year-old son, is planning to return to her full-time professional practice within the year but has concerns about her ability to cope physically. Although she has a part-time helper in the home and a supportive spouse, her energy becomes depleted very quickly on exertion, and she has no desire for pleasure. All medical diagnostic testing is negative.

After evaluating the tongue and pulse, which revealed a deficiency in the yang energy of the kidney, an aura energy assessment was done. In my practice I assess the flow of energy between the chakras and the levels of the aura using a pendulum. The following chart was developed illustrating the energy flow in this person.

Chakra/Aura	**1**	**2**	**3**	**4**	**5**	**6**	**7**
Root	❍	■	■	▲			
Sacral	■	■	■	▲			
Solar Plexus	■	▼	◆	◗			
Heart	❤	▲					
Throat							
Third Eye							
Crown							

❍ *No energy flow through the chakra on this level of the aura.*

❤ *Clockwise spin, with diminished flow of energy through the chakra and to the aura on this level of the aura.*

■ *Counterclockwise spin, with diminished flow of energy through the chakra and the aura at this level.*

▲ *Horizontal (back and forth), chaos in the flow of energy within the aura and the chakra on this particular level.*

- ◆ *Elliptical to the left, compensatory mechanism in an effort to keep chakra open.*
- ▼ *Elliptical to the right, compensatory mechanism in an effort to keep chakra open.*
- ◗ *Counterclockwise spin, with adequate flow of energy within chakra and aura. This is also a compensatory maladaptive sign reflecting a negative focus. If it continues, it will result in a blockage of the flow of energy in the chakra.*

Blank areas indicates normal energy flow to the chakra and aura. The spin is clockwise, with a three- to five-inch diameter. In diminished flow, the spin is less than three inches in diameter. If the spin is more than five inches in diameter, above a chakra, then I consider this to be in excess, and the chakra is being overused. Vertical direction of energy often can signify hara line difficulties.

The root chakra was completely blocked on the first level of the aura indicating that the problem was confined to the physical body, in and around the root center. The sacral and root chakra, on the second and third level had a counterclockwise flow, indicating an aberrant flow of energy in a effort to balance the aura and the root chakra. The solar plexus revealed an elliptical directional flow on the second and third levels of the aura and a counterclockwise flow on the first and fourth levels. The heart chakra showed compensatory chaos but was otherwise open. The throat, third eye (brow), and crown chakras all were open with normal spin in clockwise direction on all seven layers of the aura.

I further assessed the aura using my hands to sense the direction and intensity of the energy flow and to palpate for obstructions to the flow. What I discovered was a large tear in the first layer of the aura continuing into the second layer. The tear was very irregular, and tremendous amounts of energy leaked from the sacral area. The upper layers of the aura felt depleted or deficient. After discussing the findings with the patient, she confided that she had had an episiotomy; nevertheless, the baby's head was somewhat large, and she experienced a lot of tearing of her perineum during the delivery, which took several months to heal.

In this case I chose to use non-contact therapeutic healing touch and other non-contact techniques to repair the tear in the first and second level of the aura, and then apply acupuncture to stimulate and invigorate the flow of energy within the field that had become depleted from the leaking of energy through the sacral chakra. The acupuncture points used in the treatment of this patient were as follows: UB 24 (sea of energy),

Ren 4, and DU 4 to open the flow to the sacral chakra, ST 36 and Ren 12 to invigorate the blood and *Qi* energy of the body and the solar plexus chakra, SP 3 and Ren 1 to activate the energy in the root chakra and restore the communication to the earth and to stimulate the Chong Vessel. Lastly, KI 3,7, and Du 20 were used to activate the Chong and circulate the energy between the crown and the root chakras and "tonify" the kidney pulse. After three consecutive treatments the patient's energy level was restored to the level prior to her delivery. She was given breathing exercises to strengthen the chakras and circulate the energies in her aura.

The points commonly used to stimulate and activate the aura include, but are not limited to, the "tonification points" of the twelve regular meridians. The Chong Mai, Ren, and DU meridians originate in the uterus and are very effective in treating problems, physical or emotional, relating to the first and second chakras. It is very beneficial in persons with a history of childhood sexual abuse with resultant unhealed emotional scars.

Thirdly, acupuncture harmonizes and balances the aura, promoting a continuous flow of energy between the chakras, physical body, and auric levels. When the aura and the energy of the body are in balance, one experiences good health of the body/mind. In our fast-paced, technological society, many people experience a sort of spiritual poverty. This often manifests itself in the person who has "everything," so to speak, including successful career and family life, absence of physical disease, but who still cannot enjoy life. This disturbance manifests in the aura as a block in the upper three or four levels of the aura and can be successfully treated with the eight confluent points of the extraordinary vessels, the "spiritual points" and the points of the "windows to the sky."

Confluent Points

These are paired points that when needled at a shallow depth can reach beyond the body to balance the *shen* (spirit/mind) and harmonize the aura.

PC 6 — SP 4
SI 3 — UB 62
TW 5 — GB 41
LU 7 — KI 6

Window to the Sky Points

These points are effective in the treatment of psychosomatic disorders. They promote the flow of clear *Qi* within the organs, especially the brain via the cerebro-spinal fluid; they also influence the endocrine system. They are ST 9, Ren 22, Du 16, LI 18, SI 16 and 17, UB 10, TW 16, LU 3, and PC 1.

I have used the spiritual points in combination with the confluent points in treating several cases of depression or *shen* disturbance. In these persons, the aura is contracted, the chakras often contain a black tar-like substance, and in some cases the hara line is damaged. The line of the hara, described by Brennan's *Hands of Light* (1987), appears to my clairvoyant vision as a straight line, entering through the egg of the seventh chakra on the seventh level of the aura and continuing down the midline of the body, emerging through the root chakra, and continuing infinitely. I have never experienced the end of this line. When it is healthy, it appears to have a silver glow; when it is damaged, it will appear as a dull black color and may be broken or damaged.

A patient was refered to the Center for Radiant Health because she experienced constant headaches, yet all her neurological tests were normal. Energetic assessment revealed decreased energy flow to the crown chakra and a block in the posterior or yang aspect of the throat chakra. Her hara line was bent at a forty-five degree angle, protruded through the posterior throat chakra, and looked like a frayed electrical wire. There was no communication with the crown chakra. This woman, who was very kind and generous and had difficulty saying no to others, had gone to college and chosen a career that her parents desired for her, not what she wanted. The hara line aligns one with one's life purpose. This person was not very happy in her profession, and after several treatments using the window to the sky points, she began to entertain the possibility of making a career change.

The spiritual points can be found on the UB or urinary bladder channel that runs lateral to the spine. These points, as well as the window to the sky points, reach beyond the physical body to the portion of the "soul" that is said to be stored in the organs. They have a wide range of influence on the psychological well-being of a person, thereby promoting change in the aura through improved psychological functioning. These points are UB42, referred to as the door to the corporeal soul. UB 44 (mind hall) is responsible for transporting and balancing the energy between the heart and the fourth level of the aura. UB 47, called the door to the ethereal soul, harmonizes and promotes the flow of *Qi* to and from the aura and the liver. UB 49 stimulates memory and concentration and is effective in treating persons who have obsessive thoughts or who worry too much. It communicates with the aura through the spleen. UB 52 communicates with the aura through the kidneys and is called "will power room." It literally reinforces the will power in persons with weakness of will; it is also useful in certain types of depression when the person lacks the mental strength or will to get better.

There are over seven hundred acupuncture points, and all of them, in varying degrees, affect and influence the aura energetically. These acupuncture points are in themselves chakras that filter, transform, and regulate the flow of energy (*Qi*) within and without the body. As is above, so below; therefore, if the aura's energy is diminished in any way, soon the body will be affected and vice versa. All the organs of the viscera have major chakras over them that communicate with the aura. These chakras are also sites of "big acupoints" that have a direct therapeutic effect on these organs.

The acupuncture meridians lie beneath the skin and occupy the first layer of the aura. These meridians communicate with the other layers of the aura and the body via the major and minor chakra system.

This phenomenon became evident to me through clairvoyant vision while treating a twenty-nine-year-old female diagnosed with stage II Reflex Sympathetic Dystrophy (RSD) of the right forearm. Her presenting complaints were constant pain, abnormal temperature changes, muscular atrophy, and impairment of the protective nature of the right arm. She also complained of anorexia, depression, and insomnia. She had lost the function of her right arm, with resultant changes in body image and self-esteem. The only anchor she had to living were her two children, whom she loved dearly, and her spouse, who was very supportive.

The energy assessment revealed severe blockage in all of the major chakras. The chakras excreted a black, tarry substance into her aura. Her right arm, on the second level of the aura, had red lines, or streaks, consistent with the pathways of the lung, heart, and pericardium meridians. There was no energy movement in these meridians, and the *Qi* was stagnant, turbid, and obstructed. Unfortunately, I was not able to follow this patient. After only a few treatments, she relocated with her family to another state, where she continued to receive energy work. The last time

I heard from her, she was still experiencing some symptoms but was much improved.

Conclusion

There is no doubt that there is room for research in this emerging area of energy medicine that necessitates a multidisciplinary, team approach to the treatment of the patient. Within this chapter, I have proposed a model that I use in my private practice that integrates my Western medical experience with Oriental medicine and energy healing. A model, I believe, is Holistic both in theory and in practice.

CHAPTER SIXTEEN

AURAS IN THERAPY

Andrine Morse

THE DAY DAWNED BRIGHT AND SUNNY in mid-August. I sat in my office wishing I had a window so, despite my compulsion to work, I could enjoy a bit of the sun's rays. I shuffled papers from one side of the desk to the other, trying to create some focus for the tasks lined up in neat little piles. A fly began buzzing around my head. Glad to have something to do, I scrambled to roll up a few sheets of paper. Armed, I began pursuing the fly, determined to wipe its small existence off the planet.

"What did it do to you?" queried a voice.

Annoyed by the interruption, I turned around to see an old Cree womyn who had become a regular visitor to my office.

"Nothing," I said, cryptically taking another swipe at the fly.

"Then why are you killing it? Are you going to eat it? Was it going to eat you?"

I blew air out through my lips, "It was bugging me. It's a bug. Everyone kills bugs. And flies carry diseases—they're unclean."

"How did it get sick?" she asked.

By then I had lost heart for the chase, so I flopped back into my chair and glared at her. She laughed.

"Let's go for a walk," she said by way of command and not request.

I was going to say no, then stopped myself. I wasn't getting any work done, so I stood up and picked up my keys. The nice thing about working on a reserve is that there are circumstances, such as going for a walk with an elder, that suggest it is okay to hang out your "closed" sign at nearly anytime of the day.

I followed her into the brilliant sunlight and walked behind her as she took off across a field. Hers was a steady rolling gait. She turned her head slightly from side to side so her time-wizened eyes would miss nothing. The tiny, triangular tail of her colorful scarf caught the breeze, flapping in the current of air. Without warning she abruptly stopped, and I nearly collided with her back.

"See that?" she said, pointing to the ribbon of blacktop not too far in the distance. Silver rays of heat snaked into the air off of the heated asphalt.

"Yes," I said, not even sure what I was supposed to be seeing.

"You can see that around someone who's gonna be sick—have a fever."

"What?"

"Heat snakes—that," she said, pointing toward the road again. "Then you could blow a cold wind on them to take the heat away."

I shrugged and looked helplessly towards the road. She made a low sound in her throat and started walking again. The next time she stopped, she bent low to the ground, placing her knarled hands over the top of a small plant sporting tiny white flowers.

"Womyn's tea. Not ready yet," she said.

I bent, staring at the plant, noticing its soft fern-like leaves and wide clusters of flowers. I reached out my hand, attempting to understand what she was doing. I felt nothing but the soft leaf and the velvet of the flowers.

"You look around you. Everything you can see has a life inside of it. Everything you see is waiting to be useful. Maybe it will teach a lesson. Maybe it's gonna make a seed. Maybe it's gonna go back into the earth and make some dirt. Maybe it's gonna be food for something else, or maybe it's gonna be a medicine and help someone or something out."

I turned in a slow circle, taking in the rich diversity of life growing there in a field by a road in the middle of a First Nation's reserve. I looked down at the little plant with a sense of wonder at the myriad of possibilities. In a few short minutes I became extremely conscious of something that had, until then, gone surprisingly unnoticed by me—life. It was everywhere! I moved my foot and noticed that it nearly landed on a small blue flower. I placed it back where it had been and tried moving in a different direction, noticing something else growing there as well. I felt my heart start to pound. I wondered whether or not I could just step very lightly so as not to damage anything. I couldn't. I just stood there staring. For a moment I even felt as though I might begin to cry. Then the old womyn's voice shook me from my reverie.

"Get moving! You're killing things!"

I leapt into the air and hopped onto another spot, looking behind me to see small plants flattened to the ground where moments before my feet had been. I panicked and froze again.

"When you stop—when you forget to move, then you are destroying what has already grown. Look at those little ones," she ordered, pointing to the plants I had crushed with my feet. I was amazed to see one tiny leaf spring back up and then another and then another. "Everything is like that green one. Its purpose is to grow, and if nothing stops it, this is what it will do. Life is this way. Life is movement. Life is the Great Wheel. If nothing gets in its way, then it grows. This is the same for your life or any kind of life. Sickness is the same way, too. If nothing stops it, then it grows. See? Sickness and life. Sickness can stop a life, and life can stop a sickness."

The Crown of Air

In time, I learned how to place my hands over a plant, rock, animal, water, or person and to sense the life force energy radiating out from its mass. When this old Cree Grandmother spoke about "life," she was talking about that which modern science calls the electromagnetic radiation emanating from the surfaces of humans, animals, and even inanimate objects: the aura or corona.

The root or origin of the word aura is derived from Greek *aemi,* "I blow," and *aura,* "breeze." In ancient cultures, life force energy was indeed considered to be the air we breathe or the breath. Corona meant crown. Putting them together, we can conclude that this means crown of air. How do we know that this crown of air exists as electromagnetic radiation?

The easiest way is perhaps to practice with two magnets and their polarized energy. Place them near to one another, and then pass your hand or finger between the two. You will, if you are psychically attuned, feel a current of energy. This same current of energy exists around all things, animate or inanimate.

Many people can see this auric force around people, animals, and plants. Some people may experience the ability to see a full range of color similar to a rainbow, while others see only waves of energy similar to that of heat radiating off of asphalt on a summer's day. Still others sense this energy through touch or laying on of hands.

The Auric Bodies and Dis-ease[1]

The physical self has an energy layer double that is most often referred to as the etheric body. This etheric body is the mirror for the dense body's functioning. Blockages of energy occur here before the blockage manifests as disease or illness in the dense body. Those places where energy becomes blocked can no longer generate healthy cell growth, and, in time, the cells atrophy, creating dis-ease in the system. By ensuring a healthy flow of energy throughout the system, our approach to well-being becomes preventative as opposed to the current system of intervention practiced by modern medicine. This layer remains intact throughout an organism's existence. This condition means that, if due to dis-ease or accident, a leg or arm is removed, it can still be sensed on this level.

The mental and emotional bodies are mirrored in the next layer of the aura, the astral body. This layer is a person's connection between the physical body and the mind.

The third layer of the aura, known as the spiritual body, is thought to be the area of integration of all other bodies, energetic as well as dense. When a blockage occurs in the astral or spiritual body, it will be translated to the etheric body and eventually manifest in the dense physical body.

The Aura and Energy Centers

The bands of color in an aura also correspond to the energy centers in the body. These energy centers are called chakras, meaning "wheel" or "vortex." There are seven chakras, previously referred to in Chapter Seven: 1) Muladhara, root or base, red; 2) Svadisthana, vital force or sacral center, orange; 3) Manipuraka, solar plexus or lumbar center, yellow; 4) Anahatha, heart or dorsal center, pink or green; 5) Visshudha, throat or cervical center, blue; 6) Ajna, third eye or consciousness center, violet; and 7) Sahasrara, crown or wisdom center, white or gold.

When each of the seven chakras are open and balanced, the aura will appear clear and radiate like light refracted through a crystal. All the colors of the rainbow will be present and emanating from all three auric layers. Within the brilliance of this crystal rainbow light there will be a dominant show of color in three significant areas.

A dominant color displayed on the right side of your aura refers to the vibrational frequency most likely seen or felt by those around you, while a dominant color near the center of your aura or over the crown is what you experience for yourself and best describes you.

Finally, the dominant color visible on the left side of your aura refers to areas of potential you would do well to develop, as it is the vibration coming into your being. A practitioner may require the aid of a Kirlian photograph or an Aura Imaging Camera to discern these three bands of color. These colors are ones that are most often beneficial when balancing and correcting your overall field of energy.

Most individuals will not display a balanced aura, requiring work on their chakras and auric fields. Therefore, the primary goal of the practitioner is to balance the energy along the body's meridians. These meridians are pathways that circulate electromagnetic energy throughout the body and, in each chakra, create an uninterrupted emanation of energy apparent in the aura. The techniques and methods vary from one practitioner to another because there are many ways to balance energy. It is important to explore various techniques and methods to find the one with which a person is most comfortable (note chapters on energy and acupuncture).

Ways of Balancing the Aura

Some branches of alternate medicine that incorporate the balancing of the aura or energies to promote well being are: reflexology, acupuncture, acupressure, energy balancing, laying on of hands, Reiki, homeopathic medicines such as Bach Flower Remedies, aromatherapy, herbology, color therapy, crystal therapy, some massage therapies, and toning using sound.

Alice Chapman, an alternative health practitioner, explains that a physical trauma, such as a broken bone, will generally have three things attached to the original trauma. There will be the physical event itself, the emotions associated with the event, and the beliefs associated with the event. Therefore, all three bands of the aura will be affected, as if holding the memory of the break. Energy at or near the site of the break will be interrupted or cloudy. Alice (1996) says you might think of this effect as being similar to a paved road—the paved road being the meridians of energy which run through and around the body. An incident occurs, creating a bump or pothole on the road, and the practitioner assists the individual, smoothing out the bump or filling in the pothole. If this hole or bump along the energy meridians goes unattended, the blockage in the energy field will create an imbalance of energy in one or more chakras as they either begin closing down or become overactive to compensate for the blockage. This reaction may trigger other long-term physical symptoms. The sooner the trauma is dealt with on all three levels, the sooner the energy begins flowing along the meridians, creating an uninterrupted environment for healing.

Much of this information has been confirmed through the use of Kirlian photography. Through the use of Kirlian techniques, it was discovered that resonance points in the fingertips correlate to specific acupuncture passages. This technique has, according to certain researchers, revealed congested energy in certain chakras of the body (Lindgren 1975). This correlation between auras, energy centers, and acupuncture was substantiated in the early 1970s work of Inyushin and his college assistant, Nikolas Shuisky (Moss 1974).

Chakras and Organ Imbalance

The physical parts of the body impacted by the first chakra are the blood, spine, nervous system, bladder, male reproductive organs, and the vagina. Those parts influenced by the second chakra are the skin, mammary glands, female reproductive organs, and the kidneys. Imbalances in the third chakra will most likely manifest in the diaphragm, skin, digestive organs, gall bladder, liver, and adrenals.

Fourth chakra imbalances may be indicated in the heart, immune system, thymus gland, lymph glands, and the lungs. In the fifth chakra, look for indicators in the areas of the throat, thyroid, nerve tissue, ears, and muscles. Imbalances in the sixth chakra will manifest in the eyes, ears, nose, brain, pituitary gland, and pineal gland. The seventh is similar to the sixth chakra in that the areas affected are similar: the pituitary gland, pineal gland, brain, and nervous system.

Emotional Trauma and the Aura

An emotional or mental trauma, such as fear or grief, will also create an area of stress within the system, which manifests as a blockage of energy in the same manner described for physical traumas. This trauma will create interruptions in the flow of electricity along the body's meridians and may surface as physical pain, illness, or disease. If a person traces the physical manifestation to the trauma, acknowledges the emotion, and changes the belief, then the physical healing will be positively affected.

Alice (1996) says, "The first technique I would use to find the areas where the energy is blocked would be Kaliki, which is the Huna practice of opening or balancing energy centers. The Huna belief is that energy is not taken from outside of a person and put into them, rather, if someone is ill, their own energy is unbalanced or blocked. A person wants to find where the block is and unblock it.

"It is important that I talk to the person and discover what their belief is. If they believe strongly or are strongly attached to physical therapy, then I would approach it with a very physical therapy technique, such as reflexology or hands on massage. I try to focus on a person's beliefs. If they have a strong belief in energy work, then this is the approach one would take."

Releasing Energy Blockage Through Reflexology and Acupuncture

One of the physical therapies that Alice employs is reflexology. In foot-reflexology, the soles of the feet are divided into segments corresponding to the organs and glands throughout the body.

"In reflexology, the idea is that energy flows through meridians found in and around the body. If I find a place on the foot that is sensitive, I would say there was a blockage there, and, by working the area, I am unblocking it so that the energy can begin to flow along the meridian."

Another technique, acupressure massage and acupuncture, relate to a complex map of all of the bodies pressure points along energy meridians. Acupuncture is an ancient Oriental health practice based on stimulating the pressure points along the body's meridians. The acupuncturist promotes energy flow in a continuous cycle by inserting needles at certain pressure points in the body. Acupressure massage is the practice of using the middle finger on each hand to apply a deep massage to the pressure points. Alice uses a tool called an Acuhealth Meter® to stimulate these same pressure points. The Acuhealth Meter® is a hand-held apparatus used to locate blockages along the body's meridians. A small sensor near the end indicates where energy is blocked by emitting a high-pitched squeal when the sensor moves over a blocked meridian point.

"It is really effective for people as they see it and hear it, because it gives them a very strong sense of being worked on physically," says Alice (1996). When an area is located, the practitioner touches a small button on the side of the apparatus, and a pulse of electricity is emitted into the area, breaking down the blockage, such as a calcified deposit, along the meridian. If there is a lot of tension, the individual may even feel a stinging sensation. When the area is clear, the high-pitched sound lessens and eventually clears, letting both the practitioner and the individual know that the energy along the meridian point is no longer blocked.

The Beamer®

Teresa McCleod, an alternative health practitioner and reflexologist, uses a product called a Beamer® to achieve the same results. A Beamer® is a gold-plated, plastic tube filled with special gases. Each of the gases vibrates to a corresponding musical octave. These special vibrations are a high resonance energy that is broadcast into a medium such as food, beverages, herbs, vitamins, cosmetics, people, or plants. One variation looks like an oversized pencil. Another looks like a tower pyramid. Teresa explains, "The use of beamers clears energy blocks while regenerating cells at a molecular level. Beamers work on acupressure points to clear the body's meridians."

How and why? In simple terms, diseased cells contain water that is not organized or structured, while healthy cells contain structured water. A beamer's energy, using molecular resonance, organizes or structures the molecules of the receptive media into crystal lattices of information. In this way, diseased cells become healthy cells.

"I personally use reflexology and the beamers," says Teresa. "Initially, I find that people may require the physical sensation of hands on touch (reflexology). Reflexology also helps me to locate any areas of tenderness so that treatment can be focused where it is most needed. At some point a person is able to sense fine energy balances for themselves. It's at this point that they can really feel the beamer working to clear energy blocks. It does a fantastic job of just plain old relaxation."

In this process (i.e., reflexology), like acupuncture, "Kirlian photography uses reflexology points to show organic conditions in the human body. Since a blocked or weakened organ is equivalent to a blocked nerve, only a small or no electrical charge will be displayed in the reflexology points" (Fisslinger 1994, 21).

An individual beamer contains nine gases which are:

Alphanon	1st octave
Betanon	2nd octave
Gammanon	3rd octave
Helium	4th octave
Neon	5th octave
Argon	6th octave
Krypton	7th octave
Nonex	8th octave
Niton	9th octave

Moving Energy Through Reiki and Sound

Vonnie Musgrove, a Reiki practitioner and gifted voice medium, prefers working intuitively, sensing energy blockages and balancing the auric field of her clients. Vonnie begins by ensuring that the individual is relaxed. Then, moving her hands slowly four to six inches above the body, she begins feeling the energy in each chakra and in the overall aura. Energy, like water in an ice-tray, is gently moved from one chakra to the next until all are balanced and clear. If a blockage in energy is discovered, Vonnie employs sound, touch, and Reiki symbols in clearing the specific area. Vonnie uses her own voice to tone sound vibrations directly into the afflicted area. Other practitioners may use bells, tuning forks, or bowls to accomplish this.

Alice (1996) says there are three main areas to focus on, no matter what technique or method you choose to employ. "If you can increase elimination, increase circulation, and normalize body rhythms, then your body knows how to take care of itself, and there is no illness. And the major way to do that is to eliminate and/or correct stress physically, emotionally, and spiritually."

"Attention is energy," says Alice (1996). "Energy flows where my attention goes. So, if I use my attention to focus on those areas, the energy begins to flow. Our energy is also affected by the closest strongest resonate field which is around us. A person needs to surround himself with healthy strong energy to keep his health up: live foods (fresh food), crystals, plants, shapes, and symbols that would resonate strong healthy energy. This procedure increases well-being and assists one in keeping his own energy vibrating at a frequency that promotes personal wellness."

To know if a practitioner has an understanding of auras and practices any form of aura balancing, it is best to speak with them and ask the right questions. Simple and direct questions are the best route, such as, "Do you do auric cleansing or balancing?" From this point on, one can get more specific about the particular physical, emotional, or spiritual complaint and, hopefully, the practitioner will be able to assist the individual or make a referral to another practitioner who can.

Listings for practitioners can be found in many places. Some phone books will contain yellow-page listings for alternative health, and this may be the best place to start. Bookstores who specialize in stones, crystals, and spirituality will also have resource lists of persons practicing in the area. Health food stores, particularly those with homeopathic pharmacies, will usually have names of local healers.

Don't discount local indigenous healers or medicine people. Like the Cree Grandmother I spoke of, they may not have heard the word aura but may have all the skills necessary to assist one in achieving auric cleansing or balancing using their native medicines, techniques, and ceremonies to balance one's life force or spiritual energies.

It is worth mentioning again, in closing, that all things in creation have the life force energy or aura that has been discussed in relation to the human form. Energy, at varying vibrational frequencies, is present in light, sound, colors, stones, water, plants, crawlers, fish, humans, and the very air we breath. Each of these is a microcosm of the greater whole—Earth. Earth's aura, at one time radiant, is in need of our attention and healing assistance. As we help ourselves to live in balance, we are helping Earth.

Note

1. It important to mention that there are many schools of thought which further divide the mental and spiritual bodies into sub-bodies of energy and count the auric field as having nine layers. For ease of understanding I have only discussed the three major layers of the aura. It is certainly not my intention to discount the subtle layers of the aura, yet this is perhaps an area for further study and does not best serve the purpose of this introduction to aura therapy.

CHAPTER SEVENTEEN

STRENGTHENING THE CHAKRAS THROUGH HERBAL THERAPY[1]

C. E. Lindgren, DLitt
Master Herbologist

CHAKRAS, BEING THE AWARENESS ORGANS of the etheral body, are usually strengthened and cleansed through the use of a regimen of psychic healings, proper breathing, occasional fasting, correct diet, proper rest and sleep (6-8 hours), prayer, and meditation. Other areas of emphasis are a true Rosicrucian lifestyle based on honesty, selfless service, and integrity, listening to Chakra Tones, and drinking quartz crystal or magnetized water (bottled or spring).

It is seldom, however, that one thinks of these swirling energy centers as being renewed through the use of herbal preparations. For millennia, however, Ayurveda medicine has utilized certain preparations applied to the chakra regions to stimulate, or taken internally to energize, these light vortexes.

The Seven Chakras

Root Chakra *(also known as base or first chakra)*
Element: Earth
Traditional Color: Red
Sanskrit: Muladhara
Musical Note: C

Location: The base of the spine (coccyx)
Essencial Oils: Black pepper, frankincense, and vetiver
Enhancement Herbs: Ashwagandha

Ashwagandha (*Withenia somnifera*): Ashwagandha provides the body with a calming effect. The herb helps circulation and aids in the healing of broken bones. The term **Ashwagandha** literally means "to impart the strength of the horse." "It helps to nourish and strengthen the inner reserves of the human body" (Ayusherbs 1996).

Sacral Plexus Chakra *(naval or second chakra)*
Element: Water
Traditional Color: Orange
Sanskrit: Svàdahisthana
Musical Note: D
Location: Two inches below the belly button
Essential Oils: Jasmine, Tangerine, ylang ylang
Enhancement Herbs: Fennel and **Coriander**

Fennel (*Foeniculum officinale*): The qualities of this herb include anti-inflammatory, diuretic, and carminative. Strengthens the sacral plexus chakra.

Coriander (*Coriandrum sativum*): An aid to the digestive system, coriander assists in eliminating spasm pain and diarrhoea. In Ayurveda medicine, the herb aids in clearing the Chakra and providing vitality.

Solar Plexus Chakra *(third chakra)*
Element: Fire
Traditional Color: Yellow
Sanskrit: Manipura
Musical Note: E
Location: Just under the rib cage, at the diaphragm or solar plexus
Essential Oils: Lemon, rosemary, sage,
Enhancement Herbs: **Lemon Balm** and **Goldenseal**

Lemon Balm (*Melissa officinalis*): Known for its sedative qualities, the herb also is used as an anti-depressant, an antiviral, antibacterial agent, and a relaxant to the nervous system.

Golden Seal (*Hydrastis canadensis*): This expensive herb serves as a powerful astringent. Serving as a tonic, individuals should be careful in their doses as it is known to raise blood pressure.

Heart Chakra: *(fourth chakra)*
Element: Air
Traditional Color: Green
Sanskrit: Anahata
Musical Note: F
Location: Center of the chest, just under the sternum
Essential Oils: Eucalyptus, rose, mellisa, neroli
Enhancement herbs: Rose and **Saffron**

Rose (*Rosa spp.*): Serving as a tonic and cooling agent for the mind in Ayurvedic medicine, the Rose, known for it beauty and gentle scent, can be used as an antibacterial, antidepressant, aphrodisiac, and kidney tonic.

Saffron (*Crocus sativus*): According to Earl Mindell's *Herb Bible* (1992), "In 1597, English herbalist John Gerard wrote, 'For those at death's doure and almost past breathing, saffron bringeth breath again.'" In Ayurveda medicine, the spice is considered a "circulatory stimulation, kidney and liver remedy . . . and aphrodisiac" (Castleman 1991, 315). It is also used for depression (Chinese medicine).

Throat Chakra: *(fifth chakra)*
Element: Akasha/æther
Traditional Color: Sky blue
Sanskrit: Visshudha
Musical Note: G
Location: The hollow of the throat
Essential Oils: Cinnamon, eucalyptus, geranium
Enhancement Herbs: Vervain and **Cloves**

Vervain (*Verbena officinalis*): This enhancing herb aids in the elimination of stress and tension, as well as certain cases of depression. The herbal preparation, when fixed correctly, aids the throat chakra.

Cloves (*Syzygium aromaticum*): This medicinal herb may be used as a stimulant, antiseptic, and antispasmodic. This herb clears and assists in opening the fifth chakra.

Brow Chakra: *(Third eye. sixth chakra)*
Traditional Color: Indigo (dark blue)
Sanskrit: Ajna
Element: Light

Musical Note: G
Location: Just above the eyebrows, center of forehead
Essential Oils: Cedarwood, mugwort, sandelwood
Enhancement Herbs: Elecampane and **Sandalwood**

Elecampane (*Inula helenium*): Used as a tonic and antifungal. According to many, assists in strengthening the pituitary gland.

Sandalwood (*Santalum album*): Serving as a sedative and antidepressant, the medicinal herb effects the well-being of the third eye.

"Regarding herbal preparations, Water of magnanimity (an infusion of **mugwort, chicory**, and **loosestrife**) is reported to be excellent for 'opening' the third eye. It is extremely good for augmenting meditative and trance states. Another herb or smoking mixture consists of **laurel leaf**, **vervain**, and **valerian** and produces a trance like state" (Lindgren 1994, 14).

Crown Chakra: *(seventh chakra)*
Traditional Colors: Violet, white, gold
Sanskrit: Sahasra
Element: Thought/will
Musical Note: B
Location: The top of the head
Essential Oils: Frankincense, lavender, rose, sandalwood
Enhancement herbs: Nutmeg and **Goto Kola**

Nutmeg (*Myristica fragrans*): This herb serves as an anti-inflammatory, appetite stimulant, and carminative. Used by Orientals to regulate the qi flow.

Goto Kola (*Centella asiatica*): The herb is used in treating nervous disorders, memory, tonic, and longevity. Also used in Ayurvedic medicine for clarity.

Note

1. Herbs, although generally safe, can be dangerous in large amounts. As noted, some of the herbs mentioned are to be taken internally while other are used externally as compresses. For this reason, this chapter is only to be used as an example of the relationship between specific herbs and various chakras or energy centers. Before taking any herb, check with a herbologist for directions.

CHAPTER EIGHTEEN

BREATH— HEALING THE AURIC FORCE

Robert Bruce and C.E. Lindgren. DLitt

WHILE STUDYING, FOR OVER TWENTY-FIVE YEARS, the philosophies, religion, and arcane societies of the world, the writers have discerned that most have one thing in common. This commonality pertains to the importance of the breath or breathing. From Indian mystic to Rosicrucian, the Divine breath plays an important role in achieving oneness and universal perfection. With breath comes life, and in its absence is death and physical decay. Even the word animate (energize) comes from the Latin *animare,* meaning to fill with breath or breathe. This chapter will discuss several breathing techniques, drawn from Rosicrucianism, Yoga, Zen, Tao, and mystical sources. Each technique provides the same results if faithfully followed.

It is through this breath that the aura can receive energy and nourishment. Proper breathing helps to increase the force and intensity of the auric field and further changes the chakra colors from foglike, muddy, and darkened colors to pure rainbow or prismic colors relating to health and vitality.

There are many breathing techniques which facilitate the cleaning and strengthening of the chakra centers. Some are used in conjunction with meditation, prayers, or visualization. Others are beneficial to the entire auric field and bring well-being, strength, and inner-peace.

Regarding the discipline of Yoga and breathing, Beverly B. Ferguson (1996), Yoga and meditation instructor, states:

Of course, the quality of the auric fields and chakras depends on the energy and consciousness of the individual. This is determined by their complete being and lifestyle, past and present, food, environment, past experiences and thoughts, present attention, and most of all, their mind and thoughts. As the breath and the mind are one, and as Prana effects them both, all the Yogic breathing practices, under Pranayamas, have a profound effect on the aura and chakras. However, it is very important that these be a part of a total practice of Yoga and Meditation with the guidance of a Guru who has themselves practiced pranayama for many years and who has a correct understanding of these practices. It can be dangerous for anyone to take the pranayama practices from a book or teacher and try to do them on their own without also having a thorough understanding and background foundation in the entire Yoga discipline. I have met a few such people and the effects on their lives and the lives of others were not beneficial. The purpose of Yoga and Pranayams, which by the way are one of the most powerful tools in Yoga, is to realize God or one's true essential Self. To realize the answer to the question "Who am I?" not just intellectually but experientially. Without this intention in mind and heart, there would be little point in pursuing breathing practices to effect the aura or the chakras and to do so would be apt to cause more harm than good. That said, of course deep slow diaphragmatic breathing can be of benefit to everyone and would not cause any harm if pursued in a gentle and sensitive manner. That is what I recommend you discuss in your book. It calms the mind and brings healing energy into the body. If you watch an infant or an animal sleeping, you will see that such a breath is perfectly normal. We are all meant to breath that way but very few humans do. To teach people to breath "normally," deeply and slowly, would be a very great thing to do. The effects of such breathing are extremely profound on the level of body and mind. The changes in the aura and chakras of an enlightened being, saint, or yogi are a side effect of their level of consciousness and spiritual practice They are not goals to be pursued in and of themselves. Instead, they are a consequence of a life dedicated to spiritual pursuits. The purpose of human life is to realize God, or one's own true nature, not to manipulate auras or chakras. All those changes happen spontaneously as a result of proper practice. It is inner transformation that is wanted not just changes in outer image. It is not the robe that makes the messiah. Let the outer follow the inner not the other way around.

Brucian Techniques

As some parts in this book have already shown, breathing can be an effective and powerful way of drawing energy into the body. Awareness energy breathing is an extension of this that uses "bodily awareness" to draw planetary energy into the body. This stimulates the energy body and strengthens the auric field, as well as increasing vitality, which stimulates the immune system and aids self-healing. The energy I speak of is composed of many different types of energy but is easier to think of as simply "Planetary Energy" and as coming generally from the planet and atmosphere around us. The feet and hands are the main conduits into the body for this type of energy.

Storage Centres

The human energy body has three important energy storage centres where different types of planetary energy are accumulated and stored. These are quite different from the three primary energy centres (major chakras) that share the same general area, although they can be considered as being related to them.

Sub-Navel: *Position* — midway between belly button and pubic line, two inches inside body. *Function* — physical vitality energy storage.
Sub-Heart: *Position* — in centre of chest, between nipples (man) or between centre of breasts (woman), and two inches inside body. *Function* — emotional energy storage.
Sub-Brow: *Position* — between eye socket ridges in lower centre of brow, two inches inside brow. *Function* — mental and psychic energy storage.

Of these three storage centres, the only safe one to actively fill is the Sub-Navel, which will naturally overflow into the Sub-Heart, which will overflow into the Sub-Brow once the other two are full. **Warning!** Filling the two higher storage centres first is a *very* unhealthy practise and can, my research shows, cause emotional and/or mental instability. Filling the Sub-Navel can take anything from several months to several years—depending upon the state of the energy body and how strongly energy flows into it. Filling the higher Sub-Navel centres first might give you a few thrills, at first, but will not speed your overall energy development and will definitely unbalance your energy body.

Moving the Seat of Awareness[1]

The seat of human consciousness (awareness) naturally rests in the eyes. This is its natural position, but it can be easily moved to any part of the body with a simple act of will. To illustrate this, lightly scratch a small area on the back of your left hand with a fingernail, just hard enough to cause a slight stinging sensation. Close your eyes and "feel" this area with your "awareness." Do not allow your closed eyes to look in this direction while doing this, as this will weaken the action. Concentrate and "feel" this area with your bodily awareness. If you actively manipulate your awareness in this area, without allowing your muscles to respond, you will stimulate your energy body in that area. For example, move your "awareness" repeatedly back and forth over the back of the same hand, as if you were rubbing or brushing it. Hold your awareness close to your skin, using the memory of the slight sting you gave it to help zero in on this area with your awareness. You are now actively manipulating your energy body in this area.

Posture and Relaxation

No deep level of relaxation is required for any of these exercises, so just sit and relax, with shoes and socks removed. Stretch and rest your legs slightly out in front of you. Rest them on a cushion if you like, to make them comfortable, but do not cross your legs. Your legs do not have to be dead straight, just generally out in front and comfortably resting. Also, it does not really matter if you tense your muscles while doing these exercises, although you should try and keep them relaxed. Once you get the hang of these exercises you can do them anywhere, standing, sitting or lying down.

Feet

The first step is to loosen up and stimulate some of the secondary energy centres and energy exchange ports in your feet and hands, to increase the energy flow potential into your body. Using a similar but much larger awareness action, as with the back of the hand example above, repeatedly brush your awareness back and forth, covering the entire sole of your left foot, from toes to heel. This is as if you were using a large paintbrush on the sole of your foot. Rub this area with your hand or actually use a paintbrush, if you like, to help you get a "feel" for this action and centre your awareness there.

Use your breathing to aid this "awareness" action. Always breathe IN through your nose and OUT through your mouth—unless your nose is blocked. Breathe slowly and deeply, and as you breathe IN, draw your awareness from toes to heel. As you breathe OUT, draw your awareness from heel to toes. Repeat this with your right foot.

Draw your "awareness" back and forth along the top of your left foot, from the tips of your toes to the front of your ankle. Scratch this area lightly, rub it with your hand or use a brush, to help you get a "feel" for it and centre your awareness there. Draw your "awareness" from toes to ankle on the IN breath and from ankle to toes on the OUT breath.

Extend your "awareness" through your entire foot, drawing back and forth through the whole of your left foot, inside and out. Repeat this exercise with your right foot.

Splitting Awareness

Split your awareness and draw it back and forth through both feet at the same time. "Feel" both your feet, and work them both at the same time. Breathe IN as you draw your awareness from toes to backs of ankles and heels, and OUT as you move it back to toes.

Drawing Energy Through Legs

Using both legs, on the IN breath, draw your awareness from tips of toes to ankles, up shins to knees, then to the front of your hips. Draw UP your legs on the IN breath, and let go of it on the OUT breath. When you let go, quickly return your awareness to the starting point in your feet. Do NOT feel your awareness moving back down your legs; simply return your awareness to your feet, ready for the next IN breath. The whole idea is to rhythmically breathe energy "upwards" into your body.

Extend your "awareness" to fill both your legs, as you did with your feet, so you are drawing energy through the whole of your legs. "Feel" your awareness moving through your legs from feet to hips with each IN breath, and return to your feet with each OUT breath.

Arms and Hands

Repeat all the above exercises, step by step, with your hands and arms, taking energy up past your shoulders to the back of your neck.

Full Body Circuit

A full body energy circuit uses a combination of breathing and bodily awareness to stimulate the entire energy body. This aids overall development, as well as drawing energy directly into the Sub-Navel storage centre, all of which strengthens and brightens the auric field.

Continue this exercise for at least five minutes, with slow, deep breaths, holding your awareness close to your body at all times.

All the above stimulation exercises on the feet and hands should, ideally, always be done prior to the full body circuit. This may sound laborious, but with regular practise a few simple waves of awareness through feet and hands will suffice to stimulate enough energy flow to power the full body circuit.

On the IN breath, raise energy up both legs, past hips, up your back, and take it all up your back to the top of your head, and hold it there until you finish breathing IN.

On the OUT breath, take the energy down your face, chest, and stomach, and push it into your Sub-Navel storage area. Feel it flowing into your body there. At the end of the OUT breath, quickly shift your awareness back to your feet, ready for the start of the next IN breath.

Joining Arms into the Circuit

Once you are comfortable with the above part of the exercise, its time to join your arms in with the circuit. Hold your arms loose at your side, or rest your hands on your thighs. On the IN breath, raise energy up both legs and up your back to the top of your head. But, as you pass where your hands are resting, draw through your hands and up your arms as well. Let your arms' energy join into the main flow at the back of your neck, and continue to the top of your head. Do this as smoothly and naturally as you can, making it all one awareness breathing action.

On the IN breath, take energy up both legs, past back of hips to the small of your back, letting arm energy join the flow as you pass your hands. Draw ALL energy (legs and arms) up your back to join at neck, and continue on to the top of your head.

On the OUT breath, take all energy down the front into the Sub-Navel—and then quickly shift your awareness back to your feet, ready for the next IN breath.

Repeat this smoothly and rhythmically with each breath, in time with your natural breathing action, always starting from your feet as you begin the IN breath, and always starting from your head as you begin the OUT breath.

Once you are used to this action, you can do it anywhere and any time, with your arms and legs in any position. Simply split your awareness into all four limbs, drawing up both legs and both arms at the same time, to join at the back of your neck. And there is no limit as to how much energy breathing you can or should do. Try to make this a part of your life, and do it as often as possible during your daily activity.

Energy Movement Sensations

There are several peculiar, and sometimes very strong, energy sensations that can be caused by this type of energy work and breathing. It is normal, while doing the energy awareness exercises on the feet, legs, arms, and hands, to feel fairly strong buzzing and tingling sensations in them. These sensations will fade, with regular use and development, to a warm, comfortable, tingling energy flow. The degree of any energy sensations felt during energy-raising sessions depends entirely on the health and developed state of the energy body and how many energy blockages and restricted energy conduits there are. These sensations are also affected by many other factors: the strength of available planetary energy, which fluctuates daily, your location and local environment, and the atmospheric conditions around you.

The most common sensations are:

Tingling and buzzing in the toes and soles of feet.
Rushing water sensation up shins and thighs.
Bone-deep tickling inside legs, feet, and arms.
Tingling body-rush up spine.
Cobweb like tickling over face.
Pulsing or throbbing in Sub-Navel area.

Any strong sensation during awareness energy breathing indicates blockages in the energy body circuitry. These sensations will lessen as blocked energy pathways clear, widen, and re-establish themselves in response to the stronger energy flow.

The Mystery Schools

The three most used breathing techniques by esoteric schools are the two-four-two, the one-four-two, and six-twelve-six techniques. These breathing methods are used to draw the energy of the Divine or Universe.

Two-Four-Two

In two-four-two, the exercise is best done upon rising or before going to bed at night. In the morning, the student should lay in bed for about five minutes, concentrating on what he wishes to accomplish during the day. Goals and aspirations for the day should be analyzed. Then, the novice should stretch every part of his body, starting with the toes and moving upward. After doing this stretch exercise for about five minutes, arise, and take several deep breaths of fresh air, preferably from an open window with the sun striking the naked or partly clad body. While concentrating on the Divine energy of God streaming down, the student should begin the two-four-two rhythm. Taking a deep breath in through the nose, the student should hold the breath for four seconds. During this period the student should concentrate on positive and divine thoughts. Thoughts should also include needs, unselfish desires, and hopes. When exhaling through the nose, the neophyte should concentrate on sending forth good thoughts and love to others throughout the physical and spiritual universe. This exercise should be performed five to ten times.

One-Four-Two

In the one-four-two method, the student assumes an Eastern or Lotus position (full or half), with body erect. The neophyte begins a rhythm of inhaling four seconds through the left nostril (*Ida*), retaining the breath for sixteen seconds, and then exhaling for eight seconds through the right nostril (*Pingala*). While conducting this exercise, the student is to concentrate on the breath and visualize that the breath contains the life force of the Universe. Once the life force is drawn in and held, the neophyte exhales the physical breath (*Kumbakas*) while retaining its spiritual qualities. The process is then changed to the right nostril. The nostril not used is closed by pressing gently with the thumb on the nostril while resting the index and middle fingers on the third eye. This exercise is repeated five times per nostril, four times daily. This technique aids in increasing psychical powers and opening and clearing the "third eye" chakra. This exercise should be done before engaging in an auric exercise or form of meditation.

Six-Twelve-Six Technique

The six-twelve-six technique is an advanced method and requires that the participant holds his breath longer (like the one-four-two). This may initially, in some people, cause light-headedness. This is also one of the more powerful breathing techniques of the Mystery Schools. Performed like the one-four-two method, the technique is directed toward the center or third eye. While performing the technique, students will feel a buzzing or pressure sensation in the centre area slightly above the eyes. The pressure may become quite noticeable, and some people have experienced a vibrating or energy pulsation. The method should be performed in a lotus position or while sitting in a chair with back erect and feet touching the floor. The procedure should be performed ten times at each session with four sessions daily.

Conclusion

Each method provides the neophyte with benefits, and when used in conjunction with meditation, proper diet, sleep, rest, liquid intake, and thought considerations, will produce psychical and, more importantly, spiritual phenomena. Patience is of paramount importance, as the effects are not immediate and may take months or even years of training.

Note

1. Read Step 2, under "Graduated Training Method" in Chapter Twenty-One, as this explains some of the theory behind the use of "bodily awareness" to stimulate the energy body.

CHAPTER NINETEEN

ALTERNATIVE HEALING
An Introduction For Teachers

Professor Gerald Owen Grow, PhD

TEACHING TODAY IS TOO OFTEN DESCRIBED as pouring knowledge into empty heads, pounding the shapeless into shape, reinforcing desirable behaviors in unfeeling automatons, attempting crisis control in Hormone Central, meticulously promoting measurable outcomes, or functioning as the "wetware" component in a system of computer-based learning. Underlying many discussions of teaching is an implicit acceptance of the rational, scientific world view as we now know it. Few, however, seem aware that they have accepted a world view at all; what they see seems to them to be "reality," and many students are having a hard time fitting into that reality—and for good reasons. Who wants to grow up in an educational system that is permeated with the message that human beings are cosmic accidents resulting from random change produced by blind laws? The scientific world view of the late twentieth century insists that human beings have no possibility of connecting with the rest of this vast, inhuman universe. Further, the dominant view insists that each person is forever trapped inside a brain where solipsistic visions are created based on fragmentary, filtered, digitized, selective information passed to it by imperfect sense organs. Each person is seen as trapped in the inescapable hall of mirrors created by cultural conditioning and cannot even think without being secretly shaped by that culture, its folkways, the contingencies of the moment, and the insidious selectivity of language.

Continually depressed by such a view, what student, if fully aware of this message, would want to continue an education? Our system has not, like Buddhism, gone past relativism to compassion (Rahula 1959); indeed, the dangers of the implicit vision of our era seem largely invisible to the adults who embody it. Only in reactions like punk, body piercing, monastic retreat, and the growth of cults do we see symptoms that the technical rationality of our era—and the educational system that advances it—is not a complete answer to the questions of the human condition.

In spite of many public discussions of science, education, and knowledge, the world view dominating education—and the Western world—remains largely unconscious. Perhaps the only way to become aware of one's unconscious world view is to learn an alternative to it—to study in some detail a vision of the world that is so different from one's own that one's own comes to seem not reality itself, but one of many hopeful, ingenious, and imperfect maps.

This chapter uses a discussion of healing to present three alternative world views as methods of easing beyond the defined boundaries of one's usual understanding, opening to new possibilities, and realizing that the way in which we conceptualize existence determines to a surprising degree how we are capable of acting. We will consider three approaches to alternative healing—energy healing, mental healing, and spiritual healing—looking at each one's view of what goes wrong with people, its approach to setting things right, and the implications each healing method has for education. Each of the three healing methods has a long history, the shamanic probably dating back tens of thousands of years. I adopt the assumption (Csikszentmihalyi & Rathunde 1990) that anything with a long and persistent human history cannot be dismissed as mere superstition—even if it is technically incorrect—but should be examined for its meaning, its effect, and its survival function. In this case, all three traditions are very much alive and have articulate modern practitioners.

Energy Healing

This approach to healing is based on the view that a special energy moves through all things—a life energy that is the creative impetus for the universe, for all matter, and for the moment-to-moment feelings of each human being. This energy moves in pulsating rhythms that make up the seasons, the stages of the life cycle, the developmental phases of growth, the tidal rhythms of breath, the drumbeat of the heart, and the vibratory dance of the smallest particles inside each cell. Seen in terms of energy, the body consists of energy centers (chakras), energy pathways (meridians), and energy fields (auras). According to this school of thought, when energy circulates freely, people are healthy, happy, in touch with themselves, in direct energy-level communication with one another, and in tune with the universe. This energy has been called many names. The Yogic name for it is *prana*. In Taoism and acupuncture, it is known by the Chinese term *ch'i* or *qi* (Japanese, *ki*). Wilhelm Reich called the energy, "orgone."

Each theory of healing has an explanation for the nature of human difficulty and disease. In this theory, for a multitude of reasons, life-energy readily becomes blocked in human beings. The channels through which it flows can be stopped up, weakening the energy in one part of the body, building it to excessive levels in another.

Each healing system also proposes a cure: when life-energy is blocked, it must be freed in order to bring about a healing of the problems caused by that blockage—problems that include acute and chronic diseases, personality disorders, mood afflictions, psychological aberrations, anger, frustration, depression, cruelty, addiction, anxiety, indecisiveness, and all the adaptations we make to these conditions.

Life-energy may be released and rebalanced through a number of means. Acupuncturists use needles, pressure, and the application of heat to balance the flow of *ch'i* through elaborately mapped pathways called "meridians." Applied kinesiology and polarity therapy rebalance the energy through precise touch. Tai Chi and Chi Gung build, circulate, and balance life-energy through elaborate, gentle movements and prescribed postures. Hatha yoga uses physical postures, breathing, mental exercises, and diet to build and balance the centers of *prana* and their channels. Reichian therapy (which I practiced for six years) and bioenergetics release blocks and cultivate the ability to experience the fuller flow of organismic energy. Reiki and therapeutic massage manipulate muscles and move energy with the hands, not to remove muscular tension in a mechanical sense, but to clear the deep energy pathways of the body. The "healing hands" movement among holistic nurses uses touch and works with the auric field that surrounds the body.

In the ancient method of the laying on of hands, healing energy is transmitted from one person to another by touch, to re-energize or rebalance the afflicted part. The energy of healing hands can also be transmitted to others at a distance, and it can be transported by means of charged objects or a glass of charged water. Some healers use crystals to attract and focus this energy.

Perhaps the most direct method for cultivating life-energy is through working with the breath, breathing in pure energy, breathing out blocks, inhaling the energy into special centers, and breathing it from there into all parts of the body. Breath exercises can be found in yoga as well as in many recent healing methods.

Energy in Education

Consider the claims of energy healing: a life-energy runs through all things. Its free flow leads to greater health and happiness, clearer thinking, more loving relationships, and even, according to some practitioners, to a good society. Its blockage leads to illness, misery, emotional problems, alienation, and violence.

How should one properly respond to such a claim? It is easy to dismiss as unproven, unscientific, or, derisively, "pseudoscience" (Sagan 1996). But if you are willing to entertain this as an alternative, it can provide two benefits: it can help you see the view that you now hold (or, more properly, the view that now holds you), and it can suggest approaches to education unlikely to occur to someone following the more common methods.

What implications would the beliefs of energy healing have for education? How could a teacher use these concepts? In the "For the Teacher" sections, I will shift from explaining the background and address you directly as a teacher looking for new insights and methods.

For the Teacher

You cannot teach well unless you take care of your most important equipment—yourself. So the most important thing, in this view, is for you to work on your own energy. Find some healing method that enables you to keep your own energy more free and flowing. Develop the awareness necessary for identifying tension and other blocks and methods for releasing them. As your own awareness grows, you will be better able to feel and work with the energy of others and the energy of a group. Hatha yoga and Tai Chi are widely taught methods for helping your own energy flow.

Study what helps free your energy. Is it singing? Going for a walk in nature? A good talk with a friend? Deep relaxation to music? Some form of meditation? Cultivate the things that help and faithfully maintain a regular practice. Set up a support group among colleagues and friends who understand. Practice until you can choose to touch someone in a manner in which energy touches energy, without any overtones of coercion, need, sex, or even personality. It is easy to teach friends how to exchange shoulder rubs or foot massages, and your students will benefit from the relaxation these bring you.

Movement

Movement could be integrated into education in a way that helps free the flow of energy through the body, release and express emotions, integrate mental knowledge with body knowledge, and honor the rhythms of the body and the day. (This method, I understand, is the purpose of Eurythmy in Waldorf education.) Most students probably learn better when learning is integrated through movement—though normal classrooms are not well suited to working with movement. But even if there is not space to have students dance, create dramas and rituals, or do Tai Chi in a classroom, you can find room to do simple physical activities to energize, release, and balance. These might include stretching, bending forward and back, and twisting side to side. Breathing is essential and so is awareness. Exercises designed to build inner awareness and energy can be found in a number of books (Tulku 1978). Most drama teachers can teach warmups and theater games that mobilize energy, breath, voice, and feeling—and all of these mobilize learning. At least once, you should try blowing up twenty balloons, one by one, and asking students to keep them all in the air, while at the same time conducting a normal, orderly class discussion of the subject you assigned.

Many subjects can be taught kinesthetically—by having students talk, move, make gestures, use their hands, and make things. Use gestures and dance as a way of interpreting readings and as a prelude to writing (Armstrong 1994). Touching is vitally important to students of all ages, though it can be difficult to touch adolescents in a manner that does not engage sexual energy. People read one another by touching; the whole quality of a teacher can be communicated in a single touch.

Interpreting Energy Through Touch: An Experiment

If you choose to teach students openly to develop greater awareness of energy, some exercises can help. With high school students you might try this experiment in interpreting energy. Brainstorm a list of six scenarios in which the identical gesture would happen—a hand placed on the shoulder from behind. Scenarios might include warning someone not to trespass farther, comforting someone in grief, congratulating a winner, etc. Have students pair up. The one behind chooses one scenario, vividly imagines it, then places her hand on her partner's shoulder. The one being touched "reads" the touch and guesses which scenario it is from. The toucher then chooses a different scenario and places the hand identically on the shoulder again. And so on; you see how it goes. If students master this level, make it harder by having the "toucher" bring his hand one inch away from the partner's upper back, without touching, and see if the energy of intention can still be read.

Here is another example of the kind of activities you might use to teach energy awareness. Have students sit quietly, comfortably straight, with eyes closed. Then, instruct the students to: "Imagine a pearly white cloud of silky energy floating over your head. Effortlessly, imagine a soft shaft of that energy shining down on your head, through your head, through your chest, to a glowing ball in your solar plexus. Breathe in the energy and feel it grow in your middle." After a few breaths, "Continue to breathe in the energy, and as you exhale, send it out your arms for several breaths." Then up to the head. Then all around the chest and belly. Down the legs. End with a shower, washing all the energy out through the feet. Give them a moment, then ask them to open their eyes and write about the experience. Discuss, and find out if any felt more clear and energized afterwards (Weed 1968). Through exercises of this kind, students and teachers alike can develop better vocabulary for describing energy-level experiences.

Energy Through Art

Energy can be released and rebalanced through art, and almost any subject can be approached through drawing. The Waldorf method of "form drawing" can do wonders in helping focus the students' scattered attention, bringing them into their bodies, and giving them the most fundamental of all relievers of stress: focus on an intriguing task. (Though it was designed for use with elementary students, I know of one course in which form drawing was used to help junior college students focus.) If you have older students who are reluctant to draw, they might be asked to draw with big crayons using their unaccustomed hands (i.e., if right-handed, use the left). Invite (or, using a more direct paradoxical approach, require) them to draw badly, to write badly, to speak clumsily; some of the energy blocked by fear of mistakes and by perfectionism can be released this way (Grow 1987).

Humor

One of the most serious and reliable means of mobilizing hidden energy is humor (Cousins 1979). Try electing a class clown each week who gets five minutes a day to make everyone laugh. Designate one day each week for the clowns to make fun of teachers, parents, and other authority figures. Organize the humor interlude carefully and always bracket it with the same ritual, to facilitate returning to the business of the class afterward. Make a specific contract with students about when the clowning will occur, then always remember to honor it. Once or twice a month, discuss the humor and student responses.

Singing, Chanting, Breathing

Few activities free energy, open emotions, and connect people as readily as singing. If this is feasible in your setting, enlist students to identify songs that fit the subject you are studying and have them teach the class to sing them. Chants are also powerful, either unison or call-and-response. Encourage students to express the emotions they feel toward the subject they are studying. Emotions are the fundamental way energy assimilates experience. And nothing is neutral; even the learning of mathematics elicits emotional responses ranging from anger to ecstasy.

The most direct way to connect with energy is through conscious breathing. Take occasional breaks to ask students to stretch, yawn loudly, and breathe deep. Yawning helps on several levels: it brings in oxygen, activates the autonomic system, relaxes, and lets students and teacher make gentle fun of each other.

Ritual

Many of the activities I suggested throughout this chapter work best when repeated and cultivated. It is a good idea to bracket off a section of the class period just for such exercises. Enter them through a single, standardized procedure—a simple ritual, perhaps based on stretching, breathing, relaxing, and centering. And always end with the same steps that return the class to the day's business. Writing for five minutes helps make the transition from an inner activity to the outer world.

Silent Teaching Practices

There is always something you can do to free the energy of a class without calling attention to the fact that you are doing it. As your own energy flows more freely and constructively, this will encourage the energy in your students. Being in the presence of someone whose energy is balanced helps bring about balance in others. Or you can work to "tune" the energy in a class by the way you think about it. This method belongs to mental healing, but its effects are energetic: you can conduct the class while visualizing large balls of warm, caring, happy red light emerging from your heart and slowly floating around to graze everyone in the room. You can create and maintain the image of a waterfall of brilliantly sparkling, delicious, fragrant, bubbling light pouring down into the middle of the room and foaming over everyone in every direction, all through the class, bathing everyone in a sense of delight and hopefulness. If students are resistant, imagine the water rooster-tailing over a large rock, and the rock melting away before the benevolent force of the flow. Do these things while conducting class normally; do them with the part of your mind that is usually busy planning dinner, worrying about bills, struggling with student judo, or tempting you to daydream about winning the lottery.

Mental Healing

World View of Mental Healing

"Mental healing" emphasizes the interpenetration of what are usually called "mind" and "body" and makes use of the power of thought to affect the body. In the world view of mental healing, people's deeply-held thoughts make them ill or at least create the preconditions for disease and psychological problems. Healers work to remove deeply held resentments, to release unexpressed emotions, and to assuage buried terror (all of which, in this view, are caused by deeply held thoughts), in order to build self-confidence and to plant in people a positive and hopeful view of their path through life (something students need).

Mental healers insist that, just as people can make themselves sick by the way they think, the way they think can make them well again. On a simple level, a person whose self-image has led to a destructive diet that has caused medical problems may improve the problem and the diet by changing the self-image—which is a way of thinking, an intention, a mental act. Some psychologists teach people to manage depression by changing the way they think. But mental healing travels further out the continuum occupied by these easily accepted cases, to claim that all disease is caused by how we use our minds and can be improved by using our minds differently. Mental healing departs even more radically from the normal view when it holds that thoughts can change not only the body, but even the external world.

Energy-based healing methods rarely seem to employ mental activities—except for some visualizations. In energy systems, thinking is more likely to be considered part of the problem and pre-cognitive energy-flow the solution. In mental healing, thinking is both problem and cure.

Self-Talk and Affirmations

One widely used form of mental healing works to replace habitual destructive thinking with habitual constructive thinking through the use of affirmations—"seed thoughts"—that are repeated with such intensity that they become regular, recurring programs playing in the unconscious. Affirmations can also be used to nudge unconscious negative thoughts to the surface so they can be identified. Affirmations have recently gained widespread respectability through the technique of "positive self-talk" (Butler 1981; Helstetter 1987). Self-talk, however, is based on the psychological view of the world, in which each individual is isolated within a separate personality, alone and talking to one's self. Affirmations, by contrast, belong to the healing view of the world, in which the mind can affect the body and the world, and separateness is an illusion. Some practitioners claim that affirmations can also be used to "manifest" physical realities, such as money and relationships. Affirmations may be subliminal. A thriving industry sells audio tapes in which affirmations on a variety of subjects are inaudibly embedded inside sounds such as ocean waves or soothing music.

Visualization

Our culture's lack of appreciation for the power of the imagination is staggering. We can continue to inundate young children with images of violence, manipulative fantasy, and sheer weirdness, because our culture believes that the imagination is private, powerless, and basically irrelevant. Healers hold the imagination in great respect, trace many problems to its abuse, and employ the power of the imagination in healing activities.

Patients can do their own healing visualizations, or the healer can do them. Typically, the patient is taught how to enter a relaxed state, then to create vivid visual images of the desired outcome. A healer may use visualization to diagnose the client's problems, then to treat them. Such healing is premised upon the belief that powerfully held images transmit beyond the mind of the person holding those images to affect the client's mind, body, and circumstances. Many healing methods are based on the belief that there are realms of the imagination in which people's separate imaginations meet. Once you have experienced this directly, you see what power the "normal view" normally exercises in limiting our concept of what is real. The possibility that one person's imaginings can directly affect the mind of another holds profound implications for education.

Healing visualizations can be learned from many books and tapes (Gawain 1978; Epstein 1989; Rossman 1987). A form of visualization has been incorporated into the normal medical view in the Simontons' (1980) work with visualization in conjunction with the medical treatment of cancer. Autogenic Training, a systematic method of self-healing through visualization, has been widely used in Europe (Luthe 1965). Other forms of healing employ the imagination through dreams, personal journals, or creative arts such as painting, sculpture, poetry, dance, and theater. Archetypal approaches, based on the work of Jung, use the healing power of the imagination as expressed through certain symbols that are thought to be universal (Argüelles 1985).

Mental Healing in Education

Consider the claims of mental healing: thoughts and images shape or even determine what people feel and think, the world they experience, and their state of illness or health. Those thoughts and images transmit directly to others and can help heal them. What implications would these beliefs have for education? How could a teacher use these concepts?

Teacher's Own Practices

The most important mental healing for you to do as a teacher is to work on yourself. Explore affirmations and visualizations until you find methods that work for you. Then examine the phrases you habitually whisper to yourself and the images you habitually hold about yourself and the world, and begin replacing these with ones that support your deep life goals and bring you intuitive guidance.

Use mental healing to help your teaching. When alone in a deeply relaxed state, vividly visualize the class working together happily, vibrantly, deeply, caringly, with each student growing into their full potential. Visualize specific problem students and talk to them in your imagination. While visualizing, communicate your concern and caring. Ask for insight. Ask what this student needs and how you can help. Visualize the student changing, improving, coming into the fullness of being. Then let the image go, with faith that your mind and the mind of the student are working on a higher level to improve the situation.

You can perform similar mental healings on problems with administrators and other faculty, but remember: you can't make anybody do something they don't want to do. You can, though, attune yourself and another person to a higher level of common goals that may help overcome problems.

Educators already use a kind of mental healing when they work with a student's self-concept, or when they attempt to build self-esteem. Every time you say, "You can do it," every time you work to cultivate confidence, positive attitude, and students' belief in their ability, you are practicing a form of healing—using activities that are developed with greater power and discipline in mental healing.

Studying Cultural Images

If the images we hold about ourselves and the world are so powerful, what would be better than to study our culture's images of itself? And what better place to start than with the images in media?

In an appropriate course, students could use advertisements, television, film, music videos, and other sources of popular culture, to study their images of men and women and their gender roles, images of relationships, of values, of minorities. Students could ponder the influence of images of violence in children's programming and how advertisements make use of powerful images, symbols, role models, and affirmation-like phrases. Such exercises can help students free themselves from being manipulated by media images and make the power of the imagination available for more constructive uses.

Self-Talk

You could provide a valuable service by helping students learn to hear when they are using self-defeating self-talk ("I can't do *anything* right," "I *always* mess up in math"), understand the mode of thinking that lies behind it, and learn on their own to catch such thoughts and replace them with more accurate and helpful statements ("I may mess up in math from time to time, but I am steadily improving as a result of my own efforts"). This is a healing act.

Art That Makes Us Whole

Education tends to emphasize problematic literature that promotes critical thinking about societal problems. In contrast, there is a small, vibrant movement for the re-enchantment of the world (Gabelik 1991), whose adherents are trying to restore the belief that certain kinds of art can heal and unify us. Myths play a prominent role in this school of thought—myths as stories that make us whole and give our lives meaning, stories that give us images powerful enough to express what we are feeling in the present. From this perspective, art arises from the sources of transpersonal imagery and is a way of celebrating the depths of creative consciousness. Meditations with music would be a simple way to bring deeper levels of mind into the classroom in a constructive way (Bonny & Savary 1973).

Mental Healing in Medicine

You could teach a unit on contemporary medical practices that use some methods of mental healing. Dr. Carl Simonton's work with imagery and the treatment of cancer comes from a medically respectable approach, and Benson's *Beyond The Relaxation Response* presents a form of meditation that is acceptable in medical terms as a method of stress reduction. Norman Cousins' books about healing, starting with his own experience with laughter, are another reputable source. Bill Moyer's 1993 PBS video series, *Healing and the Mind,* presents many of the themes raised in this chapter as exciting possibilities on the forefront of medicine.

Spiritual Healing

Metaphysical Healing

Spiritual healing is based on the belief that life's problems are caused by the erroneous, limiting, crippling way we believe things to be. It is concerned with our vision of the universe and our place in it—a field that since Aristotle has been known as "metaphysics"—and so is often called "metaphysical healing." It is the healing of the world view. Although such distinctions are somewhat arbitrary, it is useful to distinguish mental from spiritual healing: in mental healing, the "I" is in charge; in spiritual healing, a higher power is at work. Spiritual healing begins at the point where the objects of the "imagination" take on a life of their own, provide access to new knowledge, and work harmoniously within a vision of life larger than the one we normally hold.

Spiritual healers help people identify the large-scale limiting beliefs they hold about themselves and life and replace those with a more generous vision. In the classic approach to spiritual healing, the client's normal world view is transformed by the infusion of an extraordinary alternative—an ecstatic, mystical vision of oneness with the Infinite. The world view of a spiritual healer may hold that nothing exists but God, and God is health, happiness, fulfillment, perfection. Any appearance to the contrary may be approached as an error that must be faced and re-perceived as an illusion and replaced with the direct perception that there is no reality but infinite love and perfection. In the usual approach to spiritual healing, the client learns to practice this new mode of consciousness. Another practice requires nothing of the recipient; instead, the healer "practices the presence" by seeing spiritual perfection in the client. Such healing is based on a truly remarkable premise: one can heal others simply by seeing them in a certain way—so to speak, through the eyes of God.

Someone coming to this view for the first time is likely to find it strange, for it violates so many important concepts in the normal view and creates so many complicated simplifications. But it is a widely used form of healing, best known in the form of Christian Science, also used in Science of Mind and Unity, and considered in some schools of yoga to be the highest form of healing. Books by Joel Goldsmith provide articulate modern descriptions of a spiritual healer at work (Eddy 1971; Holmes 1938; Ramacharaka 1971; Goldsmith 1959).

Spirit Guide Healing

Another form of spiritual healing that has a long history believes that the physical universe is the product of normally-unseen spiritual forces. Practitioners call upon the assistance of spiritual beings, such as angels. Some of these healers (often known as "spiritualists") go into trance while spirit guides take over. Others consciously communicate with their guides. Spirit guide healing has a lively following in England, and spiritual entities play a central role in Theosophy and the philosophy of Rudolf Steiner, and angels have recently become a topic of widespread interest among Christian writers.

Some spiritualist healers (for example, among the Navajo) attribute diseases to malevolent action by spiritual forces, which must then be dealt with on a spiritual level. This is not a game for amateurs. Some people who cannot control the influence of such spiritual powers are called possessed, or crazy; some of those who can are called shamans.

Shamanism

An ancient method for the systematic use of the imagination has recently become widely known in the adaptation of shamanism for Westerners. Helped by the rhythm of monotonous drumbeats, shamans enter an altered state of consciousness in which they may receive assistance from spirit guides (typically in animal form), discover things about people, meet one another and have shared experiences that both may later recall, receive inspiration, and perform healings. Shamanism is, in one healer's terms, a traditional technology for developing intuitive guidance in life. For our purposes, it is one of the most vivid methods for discovering that there is more to the world than Westerners ordinarily believe. A system of "core shamanism" is now being widely taught around the country as a method of personal growth (Harner 1982).

Reconnecting to the High Self

One of the basic tenets of spiritual healing is that people can lose touch with their true natures, forget who they really are, and live a partial life whose limitations hurt them. All approaches to spiritual healing help people reconnect to themselves at a very deep level (the spiritual level) and realign their lives from that level. In some spiritual healings, clients are coached to reestablish contact with (what is variously called) the high self, the true self, being, spirit, the higher power, or the soul. This true self knows who you are and what you need to do in this life; it may even have an agenda that needs to be accomplished in this lifetime—for spiritual healing often implies a world view in which souls are reborn many times, each time to learn certain lessons in a world that is a kind of school for soul-making. Healing and learning are more closely related than you might at first realize. How might it change your teaching to look out over a classroom and conceive of those young people as re-born souls here to learn vital lessons about the nature of life—and to realize that some of them are far older and wiser than you! (Moffett 1994).

Spiritual Healing in Education

Consider the claims of spiritual healing: being cut off from our true nature causes the major problems in our lives, for we then become addicted to unsatisfiable needs. The most important activity of life is to reconnect with our true nature and realign our lives around it. Healing our world view helps to heal us. How we see others helps make them sick or heal them. There are spiritual beings who want to share their wisdom and power with us, and there may be some spiritual beings who cause harm. What implications would these beliefs have for education? How could a teacher use these concepts?

For the Teacher

Again, the most important place for you to start as a teacher is to work with yourself first. Study how you view the universe and your place in it, and what effect that view has on your life. In what realms of life do you see yourself as creator? As victim? What would you have to change to see yourself as co-creator in all realms?

Educators know that their *behavior* toward students can have a crucial influence on students. Spiritual healing goes a step further and claims that the way you *see* other people—regardless of how you act—affects them directly. Not only can a teacher's beliefs hinder a student, a teacher's beliefs—independent of any action—can inspire, integrate, encourage, and heal. It therefore could be of utmost importance for teachers to develop the most expansive, inclusive, generous, and life-affirming beliefs about the nature of the universe and people, for students may be receiving the teacher's beliefs by direct psychic broadcast, hour after hour, day after day. And not just in your classroom, but all over the school, and perhaps all over the world.

Summon the Spirit of a Great Teacher

Many cultures routinely call upon their ancestors, especially when teaching essential, traditional knowledge. If you have ever had a great and inspiring teacher, consider asking him or her to come psychically to consult, plan, and teach with you. Whether or not your great (and perhaps dead) teacher is "actually there" or exists only in your mind is irrelevant; what matters is the power that can be made accessible to you by this way of focusing your intentions.

Goal Setting

Teachers and counselors engage in an activity similar to spiritual healing when they work with students on goal-setting, especially in that phase of the work that requires students to examine who they are, what brings them joy, and what they feel to be their deepest purposes in life. The healing view also suggests that teachers can help the student by visualizing the student attaining deep self-knowledge, true life goals, satisfying those goals, and becoming whole. Several authors—Brian Tracey and Shakti Gawain, to mention two—have developed goal-setting methods that begin from rational or meditative self-analysis and move toward restructuring one's world view using visualization, affirmation, and even spiritual healing techniques (Tracy 1984; Gawain 1978).

Healing by Presence

Some people claim to have been healed merely by coming into the presence of a certain person who is so powerful, holy, or spiritual that healing naturally takes place in the vicinity. Everyone is familiar with this phenomenon on a more modest level: there are people around whom things go better, meetings are more productive, people naturally concentrate on deeper issues, and conflicts arise less often. Such people need not speak to be effective. Their presence alone helps. They communicate, by their very being, vital messages about what matters most in life. Those who heal by presence carry this ability to its utmost and radiate something that can cause others to change without a word being spoken.

You also teach by your presence. On a simple level, you see students in a positive way. Students know, by the way you look at them and speak with them, that you see them as valid, important human beings with great potential.

On a higher level, you serve as a model to your students—a model of learning, mature living, health, joy, creativity, a model of how to express emotions, how to think, how to speak, how to be a person in a body in this society on this earth, moving at your own pace through your own life-cycle, as they will do through theirs. Above all, you communicate the simple, enduring, and indelible message that life is worthwhile—a message of strength shaped by delight and gratitude.

At the highest level, you teach even when you do nothing at all. You teach by presence. For in your presence, they learn about the possibilities of life. Your presence teaches them what you hold close to your heart, what you have on your mind, how much room you make for things to happen. You teach by being with them, by seeing into their hearts, seeing their accomplishments, failures, potentialities, their perfect and transitional qualities, their struggles and triumphs—and accepting them as they are in a way that inspires them to become more of what they can be. It is possible that the visible contents of education—lessons, knowledge, skills, behavioral objectives, and all the intense busyness of teaching and learning—exist mainly as a vehicle through which to communicate the nonverbal, unsymbolic messages contained in a teacher's presence. Content, of course, is important for a student's life. Perhaps even more important, though, is the outlook in which that content is wrapped. Spiritual healing addresses that level of teaching.

In Western education, teachers are too often considered conveyers of information or, increasingly, managers of the systems that convey the information. But the foundation of all knowledge is embodied knowledge, *presence*—a human being who has gained knowledge and lives it. Students learn differently and more deeply when they are in the presence of a person who embodies knowledge as a living, coping, caring human being. This simple truth has almost vanished from American education, though it is known and valued—I have been assured—in India and other places still. The study of healing shows us that education is not only about information and skills, but also about individual, profoundly interconnected people.

The Study of World Views

Spiritual healing leads naturally to the study of world views. World views are normally studied in college classes on comparative religion or cultural anthropology, but world views form the basis for the multicultural approach to education and can be studied at any age. The classic popular book on world views, their power, and the power of changing them, is Joseph Chilton Pearce's *The Crack in the Cosmic Egg* (1988), also a book about healing (see also Stevenson 1988; Redfield 1952 is a seminal study). Works on religion and anthropology would be helpful for older students, but an excellent starting point is to bring in guests who hold world views that your students would find unusual. Such people might be Native Americans, fundamentalist Christians, Hindus, Buddhists, Muslims, Rosicrucians, Rastafarians, Marxists, Jewish mystics, Jainists, witches, palm readers, or people who grew up in faraway lands where things are done differently. Start by having students write down their preconceptions in advance of the visit, then compare those with what they found.

The first payoff from such visitors is that they serve as a mirror. Students cannot know only one world view; with only one, *it* lives *them*, simply and invisibly. Only when they learn a second world view can their own become visible to them. In contrast to what the visitors say about their views of the world, students can question their own parents and friends about the nature of their own deep beliefs and casual assumptions, and they can identify the beliefs implicit in popular media, such as science shows on TV.

Ask older students to identify the world views implicit in the works of literature they are studying. For example, the attitudes toward nature expressed by Jack London and Stephen Crane make a powerful contrast to the one expressed by Henry David Thoreau. While London and Crane tell stories, they also convey a vision of the world and our place in it—a sometimes grim and modern vision. It is good not to let such visions infiltrate students' own beliefs unnoticed, for they can have—as healers point out—great power over us.

Ask of each world view: what does it make easy that is difficult or impossible in other belief systems? What *exists* in it that is unreal in other world views? At this point, many teachers will probably take the postmodern route of critical analysis and investigate how different world views maintain elite groups in power. Yet, there are no perfect world views; to compensate, each traditional world view contains methods to help people live with the limitations of that world view—things like religion, art, carnival, humor, and entertainment. At its most powerful, spiritual healing (like some forms of mysticism and Buddhism) transforms our very relationship to world views, by regrounding us in the ecstatic, holistic vision of a pre-world view—who we were, as the Zen koan goes, "before we were born." There is a transformative innocence at the heart of life that each new child summons us to rediscover.

Conclusion

The study of healing provides a model in comparison to which many normal assumptions about education become more visible. The types of healing discussed in this chapter—energy healing, mental healing, and spiritual healing—suggest practices for teachers and perhaps activities for class use. In a larger sense, healing redefines the task of education as not only to develop cognition, but also to cultivate energy; not only to impart facts, information, and skills, but also to heal ourselves, each other, and the world; not only to teach the mind to solve problems, but also to teach the imagination to create the world; not only to know and to do, but also to be.

Sections of this chapter originally appeared in *Holistic Education Review*, Vol. 7(1), Spring 1994, pp. 11-18.

SECTION V:

MECHANICS AND EXERCISES

CHAPTER TWENTY

AURIC MECHANICS AND THEORY

Robert Bruce

SO FAR IN THIS BOOK, many fine writers and researchers, with extensive scientific and metaphysical backgrounds, have given you detailed explanations—expounding upon the case for auras. Some of this is theoretical and some could even be called speculative, but a great deal of it comes from practical "hands on" wisdom from those who can not only see auras, but work with them every day. Regardless of their source, all these views have merit and worth and contribute to building a bigger picture, leading towards a greater understanding of auras and more practical and beneficial ways to work with them. This is a unique and inspirational blend of the scientific and the esoteric, combined with a strong "hands on" practical approach to understanding the nature, development, and actual mechanics involved in all forms of non-physical sight—the mystical approach.[1]

What is an Aura?

Auras are the visual representation of the myriad and complex energies of creation, existence, and life that permeate and are an integral part of all matter, living and inanimate. The human aura is both a reflection of energy activity within the body, as well as a stand alone energy field with its own substance, feel, energy circuits, and currents. The living human aura is an integral part of the energy body and both these are a part of the whole life process; one part cannot exist without the other.

Many people, understandably, are of the opinion that auras are composed of light, but at a much higher frequency than the visible part of the light spectrum, possibly ultraviolet, which is only visible to a clairvoyant. If this were true, it would surely be possible to detect and measure this light with the sophisticated electronic instruments available today (see notes for Chapter Two). There are scientific instruments used in astronomy and space research that can be tuned to detect any part of the light spectrum—no matter how refined—for example, infrared, ultraviolet, x-rays, gamma rays, etc. All these are types of light energy that are completely invisible to normal sight but are easily detected and measured with sensitive instruments—even at astronomical distances. Similar instruments have been used in attempts to measure the human aura in complete darkness—and failed to detect any light source that could possibly account for the apparent intensity of the human aura. There has been a great deal of research on bioluminescence, some of which is dealt with in Chapter Two. This shows the human body does give off minute amounts of light, in the visible part of the spectrum, but nowhere near enough to account for the size and brightness (to a clairvoyant) of the full human aura.

It is, I believe, natural and understandable to consider auras to be a type of light, because auras do look like light and do appear to be seen with the eyes. But my research shows that the human aura is not composed of any type of light, from any part of the visible or invisible light spectrum. For all the above, the human aura is definitely affected by light energy. This is partly because the human energy body which produces the living aura interacts with light and partly because light is necessary for the observer to tune into a subjects energy and observe their aura; so light definitely appears to be an integral part of the mechanics of auric sight.

Adding weight to the above argument is the well known fact that some development and stimulation of the brow centre, or some natural ability, is required to see auras clearly. This points to there being much more to the mechanics of auric sight than mere light and optics. If auras were composed of light alone, then it would, logically, be possible to see auras simply by training an observer to use the correct focus. This can be likened to learning how to see those 3-D noise pictures with the hidden images, a tricky but achievable task that anyone can learn how to do. I still can't see those 3-D noise images, but I can see auras well. Auric sight is a fickle and difficult skill for anyone to master, especially for a beginner. It can often take years of practise before enough of the aura is seen to make it a worthwhile practise—if you use traditional training methods.

The Mechanics of Auric Sight

Auric sight, as with all other forms of non-physical sight, depends heavily upon the physical eyes and the normal optical sight process, as well as on the mental habit of focusing with sight. Both physical and non-physical sight are very closely related. They are both forms of perception that allow the brain to perceive external energies as a mental sight picture. The brow center (brow chakra) is the primary non-physical energy centre linked with the eyes and the sight centre of the brain. The eyes are also non-physical organs (energy centres) in their own right and are involved with all aspects of non-physical sight. The energies responsible for auras are "detected" by the brow centre, aided by both the physical and non-physical aspects of the eyes, rather than just "seen" with the eyes alone. The energies received by this process are interpreted by the sight centre of the brain as a mental-visual picture, as colored bands of light surrounding the subject (note the technique used by the Aura Camera 3000 and 6000—Chapter Three).

Normal Sight

As explained in Chapter One, the eyes on their own do not actually see anything. They simply receive and change focused light energy into a stream of complex neuro-electrical signals that are passed, via the retina and optic nerve, to the sight centre of the brain. The brain interprets all neuro-electric signals received at its sight centre as a mental-visual picture—what we call sight.

Auric Sight

The brow centre is situated directly between the eyes and is intimately connected with the eyes and the normal optical sight process. It is capable of receiving much more subtle energies than normal light energy, but these can only be received when it is active and tuned to a receptive mode. Both the physical and non-physical aspects of the eyes are part of a complex supporting structure for the brow centre and the auric sight process. Energies received by the brow centre are passed to the sight centre of the brain, as neuro-electrical signals, in a way very similar to normal optical sight. The brain interprets "all" neuro-electrical signals it receives at its sight centre as a mental-visual picture—sight.

An individual auric color is generated within the mind of the observer by the color value given to that particular type of energy by the sight centre of the brain of the observer. The color value of each auric color is given to it by the learned mental associations of the brain of the observer and by an instinctive, subconscious, and intuitive sense of what that particular type of energy means to it. Each type of energy is thus shown, in the mind's eye of the observer, by the auric color that best represents it. When many different auric energies are received at the same time, a composite of many different colors is displayed surrounding the subject, within the mind of the observer. These auric colors are a visual representation of the color values of all the different energies the brow centre has detected surrounding and emanating from the subject (Note: If a person can see auras with their eyes closed, as some do, they are not using normal auric sight. This is a more advanced type of non-physical sight and should be considered as "mind's eye vision" and not auric sight).

The Complexity of Normal Vision

Auric sight may sound complicated, but it is really very simple when compared with normal optical sight—that simple, visual thing we all take for granted. Look around the room! What do you see? Think of all the millions of colors and shades and tones you are seeing—all at once—in spectacular three-dimensional detail. Turn around a few times and think about the enormous computer-like processing power that allows your brain to keep up with the fantastically complex and changing image you are seeing. Your eyes are passing incredible amounts of information to the sight centre of your brain, which interprets it all with ease. Normal optical sight is an incredibly complex and powerful mental ability when compared with the few simple colors and swirls of light that can be seen in a human aura. There is really no comparison between these two abilities, normal sight and auric sight; normal sight is a vastly more complex process and requires more brain power than auric sight.

Line of Sight and Aura

Supporting my earlier statements that auras are not any type of light, my research with auras shows that it is necessary for a subject to be within the field of view of the observer before its aura can be seen. If an aura was any type of light emanating from a subject, it would be possible to see this aura extending out from behind a simple barrier, with the subject only "just" hidden from sight. But, if a subject is hidden from view by a solid screen so they are only just hidden, by a quarter of an inch—which is far narrower than any aura—an observer will not be able to see any part of that subject's aura with auric sight.

The following simple test proves auric sight is dependent upon the subject being within the field of view of the observer:

Hidden Subject Test

Use a hallway opening or doorway for this test. The observer must be facing the doorway, so one side of the hallway is completely hidden from their line of sight. Mark the observer's exact line of sight, using chalk on the floor and walls and by hanging string across the hallway to mark it, so the test subject knows exactly how far they can go without being seen by the observer. This chalk line marks the HOT zone.

Set up the observer about ten feet from the opening, making sure they have no way of detecting the hidden subject other than by their aura. Have the test subject move right to the edge of the hot zone, at random

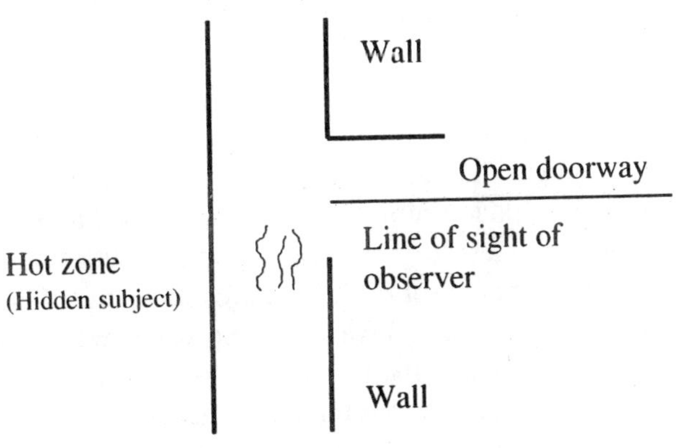

Diagram of hidden subject aura detection test

intervals, and stay there for a set time of ten seconds. The observer must not know when these times will happen. They must attempt to detect the presence of the subject by their aura alone.

Have the subject, or another observer, record hits and misses—the times when their presence in the hot zone is accurately detected and the times when they are falsely detected. There must be NO confirmation of hits and misses if this test is to be fair and objective. It is important that the observer have no other way but auric sight to detect when the subject will be in the hot zone. Make sure the observer cannot see any shadows or reflections, or hear a sound that gives indications of the presence of the subject in the hot zone. Also, to be fair, the observer should not attempt to use guesswork or intuition or any other psychic means of detection other than auric sight.

If auras were composed of any type of light that is visible to a clairvoyant, they would be able to reliably detect the presence of the test subject with auric sight—but this does not happen in practice. If you record the score of a good clairvoyant's hits and misses in this test, you will find it will not exceed what could reasonably be expected through the random guesswork of non-clairvoyant control observers.

This test goes a long way toward proving auras are not composed of any type of refined, high spectrum light. Also, it suggests that a subject must be within the observers field of view before their aura can be seen. This supports my theory that auras are seen through a complex interaction between the subject, the eyes and brow centre of the observer, and light. Once this is accepted, the true nature of aura and auric sight, as well as all other types of non-physical sight, can be better understood.

Darkness and the Aura

A further observation and test that adds weight to the above argument that auras are not light: the main human aura cannot be seen in "complete" darkness. The hidden subject test can be adapted to prove this as well. Repeat the above test in "complete" darkness, but move the "hot" zone to directly in front of the observer, in the centre of their field of view but still ten feet away. If you remove all other possible ways an observer could detect the times when the test subject is present—light, sound, smell, shadow, etc.—you will find the main aura cannot be seen.

If auras were indeed any type of light, why would it be necessary for the subject to be made visible to the observer by light in order for the observer to be able to see their aura? This shows that light, as well as normal optical sight, plays an important part in auric sight. Note: In total darkness, it is possible to see some very slight activity around the energy body, close to the skin. This is very faint and nothing at all like the main aura, looking like faint strands and tiny sparks of colored light (usually blue to white). This effect is very faint and most noticeable around the observer's own fingertips when they are brought together in front of their face (see notes at end of Chapter Two).

This type of energy sight in darkness will usually only work when observing one's own aura—depending upon the degree of development of the observer. This is made possible by focusing the brow centre and eyes with the mental habit of sight, aided by "bodily self-awareness," instead of with normal optical sight.

Everyone has a keen sense of bodily self-awareness, and everyone can feel, with their mind, exactly where every part of their body is at any one time. You can reach out within your body and feel any part of it with bodily self-awareness. Reaching out in the dark and "feeling" for your own hands with your bodily self-awareness enables the brow centre to focus on them, making a weak type of energy sight possible. Astral sight can also, in some cases, form a part of this type of energy sight.

Auric Sight and Aura Cameras

The mechanics of auric sight appears to be a complex reaction between the energy body and auric field of the subject—with visible light—with the eyes and the normal optical sight process—with the brow and crown centres—with the non-physical energy centres located in the eyes—and with the sight centre and brain of the observer. This all has to work together in just the right way for the aura of a subject to become visible to an observer.

Since all my evidence suggests auras are not composed of light, the only other way to see an aura, apart from developing auric sight, is through electronic means such as The Aura Camera 3000 and 6000, as detailed in Chapter Three. These are a new breed of ultra modern aura cameras that are light years ahead of earlier types of crude aura cameras. They use a sophisticated electronic sensing method, based upon years of scientific and clairvoyant aura research, that is capable of detecting minute changes within the energy body. They show an electronic representation of a subject's aura, based upon this research, as an elaborate, full-color display and even print hard copies of it—aura photographs. What will they think of next?

Three Basic Types of Non-physical Sight

To further understand auric sight it is important to compare it with other types of non-physical sight.

Auric Sight

Auric sight is the ability to see the energies given off by all matter and living things as an aura. Auric sight can be broken down into several different levels of perception, but these are closely related, so I have lumped them together as all being levels of auric sight. Auric sight is the first level of non-physical sight and the easiest one to develop.

Mind's Eye Sight

Mind's eye vision (commonly called clairvoyance) is the ability to perceive energies as a mental-visual picture or vision in the mind's eye of the observer. This is a higher level of energy perception than auric sight, but the way it works is very similar, the mechanics of the process being much the same. Mind's eye vision occurs when the brow centre of the observer is stimulated and active enough to receive higher, more abstract and complex types of energies than those responsible for auras. These energies are interpreted as a mental-visual sight picture by the observer's brain, in much the same way as an aura is seen. But the mental-visual picture created by the brain is, of course, much more complex because of the complex nature of the energies involved.

A mind's eye vision can be seen with the eyes open or closed, in bright light or in complete darkness. It does not depend upon visible light and the normal optical sight process to work. But the mental habit of using optical sight to focus on what is being seen is still used for focusing and tuning the brow centre.

The higher levels of auric sight, i.e., observing the spiritual aura, are partly mind's eye visions, and the symbols and signs seen within the main human aura overlay it and are combined with auric sight. This can easily be mistaken as just a part of auric sight, which can be extremely misleading for a beginner and often causes conflicting opinions among those who practise auric sight.

Astral Sight

Astral sight is the most difficult type of non-physical sight to use on its own. Pure astral sight is usually only experienced during deep meditation or a partial OOBE (Out of Body Experience). This ability becomes possible when the energy body expands enough to allow a small part of the astral body in the head and brow area to project out and literally peek out of the physical body. It is then possible to see into the astral dimension.

The part of the astral usually seen with astral sight is "The Real Time Zone." This is the closest part of the astral dimension to the physical dimension, where everything seen is a mental reflection of actual reality and set in a real time frame, i.e., everything is happening "now" and in real time. This ability, while extremely difficult to use on its own, often forms a part of what is seen with higher levels of auric sight and mind's eye vision.

Energy Centres

What They Are

The primary energy centres (chakras) are the non-physical organs of the energy body. There are at least seven primary centres, over three hundred secondary and lesser centres (according to acupuncture charts), and millions of energy exchange ports scattered throughout the human body. These are joined together by a complex network of non-physical energy circuitry and conduits called meridians. All energy centres, energy exchange ports, energy conduits and meridians, and not just the primary energy centres, radiate many different types of energies and give off many different colors values, and all add to the visible colors within the human aura (note McCurdy, Chapter Fifteen).

The Brow and Crown

My many years of personal energy and energy centre (chakras) research (using my own energy centres and raising my Kundalini to its highest level) has shown the brow and crown centres, when fully active, to be slightly larger than is commonly thought. The brow centre is about the size of the palm of a hand and covers the roughly circular area of the brow, above and between the eyes. When fully active, the brow centre is like a very definite and living extension of the crown centre and feels like a heavy, fleshy, pulsing flap, hanging down over the brow from the crown centre.

The crown centre is huge in comparison with any other centre, occupying the entire top of the head above the hairline. The crown centre, when fully active, feels like a living, fleshy, and moving extension of the brain itself, as if the brain had grown hundreds of fat, little fleshy tentacles. It is one of the most peculiar sensations I have ever experienced but extremely pleasant. The feel of it reminds me of two things: 1) having a living sea anemone extending from my brain; 2) Hindu paintings depicting the thousand petalled lotus—the crown and brow centres.

I have studied these fleshy little crown fingers (chakra petals), and they seem to act as some kind of energy antennae. When I use and direct my consciousness and will in different ways, they move slowly about, forming complex, slowly moving patterns. They appear to be sending and receiving many different types of energies at once. The full, and obviously complex, functioning of these parts of the crown centre continues to elude me. But it is obvious to me, their primary functions are the sensing, detecting, and transmission of many different types of energy. Because of this, I strongly suspect they are an integral part of auric sight, as well as being involved with all other types of non-physical perception and sensing.

The common location and similar functioning of the brow and crown centres (sight, perception, and inspiration) strongly suggests a close relationship between the eyes, the brow centre, the crown centre, and the sight centre of the brain.

The Complexity of the Energy Body

The energy body is, basically, a complete energy copy of the physical body. Every bone, muscle, vein, organ, nerve, and hair is represented in energy form. As in the physical body, all the parts of the energy body function together on an energy level, and this causes a strong energy field to reflect around them that can be perceived with auric sight as a mental-visual picture—what we call an aura.

The energy body is, in the way it functions, very similar to an electronic device. With an electronic device, energy flows into it and through connecting circuitry that is etched into a circuit board—like the meridians and bio-circuitry of the human energy body. This electronic circuitry carries energy back and forth to all its devices and components, diodes, resistors, capacitors, etc. Energy is continually changed, enhanced, and transformed by these electronic components to serve a multitude of different purposes required by the device to function properly as a whole unit. This is very similar, in principal, to how the different parts of the energy body function together as a whole interconnected unit.

The Energy Body's Effects on the Aura

The strength of the primary and secondary energy centres, energy exchange ports, and meridians in any one person depends entirely upon their individual make up and inner motivations—who and what they are. The auric color values thus generated are greatly affected by a person's nature, health, and life style, as well as by their spiritual, moral, and psychic development and surrounding life conditions. The energies generated by all the components of the energy body are reflected into the aura as color values, mixing together to form distinct patches, bands, sparks, and swirls of color. These colors are the most visible parts of the human aura and the parts most commonly seen with auric sight.

The Human Aura

The human aura is an energy field that emanates from and surrounds the human body, reflecting the subtle life energies at work within and around it. This is something like the magnetic field that surrounds a simple magnet (see Chapter Six). Like a magnetic field, an aura is generated within physical matter but is also affected by its surroundings. A magnet is affected by iron and by other magnets. It is attracted to iron and either attracted or repulsed by other magnets—depending upon the polarity of whatever magnets it comes in contact with.

The energies flowing through an aura affect, and are in turn affected by, surrounding life conditions. The magnetic-like part of the auric field is attracted and repulsed by certain life conditions and either attracted or repulsed by other auric fields—depending upon the harmonics and polarities of whatever auric fields it comes into contact with. The human aura also reflects the activity of all its internal organs, showing health and mental and emotional activity. It also shows symptoms of disease, often long before the onset of any physical symptoms.

There are three basic types of human auras and each part has many different layers striated within it.

Etheric Aura

Close to the skin is the etheric aura or vitality sheath. It is seen (with auric sight) as a pale narrow band next to the skin, outlining the body. This is usually seen as being about an inch wide but can be thinner or thicker depending upon the vitality of the subject. It looks like a dense layer of pale smoke clinging to the surface of the skin. This is the most visible part of the energy body in its contracted state.

During sleep, the vitality sheath expands, as all its energy centres and energy exchange ports change into sleep mode, becoming larger and finer to absorb and store vitality within it. This vitality energy comes from two main sources: 1) the chemical digestion of food and drink, and 2) cosmic energy from the living waters of universal energy currents.

After sleep, the energy body contracts and forms a dense sheath surrounding the body close to the skin. In its contracted state, the vitality sheath holds within it all the stored energies needed for living. In many ways, the energy body acts like a living, chemical storage battery. During sleep, like a battery that has been placed on charge, it recharges its stores of vital energy, replacing what has been used up through the activity of daily living.

Main Aura

The main human auric color values emanate from the primary energy centres and are banded around the body like strata. Imagine a person with thick, colored hoops of light dropped over them, and you get the general idea. Infused through this are all the color values generated by the secondary energy centers, energy exchange ports, and meridians. The human aura in all its glory is a spectacular sight, containing a wealth of information about the person generating it.

Spiritual Aura

The spiritual aura is a *very* complex piece of creation and is far more refined and intricate than the etheric and main human auras. It cannot be seen with simple auric sight alone, although auric sight often forms a part of the ability to see it. The spiritual aura is extremely abstract in nature and contains within it all the incredibly complex influential seeds and conditional energies of consciousness, karma, and universal law. These multi-layered energies of consciousness make us who and what we are. They form our personalities and internal realities, as well as the subtle influences and attractions and repulsions that create the conditions that shape our lives, according to universal and karmic law.

The full spiritual aura can only be seen with an extremely high level of mind's eye vision ability. Usually, only partial facets and elements of it are seen at any one time. To an observer, elements of the spiritual aura usually appears to be seen in much the same way as a normal aura is, and this can often seem to be just a part of normal auric sight. The mechanics of viewing the abstract energies within the spiritual aura are basically the same as with auric sight. But these energies cause far more complex mental-visual imagery than the simple colored bands of light caused by auric energy.

The spiritual aura generates color values, static signs and symbols, and even full "motion-picture" quality, mind's eye visions. This is "seen" in the mind's eye of the observer and can often appear to be a part of the normal aura. The amount of information that can be gleaned from the spiritual aura and the signs, symbols, and visions seen within it, depends greatly upon the connection with, and the amount of energy flowing between, the subject and the observer, as well as the development of the brow centre and skill of the observer.

Thoughts on the Aura

The etheric, main, and spiritual auras, although quite different, do have similarities. They are all caused by the energies of existence, creation, consciousness, and life, and all are seen through a remarkably similar process. All levels of the aura are affected by, and are in turn affected by, each other, as well as by surrounding life conditions and atmospheres. All three main types of aura disappear or decay soon after physical death; the main and spiritual auras vanish instantly, and the etheric aura decays gradually. This highlights the strong relationship between auras and life itself.

Understanding the principals and mechanics of auric sight and the progressive nature of developing non-physical sight will help beginners to better understand what is happening to them if they decide to apply themselves to the training and development exercises contained within this book. If you understand something better, you can use it better.

Note

1. This chapter, and the following chapter, contain some elements from my forthcoming three-part series: "Romancing the Eye."

CHAPTER TWENTY-ONE

AURIC SIGHT TECHNIQUE

Robert Bruce

All the Colors of Colors

Uniqueness

Every color has a unique and brightly colored aura all its own—having a completely different color from the original. The auras given off by bright primary colors are much brighter, denser, and are far easier to see than any other type of aura. By using the auric colors of colors as a training aid, the technique of seeing auras can be learned much faster than would otherwise be possible.

Training Aid

Whether you accept the validity of the auras of colors or not, observing this type of aura quickly teaches a beginner the basic auric viewing technique, and this speeds the overall development of auric sight. The early success with seeing this type of aura keeps interest and morale high, ensuring enough work and effort is put in to get the desired result—seeing the human aura. Once the basic viewing technique is learned and you have actual experience with seeing auras, it is a simple step to graduate to observing other living auras and, eventually, human auras.

The exact shade and tone of a color's aura varies a great deal, according to the shade and tone of that color. The auras of colors are also affected by the background against which they are observed. There are thousands of different modern colors available today, in many different shades and tones—far too many to attempt to catalogue them all—and this chart should be looked upon as a basic guide only.

Auras of Colors (chart)

COLOR	AURIC COLOR
Red	Emerald Green
Orange	Pale Green
Yellow	Violet
Green	Orange
Blue	Yellow
Indigo	Gold
Violet	Pale Gold
Pink	Iridescent Green

Afterimages and Aura

Auric colors, given off by colors, are related to and similar in appearance to common afterimages. Afterimages are an optical effect caused by staring at a brightly illuminated color and then closing your eyes or looking away. A true afterimage hangs before your eyes, closed or open, like a phantom and is the reverse color of the original.

Color Depletion

It is commonly believed that afterimages are caused by color depletion of the rods and cones in the eyes, generating the reverse or negative color of the original color. I disagree, in part, with this explanation for afterimages and for very good reason. When the ability to see auras is in its early stages, afterimages are more often seen, due to the length of time needed to see an aura. This especially happens when observing the aura of color. But once the basic viewing technique is learned, the aura of color can be seen much more quickly, and there is much less of an afterimage effect.

Slow Auric Drag

The human aura, as well as the aura of color, will sometimes drag slightly at your eyes, creating something similar to an afterimage effect.

This is especially so if an aura is studied for any great length of time. The larger, brighter parts of it can hang before your eyes for a short time when you look away or close your eyes. This is another type of afterimage but one created by staring at a living aura and not at a color. I call this type of afterimage, slow auric drag. This is caused by the colors of the human aura becoming impressed upon the mind's eye and lingering, or dragging briefly, when the observer moves his line of sight while studying an aura.

The colors of the living human aura build up from bare skin, and bare skin, especially under dim light, has NO reverse color that can possibly generate any kind of normal afterimage, let alone the many different colors seen in a living human aura. Any afterimages generated in this way are exactly the "same" color as the original aura and are not a reverse of the auric color being observed. There is no reverse color effect at all, as happens with true afterimages. Color depletion of the rods and cones in the eyes cannot alone be responsible for both these types of afterimages, because the afterimage effect is quite different in each case. The afterimage generated by observing a color's aura is of its reverse color. An afterimage generated by a human aura is of exactly the same color—two quite different effects.

A better way, I think, to describe the afterimage effect of any type of aura, including that of color, is to call it a slow auric image. By staring at an auric color of any type, living or not, the auric color of the subject can become slowly impressed upon the sight center of the brain, creating a type of afterimage effect. It does not appear to be true, in both cases, that the eyes have simply become depleted of color. It is more logical to assume that an auric color has been impressed upon the brain's sight center and is causing a lingering effect that behaves in a similar way as an afterimage.

The similarity in these two quite different afterimage effects, I suggest, rather than contradicting the validity of the case for auric colors of colors as being a genuine type of aura, supports it. Why would they be any different?

Living Aura and Afterimages

There are many critics of auras and auric sight who claim auras are just afterimages. But the way a living human aura builds up is totally unlike the way an afterimage appears. It builds up, mushrooming bright colors from and around bare skin. The aura does not just fade slowly into sight; it grows before your eyes. The colors of a living aura do not fade into view, lingering and slowly deepening and brightening. They have a consistent color, from their first appearance as a thin outline to their full size—often more than three feet thick. Auras are not just a slight outline of color but large, vivid bands of color with thickness and depth and feel and force to them. And, while an aura is building up, if you shift your focus slightly or blink, it will often disappear, only to reappear a few seconds later. An afterimage does not behave in this way. Once a normal afterimage is generated, it stays there until it fades slowly from sight—it does not flicker in and out.

Why Most People Fail: The Human Aura—Not a Good Training Ground

The most common reason why people fail to see an aura is simply the way they go about it. The human aura is not a good training ground for a beginner. This is what usually happens: the subject sits and waits, for a very long time, while the observer struggles and strains for a glimpse of their aura. They are trying to relax and concentrate and master a tricky visual-mental technique—all at the same time. They subconsciously worry about what the subject is thinking of them. Are they getting bored? Are they getting impatient? Do they think they are foolish, a failure, or both? This kind of pressure causes a build up of subtle tension within the observer that effectively negates the relaxed mental state and flow of energy needed to see a human aura. Trying to get results under this kind of pressure, as a beginner, is next to impossible.

The Auras of Color—Better for Learning

The auras of colors are far denser and easier to see than any other type of aura. This is why they are so good for training. Even a rank beginner can usually see the aura of the color blue with just a few minutes of effort. Like any other difficult skill, the mind learns fast from success, and every time auric sight is used successfully, it gets a little bit easier to see an aura.

Graduated Training Method

Step 1 — Preparation and Tips

Light

You need plenty of good, soft light to train in. Have the light come from behind and above you. It is important to not have any bright light shining or reflecting into your eyes. Any reflection or glare will distract you and make auras difficult to see. A 100-watt lamp, or similar, coming from above and behind you is perfect. Later, when viewing the human aura, a much softer light gives better results.

Blinking

When you need to blink, do so, or it will cause your eyes to tense, burn, and water. Blink normally and in a relaxed way, without changing your eyes' focus. Do not become preoccupied with it. Blinking may cause an aura to momentarily disappear, but it will reappear quickly if you stay calm and hold a relaxed gaze. Learning to hold your focus while blinking normally is an important part of auric sight.

Glasses

If you wear glasses or contact lenses, keep them on. The clearer your vision is, the more accurately your eyes and brow center will be able to focus on your subject.

Props

Get some sheets of brightly colored paper about twelve inches square, one each of the primary colors, and some sticky tape. You can also use any brightly colored objects as props for these exercises, such as clothing, kitchen canisters, toys, etc. The auras of the colors blue and red are the brightest and easiest of all to see, so are the best colors to start with.

Viewing Distances

Place your colored prop (subject) about six feet away from you. With a human aura, about eight to ten feet away is better.

Backdrop

Have a plain and fairly neutral background for your subject. Do not view them against a brightly colored wall or garish wallpaper. If the wall color is wrong, use a sheet of neutral colored paper or cloth for a backdrop.

Step 2 — Brow Center Stimulation

It is very helpful to use some type of brow center exercise to stimulate your brow center into receptive activity. It is possible for most people to see the aura of a color without stimulating the brow center, but it is very difficult to see a living aura without first doing this, unless you have a naturally active brow center. For training purposes, always stimulate the brow center as a part of any viewing exercise.

The stimulation of any energy center (chakra) is commonly called "opening" it. This is a misnomer really, as energy centers are always active, busily performing their part in life's process. To enable auric sight, you need to stimulate the brow center into a more active and receptive state than normal. One of the easiest ways to do this is to use a simple mental, bodily awareness action on the brow center. This is achieved by localizing your bodily awareness at the site of the brow center and moving your awareness there in a dynamic way. The stimulation technique I have developed, and teach here, is based upon a natural mental, bodily-awareness action that is responsible for almost all cases of spontaneous auric sight.

Remember what it feels like when you haven't slept for days and you have had to wrestle with your eyelids to keep them open? Remember lifting them, over and over, and trying to "will" them to stay open? This is a mental, bodily-awareness action, and it causes a sensation, if you observe yourself closely, much like you are trying to lift a heavy, shadowy veil in your brow and behind your eyes. When you are very tired, the muscles of your eyes do not respond very well, and the action becomes almost entirely mental. Stop for a moment and remember what this feels like, and let's take a look at what this mental bodily-awareness action does.

Wrestling with tired eyes causes a strong mental, bodily-awareness motion in the energy body at the approximate site of your brow center. This causes direct stimulation of the brow center. This action is direct, localized, and much stronger than any visualization based brow center opening technique.

Tiredness and Auric Sight

If you study case histories of spontaneous auric sight, you will find the vast majority of sightings occur when the observer is very relaxed, bored, or tired. They are often in a semi-daydream state as well as wrestling with tired eyelids and gazing but not focusing upon a subject within their field of view. These are the optimum conditions for spontaneous auric sight, when the human aura suddenly appears.

A mental, bodily-awareness action in the brow area focuses bodily awareness in the brow center. With simple tiredness, an attempted eyelid opening action is fairly widespread, usually covering the entire brow and eye area, but it is still quite effective. When your bodily awareness is focused in one part of your body and you manipulate that area with your mind, you stimulate your energy body in that area. If there is a primary energy center in that area, this will be stimulated. And, if this mental, bodily-awareness action is continued for long enough and enough mental effort is put into it, this center will become stimulated into heightened activity.

Any heightened activity in a primary energy center will cause a natural flow of energy to that area. Heightened activity in a primary energy center creates a strong energy demand that the energy body automatically attempts to fulfill. This is very similar to how the physical body's natural healing mechanism is stimulated, and blood flow is increased automatically, to an injured area of the human body.

If you carry out this mental, bodily-awareness stimulation action when you are deeply relaxed, focused, and not tired, and you have a subject in your field of view, and you are not focusing directly on your subject, controlled auric sight will begin to occur. The degree of auric sight that occurs will, of course, depend entirely upon the developed state of your brow center at that time.

Stimulation Exercises

Note: For the following exercises, your brow center should be considered to be a circular area on the front of your brow. The top of this circle is at your hairline. The bottom is the top of the bridge of your nose, where it joins your skull, just below and between your eyebrows. The center of this circle is the spot between these top and bottom points, and in line with your nose.

1: Sit comfortably and meditate for a while, or close your eyes and take a few slow deep breaths to relax and settle yourself as much as you can.
2: Lightly scratch the skin, directly between your eyes and in the center of your brow, with a fingernail. The slight stinging sensation caused by this will help you to zero in on the exact site of your brow center with your bodily-awareness.
3: Shift your bodily-awareness to the site of your brow center, where it should be stinging slightly, and feel it with your awareness. Concentrate on being aware of that area of skin.
4: To begin with, mentally lift this whole area—as if you were trying to force tired eyelids open—but do NOT allow the muscles in this area to tense up or respond in any way (use a mental bodily-awareness action only).

5: Closely observe what is happening in this area as you perform the above action. Isolate the mental command that would lift your eyelids, if you allowed it to happen. Imagine your eyes are very heavy and unresponsive, and let them close on you a few times and then force them open. Observe which muscles you use to do this, and remember what it feels like. Use this same muscle command—with your mind-based bodily-awareness in that area—but without letting your eyelid muscles obey. Repeat this rhythmically, lifting, lifting, lifting, over and over and over, as if you were lifting a heavy mental shadow from behind your eyes in your brow area, until you are familiar with this new mental, bodily-awareness action.

In the early stages, it does not matter if you feel you are lifting too large an area over your brow. Even if you are lifting right across the whole front of your forehead and eyes, it will still cause stimulation in your brow center. With practise, you will be able to narrow the area of this action to the exact brow center area and increase the degree of stimulation you are causing there.

6: When you have isolated this type of brow center stimulation, you will find one side of the heavy veil behind your eyes, as above, is easier to lift than the other (usually the right is easier). This feeling is caused by the two different hemispheres of your brain; one side is always more active and easier to use than the other. One way to overcome this is to use a more sophisticated stimulation action, so the stimulation is more even and effective.

Use a clockwise, swirling, mental, bodily-awareness action (clockwise from the inside) at the site of the brow center. Adapt this same mental command, as described above, but swirl it clockwise as if you were mentally stirring that area with an invisible, mental, bodily-awareness finger. Note: if clockwise does not seem to work for you, try counterclockwise—or alternate between them.

7: Use a clockwise action, the same as in step 6, but "feel" this action penetrating your brow to a depth of three to four inches. Stir this area clockwise, as if you were stirring your brow area deep inside with a mental bodily-awareness finger.

8: Using a similar mental, bodily-awareness action, "feel" yourself opening a tiny pair of curtains at the site of your brow center. Open these curtains, holding your awareness close on your skin. Perform this action rhythmically, over and over and over.

9: Regularly alternate between all these opening actions for maximum brow center stimulation.

These brow center stimulation exercises are very effective but depend heavily upon the manipulation of the energy body with localized bodily-awareness. You have to FEEL these mental actions on the surface of your skin and deeper inside to make them effective. If you continue these exercises, you will stimulate your brow center and eventually, cause it to become active. I suggest these exercises be done for at least a few minutes each day, and whenever auric sight is practised, to effectively speed the development of the brow center and auric sight.

Effects of Regular Stimulation

The effect of regular brow center stimulation is very progressive, and you will notice a gradual increase in auric vision, with occasional bursts of spontaneous auric sight. Increased dream activity will also occur, your dreams becoming more vivid and memorable due to the increased energy flow to your brow center.

Cobwebs

The "cobwebs" sensation is, perhaps, the most noticeable effect caused by intense brow center stimulation and energy flowing to and through it. This sensation varies in intensity, according to the degree of brow center activity and the relaxed state of the physical body and mind. It feels like there are insects crawling all over your face. The intense tickling is caused by energy flowing through the network of energy pathways connecting the brow and eye centers to the many smaller, secondary energy centers covering your face and neck. These smaller centers channel energy from the lower energy body, trunk and legs, and feed it into the brow center when an energy demand is created there.

This tickling can be *very* intense at times but must be ignored, and the itching should not, if at all possible, be scratched, as scratching interferes with the flow of energy to the brow center. Not scratching and holding your relaxed state can take a lot of willpower at times, but this has excellent training benefits—learning to stay centered and relaxed amidst distraction.

Step 3 — Viewing Technique

To see an aura you have to be able to relax your body and concentrate your mind at the same time, and there is a trick to focusing your eyes in a special way that enables your brow center to tune into and receive your subject's energy. Remember, an aura must be gazed upon and not looked at directly.

Use a bright blue prop for the first exercise, as this is the easiest to see. Relax and do the brow center stimulation exercises, as above. When you are ready, gently gaze at the blue prop. Focus your eyes about four inches to the side of the prop and just past it.

The whole idea is to totally relax the focus of your eyes and observe the prop with your peripheral or side vision. Gently hold a relaxed gaze and get used to this new focus. Do NOT allow yourself to strain or tense your eyes, eyelids, or forehead while doing this. You need to concentrate mentally but must have a very relaxed and steady gaze, similar to the daydreaming state.

Your First Aura

While gazing steadily at the colored prop, gently continue with the brow center stimulation exercises. Patiently hold this relaxed gaze, and after a while (anything from a few seconds to a few minutes, in the early stages), you will see a faint shimmering in the air around the prop. You will then see a pale, narrow band build up near the edge of the prop, on the side nearest your focussed area. Stay relaxed! Don't change your focus in any way! Don't look directly at it! Blink if you have to—it will come back quickly!

Soon, a distinct, bright-yellow aura (blue prop) will build up from the pale band around the prop. If you change your focus, tense up, or look directly at it, the aura will vanish. If it does vanish, don't worry, continue observing, and it will quickly come back into view. In the early stages, this aura will tend to appear and disappear quite a bit, and this is quite normal. Keep at it, and this will happen less and less as you master the viewing technique. The way this type of aura appears is very similar to how a living aura will behave when you graduate to observing the human aura.

Step 4 — Graduated Training Exercises

1. More Colors

Once you have completed the first exercise with the blue prop, repeat it with all the other colors you have, starting with red. Study these props, one at a time, and write down the colors you see.

2. Mixed Colors

Observe the props two and three at a time. Tape the squares of paper in a line, first with a one-inch gap between them and then with a two- and three-inch gap between them. Watch how the different auric colors mix and affect each other.

3. Plants and Trees

Get a healthy potted plant or some freshly cut flowers, and study their aura. Use the same viewing distance as with the colored props. The aura you will see around them is a living aura, but keep in mind the effect of the auric colors given off by the color of the petals and leaves. For example, the orange hue you will see around the green parts of the plant's stems and leaves will come from the auric color of green. You will see a more distinct etheric and a stronger but more subtle aura around a living plant.

Use the same lighting conditions as in the first exercises for your first viewing attempt of a plant, then lower the brightness to a quarter (about 25 watts). With less light, more detail can be seen in a living aura.

Observe the aura of a tree. Pick a good sized tree that you can view, highlighted against the sky. It is best to observe it with the sun behind you, early in the morning or late in the day—especially against a cloudless sky. If the sun, or any strong reflection, is shining in your eyes, it will make viewing very difficult.

The shimmering haze around the tree is much more imposing and intense than that of a small plant. The color of a tree's aura is influenced not only by the colors of the leaves and bark, but by the color of the sky itself. On a sunny day with a blue sky, a tree's aura will appear to be a beautiful shade of blue. On a cloudy day, it will appear as creamy-grey. A tree's aura can also be observed at night. The night sky provides a good backdrop, and the dimmer light allows more detail to be seen in the tree's aura.

Experiment with the viewing distance you use, as this varies, and the best distance depends entirely upon the size of the tree. Anything from twenty to several hundred feet with a large tree will work (note Weston's Chapter Eleven—Trees and Stars section)

4. Animals

For the next exercise use an animal, any animal, dog, cat, etc. Try and observe them while they are resting. Animal auras are not as colorful as human auras, and these are affected by the color of their coat, but this is still a good exercise. Disease can be detected in the aura of an animal, the same as with a human subject. This makes observing them very good practice for diagnosing disease in general.

5. Self-Observation

Observe your own aura. There are two ways this can be done: direct and reflected. Direct observation can be done outside with the sun behind you and using the sky as a backdrop, or inside against a neutral background. Hold your arm out and study your hand and forearm against the sky. You can also lie down and observe the aura of your feet and legs.

Reflected observation is done using a mirror. Keep in mind that the quality of the mirror will affect the quality of the observation. Stand three to six feet away from the mirror, using fairly bright lighting as with the earlier exercises. Once this is done, reduce the lighting to about 25 watts or less. A mirror does not show the main aura as clearly as a direct observation, but it is still good practice. The etheric aura and other coarse types of energy, however, do show up remarkably well in a mirror if the lighting is just right (refer to Dye's Chapter Fourteen, section "The Human Aura—Mirrors").

Step 5 — The Human Subject

Background and Lighting

The mental, visual, and energy techniques for observing the human aura are the same as used to observe any other type of aura. The main differences are background and lighting. You can see quite a bit of the human aura under fairly bright lighting conditions but not much detail. Usually only the basic hues of the main, outer parts of the aura can be seen under bright light. This, however, is quite good for diagnosis, as the shadows of disease show up quite well against a neutral background.

For clarity and depth it is best to observe the human aura under fairly dim lighting conditions (15–25 watt lamp) and with a plain black or dark grey background. A white background can also be used under these conditions to highlight shadows in the aura. I like to change backgrounds when studying an aura, first using white, then changing to black. I hang a large sheet of cloth (double bed sheet size) pegged to a screen behind my subject. I hang both sheets, white over black, and then throw the white sheet back when I am done with it, exposing the black.

The dim light and dark background are much less distracting for an observer, and these conditions also make the eyes much more sensitive and receptive to energy, and the more delicate colors and tones of the human aura show up better. This also slows the appearance of the auric colors of colors and stops the generation of afterimages. These fairly dim and gloomy conditions, against a dark background, create a colorless blur around the subject's bare skin that is perfect for viewing their aura. This colorless blur becomes a mind's eye canvas upon which the beautiful colors of the human aura are painted.

Two Stage Viewing

For your first few attempts, it is best to approach the observation of the human aura in two stages:

Stage 1. Have your subject sitting on a stool in front of you but turned slightly away. Have your subject wear a loose blue or red top that leaves their upper neck and part of their upper back area bare. Begin with the brighter lighting conditions, as previously used to see the auras of colors, but using the darker backdrop.

Relax and prepare yourself with the stimulation exercises. Observe their colored top first, until you can clearly see the aura of its color. Next, shift your gaze slightly higher to the shoulder and neck area, a couple of inches above where the top ends, but keep the top's aura in view. Keeping the aura of the top in view will help keep your gaze focused correctly. You should soon begin to see the etheric aura building up from your subject's bare skin.

Stage 2. Reduce the light to about 15–25 watts, which should be coming from several feet behind you. Do not move or change your relaxed focus, and keep sight of your subject's colored top. If you can, have someone turn down the lighting for you, or use a dimmer switch attached to a lamp. Make sure you are continuing with the stimulation exercise through all this.

Get your subject to slide their top further down off their shoulders to increase the area of bare skin, and study this larger area. The upper back area should, ideally, be completely bare, and is the best place to start your observation. With bare skin, the first thing you will see will be the etheric aura building up. This looks like creamy, pale-blue to blue-grey smoke clinging to the skin. This is quite distinct and normally about half an inch or more deep. Next, a faint, colorless shimmering effect will appear in the air above the etheric aura, extending several inches out around your subject's back. You may, at this time, see some color (usually yellow) fading into view around your subject's head. Hold your gaze steady, and observe everything with your peripheral vision—do not shift your eyes.

Relax; hold your focus; make sure you breathe slowly, regularly, and deeply—and be patient. The main auric color for that area will soon begin building up and out from the etheric aura. For the upper back, you will usually see blue high up near the shoulders and green below this. These colors will be distinct, dense, and quite beautiful.

The aura's colors will first appear as narrow, colored bands, flickering maddeningly in and out of your sight, highlighting the outer edge of the etheric aura. They will appear and disappear, growing and shrinking quite a lot. This effect is caused partly by blinking and partly by minute shifts in your focus, and it cannot be helped. This can be very frustrating, but if you concentrate, stay relaxed, and keep trying, it will steadily get easier. The colors you see will, at times, slowly expand, blossoming out several inches or more, becoming thicker and more well defined. If you hold your focus, the color will stay there, and soon, more and more colors will appear and more detail. You are now seeing your first living human aura with controlled auric sight.

Step 6—A Viewing for Two

Mutual auric observation is where the observer and subject observe each other at the same time. This is a fascinating exercise for anyone learning auric sight and studying the different aspects of aura. It has many benefits and can, for some, be easier than normal, one-sided auric viewing. When two people in harmony are focused upon each other, a strong positive energy and spiritual rapport grows between them. This rapport not only stimulates their brow centers, through shared energy, but also strengthens and brightens their auric fields. This has the added bonus, if one observer is more developed than the other, of boosting or "jump-starting" the brow center of the weaker observer.

1: Sit facing each other about eight feet apart. Have the light low and diffuse (about 15 watts). Shield the lamp, or place it behind a piece of furniture, so there is no direct light. Experiment with the lighting until you find what works best for you. All you need is enough light to be able to see each other's faces clearly.

2: Gaze gently into each others eyes, using the normal viewing method, but do NOT look to the side—gaze gently into them. Do not focus directly on each other's eyes—as if you were locking eyes—but "gaze" into them, as if you were dreamily gazing into a lovers eyes, while observing the whole person with your peripheral vision.

3: You will find this exercise tends to make you laugh a little with embarrassment, so give yourselves time to get over the sillies. A bit of laughter does not hurt, as it tends to build positive energy in the room around you, but it can be distracting. When you are both quiet, comfortable, and relaxed, intensify your gaze and concentrate, letting yourselves melt into each other's eyes. Talk freely and quietly, telling each other what you are seeing. Friendly, loving, and open communication will strengthen your spiritual rapport. This makes viewing much more profound and will open you to glimpses of your spiritual auras.

4: Continue this exercise for as long as you wish. You will be amazed at some of the things you will see and experience. Apart from the etheric aura and auric colors, signs, symbols, and even faces may appear to you both, building up from your etheric auras, sometimes even completely covering a face.

Tips

1. Auric Brightness

The brightness of a person's aura has a lot to do with their mood and how they feel. If they feel happy and full of life, their aura will be larger and brighter. Try playing your subject's favorite music, or play some Primasounds meditation music if they like it, as this is excellent for energizing the aura (note Losey's Chapter Thirteen, section "Aura Energization"). It is important that your subject likes the music you play for them, as playing something they dislike will tend to dull their aura. It also helps to crack a few jokes and have a good laugh with them. Laughter and good humor are wonderful for building up energy and energizing auras, making them much easier to see.

2. Magnets

Get a small, round, flat magnet, the type used in decorative refrigerator magnets, and tape this to the center of your brow center. Make sure you have the (-) negative side touching your skin. See Chapter Six for details about using magnets on the body and how to find the negative side of a magnet (note Lindgren's Chapter Six, section "Using Magnets").

A magnet has three effects on the brow center: 1) magnetic stimulation of the physical body and glands in the brow area; 2) direct magnetic stimulation of the brow center; and 3) drawing bodily awareness to the center of the brow area, which causes an energy flow to that area. A larger flow of energy to the brow center stimulates it and promotes its development.

It is perfectly safe to keep this magnet in place during waking hours, but please, do **NOT** sleep with a magnet in place over your brow center! Unlike other areas of the body, sleeping with a magnet taped directly to your brow center can have negative side effects. There are several negative side effects possible: severe tension headache, migraine, emotional problems, depression, mental imbalance, nightmares, and psychic attack. This warning does not come from theory but from "hard and painful" experience. I suffered severe tension headaches and nightmares myself during my early experiments with magnets many years ago. And many of my volunteers have reported some or all of these other side effects in varying degrees—some extreme. Waking up in the middle of the night with a severe tension headache is the very least that will happen if you ignore this warning.

3. Soluble Calcium

Taking a daily supplement of soluble calcium is very beneficial for brow center development. Follow the advice on the label, or consult your doctor or pharmacist for the correct dosage. This sounds like a bit of an old wives tale, I admit, but it does have a lot of merit to it. This tip was passed to me twenty-five years ago by a very good clairvoyant, Ben, a good friend and teacher—since deceased. I did not think much of it back then, until I finally tried it a few years ago. I was simply amazed at the difference it made in the strength of my auric sight and mind's eye vision. I experimented for several months, taking and then not taking the calcium, for a month at a time, and there was a definite improvement in the strength and controllability of all aspects of my non-physical sight when I was taking it.

The calcium supplement I use and recommend is of the soluble, effervescent type, and the brand name is "Sandocal." Each tablet contains: Calcium lactate gluconate - 5.23 grams and Calcium carbonate - 0.80 grams. This is equivalent to 1000 mg. of calcium per tablet.

Close

The chapters in this book represent, I think, one of the finest compilations of contemporary knowledge concerning what is known about the elusive human aura and developing the ability to see it. Taking knowledge from many different fields and disciplines and compiling it into a comprehensive and readable book is no mean feat. Everyone seems to have their own theories, based upon their own experience, and not all of these agree. But, if you look between the lines of this book, you will see a single purposeful direction and a unified cohesion of thought guiding us towards a more complete and practical understanding of the human aura.

It takes a lot of practise to see the human aura well, so please don't be disappointed if you fail or see very little of it the first few times you try. If you manage to see the auras of colors, as in the earlier exercises, you CAN learn to see the human aura—it is just a matter of using a good technique, regular brow center stimulation, practice—and above all, patience!

Twenty years ago I too was a rank beginner when it came to auric sight. My parents were spiritualists, and they taught and encouraged me according to what they had been taught. But, for the life of me, I could not see auras—and I really tried hard. I persevered, however, and eventually managed to get a few glimpses of a human aura. Many years later, I learned to see them clearly, but this was a slow process, and I learned a lot about early development problems along the way. I developed this training method, and the energy stimulation techniques within it, to save other beginners the same time-wasting pitfalls I encountered through misinformation, poor technique, and widespread misunderstanding of the mechanics of non-physical sight.

Using this training method stimulates the development of the brow center and its network of supporting centers, which are the working parts of auric sight. With time and use, these will grow in strength, and seeing auras will become progressively easier to do. It may take some time and effort and patience before you get your first proper view of the living human aura, but with practice, as I did, you can develop auric sight.

I have taught many people to see the aura using these techniques. The fast results in the early stages help to build confidence and keep interest high. These techniques ensure that enough work is put into getting the desired results—seeing the human aura. And, once you have seen your first aura, even the humble aura of a color, you have taken your first real step into a much larger, more colorful and interesting world.

Lastly, if the natural approach fails you, or if you simply cannot wait for your first full glimpse of the human aura, there is always science and ***The Aura Camera 3000 and 6000*** to fall back upon.

SECTION VI:

RESOURCES AND REFERENCES

CHAPTER TWENTY-TWO

RESOURCES FOR PERSONAL GROWTH

Blythe Arakawa

THERE'S NO SUBSTITUTE FOR direct, hands-on experience when it comes to psychic development. If you'd like to learn more about auras, chakras, and your own intuitive or psychic abilities, check out these resources suggested by this book's contributors.

This chapter includes sections on intuitive schools, spiritual healing centers, spiritual travel, books, tapes and related products, as well as our recommended reading list. You'll also find information on how to have your aura photo taken and how to contact contributors to this book for clairvoyant (psychic) readings or psychic investigation and research.

Intuitive Training Schools and Foundations

(A. R. E.) Association for Research & Enlightenment
International Headquarters
PO. Box 595, Virginia Beach, VA 23451-0595
Ph. (804) 428-3588, Fax: (804) 422-4631

A.R.E. is the international headquarters for the work of Edgar Cayce (1877-1945). Study groups and other activities, bimonthly magazine, newsletter, extracts from the Cayce readings, conferences, products, and more. Call for more information.

A. R. E. Clinic
4018 N. 40th St.
Phoenix, AZ 85018
Tel: (520) 955-0551

Same as the above A. R. E., works with the Edgar Cayce research & remedies.

Avalon Institute for Psychic Development
Chico, CA
Tel: (916) 891-0805

Teaches basic spiritual abilities and psychic tools, healing, clairvoyancy, and features a training program. Also offers seminars around the country. Call for more information.

Barbara Brennan School of Healing
P.O. Box 2005, East Hampton, NY 11937
Tel: (516) 329-0951, Fax (516) 324-9745

Founded and directed by *Hands of Light* and *Light Emerging* author, Barbara Brennan, the Barbara Brennan School of Healing is a respected educational institution dedicated to the exploration of Healing Science. Founded in 1982, the School offers a four-year Professional Healing Science certification program where students from around the world learn to work with the aura for healing on physical, emotional, mental, and spiritual levels.

Berkeley Psychic Institute
Berkeley, CA (Locations throughout the Bay Area)
Tel: (510) 848-8020

Beginning healing and meditation classes, one- or two-year clairvoyant training program, teacher training. See references to these techniques in Chapters Fourteen and Sixteen. Call for more information.

Energy Master Seminars
The Robert T. Jaffe, M.D., School of Energy Mastery
Tel: (800) 238-3060

Training in the art of advanced energy healing, enlightenment, and world service.

Healing Resource Center
P. O. Box 175
Sedona, AZ 86339
Tel: (800) 338-0112

HRC offers educational and healing experiences for individuals and groups who choose to align themselves more fully with their unconditional love, infinite power, and universal wisdom. HRC offers a three-year school of self-mastery, healing, and world service as well as several heart-based energy healing workshops and gatherings. Call for more information.

Monroe Institute (Interstate Industries)
62 Roberts Mountain Road
Faber, VA 22938
Tel: (804) 361-1252

A non-profit organizational scientific research center. One of the leaders in scientific research. Call for more information.

Pacific School of Intuitive and Holistic Studies
2822 Union Street
Oakland, CA 95408
Tel: (510) 893-5809

Offers a six-month clairvoyant training program in the Bay Area as well as seminars nationwide. Call for more information.

Phoenix Psychic Institute
Phoenix AZ
Tel: (520) 395-0651

Meditation, healing, basic psychic awareness skills, and clairvoyant training program. Call for more information.

Power to Move Center for Spiritual Learning
Englewood, CO
Tel: (303) 789-4204

Offers basic meditation, healing, and self-awareness classes, seminars, and individual sessions plus a clairvoyant training program. Call for more information.

Psychic Horizons Center
Boulder, CO
Tel: (303) 604-0990

Basic meditation and healing classes, clairvoyant training, and advanced healing classes. Call for more information.

School for Intuitive Awareness
Taos, NM
Tel: (505) 751-3469

Meditation, healing, basic intuitive awareness skills, and clairvoyant training program. Call for more information.

Scottsdale Holistic Medical Group
7350 East Stetson #128
Scottsdale AZ 85251
Tel: (520) 990-1528

Works with the Edgar Cayce research and remedies. Note above.

The Southern California Psychic Institute
Anaheim, CA
Tel: (714) 772-8269

Offers meditation, healing, and clairvoyant training classes. Call for more information.

There are many other fine psychic schools and training programs throughout the world. Check the New Age Directory or your local New Age publications to find them.

Spiritual Healing Centers

Church of Aesclepion Healing
1314 Lincoln Avenue
San Rafael, CA 94901
Tel: (415) 453-6196

Offers spiritual (energy) healing through the laying-on of hands as well as trance-channeled faith healings, working with the aura, chakras, and astral body. Healing services and lectures monthly. Long distance trance-channeled healings are available on request.

Grand Master Healer Ostad Hadi Parvarandeh
Subtle Energies & Consciousness Research Arts Institute
363 Van Ness Way Suite #401
Torrance, CA 90501
Tel: (310)-783-1999, e-mail: SECRA@aol.com

Internationally known Iranian healer who has reportably healed thousands. Dr. Parvarandeh, according to the English BBC News was recently rated as "the number one healer in the world." Call for more information.

Spiritual Travel

Deja Vu Tours
Berkeley, CA
Tel: (800) 600-3404

Transformational pilgrimages to sacred sites around the world, including England, Nepal, Peru, Brazil, the Philippines, Africa, Hawaii (dolphin adventures, Women in Business retreats), and North America. Experienced intuitive tour leaders. Workshops and events on tour. Custom tours created for your group. Ask about free travel via Travel Partners Program. Call for more information.

Lancelot's Desire Metaphysical Travel
Waimanalo, HI
Tel: (808) 259-8530

Spiritual tours led by Gwen Totterdale, Ph.D. Destinations include Australia, England, Bali, the Caribbean, and Hawaii. Swim with the dolphins, visit crop circles, sacred sites like Stonehenge, Ayers Rock, and more. Channeled sessions and workshops on tour. Call for more information.

Books, Tapes, and Related Products

Barbara Brennan Audio Cassettes (see Barbara Brennan School of Healing above for ordering information)

Brennan offers three series of inspirational audio cassettes: *Guided Visualizations*—exercises and meditations for self-healing; *Channeled Healings*—holographic healing and teachings from Barbara's guide, Heyoan; and *Lectures by Barbara Brennan*—her teachings on Healing Science and the path of healing.

Energy Anatomy
The Science of Personal Power, Spirituality, and Health
Caroline Myss, Ph.D.
Sounds True AudioTapes
Tel: (800) 333-9185

Audiocassette series on the chakras and anatomy of human energy. Myss is a medical intuitive.

ESSENTIA
100 Bronson Avenue, #1001
Ottawa, Ontario K1R 6G8 Canada
Tel: (613) 238-4437

Offers aura goggles, tapes, books, and other items including detectors, generators, Pulsor units, energizers, and body & massage tools.

Dr. Valerie Hunt
Tel: (310) 457-4694

Dr. Hunt offers auric field sound healing tapes, lecture tapes, meditations, and more. For more information, contact her office.

Legion of Light
Neil S. Cohen
Tel: (800) 543-9301 or (520) 282-0155.

Offers chakra and color charts. Call for information or to purchase chakra charts or any of the awareness guides.

Tools for Exploration
4460 Redwood Highway, Suite 2
San Rafael, CA 94903

PrimaSounds technology "use a completely new musical scale tuned to the human energy (or 'chakra') system. What results is a kind of 'vibrational bath' designed to resonate one or more of the seven primary energy centers, facilitating relaxation, enhancing consciousness, and allowing profound inner states.

"The inventor of this new musical scale is professor Arnold Keyserling of the Academy of Applied Arts in Vienna. His former student and the composer of the PrimaSound music is Ralph Losey, who has been exploring and developing chakra music over the last twenty years."

New Editions International, Ltd.
P. O. Box 2578
Sedona, AZ 86339
Tel: (520) 282-9574; Fax (520) 282-9730

International publicity and marketing resource service. Yearly trade directory (New Marketing Directory), newsletters, lists, and cooperative mailing advertising. Call for more information.

Takionic™
Tachyon Energy Research, Inc.
2200 Pacific Coast Hwy. # 304
Hermosa Beach, CA 90254
Tel: (310) 374-8777

The Takionic™ product line combining two revolutionary technologies: Optimun Resonant Materials™ and Tachyon Energy.

Recommended Reading List

These books are tremendous resources about the aura, chakras, colors, and spiritual healing. You can find most of them at your local bookstore. Many can be special ordered. Out-of-print books may be found at used book dealers or at Aura Imaging Systems, which has a walk-in lending library for rare and out-of-print books.

Aura Related Books

The Aura (first published as *The Human Atmosphere* in 1911) by Dr. Walter Kilner, 1973, Samuel Weiser, NY. One of the first books published on auras. Science-oriented—includes Kilner's observations and data about the aura. Out-of-print.

Color and Crystals by Joy Gardner, 1988, The Crossing Press. Introduction to color theory, the chakras, tarot, and other aspects of metaphysics. Fascinating case studies.

Color Energy ® for Body and Soul by Inger Naess, 1994, Energy Corporation. Booklet on the effects of color, written to accompany their products (oils & bath crystals).

Color Therapy: Healing with Color by Reuben Amber, Aurora Press. Offers therapeutic techniques on healing with colors.

Color Your Life by Howard & Dorothy Sun, Ballantine Books. A good basic book about color.

Hands of Light: A Guide to Healing Through The Human Energy Field, 1988, and *Light Emerging: The Journey of Personal Healing* 1993 by Barbara Ann Brennan, Bantam Books, NY. Brennan, a former atmospheric physicist, combines science and spirituality in these two works, which are actually textbooks for her healing school.

How to Heal with Color and *How to See and Read the Aura* by Ted Andrews, 1992, 1993, Llewellyn, New Times Press. Includes simple but fun exercises to expand your aura consciousness.

Infinite Mind: The Science of Human Vibrations by Valerie Hunt, 1989, Malibu Publishing, Malibu, CA. An excellent work covering both the science of the human aura and spiritual healing.

Life Colors by Pamala Oslie, 1991, New World Library, San Rafael, CA. Oslie works with the same system used by Barbara Bowers in *What Color is Your Aura?* Personality and aura color profile questionnaire included.

Light Medicine of the Future by Jacob Liberman, O.D., Ph.D., 1991, Bear & Co. Dr. Liberman, a doctor of optometry and pioneer in the therapeutic use of light and color, offers fascinating healing case studies. Challenges the assumption that the sun is dangerous to human well-being.

Living Rainbows: Develop Your Aura Sight by Gabriel Hudson, Rain Light Technology Publishing. Auras and the effects of color.

The Origins and Properties of the Human Aura by Oscar Bagnall, 1970, University Books, NY. Bagnall continued Kilner's work studying the human aura. May be out of print.

The Power of Color by Dr. Morton Walker, Avery Publishing. How color affects you in daily life.

The Probability of the Impossible by Dr. Thelma Moss, 1974, J.P. Tarcher, Los Angeles, CA. Moss' ground-breaking work on auras, Kirlian photography, and many other psychic experiments conducted in her lab at UCLA. May be out of print.

Seven Mansions of Color by Alex Jones, DeVoross Publications. Another explanation of the colors in your aura.

What Color is Your Aura? by Barbara Bowers, Ph.D., 1989, Pocket Books, NY. Bowers discusses her system of using the aura to understand and type personalities. Explains how the aura is a powerful key into understanding the personality. Interesting, concise, and well organized.

Wheels of Light by Rosalyn L. Bruyere, 1989, Fireside Publishing, NY. Explores the seven major chakras and their importance to our bodies, sexuality, and life energy. Interesting information on different cultures and ancient traditions.

There are many other informative books about auras, colors, chakras, and Kirlian photography. Check your local book stores and library

Bioenergy and Magnetism

Dr. Buryl Payne
PsychoPhysics Labs
4264 Topsail Ct.
Soquel, CA 95073
Tel: (408) 462-1588

Power Pulsar. This instrument produces the strongest magnetic force possible without overheating the coil. A rugged, nine-inch diameter coil can be flexibly applied to any part of the body from head to feet. Pulsing at 16 Hz, which has been found optimum for increasing blood flow, the Power Pulsar is for heavy duty problems. It is about the size of a laptop computer and has a built in rechargeable lead-acid 7amp hour battery. A two inch soft disk applicator is also supplied with the Power Pulsar.
Pulsar II. This in-between-sized unit comes with two applicators, a lightweight, six-inch diameter coil, and a two-inch applicator. The

instrument has two output jacks so both applicators can be used simultaneously. The Pulsar II also has a choice of two frequencies—16 and 8 Hz. Rechargeable batteries can be supplied by the user. A charging jack is built into the case. Other items provided by PsychoPhysics Labs include: Pocket Pulsar, Magnetic Power Pads, Magnetic Wraps, Biomagnetism Kits, the Electronic Muscle Tester, and the Biosensor.

Aura Photography

Would you like to see your own aura on film or video? Contact any one of these offices to have your aura photo taken, or find out about aura imaging photography or aura imaging video systems. These international locations offer aura photos as well as a wide variety of intuitive products, training, and services. Call Aura Imaging Systems for a location in your area, or contact one of the international locations listed below.

Aura Imaging Systems/Progen Company
International Headquarters
319 Spruce Street
Redwood City, CA 94063
***Tel: (800) 321-AURA* or (415)367-0369)**
also see our Web Site at http://www.auraphoto.com

Call for the nearest location where you can have your aura photo taken. Aura cameras are located in thirty-five countries around the globe. Information is also available about hosting an aura camera at your store or event, or purchasing an aura camera.

Asia

Hong Kong
Body Aura Shop Ltd and
The Magic Touch Publication Ltd.
Edward Li and Kent Tusi
Room 701,7/F CCI Bldg.
813-317 B Hennesy Rd.
Wan Chai-Hong Kong
Tel: (85) 2-834-1683
Fax: (85) 2-834-3271

Indonesia
Andri Bojoh-Knun
JLN.Tanjung 1/L.24
Jakarta 12530
Ranch Indah, Indonesia
Tel: (62) 21 789-3026

Japan
Michio Sasaki
Top Harajuku Dai #2 Rm, 204
5-15-1, Jingumae
Shibuyaku, Tokyo, Japan 150
Tel: (81) 354-66-0308

Malaysia
Crystal Discoveries
Keat Tan
6119A Ground Floor
Bangsar Shopping Centers
Julan Manrof, Bungsar
Kuala Lumpur, Malaysia 59100
Tel: (60) 3-253-2899

Philippines
Marianos Yupitan
2325 Golmore Cr.
Aurora Blvd.
Quezon City, Philippines
Tel: (63) 2 722-8425
Fax: (63) 2 721-8267

Singapore
Ken Crystal
Choo Yeow Chiah
111 North Bridge Road
#05-61/62 Peninsula Plaza
Singapore 0617
Republic of Singapore
Tel: (65) 339-0008

Kang Li Crystal & Accessories
Emily Ching
149 Roches Rd., #B1-05
Fu Lu Shou Complex-
Singapore 0718
Tel: (65) 337-7732
Fax: (65) 337-7065

East Light Trading
Andrew Lim
#01-01 Lucky Chinatown
211 New Bridge Rd.
Singapore 0105
Tel: (63) 2-635-4741
Fax: (63) 2-788-2834

Taiwan
Blue Rose Intl. Co., Ltd.
Chufie Tsai
Min Shen East Road Section 5
#165 11-1 FL Taipei, Taiwan
Tel: (88) 62 753-4733
Fax: (88) 62 753-4740

Thailand
Arin Chai
69/68 So Phramaemahkaroon
Tiwanon Road
Pakkrad Nonthaburi 11120 Thialand
Tel: (66) 2 583-5235
Fax: (66) 2 583-4461

Europe

Austria
Lichtzentrum
Light Centre Aura School
Rositta Virag
See Park 1
5310 Mond See, Austria
Tel: (43) 6232-6150
Fax: (43) 6232-6190

Belgium
Franz Allaert
Reigerlohstraat 11, B-8730 Beernem

Croatia
Co. Folgor Drosojewic,
B. Galenkovic, Jurisceva Nr.8,
Croatia-4100 Zagreb
Tel: (38) 5-4157- 7307

Denmark
John C. Anderson
Thorshavnsgade 4-6,
DK-2300 Kobenhavn S Denmark

England
Winfalcon Healing Center
Wendy Heart
2829 Ship Street
Brighton, Sussex BN1 1AD England
Tel: (44) 127 372-8997

France
Philimex
Daniele Laurent
58 Rue du Faubaurg Montmarte
F-75 425 Paris CEDEX 09 France
Tel: (33) 148 748-538
Fax: (33) 142 810-493

Germany
Andreas Bunkahle
Günterstalstr 14, D-79100
Freiburg, Germany
Tel/Fax: (49) 761-7070-989
email: bunka@uranus.freinet.de

Martina Gruber
Römerstr 1
D-74629 Pfedelbach-Gleichen
Tel: (49) 7949-2638
Fax: (49) 7949-2538

Italy
Elestial
Carlo Montanari
Via Vitruvio 39, I-20214
Milan, Italy 20124
Tel: (39) 2 2940 8238
Fax: (39) 2 294 06722

Netherlands
Alex van Galen
Munnikenstr.35, NL-2315 KV
Leiden
Tel: (31) 71-5225970
Fax: (31) 71-5122171

Norway
A/S Partrade Colour Energy
Inger Naess
Nordraaksgt. 8, Norway, 0260 Oslo
Tel: (47) 22 43 7001
Fax: (47) 22 43 7037

Poland
Nina Dul, Immenbusch 31,
D-22549 Hamburg, Poland
Tel/Fax: (49) 40-80-805451

Spain
Aura Imaging Systems España,
Josemarie Sanz
Gran Via Cort Catalanes 465,
E-08015 Barcelona, Spain

Switzerland
Aura Vision Schweiz
Lanz/Mühlenbecher
Brettigen, Switzerland
CH 6313 Menzingen
Tel: (41) 41 755 3202

Others

Australia
Karim Gawer
Box 5926
Gold Coast Mail Center
Queensland 4217 Australia
Tel: (61) 7 527-5195
Fax: (61) 7 570-1231

Canada
Jacques Beauchamps
365 Degoore Blvd., #814
St. Laurent, Quebec H4N2T
Montreal, Canada
Tel: 514 338-1466

Israel
Shelha Hazalam Eli
Itaneviim Str.is
Itaifa 3100 Israel
Tel: (97) 2-467-2939
Fax: (97) 2-467-2927

South Africa
Celeste Van De Merwe
P. O. Box 6013 Uniedal
7612 Stellenbossch RSA
Tel: (21) 887-6483
Fax: (21) 887-5512

Mexico
Susan Shore
Fresas 118 Apt.304-B
Mexico D F 03100
Tel: (52) 5 559-8910

Clairvoyant/Healing/Psychic Readings

Janice Dye is a certified Reiki practitioner and Intuitive counselor, and her work and spiritual interests have kept her busy and creative in Toronto for the past seven years. Recently, she has expanded her energy to encompass the global community of Internet Cyberspace and is available for readings through email at mayasweb@idirect.com. Her home on the net is the Innerspace Station, a spiritual and metaphysical resource and growing community hub. http://web.idirect.com/~innerspa.

Dayle Schear specializes in psychometry: the art of holding objects to see the past, present, and future. She has solved missing persons and murder cases with local police departments and has appeared on many national television and radio shows. Her books are *The Psychic Within*, *Dare To Be Different*, and *Tarot For Beginners*. Offices in Hawaii and Lake Tahoe, Nevada. For private consultations: call (702) 588-3337.

Psychic Investigator/Researcher

C. E. Lindgren provides scientific research in all fields of psychic phenomena, arcane societies, Rosicrucianism, and occult topics. He has seven university degrees and twenty-five years of experience. As a adjunct professor of parapsychology and medieval history, he also teaches correspondence courses in PSI investigation, leading to certificates in parapsychology and psychic development. He consults with clients worldwide concerning all areas of psychic happenings. Rev. Lindgren, FCP, DLitt, DEd (c) may be reached at lindgren@panola.com Tel: (662) 563-8954.

CHAPTER TWENTY-THREE

REFERENCES AND OTHER RELATED WORKS

Alessandra, P. 1995. *Seeing Auras*, A. Priori, 6524 San Felipe #323, Houston, TX 77057 USA (email: aprioripa@aol.com).

Allan, G. 1996. Interview by author.

Alvino, G. 1996. Quoting "A Study of Structural Neuromuscular Energy Field and Emotional Approaches" by Dr. Valerie Hunt, 1988, in "The Human Energy Field in Relation to Science, Consciousness, and Health." (http://www.vxm.com/21R.43.html.)

Anderson, M. 1975. *Color Healing*. Samuel Weiser Inc.

Argüelles, J. & Miram. 1985. *Mandala.* Boston: Shambhala.

Armstrong, T. 1994. *Multiple Intelligences in the Classroom.* Alexandria, VA: Association for Supervision and Curriculum Development.

Aurobindo, S. 1958. *On Yoga II*, Tome One. Pondicherry, India: Aurobindo Ashram Press.

Ayusherbs. 1996. Bellevue, WA: Ayush Herbs, Inc. [pamphlet] (www.ayush.com)

Bagnall, O. 1970. *The Origin and Properties of the Human Aura.* New York: University Books, Inc. [Rev. edition from 1937]

Bailey, A. 1922. Letters on Occult Meditation.

Bailey, A. 1953. *Esoteric Healing.* New York: Lucis.

Bartlett, L. E. 1981. *Psi Trek.* New York: McGraw-Hill Book Co.

Beal, J. B. 1974. "The Emergence of Paraphysics: Research and Applications." *Psychic Exploration: A Challenge for Science.* Edited by John White. New York: G. P. Putnam's Sons.

Becker, R. 1985. *The Body Electric.* Quill.

Becker, C. B. 1993. *Paranormal Experience and Survival of Death.* NewYork: State University of New York Press.

Bentov, I. 1988. *Stalking the Wild Pendulum: On the Mechanics of Consciousness.* Rochester, VT: Destiny Books.

Boddington, H. 1946. *The University of Spiritualism.* London: Spiritualist Press.

Bohr, N. 1934. *Atomic Physics and the Description of Nature.* Cambridge, England: Cambridge University Press.

Bonny, H. L. & Savary, L. M. 1973. *Music and Your Mind: Listening with a New Consciousness.* Station Hill Press.

Braud, W. G. & Schlitz, M. J. 1991. " Consciousness Interactions with Remote Biological Systems: Anomalous Intentionality Effects." *ISSSEEM Journal*, Vol. 2 (1), abstracts.

Brennan, B. A. 1987. *Hands of Light.* Toronto & New York: Bantam Books.

Brennan, B. A. 1988. *Hands of Light.* New York: A Bantam Book.

Brennan, B. A. 1993. *Light Emerging.* New York: Pleiades Books.

Brennan, J. H. 1972. *Experimental Magic.* Wellingborough, Northamptonshire: The Aquarian Press.

Bruce, R. 1994. *How to See Auras.* Email: rsb@tower.net.au.

Butler, P. E. 1981. *Talking to Yourself: Learning the Language of Self-Support.* New York: Harper & Row.

Bruyere, R. L. 1989. *Wheels of Light: Chakras, Auras, and the Healing Energy of the Body.* New York: "A Fireside Book," Simon and Schuster.

Campbell, J. 1986. *The Inner Reaches of Outer Space: Metaphor as Myth and as Religion.* San Francisco: Harper & Row Publishers, Inc.

Capek, M. 1961. *The Philosophical Impact of Contemporary Physics.* Princeton, NJ: D. Van Nostrand.

Castleman, M. 1991. *The Healing Herbs.* Emmaus, PA: Rodale Press.

Chapman, A. 1996. Interview by Andrine Morse.

Coggins, G. 1994. Interview by C. E. Lindgren.

Coggins, G. 1996. Interview by Susana Madden.

Cohen, D. 1974. *The Far Side of Consciousness.* New York: Dodd, Mead & Company.

Copenhaver, B. P., Ed. & Trans. 1992. *Hermetica: The Greek Corpus Hermeticum and the Latin Asclepius.* Cambridge, England: Cambridge University Press.

Corliss, W. R. 1996. "Slamming the Door on Parapsychology." *ARPR Bulletin* (Academy of Religion and Psychical Research). September, vol. 5(3):1. [From W. R. Corliss in *Science Frontiers*, July-August, 1996 from an exchange of letters in *Physics Today* (April)].

Cosmic Awareness. 1969. The Tattvic Tides.

Cousins, N. 1979. *Anatomy of an Illness*. New York: Bantam.

Cozort, D. 1986. *Highest Yoga Tantra: An Introduction to the Esoteric Buddhism of Tibet*. Ithaca, NY: Snow Lion Publications.

Crosland, M. P. (Ed.). 1971. *The Science of Matter*. History of Science Readings. Baltimore, MD: Penguin Books.

Csikszentmihalyi, M. & Rathunde, K. 1990. "The Psychology of Wisdom: An Evolutionary Interpretation," in Robert J. Sternberg (Ed.), *Wisdom*. New York: Cambridge.

de Nicolás, A. T. 1976. *Avatara: The Humanization of Philosophy Through the Bhagavad Gita*. New York: Nicolas Hays, Ltd.

Dumézil, G. 1973. *Gods of the Ancient Northmen*. Berkeley, CA: University of California Press.

Duncan, L. & Roll, W. 1995. *Psychic Connections: A Journey into the Mysterious World of Psi*. New York: Bantam Doubleday Dell Books.

Dychtwald, K. 1977. *Bodymind*. New York: G.P. Putnam's Sons.

Dyczkowski, Mark S. G. 1987. *The Doctrine of Vibration: An Analysis of the Doctrines and Practices of Kashmir Shaivism*. Albany, NY: State University of New York Press.

Eddy, M. B. 1971. *Science and Health, with Key to the Scriptures*. Boston: First Church of Christ, Scientist, 1971 (many editions).

Eidelman, W. S. 1995. "The Bio-Energy Revolution." (http://maui.net/drbill/hompsciv.html)

Eliade, M. 1961. *Images & Symbols: Studies in Religious Symbolism*. Trans. Philip Mairet. Mission, Kansas: Sheed Andrews and McMeel, Inc.

Eliade, M. 1969. *Yoga: Immortality and Freedom*. Trans. Willard R. Trask. Bollingen Series LVI. Princeton, New Jersey: Princeton University Press.

Epstein, G. 1989. *Healing Visualizations: Creating Health Through Imagery*. New York: Bantam.

Ferguson, B. B. 1996. Personal correspondence, Yoga and Meditation Instructor. (web-site: http://www.holistic.com/listings/om.html).

Findlay, A. 1947. *The Psychic Stream or the Source and Growth of the Christian Faith*. London: Psychic Press, Ltd.

Fisslinger, J. 1994. *Aura Imaging Photography*. Trans. from German by Daniela Rommel-Hathaway. Iowa: Sum Press.

Gablik, S. 1991. *The Re-Enchantment of Art*. New York: Thames and Hudson.

Gardner, K. 1990. *Sounding the Inner Landscape: Music as Medicine*. Stonington, MA: Caduceus Publications.

Gawain, S. 1978. *Creative Visualization* (book and tape). Berkeley: Whatever Publ.

Gerber, R. 1988. *Vibrational Medicine*. Ingram.

Goldberg, J. 1989. *Anatomy of a Scientific Discovery: The Race to Discover the Secret of Human Pain and Pleasure*. Toronto: Bantam Books.

Goldsmith, J. 1959. *The Art of Spiritual Healing*. New York: Harper.

Green, E., Parks, P. A., Guyer, P. M., Fahrion, S. L. & Coyne, L. 1991. "Anamalous Electrostatic Phenomena in Exceptional Subjects," *ISSSEEM Journal*, Vol. 2 (3), abstracts.

Grim, P., Ed. 1982. *Philosophy of Science and the Occult*. Albany, New York: State University of New York Press.

Grimes, J. 1989. *A Concise Dictionary of Indian Philosophy: Sanskrit Terms Defined in English*. Albany, New York: State University of New York Press.

Grof, S. 1988. *The Adventure of Self Discovery: Dimensions of Consciousness and New Perspectives in Psychotherapy and Inner Exploration*. Albany, NY: State University of New York Press.

Grog, S. *The Holotropic Mind*.

Grow, G. 1987. "Teaching Writing through Negative Examples." *Journal of Teaching Writing*, Winter.

Hannemann, H. 1990. *Magnet Therapy*. NY: Sterling Publ. Co.

Harner, M. 1982. *The Way of the Shaman*. New York: Bantam.

Heisenberg W. 1958. *Physics and Philosophy*. New York: Harper Torchbooks.

Helstetter, S. 1987. *The Self-Talk Solution*. New York: Morrow.

Hines, T. 1988. *Pseudoscience and the Paranormal*. Buffalo, NY: Prometheus Books.

Holmes, E. 1938. *Science of Mind*. New York: Dodd, Mead.

Hurkos, S. 1996. "Aura Imaging Photography." [pamphlet]

Janiger, O. & Goldberg, P. 1993. *A Different Kind of Healing*. New York: G.P. Putnam's Sons.

Jeans, J. 1951. *The Growth of Physical Science.* Cambridge, England: Cambridge University Press.

Johnson, M. 1987. *The Body in the Mind: The Bodily Basis of Meaning, Imagination, and Reason.* Chicago, IL: The University of Chicago Press.

Joy, B. 1979. *Joy's Way.* Los Angeles, CA: Jeremy P. Tarcher, Inc.

Julien, L. 1996. Interview by Jennifer Baltz.

Kaku, M. 1994. *Hyperspace: A Scientific Odyssey Through Parallel Universes, Time Warps, and the Tenth Dimension.* New York: Oxford University Press.

Kalupahana, D. J. 1976. *Buddhist Philosophy: A Historical Analysis.* Honolulu, HI: The University Press of Hawaii.

Kaplan, R. *Seeing Beyond 20/20*

Karagulla, S. 1967. *Breakthrough to Creativity.* Los Angeles: DeVorss & Co.

Kerényi, K. 1976. *Hermes Guide of Souls: The Mythologem of the Masculine Side of Life.* Trans. Murray Stein. Zurich: Spring Publications.

Kilner, W. J. 1965. *The Human Aura.* New York: University Books.

Kilner, W. J. 1973. *The Aura.* New York: Weiser.

Klein, A. 1979. *The Healing Power of Humor.* Los Angeles: Tarcher.

Krippner, S., Ed. 1979. *Psychoenergetic Systems: The Interaction of Consciousness, Energy and Matter.* New York: Gordon and Breach Science Publishers.

Krippner, S. & Rubin, D. 1972. *Galaxies of Life.* New York: Gordon & Breach.

Krishna, G. 1967. *Kundalini: The Evolutionary Energy in Man.* Berkeley, CA: Shambhala.

Kul, D. 1974. *Intermediate Studies of the Human Aura.* Los Angeles, CA: Summit University Press.

Lawlor, R. 1982. *Sacred Geometry: Philosophy and Practice.* NY: The Crossroad Publishing Company.

Lazarus, R. S. 1991. *Emotion and Adaptation.* Oxford: Oxford University Press.

Leadbeater, C.W. 1987. *Man Visible and Invisible.* Wheaton, IL, London, & Madras: The Theosophical Publishing House (A Quest Book). [First printing, 1925]

Lehmann, A. 1924. *Aberglaube und Zauberei.* Leipzig.

Lenzi, M. 1940. "A Report of a Few Recent Experiments on the Biological Effects of Magnetic Fields." *Radiology, 35*(3), 307.

Lindgren, C. E. 1975. "The Correlation Between Specific Acupressure Points and Chakra Energy Congention." *The Journal of the Advanced Institute for Psychic Research.* University of Mississippi.

Lindgren, C. E. 1994. "Beyond Smart Drugs: Psychological & Parapsychological Entergisers." *Intuitive Explorations.* November/December, 13-14.

Luthe, W., Ed. 1965. *Autogenic Training.* New York: Grune & Stratton.

McClain, E. G. 1976. *The Myth of Invariance: The Origin of the Gods, Mathematics and Music from the Rg Veda to Plato.* York Beach, Maine: Nicolas-Hays, Inc.

McCleod, T. 1996. Interview by Andrine Morse.

Maciocia, G. 1989. *The Foundations of Chinese Medicine.* New York, NY: Churchhill Livingston, Inc.

Madden, S. 1995. "Aura Imaging Photography: Building Bridges Between Modern Science and the Healing Arts." Unpublished manuscript.

Mann, A. T. 1991. *The Divine Plot.* New York: Element Inc.

Matsumoto, K. & Birch, S. 1988. *Hara Diagnosis: Reflexation on the Sea.* Brookline, MA: Paradigm Publ.

Mindell, E. 1992. *Earl Mindell's Herb Bible.* New York: A Fireside Book, Simon & Schuster.

Moffett, J. 1994. *The Universal Schoolhouse: Spiritual Awakening Through Education.* Jossey-Bass.

Mormon. 1981. *The Book of Mormon.* Trans. By Joseph Smith. First English trans. 1830. Salt Lake City, UT: The Church of Jesus Christ of Latter-day Saints.

Moss, T. 1974. "Psychic Research in the Soviet Union." *Psychic Explorations: A Challenge for Science.* Edited by John White. New York: G. P. Putnam's Sons.

Motoyama, H. 1978. *Science and the Evolution of Consciousness.* Brookline, MA: Autumn Press, Inc.

Motoyama, H. 1981. *Theories of the Chakras: Bridge to Higher Consciousness.* Wheaton, IL: The Theosophical Publishing House.

Motoyama, H. 1990. *Toward a Superconsciousness: Meditational Theory and Practice.* Trans. Shigenori Nagatomo & Clifford Ames. Berkeley, CA: Asian Humanities Press.

Muller-Ortega, P. E. 1989. *The Triadic Heart of Siva: Kuala Tantricism of Abhinavagupta in the Non-Dual Shaivism of Kashmir.* Albany, NY: State University of New York Press.

Musgrove, V. 1996. Interview by Andrine Morse.

One of the Brethren. 1950. *The Mystery of the Human Aura.* Kingston, NY: Society of Rosicrucians, Inc. (*Societas Rosicruciàna in America*) [Reprint 1987]

Opsopaus, J. 1995. "The Rotation of the Elements." *Caduceus: The Hermetic Quarterly*, I(2):2-10.

Payne, B. 1988. *The Body Magnetic.* Santa Cruz, CA: Buryl Payne.

Payne, B. 1991. *The Body Magnetic.* Boulder, CO: Buryl Payne.

Pearce, J. C. 1988. *The Crack in the Cosmic Egg: Challenging Constructs of Mind and Reality.* New York: Julian.

Pehek, J., Kyler, H. & Faust, D. 1976. "Image Modulation in Corona Discharge Photography." *Science*, 194:263-70.

Philpott, W. H. & Taplin, S. 1990. *Biomagnetic Handbook.* Choctaw, OK: Enviro-Tech Products.

Pollack, R. 1988. *The Haindl Tarot. Volume 1: The Major Arcana.* North Hollywood, CA: Newcastle Publishing, Inc.

Progen. 1990. *BioFeedBack Field Photography.* [video production]

Radhakrishnan, S. & Moore, C.A., Eds. 1957. *A Source Book in Indian Philosophy.* Princeton, NJ: Princeton University Press.

Raju, P.T. 1985. *Structural Depths of Indian Thought.* Albany, NY: State University of New York Press.

Ramacharaka, Yogi. 1971. *The Science of Psychic Healing.* London: Fowler. [First published, 1909]

Randolph, P. B. 1867. *The Guide to Clairvoyance, and Clairvoyant's Guide: A Practical Manual for Those Who Aim at Perfect Clear Seeing and Psychometry . . .* Boston: Rockwell & Rollins.

Regardie, I. 1989. *The Middle Pillar.* St. Paul, MN: Llewellyn Publications.

Richards, S. 1992. *Invisibility: Mastering the Art of Vanishing.* London & San Francisco: Aquarian/Thorsons.

Robinson, D. 1981. *To Stretch a Plank.* Chicago: Nelson-Hall.

Rossman, M. L. 1987. *Healing Yourself: A Step-by-Step Program for Better Health Through Imagery.* New York: Simon Schuster.

Sagan, C. 1966. *The Demon-Haunted World.* New York.

Samuels, M. 1974. *Spirit Guides: Access to Inner Worlds.* New York: Random House.

Sanders, P. 1989. *You Are Psychic:The Free Soul Method*. New York: Rawson Associates.

Schwartz, S. A. 1990. "Editorial Essay: Creativity, Intuition, and Innovation. *ISSSEEM Journal*, Vol. 1(2) abstracts, (http://www.vitalenergy.com/issseem/vol1no2.html).

Scott, M. 1983. *Kundalini in the Physical World*. London: Routledge & Kegan Paul.

Shepard, L., Ed. 1978. "Aura." *Encyclopedia of Occultism & Parapsychology*. Detroit: Gale Research Co.

Schilpp, P. A., Ed. 1949. *Albert Einstein: Philosopher-Scientist*. Evanston, IL: The Library of Living Philosophers.

Schrodter, W. 1954. *Geheimkunste de Rosenkreuzer*. Baumgartner-Verlag.

Silburn, L. 1988. *Kundalini: Energy of the Depths*. Trans. by Jacques Gontier. Albany, NY: State University of New York Press.

Simonton, C. O. 1980. *Getting Well Again: A Step-by-Step, Self-Help Guide to Overcoming Cancer for Patients and their Families*. New York: Bantam.

Singer, B. 1981. "Kirlian Photography." In G. Abell and B. Singer (Eds.), *Science and the Paranormal*, 196-208.

Sivananda Radha, Swami. 1978 & 1993. *Kundalini Yoga for the West*. Spokane, WA: Timeless Books.

Sivananda Radha, Swami. 1991. *In the Company of the Wise: Remembering My Teachers Reflecting the Light*. Palo Alto, CA: Timeless Books.

Steiner, R. 1947. *Knowledge of the Higher Worlds and Its Attainment*. Trans. by H. B. & L. D. Monges, New York.

Stenger, V. J. 1992. *The Humanist*. May/June, Vol. 53(3), 13-15.

Stevens, E. J. 1924. *Science of Colors and Rhythm. . . .* San Francisco: E. J. Stevens Light, Color and Tone Research Laboratories.

Stevenson, L. 1974. *Seven Theories of Human Nature: Christianity, Freud, Lorenz, Marx, Sartre, Skinner, Plato*. New York: Oxford University Press.

Stewart, R. J. 1987. *Music and the Elemental Psyche: A Practical Guide to Music and Changing Consciousness*. Rochester, VT: Destiny Books.

Sun, H. & Sun, D. 1993. *Color Your Life*. New York: Ballantine Books.

Suzuki, D. T. 1968. *The Essence of Buddhism*. Kyoto, Japan: Hozohan.

Svoboda, R. E. 1986. *Aghora: At the Left Hand of God*. Albuquerque, NM: Brotherhood of Life, Inc.

Svoboda, R. E. 1993. *Aghora II: Kundalini*. Albuquerque, NM: Brotherhood of Life Publishing.

Takionic Products. 1996. "Tachyon Field Theory." (http://www.commercial-directory.com/health/index2.htm)

Tompkins, P. & Bird, C. 1989. *The Secret Life of Plants*. New York: Perennial Library Edition. From 1973, New York: Harper & Row Publishers.

Townsend, L. 1996. "Energy Harmonization." (http://infousa.com/member/lthealth/lthealth.htm)

Tracy, B. 1984. *The Psychology of Achievement* (audiotapes). Chicago: Nightingale-Conant Corporation.

Tromp, S. W. 1949. *Psychical Physics*. New York: Elsevier Publ. Co.

Tulku, T. 1978. *Kum Nye Relaxation: Part 2, Movement Exercises*. Berkeley, CA: Dharma Publishing.

Turner, F. 1991. *Beauty: The Value of Values*. Charlottesville, VA: University Press of Virginia.

Tyson, D. 1987. *The New Magus: Ritual Magic As a Personal Process*. St. Paul, MN: Llewellyn Publications.

Varela, F. J., Thompson, E. & Rosch, E. 1991. *The Embodied Mind: Cognitive Science and Human Experience*. Cambridge, MA: The MIT Press.

Versluis, A. 1986. *The Philosophy of Magic*. Boston, MA: Arkana Paperbacks.

Walpola, R. 1959. *What the Buddha Taught*. New York: Grove-Weidenfield.

Waters, F. 1963. *The Book of the Hopi*. New York: Viking Press.

Weed, J. J. 1968. *Wisdom of the Mystic Masters*. West Nyack, NY: Parker.

Whitehead, A. N. 1978 [1929]. *Process and Reality: An Essay in Cosmology*. Corrected edition. New York: The Free Press.

Whitehead, A. N. 1938. *Modes of Thought*. New York: The Free Press.

Wilber, K. 1983. *Up From Eden: A Transpersonal View of Human Evolution*. Boulder, CO: Shambhala.

Wildiers, N. M. 1982. *The Theologian and His Universe: Theology and Cosmology from the Middles Ages to the Present*. New York: The Seabury Press.

Winfree, A. T. 1987. *When Time Breaks Down: The Three-Dimensional Dynamics of Electrochemical Waves and Cardiac Arrhythmias.* Princeton, NJ: Princeton University Press.

Wirth, D. P. 1990 "The Effect of Non-contact Therepeutic Touch on the Healing Rate of Full Thickness Dermal Wounds." *ISSSEEM Journal,* Vol 1, No.1 Abstracts.

Woodroffe, J. (Arthur Avalon). 1919. *The Serpent Power: The Secrets of Tantric and Shaktic Yoga.* New York: Dover Publications, Inc.

Wulff, D. M. 1991. *Psychology of Religion: Classic and Contemporary Views.* New York: John Wiley & Sons.

Zimmer, H. 1951. *Philosophies of India.* Ed. By Joseph Campbell. Princeton, NJ: Bollingen Foundation.

Zukav, G. 1979. *The Dancing Wu Li Masters: An Overview of the New Physics.* William Morrow and Co.

CONTRIBUTORS

Contributing Editor:

Professor, The Chev. C.E. Lindgren, DEd, is Chair of History and Education at Greenwich University and soon to be Dean of the School of Arts and Sciences at Eastern American University. Prof. Lindgren has written six books and over two hundred magazine and journal articles. He is also a Fellow of the Royal Society of Arts, Royal Asiatic Society, College of Preceptors in England, and Master Herbologist. His upcoming works include *Spiritual Alchemists: Rosicrucians, the Brotherhood of Light* and *Spirits of the Afterlife*. Lindgren resides in north Mississippi. He may be contacted at lindgren@panola.com or (662) 563-8954. His background in psychical research includes over twenty-five years of study, teaching, and research with membership in the Academy of Religion and Psychic Research and the Society for Psychical Research (London). Lindgren's Web page is <http://www.geocities.com/Paris/Cathedral/4800/index.html>.

Contributors:

Blythe Arakawa works with many psychics, healers, writers, researchers, and artists worldwide. Born and raised in Hawaii, he divides his time between Lake Tahoe and Hawaii. According to Blythe, "I feel one of my purposes in life is to help network people together."

Jacques Beauchamp began his personal journey thirty years ago, at age fourteen, through yoga, relaxation meditation, and joining a metaphysical study school. Today, after studying Tai Chi, N. L. P., hypnotherapy, Solution Focused Therapy, and Reiki (Master), Jacques uses the Aura Imaging Camera as a reference tool for analysis of various physiological conditions. He is currently International Representative and Trainer for Progen Aura Imaging Technology.

Robert Bruce is an internationally known mystic, healer, writer, backyard scientist, and "hands-on" metaphysical researcher. Born in the UK in 1955, but living most of his life in Australia, he has run a free Internet consulting service, since 1993. The service offers practical advice for all types of paranormal and developmental problems. He specialises in the "mechanics" of the paranormal, especially with astral projection, the human energy body, non-physical sight, and psychic self-defence. He has worked extensively in the paranormal field for over twenty years, mainly hands-on field work, but never for hire, preferring to use his extensive abilities helping others and as research tools. Robert has a popular WWW page "THE ASTRAL PULSE" at <http://www.tower. net.au/ ~rsb/>. This WWW page carries a lot of his earlier written work, free for download. His email address is: rsb@tower.net.au

Fritjof Capra, PhD, has conducted research in theoretical high-energy physics at Stanford University, the University of Paris, the University of California, and Imperial College in London. Currently Dr. Capra lectures at the University of California, Berkeley, and is promoting his new book, *The Web of Life*. Besides these obligations, Capra is still engaged in educational work at the Center for Ecoliteracy. His other works include *The Turning Point* and *Uncommon Wisdom*.

Guy Coggins, noted inventor and technological researcher, has numerous inventions to his credit including Aura Imaging Camera 3000 & 6000, aids for the blind. Second Vision (an interactive video aura camera), AuraVoir software, and the Auracle biosensor glove. Besides his research, Mr. Coggins is president of Progen Company, which specializes in high voltage power supplies, aura imaging, and ion systems.

Ruby K. Corder, a Christian consultant, serves as executive secretary of Educational Consultants of Oxford, Inc. and lay worker for the Rose Cloister Interfaith Outreach Service. She currently lives in North Mississippi, where she writes, edits, and conducts research.

Janice Dye is a certified Reiki practitioner and Intuitive counselor, and her work and spiritual interests have kept her busy and creative in Toronto, ON, Canada for the past seven years. Recently, she has expanded her energy to encompass the global community of Internet Cyberspace and is available for readings through email at mayasweb@ idirect.com. Her home on the net is the Innerspace Station, a spiritual and metaphysical resource and growing community hub. <http://web. idirect.com/~innerspa>

Prof. Gerald Owen Grow, PhD, is Professor of Magazine Journalism at Florida A&M University. He graduated from Harvard in 1964 and received a Ph.D. in English from Yale in 1968 (in the peaceful days before Deconstruction), with a dissertation on Shakespeare's tragedies and Milton's *Paradise Lost.* He spent a year of postgraduate study at Pembroke College, Cambridge. He has taught at Yale, San Francisco State, St. Mary's College of California, Florida State University, and Florida A&M University—where he coordinates the magazine program and advises *Journey,* the FAMU student magazine. Dr. Grow is a long-time student of alternative healing. He may be reached at P.O. Box 4282, Tallahassee, Florida 32315. Prof. Grow's Web page is <http://www.longleaf.net/ggrow>.

Professor Arnold Keyserling is the discoverer of Chakra Music and Professor of Religious Philosophy, Academy of Art, University of Vienna, Austria. He also serves as Director and Facilitator of the School of Wisdom. Besides his other duties, Prof. Keyserling is an author, public speaker, historian, philosopher, and music theorist. He has authored over fifty books and in the 1980s, served as president of the European Humanistic Psychology Association.

Ralph Losey, JD, is a philosopher, çomposer, and attorney in private practice. He is the author of numerous legal publications and articles on the law, music, and philosophy. He recently wrote the chapter on Internet Law in two books for Macmillian Publishing: "Que Special Edition, Using the Internet with Windows 95" (Macmillian, 1995) and "Que Special Edition - Using the Internet" (Macmillian 3rd ed. 1996). Ralph is the founder of the first branch of School of Wisdom in the U.S.A., where he and his wife, Molly Losey, and others, teach weekly classes and offer periodic workshops. The SOW is a non-profit institute for global philosophy, teaching the underlying unity of differing spiritual traditions. The SOW was founded in Europe in 1920 by Count Hermann Keyserling. Its past teachers include the psychiatrist, Carl Jung, and the translator of the I Ching, Richard Wilhelm. The SOW has a major website on the Internet where Ralph is the Webmaster. <http://www.schoolofwisdom.com/welcome.html> and <http://www.sun-angel.com/emporium/sow/sow.html>.

William T. McClellan, BA, MAR, PhD (cand.), has been curious about psychic phenomena and esoteric systems of thought since high school days, finding in them things that challenge what are commonly perceived as disjunctions between religion and science. His undergraduate degree (Goddard College, 1968) is in philosophy, with a psychology minor. He holds an M.A.R. from Yale Divinity School (1981) and has completed all course work and exams toward a Ph.D. in Philosophy of Religion and Theology from the Department of Religion at Claremont Graduate School. He lives in Claremont, California, with his wife and two children.

Rosalee Elizabeth McCurdy, RN, AP, MSc, DOM, Diplomate in Acupuncture (NCCA), is a doctor of Oriental Medicine with a private practice at The Center For Radiant Health in South Miami, Florida. She is adjunct professor at Miami Dade Community College and teaches Therapeutic Touch (Kreiger/ Kunz method) to medical professionals and lay persons. She has also been an instructor in the Department of Natural Healing Arts and Sciences at St. John's University in Louisiana.

Susana Madden is a freelance writer and photographer who has traveled extensively throughout the U.S. and Canada to holistic expos and events, photographing auras. Ms. Madden is also a noted California artist.

Andrine Morse is Community Relations Director for a non-profit organization which offers twenty community-based services and counseling programs. The organization is largely government funded with an annual budget of $2.5 million. Ms. Morse is responsible for operationalizing priorities of the board and executive director: public relations, funding, program research, and proposal development. Although trained in behavioral modification, family systems theory, and art and play techniques, she incorporates the use and teaching of the Great Wheel of Life. This method is a tool taught to her by Elder Cree women of the First Nation reserve at Hobbema, Alberta. She may be reached at amorse@ pris.bc.ca.

Buryl Payne, MS, PhD, is a Phi Beta Kappa graduate of the University of Washington and holds advanced degrees in psychology and physics. His research work includes designing and patenting GSR type biofeedback technology, as sold by Radio Shack and Thought Technology. A former faculty member of Goddard College and Boston University, he currently designs magnetic field devices.

Margo von Phul, BFA, is an accomplished artisan/commercial designer, with over twenty-five years of free-lance experience in a variety of mixed media. Ms. von Phul obtained a Bachelor's Degree in Graphics from the University of California, Santa Barbara, in 1975.

Chip Weston, BA, has been a meditation instructor since the late 1960s. He was trained as a "non-leader" and led encounter groups in Florida and in Berkeley, CA. He studied different forms of yoga, martial arts, co-counseling, diet, and fasting and has undergraduate training in behavioral science and post graduate work in liberal studies. Chip has extensive training in Kriya Yoga and has developed an eclectic practice which includes yoga meditation, intense physical training, Chi Gong, and visualization techniques. He has led yoga groups and workshops in Orlando, Florida for over twenty years. Mr. Weston opened Weston Studios in 1974 and works in the fields of advertising, theme park, film, video, and radio. He has an eclectic background in many different areas of creativity, art, and music and is knowledgeable in new materials, color theory, symmetry, archetypal imagery, symbolism, and sublimation. He is on the board of directors of the local public library and works with the State of Florida to develop library technology and information services. He may be reached at chi@gdi.net.

Richard Bernard Wigley, BA, of St. George, Utah, is a professional astrologer, writer/lecturer, editor, and business consultant. A graduate of the University of California, Santa Barbara, in Religious Studies, he has continued for the past twenty-two years to refine and focus the connections between ancient wisdom and current scientific models. This eclectic philosophy shines through his own words; "Human reality is a synthesis of astro/quantum physics, mind/body consciousness, technology, genetics, philosophy/religion, and personal insight." Richard Bernard's creative focus consists of following the well forged course of human philosophic endeavor, learning, teaching, and listening for wisdom. Richard may be contacted at rysa@sisna.com.